Drugs and Health

A Conference Sponsored by the
American Enterprise Institute for Public Policy Research

Drugs and Health

Economic Issues and
Policy Objectives

Edited by Robert B. Helms

American Enterprise Institute for Public Policy Research
Washington and London

Library of Congress Cataloging in Publication Data

Drugs and health.

(AEI symposia ; 81B)
Proceedings of a conference sponsored by AEI's Center for Health
Policy Research.
1. Pharmaceutical research—Economic aspects—Congresses. 2.
Pharmaceutical policy—Congresses. 3. Drug trade—Congresses. I. Helms,
Robert B. II American Enterprise Institute for Public Policy Research.
Center for Health Policy Research. III. Series: American Enterprise Institute
for Public Policy Research. AEI symposia ; 81B.
[DNLM: 1 Drug industry——Economics——United States—Congresses. 2.
Public policy—United States— Congresses. 3. Research—United States—
Congress. 4. Legislation, Drug—United States— Congresses. QV 736 D795
1981]
HD9665.5.D78   615.1'068'5   80–388 80–28825

ISBN 0–8447–2201–4
ISBN 0–8447–2202–2 (pbk.)

AEI Symposia 81B

Printed in the United States of America

3003 85

Dr. Michael Halberstam was murdered at the age of forty-eight in the course of a robbery in Washington, D.C., on December 5, 1980. His death means the loss to society of a true Renaissance man, one highly skilled in the practice of medicine, a writer, a participant in the public policies of medicine, and an invaluable member of the AEI advisory committee on health policy. As a small token of our friendship and esteem, this volume is dedicated to Mike.

The uniqueness of Dr. Halberstam lay in his ability to communicate the problems of medical practice to other practitioners and to his patients. He was, in fact, a professional writer, having published a successful novel, a book of personal experiences, and a third on *The Pills in Your Life*. For AEI's Center for Health Policy Research he participated in several official conferences, including this one (see his commentary in part 4, "The Economics of Drug Choice"). His article "Too Many Drugs" (1979) appears in the AEI reprint series. As editor of *Modern Medicine*, he reached a vast audience with his editorials. He pursued his interests in sports, politics, and education with the same tireless enthusiasm with which he practiced medicine.

The loss of Mike is especially lamentable because there are so few of his kind. He bridged the wide gaps that prevail between medical practice, academic medicine, and government. And he did it with charm, always sharpened by his wit, good sense, and unfailing honesty. With a mind forever boyishly curious and extraordinarily retentive, he could make masterly use of the phrase "for instance," having a rich accumulation of experiences from which to draw.

It is a small honor that we proffer. We would have preferred to confer it during his lifetime. Our tribute to Mike is slight in comparison to what he gave us during his relatively short life. All of us who knew and worked with him will always cherish the memory of his friendship and his knowledge.

IRVINE H. PAGE

Chairman, Advisory Committee
Center for Health Policy Research
Hyannis Port, Massachusetts

Contributors

Barry M. Bloom
President
Pfizer Central Research

Yale Brozen
Professor of Business Economics
University of Chicago

Kenneth W. Clarkson
Professor of Economics
Law and Economics Center
University of Miami

William S. Comanor
Director, Bureau of Economics
Federal Trade Commission

J. Richard Crout
Director, Bureau of Drugs
Food and Drug Administration

George Eads
Council of Economic Advisers

John F. Geweke
Professor of Economics
University of Wisconsin

Henry G. Grabowski
Professor of Economics
Duke University

Michael Halberstam, M.D.
Editor, *Modern Medicine,* and
physician in private practice

Ronald W. Hansen
Professor of Economics
University of Rochester

Robert B. Helms
Director of Health Policy Studies
American Enterprise Institute

Mark C. Hornbrook
Senior Research Manager
National Center for Health Services Research
Department of Health and Human Services

Louis Lasagna, M.D.
Professor of Pharmacology and Toxicology
University of Rochester

David F. Lean
Bureau of Economics
Federal Trade Commission

William C. MacLeod
Law and Economics Center
University of Miami

W. Duncan Reekie
Professor of Economics
University of Edinburgh

Michael A. Riddiough
Senior Analyst
Office of Technology Assessment

F. M. Scherer
Professor of Economics
Northwestern University

Leonard Schifrin
Professor of Economics
College of William and Mary

Meir Statman
Professor of Economics
University of Santa Clara

Lester G. Telser
Professor of Economics
University of Chicago

Peter Temin
Professor of Economics
Massachusetts Institute of Technology

John Vernon
Professor of Economics
Duke University

John R. Virts
Corporate Staff Economist
Eli Lilly and Company

Burton A. Weisbrod
Professor of Economics
University of Wisconsin

J. Fred Weston
Professor of Business Economics and Finance
University of California, Los Angeles

Steven N. Wiggins
Professor of Economics
Texas A&M University

Harry R. Woltman
Director of Economic Staff
Food and Drug Administration

S. Y. Wu
Professor of Economics
University of Iowa

*This conference was held at
the American Enterprise Institute for Public Policy Research
in Washington, D.C., on November 15–16, 1979*

Contents

FOREWORD xvii
    William B. Baroody, Jr.
PREFACE xix
    Robert B. Helms

PART ONE
THE RESEARCH AND DEVELOPMENT PROCESS: THE IMPACT OF ECONOMIC FACTORS

The Determinants of Research and Development Expenditures in
the Pharmaceutical Industry 3
    Henry G. Grabowski and John Vernon

Expectations and the Allocation of Research and Development
Resources 21
    John R. Virts and J. Fred Weston

Commentary
    F. M. Scherer 46
    Harry R. Woltman 49

PART TWO
THE RESEARCH AND DEVELOPMENT PROCESS: DECISION MAKING IN A REGULATED INDUSTRY

The Pharmaceutical Research and Development Decision
Process 55
    Steven N. Wiggins

Reducing the Drug Lag: Enterpreneurship in Pharmaceutical Clin-
ical Testing 84
    Kenneth W. Clarkson and William C. MacLeod

Commentary
>   Barry M. Bloom   114
>   J. Richard Crout   117

PART THREE
COMPETITION AMONG DRUGS: THE ROLE OF PRICES AND PATENTS

Price and Quality Competition in Drug Markets: Evidence from the United States and the Netherlands 123
>   W. Duncan Reekie

The Effect of Patent Expiration on the Market Position of Drugs 140
>   Meir Statman

Commentary
>   Mark C. Hornbrook   152
>   Leonard Schifrin   166

PART FOUR
THE ECONOMICS OF DRUG CHOICE

Physician Prescribing Behavior: Is There Learning by Doing? .. 173
>   Peter Temin

The Market for Research and Development: Physician Demand and Drug Company Supply 183
>   Lester G. Telser

Commentary
>   Michael Halberstam, M.D.   222
>   David F. Lean   227

PART FIVE
THE SOCIAL RETURNS TO PHARMACEUTICAL RESEARCH AND DEVELOPMENT

Some Economic Consequences of Technological Advance in Medical Care: The Case of a New Drug 235
>   John F. Geweke and Burton A. Weisbrod

Pharmaceutical Innovation, Product Imitation, and Public Policy   272
>   S. Y. Wu ....

Commentary
    Michael A. Riddiough 290
    Ronald W. Hansen 293

PART SIX
DRUGS AND HEALTH: WHAT RESEARCH AGENDA FOR PUBLIC POLICY? A PANEL DISCUSSION

Introduction 303
    Robert B. Helms, Moderator

Statements
    Yale Brozen 305
    William S. Comanor 308
    George Eads 311
    Louis Lasagna, M.D. 312

Highlights of the Discussion 317

Editor's Postscript 343
    Robert B. Helms

Foreword

This volume is one of a series of studies and conference proceedings that have been published by AEI's Center for Health Policy Research over the last several years.[1] All of these publications have presented academic research on the economic performance of the pharmaceutical industry and the effect of government regulation on that performance. More recently, in response to the intensified discussion of possible reforms of U.S. regulatory policy, AEI undertook a special project to present analysis and discussion of several of the major issues involved in the debate. In addition to publishing an analysis of the major legislative proposals, *Proposals to Reform Drug Regulation Laws,*[2] AEI held two conferences. The first concentrated on international issues, such as the effects of U.S. and foreign regulation on the international marketing of drugs, the role of patents and proprietary information on research and international competitiveness, and the special problems of supplying drugs to developing countries. The proceedings of this conference, *The International Supply of Medicines,* were published recently by AEI.[3]

The proceedings of the second of the two conferences, contained in this volume, concentrate on domestic policy issues. A major objective of the volume is to provide empirical evidence and expert analysis that will prove useful to policy makers and others attempting to improve the process of supplying and regulating drugs. This volume will also be useful to policy analysts interested in any aspect of health and safety regulation. The papers and discussion deal with such topics as the economic measurement of the effects of regulation, the controversial issue of how to ensure consumer safety without inhibiting scientific progress, the measurement of benefits and costs of risky products, and the direction of policy-related research in health and safety regulation. All are

---

[1] Sam Peltzman, *Regulation of Pharmaceutical Innovation,* 1974; William M. Wardell and Louis Lasagna, *Regulation and Drug Development,* 1975; Robert B. Helms, ed., *Drug Development and Marketing,* 1975; David Schwartzman, *The Expected Return from Pharmaceutical Research,* 1975; Henry G. Grabowski, *Drug Regulation and Innovation,* 1976; William M. Wardell, ed., *Controlling the Use of Therapeutic Drugs: An International Comparison,* 1978; and Jack Behrman, *Tropical Diseases: Responses of Pharmaceutical Companies,* 1980.

[2] *Proposals to Reform Drug Regulation Laws,* AEI Special Analysis, 1979.

[3] Robert B. Helms, ed., *The International Supply of Medicines* (Washington, D.C.: American Enterprise Institute, 1980).

topics that are being intensely studied by scholars, policy makers, and industrial strategists concerned with the broad field of government regulation.

As Robert Helms has stated in his preface to this volume, "The central question of the [regulatory reform] debate is not the simplistic one of how to maximize safety. Rather, it is the more complex question of how to establish a workable system of research, regulation, and drug delivery that will effectively balance the benefits of drugs against the risks." The informed reader knows that this is no easy task since drug regulation presents us with a classic example of a dilemma, that is, choosing between equally unsatisfactory alternatives. But AEI has never chosen to avoid controversy or dilemmas. The institute remains dedicated to the proposition that informed and wise public policy choices should be made on the basis of the best information and analysis that scholars and other informed thinkers have to offer.

One informed thinker was the late Dr. Michael Halberstam, to whom this volume has been dedicated. For the last five years we have benefited from Dr. Halberstam's participation on the advisory committee for our Center for Health Policy Research. His discussion of physician prescribing practices in part 4 of this volume is an example of the interest he took in a wide range of health policy issues. We shall all miss his special way of reminding us that the health and welfare of all of us are affected, not only by the way physicians practice medicine, but by the actions of government. We are all indebted to his informed evaluations of public policies.

WILLIAM J. BAROODY, JR.
President
American Enterprise Institute
for Public Policy Research

Preface

The regulation of drugs has been subjected to periodic public debate since the first decade of this century. As the public's knowledge and concern about the effects of drugs have changed, so too has the focus of the debate. Concerns about poisons in patent medicines have given way to the more complex issue of efficacy. This volume is a response to the latest phase of this long public discussion, a concern that our present system of regulation may have become too rigid and may be reducing the potential benefits of drugs. This response reflects a renewed willingness to consider an even more sophisticated and complex issue, the ability of regulation to strike a more realistic balance between the benefits and the risks of drugs.

This preface, rather than being a detailed summary of the volume, considers several aspects of drug markets that the editor believes are important in the debate about the reform of drug regulation. These topics include a discussion of why drug regulation has always been so controversial; some views on why regulators undervalue the potential benefits of drugs, as opposed to the potential risks; and a number of possible reforms that might address the regulatory imbalance.

Why the Controversy about Drug Regulation?

The process of drug regulation is controversial for a simple and obvious reason—we cannot predict the future. There is no certainty that the future effects of new medicines will be beneficial or harmful. Guided by the history of the development of existing pharmaceutical products, we can predict only one thing—that new drugs, when used by large numbers of people, will have unpredictable effects. Some of these may be unexpected side effects with various degrees of adverse consequences for some patients. Such results can be tragic, a fact of history of which proponents of more stringent regulation keep reminding us. But less well known, especially outside the medical professions, is that some unexpected effects can be beneficial. Serendipity is indeed important in drug development. Not only may new drugs be more beneficial than expected in their intended uses, but they may have entirely unpredictable benefits for some patients. Or they may have unpredictable effects that provide researchers with the clue to the development of even more effective and safer drugs.

This controversy sets the stage for the debate about regulatory reform of our drug laws. The central question of the debate is not the simplistic one of how to maximize safety. Rather, it is the more complex question of how to establish a workable system of research, regulation, and drug delivery that will effectively balance the benefits of drugs against the risks. As would be expected, those on the side of more stringent regulation place greater emphasis on the past adverse effects of drugs than on the beneficial effects. Those arguing for less stringent regulation emphasize beneficial drugs, but they enter the debate with two strikes against them. Because of the uncertainty about future effects and the long-term nature of the drug development process, there is an imbalance in the public's perception of drug safety that has a profound effect on the politics of drug regulation reform.

The Asymmetry of Public Information

To understand why the public debate on drug regulation emphasizes the risks of drugs more than the benefits, consider briefly the decisions that are typically made by researchers (academic, industrial, and governmental) and the government regulatory officials who review this research.[1] For simplicity, assume that a drug, on the basis of research, animal and human tests, and actual use after marketing, can be found to be unequivocally either beneficial or harmful.[2] In addition, assume that research and regulatory personnel decide either to place a new drug on the market or to abandon it. This amounts to assuming, unrealistically, that decision makers, both private and public, never have doubts about their decisions and never procrastinate or make qualified decisions. Under such simplifying assumptions, we can catalog four possible outcomes of the combination of decisions made during the development and approval process: (1) a beneficial drug is approved for marketing; (2) a harmful drug is rejected for marketing; (3) a harmful drug is approved for marketing; and (4) a beneficial drug is rejected for marketing. In retrospect it would be possible to classify the first two cases as "correct" decisions, the kind of outcome all can agree is desirable. On the other hand, the last two decisions could be classified as "wrong" decisions, the kind of results public policy would like to avoid.

---

[1] For a more detailed description of the drug development and approval process, see William M. Wardell and Louis Lasagna, *Regulation and Drug Development* (Washington, D.C.: American Enterprise Institute, 1975), pp. 19–44.

[2] That a drug could turn out to be neither, that is, ineffective and harmless, is of considerable practical importance but only distracts from the central point to be made.

Although actual decisions about drugs never fit neatly into these four categories, let us consider some examples of the public and political reaction to these decisions.

The most dramatic and well-known example of a correct decision is that of an FDA medical examiner, Dr. Frances Kelsey, who in 1961 declined to approve the new tranquilizer thalidomide. Once the public saw pictures of deformed babies whose mothers had taken thalidomide in Europe, it heaped well-deserved praise on Dr. Kelsey.[3] The European experience with thalidomide illustrates the marketing of an obviously harmful drug. The public reaction was so strong that it profoundly affected the U.S. drug regulatory system.[4] Long-lasting condemnation was directed, not only at the German company that marketed thalidomide in Europe, but at all drug firms, which were judged guilty regardless of their attempts to ensure the safety of their products. The company decision makers did not know, at least at first, of thalidomide's tragic effects on fetuses since this information emerged slowly in the midst of numerous pieces of conflicting information. Thalidomide was marketed with high hopes that it would be a great improvement over the other tranquilizers then available. Once a definite connection had been made between thalidomide and phocomelia, the condition of fetal deformity, it was easy for writers to picture those on the side of caution as heroes and those on the side of continuing use as villains.

The marketing of drugs that turn out to be harmful is not the only kind of wrong decision. Some wrong decisions prevent beneficial drugs from being discovered, developed, and marketed. And just as in the thalidomide case, the decisions that prevent people from receiving beneficial drugs can be made by both industry and government officials. Again, the public is given a simplistic perception of the situation, but not in quite the way that may first seem apparent.

As a counterpart to the thalidomide decision, we might select one of the many rags-to-riches stories of the development of medicines— stories in which the industry or the academic scientist is the hero and the FDA the villain. There are several examples of hard-working physicians and scientists who have had new ideas that were simply not taken seriously by their peers.[5] Not only are such persons unable to attract

---

[3] For one review of the thalidomide episode, see Walter S. Ross, *The Life/Death Ratio* (New York: Reader's Digest Press, 1977), pp. 18–47.

[4] For two accounts of the role thalidomide played in the passage of the 1962 Kefauver amendments to the Pure Food and Drug Act, see David Seidman, "The Politics of Policy Analysis: Protection or Overprotection in Drug Regulation?" *Regulation*, vol. 1, no. 1 (July/August 1977), pp. 23–24; Paul J. Quirk, "Food and Drug Administration," in James Q. Wilson, ed., *The Politics of Regulation* (New York: Basic Books, 1980), pp. 197–99.

[5] For examples, see Louis Lasagna, "Who Will Adopt the Orphan Drugs?" *Regulation*, vol. 3, no. 6 (November/December 1979), pp. 27–32.

private capital to test their ideas fully, they may also be subjected to professional ridicule. Or, the story may go, short-sighted bureaucrats at the FDA may not approve a new drug, regardless of the good it does for most patients, because the evidence is not strong enough that there are no harmful side effects. As the plot thickened, however, the scientist would use overseas experience with the drug to prevail against the forces of ignorance, bureaucratic inefficiency, and special interests. In the end, he would earn the acclaim of the public and his peers, and perhaps even a Nobel prize. The happy ending of such a plot is familiar to all who read bedtime stories to their children.

While such situations do occur in part in medicine, they are not parallel to the thalidomide example. They do not illustrate the usual outcome of a wrong decision about what later turns out to be a beneficial drug. When a decision (either public or private) is made to abandon a drug during the long discovery and development process, the usual outcome is simply greater uncertainty, rather than dramatic evidence of success or failure. We simply stop producing information upon which to make a definitive judgment. When a project is dropped by a company or by an academic research director because of lack of funds, all that remains is the lingering doubt of a few knowledgeable scientists about what *might have been*. News editors do not pick stories with such un-dramatic conclusions.

Thus, there is an asymmetry of information presented to the public about the effects of the two types of wrong decisions. In the first case, when the decision is made to develop and market a drug that turns out to be harmful, its dramatic results can be used to ridicule and punish both the private decision makers who developed the drug and the public officials who allowed it to be marketed. In the second case, when the decision is made to abandon a drug that would have benefits, we are left only with uncertainty and a lack of information. There is no direct evidence that the continuing suffering of patients is avoidable.

This asymmetry of information also shows up in statistical studies. If we study a large sample of drugs that have entered the development process, we find that some drugs have been abandoned because of lack of effectiveness or potential harmful effects. Among the drugs that are marketed, we can find both beneficial and adverse effects from actual use. Among the drugs abandoned in the research and development process, however, we cannot measure what benefits would have accrued if the drugs had been put to actual use.

Thus, as the benefits of drugs are systematically undervalued relative to the risks, those of us who would make a case for the potential benefits of private research and development are put on the defensive. Several types of research have been marshaled to attempt to overcome this distorted public perception. Economic measurements have shown that the 1962 amendments have had such a detrimental effect on drug discovery that the costs of the regulation exceed the benefits of improved safety.[6] Other studies have measured the increased cost of marketing new drugs[7] and the effects of regulation on private investment in research and development.[8] Others have documented the greater delay of the FDA approval process compared with that in other countries[9] or shown the importance of serendipity in industrial drug research by tracing the history of the discovery and development of important drugs.[10] Although this body of research has been carefully and objectively done, it has amounted to a weak charge in the uphill battle against the public and political perception of drugs and the drug industry. Those who must rely on hypothetical benefits in the debate about new drugs are at a distinct disadvantage against those who can point to real and dramatic evidence of the harm that drugs occasionally do.

Living with Uncertainty: A Choice of Institutions

But all is not lost. Congress's votes to prohibit the FDA from banning saccharin[11] and the Supreme Court's recent benzene decision[12] suggest a willingness to reconsider our attempts to achieve a riskless society. As Paul Johnson, the distinguished British journalist and historian, has observed about U.S. health and safety regulation:

> It is perhaps natural that America, whose public life has sought to express absolute moral ideals, should bring to the regulation of risks a quasi-religious zeal and intransigence. This has con-

[6] Sam Peltzman, *Regulation of Pharmaceutical Innovation* (Washington, D.C.: American Enterprise Institute, 1974).

[7] Ronald W. Hansen, "The Pharmaceutical Development Process: Estimates of Development Costs and Times and the Effects of Proposed Regulatory Changes," in Robert I. Chien, ed., *Issues in Pharmaceutical Economics* (Lexington, Mass.: Lexington Books, 1979), pp. 151–81.

[8] Henry G. Grabowski, "The Determinants of R&D Expenditures in the Pharmaceutical Industry," in this volume; and "Regulation and the International Diffusion of Pharmaceuticals," in Robert B. Helms, ed., *The International Supply of Medicines* (Washington, D.C.: American Enterprise Institute, 1980), pp. 5–36.

[9] Wardell and Lasagna, *Regulation and Drug Development*, pp. 51–123; William M. Wardell, "Rx: More Regulation or Better Therapies?" *Regulation*, vol. 3, no. 5 (September/October 1979), pp. 25–33.

[10] Larry L. Deutsch, "Research Performance in the Ethical Drug Industry," *Marquette Business Review*, vol. 17 (Fall 1973), pp. 129–42; Michael Halberstam, "Too Many Drugs?" *Forum on Medicine*, vol. 2, no. 3 (March 1979) and no. 4 (April 1979).

[11] Public Law 96–273.

[12] Industrial Union Department, AFL–CIO, v. American Petroleum Institute et al., no. 78–911, decided July 2, 1980, 448 U.S.

siderable value in the first phase of a reforming program, the value of impressing on all concerned the importance and urgency of the issue. But there comes a time when national computation must replace primitive zealotry.[13]

Even the FDA has shown some concern about the burden it imposes on research and development. As Paul Quirk reports, the FDA has shown some willingness to consider foreign testing data and has resisted demands by some consumer groups for more stringent animal tests before human tests.[14] In addition, the FDA has attempted to speed the approval of drugs *it* considers (and therein lies another controversy) to provide significant advances in therapy.

In the editor's opinion, any reassessment of this country's process of drug regulation should begin with the realization that we are not now effectively applying new scientific information to the discovery and development of therapeutic agents. This is due to a political attitude in Congress, at the FDA, and among the public that has systematically placed excessive emphasis on avoiding the risks associated with new drugs. Certainly drugs will have unpredictable effects in use. Consequently, the regulatory reform debate should concentrate on learning to live with uncertainty by establishing a set of institutions, both public and private, that could help to strike a more efficient balance between the potential risks and benefits of new products.

The literature on drug regulation, including that published by the American Enterprise Institute, contains a number of ideas that should be considered in this reassessment. The costs of regulation imposed on both academic and industrial researchers should be reduced to increase the incentives to investigate important scientific leads. With lower costs of research from any source including lower regulatory costs, a larger proportion of scientific possibilities can be investigated, producing more information about risks and benefits. In addition to reducing costs, we should develop institutions to gather more accurate information about the effects of drugs in actual use.[15] Information on the benefits of drugs should be collected, even though it may be more difficult to obtain and interpret than information on adverse reactions.

The legislative mandate to FDA officials should also be reconsidered: they should not be forced into the inefficient strategy of seeking

---

[13] Paul Johnson, "The Perils of Risk Avoidance," *Regulation*, vol. 4, no. 3 (May/June 1980), p. 18.

[14] Quirk, "Food and Drug Administration," pp. 219–20.

[15] For a discussion of drug utilization surveillance, see William M. Wardell, ed., *Controlling the Use of Therapeutic Drugs: An International Comparison* (Washington, D.C.: American Enterprise Institute, 1978), especially pp. 1–28.

zero risk. A common myth in the regulatory reform debate is that regulation may be imposed simply by replacing the present regulators with better qualified ones. Most serious analysts of drug regulation, however, have not blamed the poor performance of the FDA on the people as much as on the incentives established by the legislation. They argue that the present agency personnel are not the real problem, they are just as dedicated and hard working in attempting to reduce risk as any other professionals in public or private institutions. The trouble is that Congress has given the FDA and other health and safety regulatory agencies a single mandate to reduce risk to consumers. Some analysts feel that this bias in favor of reducing risk, regardless of the cost of forgone benefits, should be substantially changed: the mandate should also consider the costs of agency decisions and, in the case of drugs, the potential benefits of new drugs to patients. Because, as the saying goes, "there is many a slip 'twixt the cup and the lip," the implementation of such a mandate should be carefully monitored to ensure that the intent of Congress is not altered.[16]

The regulatory reform debate should also note that the model of prior market approval by a single government agency is not the only way to ensure protection of consumers. Competition should be introduced into the approval process by establishing some combination of government and private testing facilities to produce information about risks and benefits. Such competing testing authorities should have the advantage of providing the scientific community and consumers with more objective information and a more open discussion of the mechanisms of testing procedures.

The sale of insurance is a typical market response to other situations where consumers know they face a risk, but one that is actuarially definable. To a certain extent, pharmaceutical industry research and sale of products under a company brand name are ways of selling drugs with an implied insurance policy attached. The company attempts to determine the patient's medical risk and its own financial risk through its research. The consumer's identification of the product with the company name implies an acceptance by the company of product liability. The greater the company's liability in case of adverse effects, the greater its incentives to market only safe products. We should consider how to increase these private incentives to market only safe and beneficial products.

---

[16] For a discussion of how regulatory agencies, especially the FDA, respond to legislative mandates, see Jerry L. Mashaw, "Regulation, Logic, and Ideology," *Regulation*, vol. 3, no. 6 (November/December 1979), pp. 44–51; see also Thomas Sowell, *Knowledge and Decisions* (New York: Basic Books, 1980), pp. 140–49.

Conclusion

Exactly how we should reform drug regulation is still open to considerable debate. It is the editor's opinion that, regardless of how one views the present situation, the papers and proceedings in this volume make a real contribution to this debate. The reader will not find agreement about the future of drug regulation, and certainly not agreement with the views expressed by the editor in this preface, among all of the contributors to this volume. What the reader will find is a penetrating discussion of the issues by an informed group of analysts. I would like to thank all of them for their hard work on their contributions and for the cooperation they have given me and others at AEI in the preparation of this volume.

ROBERT B. HELMS
Director
Health Policy Studies
American Enterprise Institute
for Public Policy Research

PART
ONE

The Research and Development
Process: The Impact of Economic
Factors

The Determinants of Research and Development Expenditures in the Pharmaceutical Industry

Henry G. Grabowski
and
John Vernon

The pharmaceutical industry has been among the most innovative industries in the United States economy over the post–World War II period. A number of studies, however, have pointed to declining innovational outputs and lower research and development (R&D) productivity in this industry over the past several years.[1] Our main objective in this paper is to analyze the reaction of the major pharmaceutical firms to these developments in terms of their allocations for research and development activities. In particular, we wish to examine empirically how firm research intensities have been responding to factors such as the expected returns from R&D and the availability of funds to undertake R&D. To investigate this question, we utilize a model similar in structure to that previously estimated by Grabowski for the pharmaceutical industry over the earlier period 1959 to 1962.[2]

The section of the paper that immediately follows discusses the hypotheses to be tested as well as the general specification of the model. The second section presents the empirical estimates. The final section discusses the main conclusions and implications of the analysis.

Model Specification

The R&D Decision Process in Pharmaceuticals. From the standpoint of the pharmaceutical firm, R&D for new drug products constitute a long-term investment decision process. As a first step in modeling this process, we briefly review the investment theory of the firm and then discuss its general applicability to R&D decisions in the drug industry.

---

[1] See, for example, the discussion of these adverse trends and the hypotheses concerning their causes in Henry G. Grabowski, John M. Vernon, and Lacy G. Thomas, "Estimating the Effects of Regulation on Innovation: An International Comparative Analysis of the Pharmaceutical Industry," *Journal of Law and Economics*, vol. 21 (April 1978), pp. 133–40; and also in Henry G. Grabowski, *Drug Regulation and Innovation* (Washington, D.C.: American Enterprise Institute, 1976), chaps. 2 and 3.

[2] Henry G. Grabowski, "The Determinants of Industrial Research and Development: A Study of the Chemical, Drug, and Petroleum Industries," *Journal of Political Economy*, vol. 76 (March/April 1968), pp. 292–306.

To determine the optimal level of R&D investment using the economist's rate-of-return analysis, the firm must first estimate the expected time streams of costs and revenues for each of its potential R&D projects. This information can then be used to construct a marginal-return-on-investment schedule (*mrr*) by arranging projects in order of decreasing rates of return (appropriately adjusted for risk). The intersection of *mrr* and the cost-of-capital curve (*mcc*), which reflects the opportunity cost of alternative investments for the firm and its shareholders, determines the optimal level of R&D investment, R^*.

In algebraic terms, the optimal level of R&D investment, R^*, is given by solving the equation

$$mrr(R, X) = mcc(Z) \qquad (1)$$

where R = investment expenditures in R&D; X = vector of variables influencing the rate of return from new drug R&D; and Z = vector of variables influencing the opportunity cost of investing in new drug R&D.

Equation (1) yields a determinant function for R^* of the general form

$$R^* = f(X, Z) \qquad (2)$$

so that changes in the optimal level of R&D occur as a result of shifts in either the marginal return on investment (the X factors) or the cost-of-capital schedules (the Z factors).

We feel these basic factors influence the level of pharmaceutical R&D expenditures as in the case of other investment decisions, but one should also keep in mind some special characteristics of the R&D process in this industry. As industry managers frequently point out, the discovery and development of a new chemical entity (NCE) are characterized by great uncertainty and normally take several years to pass through all the different phases of research, clinical testing, and regulatory reviews.[3]

Basic research must first be undertaken before specific NCEs can even be identified. After a new product candidate is synthesized, it is

---

[3] The quantitative characteristics of the R&D process in drugs (e.g., attrition rates, residence times, and costs in different stages) have been examined in a recent National Science Foundation research study at the University of Rochester under the direction of Professor William Wardell and Louis Lasagna. See, for example, Ronald W. Hansen, "The Pharmaceutical Development Process: Estimates of Development Costs and Times and the Effects of Proposed Regulatory Changes," in Robert I. Chien, ed., *Issues in Pharmaceutical Economics* (Lexington, Mass.: Lexington Books, 1979), pp. 151–82; and W. Wardell, M. Hassar, S. Anavekar, and L. Lasagna, "The Rate of Development of New Drugs in the United States, 1963 through 1975," *Clinical Pharmacology and Therapeutics*, vol. 24 (August 1978), pp. 133–45.

then screened on animals to obtain some idea of its properties in man. Typically, hundreds of drugs are screened for every one clinically tested in man. Those drugs that are taken into clinical testing come under the regulation of the Food and Drug Administration (FDA) and must pass through a number of development stages designed to illuminate their therapeutic and toxic effects in man. Wardell's recent analysis of the clinical investigation process in drugs indicates a high attrition rate here as well. Only about one drug in eight passes through all the stages to the point of filing a new drug application (NDA) with the FDA.[4]

Given this situation, industry managers indicate that it is only after the initial clinical tests are completed that sufficient information becomes available on a drug's therapeutic and toxic effects to allow them to perform a formal rate-of-return analysis. A firm also has considerable economic incentive to do so at this point because the R&D costs for a project begin to escalate rapidly in the more advanced stages of development.[5] It is also true, however, that there are many more projects at the discovery and early clinical stages. In the aggregate, these constitute a major share (more than half) of the industry's total R&D investment expenditures.[6]

Given the difficulties of estimating returns for discovery research projects and in early clinical development trials, how do firms allocate resources to these projects and determine their total R&D budgets? Interviews with industry managers indicate that, in the short run, drug firms accord considerable attention to rule-of-thumb relationships.[7] In particular, they tend to focus on the R&D-to-sales ratio as a device for budgetary control and the allocation of resources to R&D. This is a short-run management device for dealing with the high levels of uncertainty associated with drug R&D, and it also provides some underlying stability in the growth (or contraction) of scientific personnel and other R&D inputs.

Nevertheless, it is also clear from examining data on the pharmaceutical industry that firm R&D-to-sales ratios or research intensities

---

[4] Wardell et al., "Rate of Development," p. 133.

[5] Hansen, "Pharmaceutical Development Process," p. 165.

[6] David Schwartzman, for example, estimates that discovery research by itself accounts for approximately half of the industry's R&D expenditures. See David Schwartzman, *Innovation in the Pharmaceutical Industry* (Baltimore: Johns Hopkins University Press, 1976), p. 70.

[7] The decision-making process in this regard was examined by Grabowski in his doctoral dissertation, "The Determinants and Effects of Industrial Research and Development Expenditures" (Princeton University, 1967), and more recently in a doctoral dissertation by Erol Caglarcan, "Economics of Innovation in the Pharmaceutical Industry" (George Washington University, 1977).

do change over time and that there is also a considerable variance in these ratios across firms at any point in time.[8] It seems reasonable to hypothesize that firms will attempt to adjust their research intensity over time in accordance with the factors specified in the investment model given above; that is to say, we would expect that firm research intensity would change in accordance with management perceptions of the prospective returns to R&D relative to the cost and availability of investment funds (namely, the X and Z factors in equations (1) and (2) above).

In this paper, we plan to develop and estimate a model of the determinants of firm research intensity in the pharmaceutical industry using this general methodological framework. Our analysis of firm research intensity builds directly on an earlier empirical study on this subject by Grabowski for the 1959–1962 period.[9] The current study will investigate the determinants of research intensity for a sample of ten major pharmaceutical firms over the more recent period 1962 to 1975.

An investigation of the determinants of drug firm research intensity for the post-1962 period would seem desirable on a number of counts. First, there have been a number of important structural changes affecting the pharmaceutical R&D process since 1962, including the Kefauver-Harris amendments to the Food and Drug Act. Second, there are some new data sources that can be employed to formulate some of the determinant variables in a form conceptually superior to what was previously possible. Finally, there are a number of important policy developments now taking place in the pharmaceutical industry, such as the passage of state substitution laws, which could influence significantly the incentives for R&D over the immediate future. To gain insights into the likely quantitative effects of these developments, however, R&D determinant equations estimated on current rather than historical data are necessary. Because there have been no published studies to our knowledge on R&D determinants specific to the pharmaceutical industry for the post-1962 period, we undertake such an empirical study here.[10]

Data Sample Characteristics. Data on firm R&D expenditures were obtained from the Standard and Poor Compustat Tape. Two major

---

[8] Data supporting this point are discussed in the next section and are also presented in the data appendix at the end of this paper.

[9] Grabowski, "Determinants of Research and Development," passim.

[10] Ben Branch has published a study of the determinants of R&D for drugs and other industries, using patents as a proxy for R&D inputs, that also focuses on the earlier time period, 1950 to 1965. See Ben Branch, "Research and Development Activity and Profitability: A Distributed Lag Analysis," *Journal of Political Economy*, vol. 82 (September/October 1974), pp. 999–1011.

6

considerations in selecting the sample of firms to include in the study were the availability of R&D expenditures for the complete 1962–1975 period and the degree of specialization of the firm in ethical drugs. Only firms with 40 percent or more of their total sales accounted for by ethical drug sales were included. (In addition, we included this percentage as an explanatory or control variable in the regressions.) These two conditions resulted in a sample of ten major pharmaceutical firms for the period 1962–1975.

Further details on this sample are presented in the data appendix. At this point, however, we should note that there is a wide variance in the research intensity for these ten sample firms. In the initial year of the sample, for example, R&D expenditures as a percentage of sales vary from a low of 3.8 percent to a high of 11.6 percent. Another interesting fact is that the R&D-to-sales ratio exhibited a decided downward trend over time between 1962 and 1975 for most of the firms in our sample.[11]

It is instructive in this regard to examine the time pattern of R&D expenditures and research intensities obtained by aggregating the individual firm data over the group of firms in our sample. These aggregate figures are shown in figure 1. R&D expenditures for this group of ten firms, measured in constant dollar terms, grew at a rapid rate over the 1960s but increased at relatively low rates during the 1970s.[12] In contrast to this pattern for absolute dollar outlays, however, the aggregate R&D-to-sales ratios for this group of firms peaked in the 1961 to 1963 period and exhibited a general decline over the remainder of this sample period. Hence, in contrast to the studies of R&D determinants previously done for the period of the 1950s and early 1960s, we are investigating here a period of generally declining rather than rising firm research intensities. It will be interesting to see how this affects the empirical estimates.

Explanatory Variables and Model Hypotheses. *Past R&D success.* A key question is how firms form expectations on the returns from R&D, given the high degree of uncertainty that characterizes the large share of projects in the discovery and early clinical development stages. A basic assumption made in Grabowski's earlier study was that firm expectations

---

[11] This was true for seven of the ten firms in the present sample. Furthermore, the three firms with a positive trend in R&D-to-sales ratios were the three with the lowest R&D-to-sales ratios in the beginning year, and their R&D-to-sales ratios remained significantly below the sample mean throughout the full period.

[12] Absolute R&D expenditures were transformed to constant 1967 dollars using the wholesale price index as the deflator. It is generally acknowledged that R&D costs have risen at a faster rate than this price index. Hence, the very low positive rates of growth for R&D expenditures over recent years observed in figure 1 could actually be negative if a better deflator of R&D expenditures were available to transform these data.

FIGURE 1
TIME TREND IN R&D VARIABLES FOR AGGREGATE SAMPLE

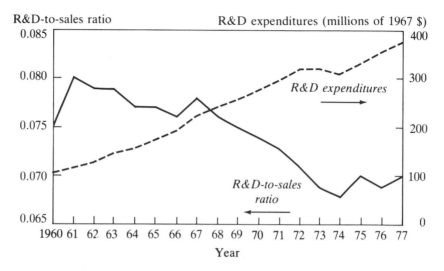

are significantly influenced by past successes or failures from R&D. Under this hypothesis, expectations change over time as a result of the firm's cumulative track record from R&D. Significant differences in attitudes and expectations concerning R&D can be expected to arise across firms from this adaptive type of process.

In Grabowski's earlier study, a variable indexing a firm's past "research productivity" was constructed to test this hypothesis. This variable was formulated as a moving average of the patents received by a firm relative to its R&D employees over a prior period of several years. Although this variable was highly significant, there are a number of obvious conceptual problems associated with using patents as one's basic index of R&D outputs.[13]

In the current study, an R&D productivity variable is constructed that has new product sales rather than patents as the basic measure of R&D output. In particular, the R&D productivity variable is formulated as a moving average of a firm's introductory sales of NCEs over a prior five-year period divided by its R&D expenditures over this period. This is a much better proxy variable for a firm's past return from R&D. It therefore should provide a better test of the expectational hypothesis above.

In addition, it will be especially interesting to see how this past

---

[13] These are discussed by Grabowski in "Determinants of Research and Development," pp. 294–95.

FIGURE 2

TIME TREND IN R&D PRODUCTIVITY INDEX FOR AGGREGATE SAMPLE

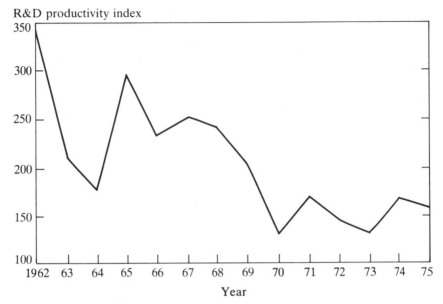

R&D productivity index

Year

success variable performs in the period under analysis, given the fact that a number of recent research studies point to sharply declining private rates of return to drug R&D activity in the post-1962 period. Martin Bailey, for example, found (pretax) rates of return to R&D in the pre-1962 period of approximately 30 percent while projecting rates of return in the post-1962 period to have declined to less than half this level.[14] David Schwartzman, in an extensive study of this question, estimated an (after-tax) return to drug R&D for the 1966–1972 period to be in the range of 3.3 to 7.5 percent, also down significantly from his pre-1962 estimated (after-tax) return of 11.4 percent.[15]

In figure 2, we have plotted the trend over time in our past R&D success variable that was obtained by summing the values on new product sales and R&D expenditures over all ten firms in our sample. Although there is considerable year-to-year fluctuation in this aggregate index, the long-term trend over the 1962 to 1975 period is clearly downward. The value in the terminal year is roughly half what it was in the

---

[14] Martin N. Bailey, "Research and Development Costs and Returns: The U.S. Pharmaceutical Industry," *Journal of Political Economy*, vol. 80 (January/February 1972), p. 83.

[15] David Schwartzman, *The Expected Return from Pharmaceutical Research* (Washington, D.C.: American Enterprise Institute, 1975).

9

initial year. The behavior of this aggregate variable over time therefore appears consistent with results from the formal rate-of-return studies cited above.

From a disaggregative perspective, of course, some of the firms in our sample experienced significant new product successes during this period while others did not, and this should be reflected in their R&D behavior if the hypothesis above is correct.

Diversification. A second determinant variable of research intensity included in Grabowski's early study was an index of firm diversification. This variable was included to test Richard Nelson's hypothesis that firm diversification will positively influence profit expectations from R&D.[16] The basic idea is that a more diversified firm will be better able to exploit serendipitous research findings than one with a narrow base of operations. Hence, it will have the incentive to undertake more R&D, especially basic or discovery research activity.

In Grabowski's earlier study, the measure of firm diversification used was the number of separate five-digit standard industrial classification (SIC) pharmaceutical products produced by the firm. This variable was statistically significant in his study. At the same time, however, diversification measures have exhibited a mixed performance in other studies of R&D expenditures and outputs. Some studies have found a positive effect for diversification, but others have found insignificant or even negative relationships.[17]

In the current study, we include firm diversification as a determinant variable of research intensity. Instead of counting the number of five-digit classes to construct this variable, however, firm data on market share by therapeutic product classes were assembled to construct a Herfindahl-type measure of diversification. This is a conceptually superior measure of this structural characteristic and should provide a better test of the effect of diversification on firm research intensity.[18]

---

[16] Richard Nelson, "The Simple Economics of Basic Scientific Research," *Journal of Political Economy*, vol. 67 (June 1959), pp. 297–306.

[17] The results of these studies are summarized in M. J. Kamien and N. L. Schwartz, "Market Structure and Innovation: A Survey," *Journal of Economic Literature*, vol. 13 (March 1975), pp. 26–27. In addition, an alternative measure of diversification based on the number of separate therapeutic categories in which a firm performs R&D has also been employed in past analysis. See Erol Caglarcan, Richard E. Faust, and Jerome E. Schnee, "Resource Allocation in Pharmaceutical Research and Development," in Samuel A. Mitchell and Emery A. Link, eds., *Impact of Public Policy on Drug Innovation and Pricing* (Washington, D.C.: American University, 1976), pp. 331–48.

[18] The Herfindahl Index, which is formally defined in the next section and illustrated in the data appendix, is generally considered a more discriminating measure of diversification because it takes account not only of the number of different product classes in which a firm produces but also of its level of production in each class.

Cash flow. In addition to expected returns, the cost and availability of investment funds are another basic set of factors influencing long-term R&D investment decisions (that is, the Z factors in equation 2). In Grabowski's earlier study, a highly significant relation was found between a firm's research intensity and its cash flow margin (measured as the ratio of lagged profits plus depreciation to sales). The basic rationale for including such a cash flow variable is the hypothesis that firms impute a lower cost of capital to internal funds, because of the lower transactions costs and risks compared with those from external sources.

The general relation between firm investment expenditures and cash flow availability has received considerable attention in the empirical literature on investment determinants. A number of studies have found results consistent with the hypothesis above, whereas others have disputed its validity.[19]

In the case of the relation of R&D investment in the pharmaceutical industry to cash flow availability, however, there are some particular factors that should be kept in mind. First, the industry invests relatively large sums in the search for new drug products and in the promotion of new products after they enter the marketplace. At the same time, the industry is not very capital-intensive in terms of fixed capital assets (that is, investment in plant and equipment). Hence, a large share of a firm's investment is in so-called intangible capital,[20] which generally involves above average riskiness.

This latter point is supported by recent research studies that indicate that the distribution of returns to drug R&D is highly skewed.[21] In particular, it is not uncommon for major firms to go several years without any commercially successful NCEs while, at the same time, a few new drugs have earned spectacular returns. Furthermore, the capital value of an established drug product can erode very quickly in pharmaceuti-

---

[19] Perhaps the most supportive empirical study of the general hypothesis underlying this relation is given in a paper by W. Baumol, P. Heim, B. Malkiel, and R. Quandt, "Earnings Retention, New Capital, and the Growth of the Firm," *Review of Economics and Statistics*, vol. 52 (November 1970), pp. 345–55. They find much lower average returns for investments financed by retained earnings compared with debt or new equity. For a review of studies specifically focused on the effects of cash flow on R&D investment, see the review in Kamien and Schwartz, "Market Structure and Innovation," pp. 24–26.

[20] This result emerges in studies by Kenneth W. Clarkson, *Intangible Capital and Rates of Return* (Washington, D.C.: American Enterprise Institute, 1977), and Henry G. Grabowski and Dennis C. Mueller, "Industrial Research and Development, Intangible Capital Stocks, and Firm Profit Rates," *Bell Journal of Economics*, vol. 9 (Autumn 1978), pp. 328–43.

[21] This finding, for example, is emphasized by Schwartzman in *The Expected Return*, pp. 137–39, and also in the paper by John Virts and Fred Weston, "Expectations and the Allocation of Research and Development Resources," herein.

cals, if a competitor comes out with a product clearly superior in the eyes of physicians.

Given these circumstances, it is not implausible that firm managers in the drug industry would have a strong desire for secure financial underpinnings to their investments in R&D and that a positive link between R&D outlays and cash flow availability would occur. This hypothesis is also consistent with the very low debt-to-equity ratios traditionally observed for this industry.[22]

In the current study, we therefore include cash flow availability as another determinant variable of drug R&D investment. Because the dependent variable in our analysis is research intensity, the cash flow variable is also deflated by firm sales.[23] Hence, we are testing the hypothesis that a firm's research intensity is positively related to its (lagged) cash flow margin. The trend over time in this cash flow margin variable for our aggregate ten-firm sample is shown in figure 3.

Basic Model Specification. The basic model that is to be estimated in our regression analysis for the 1962 to 1975 period is therefore the linear functional form of the following equation:

$$RDS_{it} = f(NR_{it}, DVR_i, CFM_{it}, PC_{it}) \qquad (3)$$

where the variables are defined as follows:

RDS_{it} = research and development expenditures divided by sales for the ith firm in year t

NR_{it} = index of past R&D success for ith firm in year t—in particular, it equals sales of firm's new product introductions, during first three years of product's commercial life, for all its introductions in years $t = 0, -1, \ldots, 4$, divided by R&D expenditures in year $t - 2$

DVR_i = a Herfindahl-type index of ith firm's diversification that equals $1 - \Sigma S_j^2$ where S_j = fraction of firm's ethical drugs sales in jth class, calculated at a midpoint year of the sample

---

[22] Stewart Myers argues that firms that tend to invest in assets that take a relatively long term to realize returns and are not easily salable (i.e., R&D as opposed to plant and equipment) are less likely to finance with debt instruments. See Stewart Myers, "Determinants of Corporate Borrowing," *Journal of Financial Economics*, vol. 5 (November 1977), pp. 147–75.

[23] By expressing these variables as intensity measures or size-deflated ratio variables, one also avoids the econometric problem of heteroscedasticity that is generally present in cross-sectional models estimated on absolute values.

FIGURE 3

TIME TREND IN CASH FLOW MARGIN FOR AGGREGATE SAMPLE

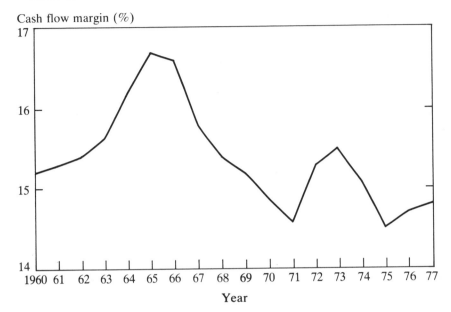

CFM_{it} = cash flow margin for ith firm in year t—in particular, it equals lagged profits after taxes plus depreciation divided by sales

PC_{it} = percentage of ith firm's total sales accounted for by ethical drug sales during year t

This is essentially the same structural model previously estimated by Grabowski for the 1959 to 1962 period. In the present analysis, however, we have constructed the past R&D success as well as the diversification variables in a conceptually superior form. The percentage of firm's sales accounted for by pharmaceuticals has also been included as a control variable to take account of the fact that firms have secondary, but nonsignificant, operations in other industries that will affect their overall research intensity.[24]

Several variants of this basic equation will also be estimated and discussed in the next section on empirical results.

---

[24] Because the pharmaceutical industry is among the most research-intensive sectors, diversification to other product areas generally implies lower overall firm research intensity. Hence, a positive coefficient is expected for the PC control variable in this regression equation.

13

Empirical Results

In table 1, we present the linear regression coefficient estimates for the model specified in equation (3). The coefficients are estimated on the pooled sample for the ten pharmaceutical firms taken over the entire fourteen-year period 1962–1975 and also for the two seven-year subintervals, 1962–1968 and 1969–1975.

As in the earlier study, both the cash flow and the R&D productivity variables are positive and statistically significant at normal confidence intervals. The diversification variable takes on the expected positive sign. It is statistically significant, however, only at the 10 percent level for the fourteen-year period and insignificant in the subinterval equations. Finally, the variable indicating the percentage of firm sales volume accounted for by pharmaceuticals, which has been added to present specification as an additional control factor, also has the expected positive coefficient and is statistically significant in all cases.

The present set of estimates is very similar in character to the previously published results. Thus, the model appears to be quite robust.

TABLE 1

LINEAR REGRESSIONS EXPLAINING R&D/SALES RATIOS FOR TEN PHARMACEUTICAL FIRMS

Equation Number	Intercept	CFM	NR	DVR	PC	R^2/F	Period
(1–1)	−.051	.268	.019	.045	.063	.49/32.6	1962–1975
	(−1.86)	(6.07)	(3.80)	(1.73)	(5.11)		
(1–2)	−.005	.224	.015		.064	.48/41.9	1962–1975
	(−.73)	(6.16)	(3.36)		(5.18)		
(1–3)	−.057	.282	.016	.035	.084	.53/18.9	1962–1968
	(−1.36)	(4.38)	(2.49)	(.88)	(5.01)		
(1–4)	−.021	.249	.013		.085	.53/25.1	1962–1968
	(−1.81)	(4.76)	(2.45)		(5.10)		
(1–5)	−.033	.255	.029	.042	.041	.44/13.1	1969–1975
	(−.85)	(3.81)	(1.96)	(1.09)	(2.18)		
(1–6)	.007	.209	.030		.043	.43/17.1	1969–1975
	(.72)	(4.01)	(2.01)		(2.30)		

NOTE: *t*-statistics are given in parentheses; *CFM* (cash flow margin) = profits after taxes plus depreciation divided by sales, all lagged two years; *NR* = sum of *NPS* (*t*) for $t = 0, -1, -2, -3, -4$, divided by R&D expenditures in $t -2$, where *NPS(t)* = sales of new chemical entities introduced in year t in $t + 1$, $t + 2$, and $t + 3$; *DVR* = index of diversification, which equals $1 - \Sigma s_i^2$, where s_i = share of prescriptions in ith class; *PC* = percentage of total firm sales accounted for by pharmaceutical sales.
SOURCE: See appendix.

Moreover, its robustness over the current fourteen-year sample period is illustrated by the high degree of stability in the coefficients when estimated over the two seven-year subintervals. Using the standard F-test devised by Chow, we were unable to reject the hypothesis that the estimated coefficients were identical over the two periods (with $F = 1.10$).[25]

Because the formulation of the R&D productivity variable as a five-year moving average of a firm's prior NCE introductions is quite arbitrary, we experimented with several variants of this variable. First, we tried constructing this variable as a moving average using shorter time intervals (three and four years) but found that the five-year period performed somewhat better from a statistical standpoint. Second, we estimated this variable using an Almon polynomial distributed lag approach. This relaxes the constraint of a uniform lag structure implicit in our moving average formulation. The pooled samples used in the present analysis do not provide the best basis for discriminating between alternative lag structures because of the short time intervals involved here. The general pattern emerging from the Almon lags estimates, however, indicated a declining lag structure as one moves backward in time. This is a plausible lag structure for this variable. Nevertheless, the five-year moving average formulation, which uses up fewer degrees of freedom, performs about as well from the standpoint of explanatory power. It therefore appears to be a reasonable formulation of this variable in the present situation.

We also investigated some alternative lag formulations for the cash flow margin variable. In particular, we estimated equation (3) with the cash flow margin separately lagged zero, one, and two periods and also with all of these lagged terms put simultaneously in one equation. We found all three lag specifications had similar coefficients when entered separately, but the two-period lag performed marginally better in terms of statistical significance. The two-period lag also dominated statistically when all three lag terms were entered simultaneously; so this particular lag term was selected for our summary results in table 1.[26]

---

[25] We should also observe that because the data involve a pooling of cross sections, the usual Durbin-Watson coefficient cannot be used to test autocorrelation. Theoretically, an estimate of the autocorrelation parameter for the error terms of each of the ten firms might be appropriate, yielding ten parameters to be used in transforming the data. A visual examination of the residuals, however, indicated that serial correlation did not appear to be a problem in the present situation. This contention was given further support by estimating regressions using observations for the years 1962, 1969, and 1975 only for each firm. The coefficients were quite close to those in table 1.

[26] There is such a high degree of correlation between these lag terms in our pooled cross-sectional sample that attempts to estimate more complex lag structures were not feasible. Nevertheless, it is interesting to note that when we entered these lag terms simultaneously, the sum of the regression coefficients was approximately equal to the value observed when the lag terms were estimated separately.

It is interesting to point out that the coefficient estimates for the cash flow margin variable in table 1, and also for the alternative lag term formulations, are quite close to the 0.24 coefficient estimate on this variable in Grabowski's early study. These estimates imply that a $1 million increase (decrease) in cash flow will lead approximately to a quarter-million increase (decrease) in R&D expenditures. Moreover, estimates on the magnitude of this coefficient have remained stable for an extensive period in which a number of important structural changes have occurred in the industry.

We should emphasize at this point that the effects on R&D investment of the past R&D success and cash flow variables are interrelated. In particular, past R&D success influences not only a firm's expected future returns to R&D but also its level of cash flow availability to undertake R&D. We investigated this point by estimating distributed lag relations between the cash flow margin and past R&D productivity measures. We found a statistically significant relation between these variables that was characterized by relatively long mean lags—namely, seven to nine years. Hence, there is a long-term interactive relation between these variables and R&D. Specifically, if a firm's research productivity remains low for a number of years, its cash flow will also eventually be significantly affected, and there will be further negative impacts on its R&D investment.[27]

The diversification variable was not statistically significant in the present analysis, in contrast with the earlier study. One problem with this variable in the current case is that all ten firms turned out to be very diversified across ethical drug classes. Hence, there is not much sample variation to investigate this hypothesis.[28] As discussed above, this variable has also performed in a mixed fashion in several related studies by other investigators.

In addition to the linear regression specification given in table 1, we also estimated a logarithmic specification of this model. This specification was confronted by a basic problem not applicable to the linear case—namely, the presence of some zero observations in the R&D productivity variables. We circumvented this problem by the standard

---

[27] The observed coefficient on the cash flow variable can also be expected to be altered, over the long run, by the firm's expected return to R&D. Whereas we have estimated the parameter using a linear specification over the relatively short period under study, a firm's investment allocations from its cash flow should change in accordance with its long-run perceptions of relative returns from different investment activities. Thus, if a firm were to become convinced over time that the expected returns from R&D were generally going to remain below those of other investment activities, one would also expect to see the share of cash flow devoted to R&D diminish.

[28] This point can be seen from the data presented in the appendix. The sample mean for the diversification variable is 0.84, and its coefficient of variation is only .08. Eight of the ten firms are concentrated in the narrow interval from 0.83 to 0.91.

(but ad hoc) procedure of assigning arbitrary low values to these zero observations. Two firms had so many zero values that they were omitted from the analysis. Nevertheless, the resulting estimates were generally supportive of the linear equation specification, in the sense that both the cash flow and the past R&D success variables were statistically significant.

In sum, the empirical results presented here generally confirm the investment model presented in the first part of the paper. They are also broadly consistent with Grabowski's empirical findings for the earlier 1959 to 1962 period.

Conclusions and Implications

As noted at the outset, drug innovation has been characterized by a number of adverse trends over the last two decades, including higher research costs and development times and fewer new product introductions. Several researchers have formally investigated the private rate of return to pharmaceutical R&D over this period, and they have generally found low average returns on R&D. Nonetheless, these rate-of-return studies also give rise to a somewhat paradoxical question: Why have drug firms continued to maintain such high levels of investment in R&D if the expected returns are as low as these studies seem to indicate?

The analysis of R&D determinants undertaken here provides some insights into this question. Our regression results indicate that firms do react to lower realized returns on R&D in the expected manner, but the adjustment process is a very gradual one with relatively long lags. This is perhaps not surprising, given the fact that new product innovation has historically been a central and quite profitable mode of competition for the industry dating back to the pre–World War II era. Moreover, the high degree of uncertainty and serendipity that characterizes discovery research and early clinical development trials in pharmaceuticals is also consistent with a cautious response to lower realized returns on past R&D efforts. Future returns may be very different from current or past returns, especially for individual firms. Although the major drug firms have not generally responded to lower returns by decreasing the *absolute* size of their R&D personnel and other inputs, the research intensities of these firms have been gradually declining over the past two decades, and there have been increased investment and diversification in nonpharmaceutical areas.

Our regression results also indicate that the general availability of internal funds, or cash flow, is another important factor that influenced R&D behavior over this period. We found a statistically significant, stable positive relation between firm research intensities and their lagged

17

cash flow margins. Moreover, these margins were relatively high over much of the period under study as a result of the record number of products introduced in the 1950s. These products remained under patent protection and generated high cash flows for the innovating firm well into the 1960s, and even 1970s, in many cases.[29]

We can therefore infer from our analysis that the relatively high levels of internal cash flow over much of the post-1962 period operated to moderate the observed decline in firm research intensities. Whether this will be the case in the future, however, is not at all obvious. Industry cash flow margins are now well below the peak of earlier years. Furthermore, there are a number of institutional and structural changes taking place in the industry that are likely to have negative effects on both the expected returns to R&D and the cash flow margins of the research-intensive firms in the future. These changes, which we have analyzed elsewhere, include much shorter effective patent lives on current new product introductions,[30] as well as the likelihood of increased competition from generic products in the postpatent period as a result of the new state substitution laws and the maximum-allowable-cost program on government purchases of drugs.[31]

Should policy makers be concerned about declining research intensity in the pharmaceutical industry and the prospect that such trends may accelerate if the private returns on R&D remain low? The answer to this question depends on whether current levels of private R&D expenditures are too high or too low from the perspective of overall *social* benefits and costs. The positive analysis of R&D behavior undertaken here does not directly address this question.

We might close, however, by noting that it is generally presumed in the theoretical literature that social rates of return will usually be

---

[29] This general point is illustrated by examining the trend on the aggregate cash flow margin for the ten firms in our sample that is plotted in figure 3. This variable was still increasing for several years into the 1960s while the level of sales per R&D input had peaked and was trending sharply downward (as reflected in the behavior of the research productivity variable in figure 2).

[30] The University of Rochester's Center for the Study of Drug Development has undertaken an analysis of average effective patent life for new introductions over recent years. They found that average patent life for an NCE introduced in 1966 was 13.8 years, but by 1977 the average patent life for an NCE had declined to 8.9 years (Martin Eisman, University of Rochester, private correspondence, 1978). The short effective patent lives on new drug products reflect the long development and regulatory approval times and the fact that a patent is normally granted several years before a typical NCE is approved for marketing.

[31] In a recently published paper, we perform a sensitivity analysis that examines the joint effect of shorter patent lives and increased substitution on the incentives for R&D: "Substitution Laws and Innovation in the Pharmaceutical Industry," *Law and Contemporary Problems*, vol. 43 (Winter-Spring 1979), pp. 43–66.

TABLE 2

DATA VALUES FOR ALL VARIABLES, 1970

Firm	R&D/SALES	CFM	NR	DVR	PC
Abbott	0.058	0.115	0.4	0.88	0.72
Eli Lilly	0.103	0.174	154.8	0.89	0.71
Merck	0.092	0.197	52.2	0.83	0.90
Pfizer	0.035	0.120	411.6	0.84	0.48
Robins	0.044	0.135	6.5	0.86	0.70
Schering-Plough	0.054	0.150	192.7	0.88	0.63
SmithKline	0.090	0.171	15.3	0.91	0.62
Syntex	0.119	0.301	186.1	0.63	0.74
Upjohn	0.105	0.135	205.6	0.86	0.86
Carter-Wallace	0.063	0.102	0.0	0.86	0.42

Definition of variables and sources:
- R&D/SALES = research and development expenditures divided by sales; obtained from Standard and Poor's Compustat Annual Data Tape.
- CFM (cash flow margin) = profits after taxes plus depreciation divided by sales, all lagged two years; obtained from the Compustat Tape.
- NR = sum of $NPS(t)$ for $t = 0, -1, -2, -3, -4$, divided by R&D expenditures in $t - 2$; where $NPS(t)$ = sales of new chemical entities introduced in year t in $t + 1$, $t + 2$, and $t + 3$. Units are normalized for descriptive purposes (see figure 2). List of new chemical entities each year obtained from Paul de Haen, *Nonproprietary Name Index*, and special reports by de Haen. All data on sales of new chemical entities obtained from Intercontinental Medical Statistics.
- DVR = index of diversification, which equals $1 - \Sigma s_i^2$ where s_i = share of prescriptions in ith class. This index was constructed using data from a marketing research firm, Lea Associates. In a special report for the year 1968, an analysis of pharmaceutical manufacturers was prepared in which each firm's total prescriptions were distributed among twenty-two classes (for example, infective and parasitic diseases, neoplasms, allergic disorders). Hence, DVR values for 1968 were assumed to hold for the entire period.
- PC = percentage of total firm sales accounted for by pharmaceutical sales. The value of PC for 1970 was obtained from NEDO Chemicals, *E.D.C. Focus on Pharmaceuticals*, September 1972. Values of PC for 1975 were obtained from *Scrip*, January 8, 1977. Hence, the 1970 PC values were applied to all prior years, and succeeding years were found by linearly interpolating between 1970 and 1975 values.

greater than private rates of return on R&D activity for a number of well-known reasons.[32] Furthermore, Mansfield et al. recently investigated this question empirically for a sample of seventeen (nonpharmaceutical) innovations and found the social rate of return on average

[32] A classic article in this regard is Kenneth Arrow's paper, in the National Bureau of Economic Research conference volume, "Economic Welfare and the Allocation of Resources to Invention," in R. Nelson, ed., *The Rate and Direction of Inventive Activity* (Princeton: Princeton University Press, 1962).

to be roughly double the private rate.[33] The case study analysis by
Weisbrod and Geweke[34] to be presented later in this volume also indicates relatively high social returns to R&D. Although considerable
research remains to be done in this area, these initial results suggest that
policy makers should at least examine the basic factors underlying the
declining levels of drug firm research intensities and innovations and
should also consider possible policy options for dealing with this situation.

Data Appendix

The data used in this study were obtained from various sources, as will
be described. Table 2 contains values for the variables for the year 1970
to provide the reader with an understanding of the relative magnitudes.
The ten firms selected were all firms for which complete data were
available for the 1962–1975 period. Generally, the unavailability of data
on R&D expenditures was the primary reason that most other firms
failed to be included.

---

[33] Edwin Mansfield, J. Rapoport, A. Romeo, S. Wagner, and G. Beardsley, "Social and
Private Rates of Return from Industrial Innovation," *Quarterly Journal of Economics*,
vol. 91 (May 1977), pp. 221–40.
[34] John F. Geweke and Burton A. Weisbrod, "Some Economic Consequences of Technological Advance in Medical Care: The Case of a New Drug," herein.

Expectations and the Allocation of Research and Development Resources

John R. Virts and J. Fred Weston

Introduction

The determinants of and the results from research and development (R&D) have been an important area of theoretical and empirical research for economists.[1] An important aspect of the findings of this research is that the innovation that results from R&D can in turn affect the structure of an industry.[2] Standard economic theory predicts that a major determinant of the amount of research and development activity, and its resulting innovative output, is the expectations of the future net returns of that activity compared with alternative investments.

It is the expected rate of return that is the key element in the allocation of resources among all activities in the economy; but economists have not been able to observe expected rates of return and therefore they have been forced to observe ex post accounting rates of return. By combining these observations with observations concerning the movement of resources, inferences about the relative magnitude of the expected rate of return as well as the allocative efficiency of particular economic activities have been drawn. For example, if accounting rates of return on an activity are observed to be high at some point in time, relative to other activities, and if this attracts resources into the activity, it subsequently causes an erosion of the accounting returns. Here it is concluded that there is relative allocative efficiency because resources are shifted, which reduces the accounting rate of return.

Alternatively, if the observed accounting rate of return for a particular economic endeavor is low and this causes a reduction in the amount of resources devoted to that activity, which in turn generates an increase in the accounting rate of return, then it is felt the expected

An earlier version of this paper appeared in *Managerial and Decision Economics*, vol. 1, no. 3 (September 1980), pp. 103–11. We are indebted to Douglas L. Cocks, Yale Brozen, Robert B. Helms, and Richard L. Smith for assistance and comments.

[1] For a comprehensive survey of this research, see M. J. Kamien and N. L. Schwartz, "Market Structure and Innovation: A Survey," *Journal of Economic Literature*, vol. 13 (March 1975), pp. 1–37.

[2] Ibid., p. 11.

rate of return was low. Again, it is inferred that allocative efficiency is achieved because of the movement of resources.

If we combine the theory of expected profitability and empirical observation, using accounting measures can also create some ambiguities. If accounting rates of return remain persistently high and entry does not occur, for example, there are at least two possible explanations: (1) the accounting rate of return reflects the economic rate of return, but entry barriers prevent the flow of resources from forcing down the expected rate of return; (2) accounting rates of return do not reflect expected economic rates of return, and the lack of resource movement reflects an average level of expected economic rates of return.

The measured rate of return for the pharmaceutical industry has been of some interest to economists. The early literature exphasized that the accounting rate of return of the industry was persistently higher than that of other U.S. manufacturing industries. When aligned with information on the structure and behavior of the industry, these accounting rates were considered to be the primary indicator of resource misallocation.[3]

The more recent literature on the economic rate of return of the pharmaceutical industry has been concerned with the idea that the accounting rates of return reported in annual reports and other published sources do not accurately reflect the economic rate of return. This occurs because accounting measures generally do not treat expenditures for research and development as an asset, and therefore accounting rates do not represent economic rate of return.[4] The various studies that were concerned with this issue made adjustments to accounting numbers such that R&D are treated as an investment. With these adjustments, the rates of return are significantly reduced and approach the rates for many industries.[5]

---

[3] P. M. Costello, "The Tetracycline Conspiracy: Structure, Conduct, and Performance in the Drug Industry," *Antitrust Law and Economic Review*, vol. 1 (Summer 1968), pp. 13–44; Leonard Schifrin, "The Ethical Drug Industry: The Case for Compulsory Patent Licensing," *Antitrust Bulletin*, vol. 12 (Fall 1967), pp. 893–915; and H. Steele, "Monopoly and Competition in the Ethical Drug Market," *Journal of Law and Economics*, vol. 5 (October 1962), pp. 131–63.

[4] The Federal Trade Commission has stated that the capitalizing of R&D is an important aspect of an industry that must be considered when assessing economic rates of return; see Bureau of National Affairs, Inc., "FTC Annual Line of Business Report Program," *Securities Regulation and Law Report*, August 22, 1973, D-1–D-10.

[5] See R. Ayanian, "The Profit Rates and Economic Performance of Drug Firms," in R. B. Helms, ed., *Drug Development and Marketing* (Washington, D.C.: American Enterprise Institute, 1975), pp. 81–96; Harry Bloch, "True Profitability Measures for Pharmaceutical Firms," in J. D. Cooper, ed., *Regulation, Economics, and Pharmaceutical Innovation* (Washington, D.C.: The American University, 1976), pp. 145–57; Kenneth

Although these more recent analyses of rates of return to the pharmaceutical industry have been valuable, they still contain difficulties when the assessment of economic rates of return as seen as expected returns is desired. First, these, like accounting measures, may or may not reflect these expected rates of return. Second, these returns reflect average rates of return. Third, these measures do not reflect the return on research and development, which is a crucial element, especially when public policy is being considered.

To overcome some of these difficulties, David Schwartzman has attempted to measure the internal rate of return to pharmaceutical R&D. Schwartzman estimates that this internal rate of return is well below a "normal" alternative return.[6] The type of internal-rate-of-return calculation conducted by Schwartzman is also faced with some difficulties. The estimates require some fairly broad assumptions coupled with broad aggregate data for the industry. Schwartzman's estimates are inherently averages, as are the calculations from previous studies.[7] The Schwartzman estimates are ex post, and as such they do not adequately reveal the elements upon which expectations are formed in generating expected rate of return estimates.[8]

It is the purpose of this paper to generate an inferred judgment concerning the relative magnitude of the current (1976) expected rate of return for pharmaceutical research and development. In making this assessment, an actual numerical calculation of the expected rate of return will not be made. Given the numbers that are available, it would be possible to make such a calculation, but the result would be fraught with as many difficulties as have been experienced from the earlier studies. Instead, the focus of attention will be on the formation of the expectations that are the basis of determining the expected rate of return. An important aspect of this expectations formation process is the impact of public policy on it.

In this context, there are two sets of expectations. In both, differing sets of public policies are operating. One set of expectations relates to the cost of developing new pharmaceutical products. Here the primary public policy impact operates through the regulation of drug development and testing by the Food and Drug Administration (FDA). This

W. Clarkson, *Intangible Capital and Rates of Return* (Washington, D.C.: American Enterprise Institute, 1977); and T. R. Stauffer, "Profitability Measures in the Pharmaceutical Industry," in Helms, *Drug Development.*

[6] David Schwartzman, *Innovation in the Pharmaceutical Industry* (Baltimore: Johns Hopkins University Press, 1976), pp. 136–61.

[7] F. M. Scherer, "Commentaries" (comments on seminar papers, "Factors Affecting Drug Companies' Incentives and Performance"), in Helms, *Drug Development,* p. 122.

[8] Cf. Sam Peltzman, "Review of David Schwartzman's *Innovation in the Pharmaceutical Industry,*" *Journal of Economic Literature,* vol. 16 (March 1978), pp. 149–50.

impact is manifested in the sheer burden of complying with the structure of FDA regulation.

The second set of expectations relates to the expected revenues from new pharmaceutical products. In many cases the public policies that affect revenue expectations are much more subtle, and therefore not as discernible, but they would include things such as state formularies, maximum-allowable-cost (MAC) programs, repeal of antisubstitution laws, and other methods that would reduce product revenues. In addition, FDA regulations that affect patent life and competitive positions of individual products would also affect revenue streams.

It is the intent of this paper to look separately at both the cost and the revenue sides of new drug development and to see how the two expectational sets are shaped. On the cost side, we assume expectations are based on patterns of historical data on cost experience and trends in the costs per new chemical entity (NCE) produced. For revenue expectations, we look at the historical sales patterns along with marketing forecasts of future sales rates of the NCEs introduced during the ten-year period 1967–1976. We also consider the ways public policy affects these expectational sets, and we analyze changes in the structure of the industry. By combining the assessment of changed expectations with the assessment of structural change, it will be possible to infer the relative magnitude of the expected returns to pharmaceutical R&D. The importance of this consideration is seen by the fact that the private pharmaceutical industry is the primary source of new drug innovation. Studies of new drugs introduced into the United States between 1940 and 1977 show that over 90 percent originated in private pharmaceutical firms.[9]

Before we proceed to the analysis of the factors that affect expected rates of return to pharmaceutical research and development, a discussion of one of the basic assumptions of this paper is necessary. In recent years there has been some discussion about the extent to which pharmaceutical innovation is limited by the exhaustion of knowledge.[10] In economic terms it is felt by some that the production of drug innovation has reached the point of diminishing returns. It is assumed in this paper that the point of diminishing returns has not been reached in the production of drug innovation. That this assumption is felt to be valid is primarily due to the very nature of pharmaceutical R&D. Unlike many sciences—physics, for example—the pharmaceutical sciences have been characteristically empirical. The recent development of medicinal sci-

---

[9] PMA Fact Book, 1978 (draft).

[10] Henry G. Grabowski, *Drug Regulation and Innovation* (Washington, D.C.: American Enterprise Institute, 1976).

ence appears to be in the direction of establishing relevant theories concerning chemical and therapeutic activity. Therefore, it is hypothesized that as this theory evolves, a greater number of drug innovations will be possible.

The Pharmaceutical Development Process and the Cost of Innovation

Basing his calculations on a sample of NCE testing records supplied by fourteen firms covering the period 1963–1975, Ronald Hansen developed data on the length of time and the costs required to complete the various phases of testing in the process of seeking FDA approval of a new drug.[11] Following is a summary of the eight stages of the drug development process identified by Hansen:

1. *Discovery phase*: This stage involves basic research syntheses of new chemicals and early studies of chemical properties to identify specific new chemical entities that are worthy of further testing. Three durations have been assumed for this stage. A three-year period is picked for the cost analysis. The total identifiable testing expenditures are estimated to be $1.1 million in 1967 dollars.

2. *Preclinical animal testing*: During the early development stage after the discovery of new chemical entities, short-term animal toxicity tests are performed for evidence of safety in preparation for human testing. The average reported duration for this stage is 13.7 months, with an average cost of $97,000 in 1967 dollars.

3. *IND filing*: If the findings in the prior stage are favorable, a request is made for authorization to begin human testing by filing a notice of claimed investigational exemption for a new drug (IND). Usually, it takes thirty days to get the authorization.

4. *Phase I clinical testing*: This is the first of three sequential tests that are conducted directly on human bodies. Doses of the NCE in testing are given to healthy volunteers for evidence of toxicity in humans. Started right after the discovery phase and the authorization of human testing, this stage lasts for an average 9.1 months in Hansen's sample, with an estimated cost of $166,000 in 1967 dollars.

5. *Phase II clinical testing*: Only 50 percent of the testings performed during the last stages in Hansen's sample turned out to be positive and were continued in this phase to evaluate therapeutic values of the NCEs. The average testing time and expenditures were 23.2 months and $881,000.

---

[11] R. W. Hansen, "The Pharmaceutical Development Process: Estimates of Development Costs and Times and the Effects of Proposed Regulatory Changes," in R. I. Chien, ed., *Issues in Pharmaceutical Economics* (Lexington, Mass.: Lexington Books, 1979).

6. *Phase III clinical testing*: Nineteen percent of all the sampled NCEs that entered the human clinical testing passed the prior test and were further tested in this period. Large-scale tests are conducted in human bodies to uncover unanticipated side effects. All the extensive tests should be conducted before the final new drug application (NDA) is approved. An average testing time of 33.6 months is reported. The average cost for this phase is $1,546,000 in 1967 dollars.

7. *Long-term animal studies*: About 29 percent of NCEs tested in phase II were advanced here to check the effects of prolonged exposures and the effects on subsequent generations. Such studies are typically started six months after the beginning of phase II testing and last for 36.8 months. The average expenditures are around $420,000 in 1967 dollars.

8. *NDA approval*: This is the application to the FDA for approval of commercial marketing of the new drug after it has completed all the tests above. The approval is granted for about one out of eight of the original NCEs for which an IND was issued in the sample reported by Hansen. The average NDA submission date is 22.6 months after the start of phase III. The average time for an approval decision is 24 months.

Based on Hansen's work, table 1 shows the expected monthly expenditures for each stage. Column (1) is the average cost for testing during each phase. The probabilities of the original NCE's reaching each phase are given in column (2). Average durations of each stage are shown in column (3). The expected monthly expenditures in Column (4) are derived by first multiplying columns (1) and (2) and then dividing by column (3). In table 2, column (1) is the duration of each phase in months. Column (2) shows the time period from the end of each phase to the NDA approval.

The data of tables 1 and 2 are used in the cost analysis in table 3. Column (1) in table 3 is from column (4) in table 1, and column (5) in table 3 is from column (2) in table 2. An 8 percent cost of capital is assumed by Hansen as a high reference case. The future value interest factor of annuity (FVIFA) at an 8 percent cost of capital and for the duration in column (2) is calculated for each stage in column (3). By multiplying the expected monthly expenditures in column (1) by FVIFA, we get the expected capitalized costs for each phase in column (4). In column (6), the future value interest factors (FVIF) at the same cost of capital and for the durations in column (5) are generated. The expected capitalized costs to the point of marketing approval for each phase are then derived by multiplying column (4) by column (6).

The total estimated costs and the methods of calculation for each

TABLE 1

EXPECTED MONTHLY INVESTMENT OUTLAYS FOR DEVELOPING A
NEW DRUG
(thousands of 1967 dollars)

	Phase	Average Cost for Testing during Phase (1)	Probability of NCE's Reaching Phase (%) (2)	Duration of Phase in Months (3)	Expected Monthly Expenditures (1) × (2) ÷ (3) (4)
(a)	Three-year discovery phase	$1,100	100	36.0	$30.56
(b)	Preclinical animal toxicity	97	100	13.7	7.08
(c)	Phase I clinical	166	100	9.1	18.24
(d)	Phase II clinical	881	50	23.2	18.99
(e)	Phase III clinical	1,546	19	33.6	8.74
(f)	Long-term animal studies	420	29	36.8	3.31

SOURCE: Hansen, "Pharmaceutical Development Process," pp. 151–88.

major stage are shown in rows (g), (h), and (i). The cost per marketable NCE (which is one of eight successful INDs) is the product of the total cost for each successful IND in row (i) times eight and is shown in row (j). Using the price index of 1.829 for 1976 with the 1967 price level as the base, we can convert the cost in row (j) to get the total expenditures for each marketable NCE in 1976 dollars, which gives $54.2 million in row (k).

The estimate of $54 million as the cost of developing a successful NCE in 1976 is a reference number. It is, of course, subject to variation in both directions. A number of types of sensitivity analysis could be performed. We were particularly interested in the issue of drug lag because the 1962 amendments appear to have roughly doubled the time for FDA approval to about three years. We, therefore, examined the effects of reducing the lag by twelve months. We accordingly reduced the number of months in column (5) of table 3 by twelve months for all rows except row (e). For column (2) we reduced the duration by twelve months for only rows (d), (e), and (f). The result was to decrease the

TABLE 2

TIME PROFILE OF EACH R&D PHASE

Phase	Duration of Phase (1)	End of Phase to Marketing Approval (2)
(a) Three-year discovery phase	36.0	78.9(d + e + f + h2)
(b) Preclinical animal toxicity	13.7	79.9(c + d + e + f + h2)
(c) IND filing	1.0	78.9(d + e + f + h2)
(d) Phase I clinical	9.1	69.8(e + f + h2)
(e) Phase II clinical	23.2	46.6(f + h2)
(f) Phase III clinical	33.6	13.0(h2)
(g) Long-term animal studies	36.8	27.0(e + f − 6^a − g + h2)
(h) NDA approval	24.0	0
1. Before the end of phase III	11.0	
2. After the end of phase III	13.0	

^{a} Subtracted to allow for overlap with other phases.
SOURCE: Same as table 1.

estimated capitalized cost of an NCE to $43 million, a reduction of approximately 20 percent.

As another check, explicitly heuristic and less rigorous, on the $54 million estimate of the cost of an NCE in 1976, we analyzed R&D outlays per NCE for the period 1961 through 1977, using the data shown in table 4. We recognize, of course, that lead-lag relationships are involved, so we focused our analysis on the final column, which is a three-year moving average of R&D outlays per NCE. The average is related to the middle year of the three-year period. Thus we have data for 1962 through 1976. The R&D outlays per NCE increase at a compound annual rate of 14 percent per annum. The issue posed by this figure is whether prospective returns from NCEs have increased at the same 14 percent rate.

Although the $54 million from the Hansen analysis represents capitalized costs to the point of marketing approval, the annual company-financed R&D expenditures shown in table 4 are more properly related to NCEs to appear in future years. We note, however, that the R&D expenditures per NCE shown in table 4 are of the same order of mag-

TABLE 3

REPLICATION OF HANSEN'S ESTIMATES
(thousands of dollars)

Phase	Expected Monthly Expenditures (1)	Duration of Phase in Months (2)	FVIFA at 8% (3)	Expected Capitalized Costs for Each Phase (1) × (3) (4)	End of Phase to Marketing Approval (5)	FVIF at 8% (6)	Expected Capitalized Costs to Marketing Approval (4) × (6) (7)
(a) Three-year discovery phase	$30.56	36.0	40.5356	$1,238.77	78.9	1.6892	$ 2,093
(b) Preclinical animal toxicity	7.08	13.7	14.2953	101.21	79.9	1.7005	172
(c) Phase I clinical	18.24	9.1	9.3496	170.54	69.8	1.5901	271
(d) Phase II clinical	18.99	23.2	25.0005	474.76	46.6	1.3629	647
(e) Phase III clinical	8.74	33.6	37.5212	327.94	13.0	1.0902	358
(f) Long-term animal studies	3.31	36.8	41.5511	137.53	27.0	1.1965	165
(g) Total post-IND [(c) + (d) + (e) + (f)]							1,441
(h) Total including preclinical [(b) + (g)]							1,613
(i) Total including discovery phase [(a) + (h)]							3,706
(j) Total cost per marketed NCE [(i) × 8]							29,648
(k) Total cost per marketed NCE in 1976 dollars [(j) × 1.829]							54,226

SOURCE: Same as table 1.

29

TABLE 4

R&D OUTLAYS PER NEW CHEMICAL ENTITY, 1961–1977
(millions of dollars)

	Company-Financed R&D Expenditures for Human-Use Pharmaceuticals (1)	Number of NCEs Excluding Salts (2)	R&D Outlays per NCE (3)	Three-Year Moving Average of R&D Outlays per NCE (4)
1961	$227.3	36	$6.3	—
1962	237.8	26	9.2	$10.7
1963	267.1	16	16.7	14.1
1964	278.3	17	16.4	15.8
1965	328.7	23	14.3	20.6
1966	374.4	12	31.2	20.7
1967	412.4	25	16.5	29.5
1968	449.5	11	40.9	37.9
1969	505.8	9	56.2	44.2
1970	565.8	16	35.4	45.5
1971	628.8	14	44.9	47.0
1972	666.8	11	60.6	48.4
1973	752.5	19	39.6	49.3
1974	858.5	18	47.7	49.4
1975	973.5	16	60.8	59.9
1976	1,067.8	15	71.2	65.9
1977	1,181.8	18	65.7	—

SOURCES: Column (1) and 1961, 1962 for column (2): Grabowski, *Drug Regulation*, table 1, p. 18, table 3, p. 43; and PMA, *Annual Survey Report: Ethical Pharmaceutical Industry Operations*, various years. Column (2), 1963–1977: Paul de Haen, Inc., New York, N.Y., various annual publications.

nitude (but somewhat larger) than the Hansen $54 million for 1976. Relative to expectations and the allocation of resources, the key point is whether prospective revenues from NCEs have kept pace with the 14 percent compound annual rate of increase in R&D outlays per NCE over the last fifteen years to achieve recovery of the $54 million investment. Therefore, we next turn to an analysis of prospective cash flows from NCEs.

Prospective Cash Flows from Pharmaceutical Innovation

In the decade 1967–1976, over 150 NCEs (some in the form of several products by one or more manufacturers) were introduced in the U.S.

market, of which 119 represent primarily outpatient (nonhospital) therapy, so that drugstore prescription sales constitute nearly all of the sales of products based on these NCEs. These 119 NCEs were selected for study because data concerning prescription sales would reflect virtually all sales.

Audits of drugstore prescription sales (including both new and refill prescriptions) and of drugstore purchases of prescription drugs from manufacturers and distributors are routinely conducted by the market research firm IMS America. These audits were used to study the number of prescriptions and the drugstores' purchase cost of the products—the drugstore purchase cost is used here as the manufacturer's (NCE owner's) selling price.

The following numbers of studied NCEs were introduced in each of the ten years 1967–1976:

1967	21	1973	16
1968	9	1974	15
1969	8	1975	16
1970	8	1976	7
1971	10		
1972	9	Total	119

This group of 119 products closely matches the approved NDAs from sets of R&D projects analyzed in the cost data reported in the previous section. For each of the ten cohorts of products introduced in a particular year, sales data were collected for each of the years since introduction through 1976. (There were, thus, ten years of data for twenty-one products, nine years for nine, and so forth, with only one year of data for the seven NCEs introduced in 1976.) The pattern of sales for these NCEs, as well as other historical studies, indicates a growth curve for the first ten years of a new drug product's life exhibiting the S-shaped growth characteristic. On this experience basis, projections were made for each set of products as required to derive ten years of data. (Table 9 in the appendix shows the summary data and projections.) From these data, the properties of an average NCE from these 119 can be derived for an average year of its first ten years in the market. In addition, the distribution of NCEs around this average was calculated for prescription volume, manufacturer's selling price per prescription, and sales, as summarized in table 5.

These data are used to develop estimates of the distribution of the prospective dollar returns as shown in table 6. The results obtained in table 6 reflect the application of the following procedures:

1. Selling price data (row 1) are taken from table 5.

TABLE 5

MARKET PERFORMANCE OF 119 NEW CHEMICAL ENTITIES,
1967–1976

	Number of Prescriptions per NCE (millions)	Manufacturer's Selling Price per Prescription	Annual Sales per NCE ($ millions)
Average	1.333	$5.16	$ 6.9
Average of top 25%	3.937	5.36	21.1
Average of low 75%	0.493	4.65	2.3

NOTE: The sample includes over 75 percent of the NCEs introduced during the decade.
SOURCE: Compilations by the authors from IMS America data.

2. From a review of the financial reports of pharmaceutical companies, we observe that all costs excluding depreciation, R&D, interest, taxes, and profits constitute 70 percent of the manufacturer's selling price. This is a strong modal relationship, only one or two companies having lower or higher cost ratios.

3. Net cash flows composed of depreciation, R&D, interest, taxes, and profits constitute 30 percent of the manufacturer's selling price.

4. Studies indicate that the average transaction price per dosage unit of ethical drugs increased at a 2.2 percent annual rate over the period 1968–1978.[12] The Firestone price index for the same period increased at an annual rate of 2.9 percent.[13] Making allowance for a somewhat higher rate of future inflation, we employed a price change estimate of 3 percent. The average year's inflated margin was computed by multiplying row 3 by $(1.03)^5$ to obtain row 4.

5. Because most NCEs are sold in foreign markets as well as in the United States, the number of prescriptions from the U.S. study, above, is multiplied by 1.6, the ratio of worldwide sales to U.S. sales for the typical U.S. firm reported by the industry association (PMA), resulting in row 5.[14]

6. Our data in appendix table 9 indicate that the real growth in prescribing varies greatly with the cohort of NCEs introduced in a particular year. On the basis of inferences from the data in the table, we assumed a 14 percent annual growth rate for the high-success NCEs.

---

[12] Gordon R. Trapnell, *National Health Insurance Issues* (Nutley, N.J.: Roche Laboratories, 1979), p. 86, table B–1.

[13] J. M. Firestone, "Pharmaceutical Price Indexes," Annual Reports to the Pharmaceutical Manufacturers Association, Washington, D.C.

[14] Pharmaceutical Manufacturers Association, "Annual Survey Report," *Medical Marketing & Media*, March 1978, p. 20.

TABLE 6
ANALYSIS OF PROSPECTIVE RETURNS TO R&D ON NCE DRUG PRODUCTS

	Average NCE	Low-Probability, High-Success NCEs (top 25%)	High-Probability, Low-Success NCEs (low 75%)
1. Manufacturer's selling price per prescription	5.16	5.36	4.65
2. Costs excluding depreciation, R&D, interest, taxes, and profits at 70%	3.61	3.75	3.25
3. Net cash flows (depreciation, R&D, interest, taxes, and profits) at 30%	1.55	1.61	1.40
4. Margin with inflation at 3%	1.80	1.87	1.62
5. Number of prescriptions, adjusted for international sales, in millions	2.133	6.299	0.789
6. Number of prescriptions, adjusted for annual growth	at 6%: 2.854	at 14%: 12.126	at 2%: 0.871
7. Annual cash inflows (row 4 × row 6), in millions	5.14	22.68	1.41
8. Present value factor at 8%	6.710	6.710	6.710
9. Gross present value (row 7 × row 8), in millions	34.5	152.2	9.5

33

To estimate growth rates for the less successful NCEs, we first considered the pattern of trends in the utilization of prescription drugs overall. The data show virtually no growth in the total number of prescriptions dispensed over the period 1972–1978.[15] When adjustment is made for the size of prescriptions, the total number of medications dispensed grows at an annual rate of 3.3 percent.[16] For the average NCE we used a growth rate roughly double the average when adjustment is made for prescription size, that is, a 6 percent annual rate. For the low-success NCEs we used a growth rate slightly under the trend for 1972–1978, 2 percent per annum.

7. The average annual cash flow (row 7) is the product of average margin per prescription (row 4) times prescription volume (row 6).

8. To arrive at the present value of the ten-year stream of cash flows, we applied the same 8 percent discount factor used in the cost estimates. This is the present value factor of 6.710 of row 8.

9. Row 9 is the gross present value of cash flows to R&D on NCE drug products.

A question may be raised with respect to the use of a ten-year period for future revenues when sales are likely to continue for additional years—beyond the ten-year remaining effective patent life.[17] Previous studies indicate that strong competition from substitute drugs is highly probable by the tenth year.[18] Firms seek to maintain capacity utilization on the older drugs by efforts to sustain the physical volume of sales through price cutting. The price declines on the older drugs will reduce the profit margins assumed to grow over the ten-year period. Industry expectations from such developing governmental influences as MAC, changing substitution rules, and NDA requirements also would seem to support the use of a period of stable profit margins of no longer than ten years.

We could have performed the calculations by reducing the profit margins over time and extending the period for duration of sales of a group of NCEs introduced in a particular year. The present value factors,

---

[15] Trapnell, *National Health Insurance Issues*, p. 27, table 4.

[16] Ibid.

[17] This ten-year period is also consistent with recent evidence on the effective life of drug patents. See Meir Statman, "The Effect of Patent Expiration on the Market Position of Drugs," herein.

[18] See D. L. Cocks, "Product Innovation and the Dynamic Elements of Competition in the Ethical Pharmaceutical Industry," in Helms, *Drug Development*, pp. 225–54; D. L. Cocks and J. R. Virts, "Pricing Behavior of the Ethical Pharmaceutical Industry," *Journal of Business*, vol. 47 (July 1974), pp. 349–62; W. D. Reekie, "Price and Quality Competition in the United States Drug Industry," *Journal of Industrial Economics*, vol. 26 (March 1978), pp. 223–37; and J. F. Weston, "Pricing in the Pharmaceutical Industry," in Chien, *Issues in Pharmaceutical Economics*, pp. 71–95.

however, drop below 0.5 by the tenth year and below 0.25 by the seventeenth year. Also, it is profit margins, not sales, that produce net revenues. Hence, our procedures, which use growing profit margins for ten years, produce the same approximate revenue forecasts with fewer explicit assumptions than attempting to project declining profit margins over an extended period when present value factors are quite small.

Under the assumptions used here, the results indicate that the average NCE experience would not create adequate revenues for the R&D investments to earn their cost of capital. Assumptions more optimistic than historical patterns would be required to recover a $54 million investment. The high-probability, low-success experience would require much more optimistic assumptions about higher prices or volumes for adequate investment returns. Good performance for an individual company requires strong participation in the low-probability, high-success NCEs. This is also supported by evidence of a high correlation between relative sales success of individual companies and the number of introductions of important NCEs.[19] It follows that the profitability rate is also correlated with the number of significant NCEs introduced.

The present value of the cash flows (ten-year investment horizon) of the average or "expected" NCE, then, compares unfavorably with Hansen's $54 million estimate of the economic cost of discovering and bringing such a product to market. The implications are that the prospective average return on investment (ROI) to pharmaceutical R&D has been significantly less than 8 percent and that these results have varied markedly among individual NCEs. Clearly, the owners of those NCEs falling in the top 25 percent in market performance have achieved much higher returns, and the average ROI to R&D for those companies exceeds the average for the drug industry and for all manufacturing companies. On the other hand, most NCEs have apparently failed to generate cash flows sufficient to earn a conservative estimate of the cost of capital (or applicable discount factor) for the investment outlays, or perhaps even to recover the capital outlays made.

We recognize, of course, that estimates were used at a number of stages in the development of the results in table 6. The high-probability, low-success NCEs, however, fall far short of achieving gross present values close to the present capitalized costs of developing an NCE. When the low-probability, high-success NCEs are included, the average NCE still achieves a gross present value substantially short of plausible estimates of the capitalized costs of developing an NCE. Substantial modifications in the relationships we employed would be required to reduce the indicated gap between the present value of inflows and the present value of outflows in analyzing the returns from NCEs.

---

[19] Cocks, "Product Innovation," pp. 237–42, tables 1 and 3.

Our result is not that all pharmaceutical R&D investment is no longer profitable. Individual NCEs with favorable prices and volumes will earn above average rates of return. Ex ante, it is not possible to predict what the actual return on a specific R&D investment project will be. Our concern is whether changing expectations of industrial R&D investment decision makers about probable future returns are likely to have significant effects on industry resource allocation and industry structure. Our estimates of the increases in current investment costs along with the prospective market performance of a new NCE suggest that the probability distribution of returns to R&D must now be viewed less favorably. The data suggest that, from a probability standpoint, investment in pharmaceutical R&D is less likely to earn its cost of capital in the present environment.

We now look at some evidence related to our estimates. If R&D has been earning handsome returns for the industry participants, expectations are likely to be favorable, and no changes in resource allocation or industry structure would be observed. If, however, returns to R&D have become less favorable and especially if the probability of inadequate returns is high, we should expect to see some industry adjustments. Our results suggest the likelihood that in the allocation of corporate resources pharmaceutical companies must now view R&D outlays as relatively less attractive, compared with alternative uses of corporate funds. In the remainder of the paper we shall consider a number of types of evidence to test these predictions that follow from our estimates of investment costs and returns from pharmaceutical R&D activity.

In presenting the relevant evidence, we shall first summarize the findings of other studies, then report in the later sections of this paper some new materials that we have developed. Earlier studies analyzed trends in the production of NCEs and include evidence of structural shifts related to the possible effects of U.S. regulation on expectations of the ROI to R&D and thus on resource allocation.

Factors Relating to the Return to R&D: Previous Studies

With regard to the production of NCEs, Grabowski, Vernon, and Thomas found that the number of new chemical entities introduced dropped from forty-seven per year in 1957–1961 to nineteen per year in 1962–1966 to fifteen per year in 1967–1971.[20] Although the average annual sales per NCE during the first three marketed years rose over

---

[20] H. G. Grabowski, J. M. Vernon, and L. G. Thomas, "The Effects of Regulatory Policy on the Incentives to Innovate: An International Comparative Analysis," in S. A. Mitchell and E. A. Link, eds., *Impact of Public Policy on Drug Innovation and Pricing* (Washington, D.C.: The American University, 1976), p. 51.

TABLE 7

STRUCTURAL SHIFTS IN THE RELATION OF INNOVATION TO FIRM SIZE
FOR U.S. AND U.K. PHARMACEUTICAL INDUSTRIES

Period	Total NCEs (1)	Share of NCE Sales in Total Sales (2)	Number of Firms with an NCE (3)	Largest Four Firms		
				Share of innovation (4)	Share of sales (5)	Ratio of innovation share to sales share (6)
United States						
1957–1961	233	20.0	51	24.0	26.5	0.91
1962–1965	93	8.6	34	25.0	24.0	1.04
1967–1971	76	5.5	23	48.7	26.1	1.87
United Kingdom						
1962–1966	115	13.3	48	39.9	26.9	1.48
1967–1971	95	12.9	44	14.5	29.5	0.49

SOURCE: Grabowski, *Drug Regulation*.

the period studied, the total sales of all NCEs as a percentage of total ethical drug sales dropped from 20 percent in 1957–1961 to 5.5 percent in 1967–1971. These changes could reflect reduced R&D efforts or lower success ratios or both.

In addition, Grabowski finds that the ratio of foreign research and development to total research and development of U.S. pharmaceutical companies increased from 5 percent in 1961 to 15.4 percent in 1974.[21] This suggests that *relatively* more inflexible regulation in the United States has produced a shift of domestic research and development in pharmaceuticals to undertaking the activity in foreign countries. Grabowski also presents data consistent with the conclusion that drug regulation, though increasing both in the United States and abroad since the early 1960s, was relatively more stringent in the United States.[22] Table 7 shows that NCE introductions in both the United States and the United Kingdom declined in the 1967–1971 period from those in earlier time segments. The share of NCE sales in total sales, however, declined much more sharply in the United States than in the United Kingdom. The number of firms with an NCE in the United Kingdom was almost double that in the United States.

The evidence is consistent with an impact of fewer rich innovational opportunities available after the mid-1960s for both countries. Never-

---

[21] Grabowski, *Drug Regulation*, p. 43.
[22] Ibid., pp. 21–23.

theless, the differentially more favorable experience in the United Kingdom suggests that the impact of less flexible approval procedures in the United States created a less favorable environment in this country for R&D activity in pharmaceuticals than in the United Kingdom.

The comparative data in table 7 also exhibit a significant structural shift, perhaps providing evidence of regulatory effects favoring firms of larger size. The largest four firms in the United States increased their share of innovation from 24 percent in 1957–1961 to over 40 percent in 1967–1971. The share of the top four in the United Kingdom, however, declined from around 40 percent in 1962–1966 to 14.5 percent in 1967–1971. Indeed, the ratio of the share of innovation to the share of sales for the largest four firms increased from less than one for the United States to almost two, while the ratio for firms in the United Kingdom declined from about 1.5 to less than 0.5.

These structural patterns are consistent with the evidence on the greater absolute amount of R&D investment required to achieve an NCE in the new U.S. regulatory environment after 1962. Since the risks of not achieving a commercially profitable NCE are also greater, this reinforces the advantage of large size. Simply to make the large investment requires a firm of large absolute size; but risk is reduced if a firm has a portfolio of new NCE possibilities. It is more likely to avoid having only "dry holes" in a large diversified portfolio of NCE efforts.

Further Evidence of Resource Reallocation or Structural Shifts: Decline in Real R&D Investment Rate

The Pharmaceutical Manufacturers Association has collected and published data on R&D spending intensity.[23] R&D spending by U.S. member firms rose from $245 million in 1961 to $1,164 million in 1976. R&D spending remained in the range of 9 to 10 percent of worldwide sales throughout the period. In the face of increasing R&D costs—mainly the wages and salaries of researchers—and relatively declining drug prices, however, the R&D-to-sales ratio would have had to increase if the relative flow of "real" funds to R&D were to remain constant. Deflating R&D spending with the gross national product deflator reveals an increase of 146 percent in real R&D spending over the period 1961–1976, whereas the same manufacturers' worldwide sales, deflated by an index of wholesale pharmaceutical prices, increased by over 300 percent. The percentage of sales in constant dollars devoted to R&D in constant dollars fell from about 10 percent to about 6.6 percent over the period.

---

[23] "Annual Survey Report," p. 17.

This indicator of relative resource flow is also consistent with our previous evidence on an unfavorable shift in prospective returns from R&D investment in the United States.

Further Evidence of Structural Shifts in Sources of Pharmaceutical Innovation: Number of Firms

Another measure of structural change in the pharmaceutical industry is the effect on the number of independent firms achieving new product introductions and the entry and exit of firms able to achieve a new product introduction. Our compilations of data on these points are summarized in table 8. The first section of table 8 shows the number of independent firms adding new chemical entities to the U.S. market in each of the three five-year periods studied. There were nearly 20 percent fewer firms achieving such R&D output—including meeting the scientific and regulatory requirements for demonstration of safety and efficacy—in the period immediately following the passage of the 1962 drug amendments and the resulting changes in regulation. The phenomena

TABLE 8

INDEPENDENT FIRMS ADDING NEW CHEMICAL ENTITIES AND OTHER PHARMACEUTICAL PRODUCTS TO THE U.S. MARKET

	Number of Independent Firms	Foreign Firms (%)	Total Exits	Exits by Merger	Entrants
NCEs added to U.S. market					
1954–1958	51.0	14	—	—	—
1963–1967	41.0	17	22	2	12.0
1972–1976	40.5	27	17	4	16.5
New pharmaceutical products					
1954–1958	163	6	—	—	—
1963–1967	106	10	74	29	17
1972–1976	76	21	43	16	13

SOURCE: Tabulations are based on the definition of NCEs and new products as reported in the de Haen *New Drug Analysis, USA*, vol. 13, 1972–1976, and vol. 4, 1963–1967, and the de Haen *New Product Surveys* for the years 1954–1958. These sources are also used to determine attribution to innovating company. The data used are in the form of names of firms adding one or more NCEs or new products in a designated year or years. Determination of domestic (foreign) ownership and of whether a de Haen–listed firm represented, in a particular time period, a single free-standing firm, a parent firm, or a subsidiary (division) of another firm was made by the authors for the purpose of this analysis—using a number of different reference sources.

of declining NCEs introduced and of a declining number of firms achieving an introduction are related.

Although the total number of independent firms adding at least one NCE in the most recent period is not markedly lower than in 1963–1967, the number of independent *domestic* firms continued to decline. More than one-quarter of the successful NCE-adding firms are now foreign owned and based—but usually with a substantial U.S. division or subsidiary. Four (over 40 percent) of the nine and a half firms adding one or more NCEs in 1972–1976 but none in 1954–1958 were foreign owned. Foreign entry was achieved mainly by acquisition of domestic firms. One U.K. pharmaceutical company entered the market directly, as did the joint venture of an Italian conglomerate and a U.S. conglomerate not previously in the drug business.

The net loss of firms between the two time periods reflects the fact that a greater number of independent firms failed to achieve NCE additions, even though some new firms did achieve such additions. Some firms that added one or more NCEs in the period 1954–1958 failed to do so in the second period studied and then were again successful in the 1972–1976 period. If we view the entire period from 1954–1958 to 1972–1976, twenty (nearly 40 percent) of the original fifty-one firms adding at least one NCE in an earlier period failed to achieve such an addition in recent years. Only seven of these firms exited by reason of merger with another firm subsequently achieving NCE additions. The force of acquisition-merger contributed to independent firm exit; but, clearly, other more important forces have been at work.

It is likely that the increased time to conduct the R&D necessary to receive an approved NDA has somewhat decreased the probability that a firm pursuing such R&D will achieve an introduction in a five-year period. These data, however, add to the body of evidence of the movement of resources away from this most important investment activity for the pharmaceutical industry.

Examination of the number of firms adding a "new product" (not necessarily an NCE but still one requiring R&D capability) reveals an even stronger pattern. The numbers of independent firms adding new pharmaceuutical products in each of the five-year periods studied are shown in the second part of table 8. The time pattern of net exit of firms adding new products is different from that of the firms failing to achieve an NCE addition from period to period.

The percentage loss of firms from the 1954–1958 period to the period immediately following the 1962 drug amendments was only slightly greater than the percentage reduction in firms from the

1963–1967 period to the 1972–1976 period (35 percent versus 28 percent). The increasing penetration of foreign-owned and -based firms into this aspect of the U.S. pharmaceutical market is at least as strong as into NCE addition, although domestic firms remain a somewhat higher proportion of the total firms engaged.

Viewing the entire period 1954–1958 to 1972–1976, we see that the force of acquisition and merger was somewhat more important for adding a new product than for adding NCEs. Nearly one-half (49 percent) of the firms exiting this activity did so because of merger with another firm conducting similar activities. It is still apparent, however, that additional forces are at work, because fifty-two (nearly one-third) of the independent firms adding new products in 1954–1958 failed to achieve such an addition in later years for some reason other than acquisition or merger. Again, the evidence is that fewer firms have been successful in developing new products, and various structural adjustments have been induced. This parallels the evidence on NCE introductions. Together, these materials on the reduced ability of firms to function successfully in the industry's most important activity suggest that economic returns have been inadequate for some firms and prospectively less favorable even for the successful.

Further Evidence of Structural Shifts or Resource Reallocation: Trends in Pharmaceutical versus Nonpharmaceutical Revenues

Another way to test whether R&D efforts on pharmaceuticals are becoming less attractive in the United States is to investigate trends in the allocation of corporate resources to pharmaceutical activity as compared with nonpharmaceutical business activities. We start with the list of companies that had achieved a position among the top fifteen firms in IMS America–reported drugstore and hospital purchases of prescription drugs in *each* of the years 1957 (the earliest year of IMS America reporting), 1962, and 1977. Firms were eliminated from consideration for this purpose for only three reasons: unavailability of data because of foreign ownership and non–U.S. reporting; ownership by a conglomerate whose sales were principally in lines other than pharmaceuticals; or subsequent acquisition. Eight leading firms remain on the list: Abbott, Lilly, Merck, Pfizer, Schering-Plough, SmithKline, Squibb, and Upjohn. If we aggregate these companies' reported segmented worldwide sales most closely approximating pharmaceutical sales and aggregate their worldwide total corporate sales, the ratios of these aggregates for each year are as follows:

Year	Percentage of Leading Firms' Total Sales in Pharmaceuticals
1973	58.9
1974	57.3
1975	57.3
1976	56.4
1977	55.3
1978	55.3

Not every firm's ratio declined—but the segmented-sales reporting requirements are such that diversification away from (or into) human prescription drugs can be obscured by a firm's need to report human health, or human and animal health products, as an aggregate. On average, a persistent year-to-year shift to revenues from nonpharmaceutical products is shown by the data, at least through 1977. Although the decline is only 3.6 percentage points, it represents almost one-half billion dollars of the $12.7 billion of 1978 revenues of the eight companies. Because these firms are established, long-term leaders in pharmaceutical sales, these data provide further evidence of a shift in resource flows reflecting relatively unfavorable changes in returns from pharmaceutical investments.

Conclusions

The formation of expectations of returns to a particular economic activity is the essence of resource allocation in a market economy. The aim of this paper has been to estimate the expected returns to pharmaceutical research and development. The general conclusion from this assessment is that for the pharmaceutical industry as a whole the current expected returns to R&D have shifted unfavorably compared with what can be earned on alternative investments. Evidence is that resources are being diverted away from pharmaceutical R&D and that pharmaceutical sales as a percentage of total revenues are declining.

Many factors affect the formation of expectations about investments. These include the usual market characteristics as well as "exogenous" factors in the economic and political environments. It is recognized that it is not really possible to untangle the interactive effects of these factors to determine how each operates on expectations. There is reason to believe, however, that one of the exogenous factors that is becoming increasingly important in the U.S. economy is government regulation.

If the constraints imposed by regulation are the same across all industries, then the relative allocation of resources may be unaffected, and only the total amount of resource use will be changed. Regulatory constraints are not the same across industries, however, and they appear to bear relatively more heavily on the pharmaceutical industry. In addition, public policy applied to the industry is disjointed in that the interaction of various regulations is not assessed or even recognized. On the supply side, regulation through the FDA determines what products can be marketed; the FDA controls the R&D process itself; and the FDA regulates many of the aspects of production and distribution of pharmaceuticals. On the demand side, there is a growing set of regulations reflected in various forms of price controls, restricted lists of products, and governmental assessment of quality and equality of products. It is a plausible hypothesis, therefore, that regulatory factors have had an important role in shifting unfavorably the returns to pharmaceutical R&D. Consequently, it is also plausible that the observed resource and industry structural changes have resulted from these same regulatory forces.

The data presented in this paper indicate that there are relatively unfavorable forces operating on investment decisions of the pharmaceutical industry. Although individual firms are influenced by these forces, there are many possible ways for a firm to respond so as to maintain or even enhance its performance. Some responses by firms result in the shifts in the industry's structure and in resource allocation decisions that we have described. Society can be less well off as a result of such responses, even though individual firms may be able to make adjustments to mitigate or offset unfavorable developments in their environment.

Appendix

In table 9, data above the "stair steps" are actual average sales per year per NCE for the NCEs introduced in the indicated years. The data below the stair steps are projections by marketing personnel. The numbers immediately above the stair steps are the 1976 prescription sales. The 1976 sales occur in the tenth year after the 1967 NCE introductions; for the 1976 NCE introductions, the 1976 sales occur in year 1.

Our previous studies of the historical sales patterns of individual NCEs suggest S-shaped growth patterns. After moving past some threshold level of sales, the growth rate in sales of new products increases at an increasing rate. The introduction of substitute products causes the dollar value of sales of products introduced earlier to begin to grow at a reduced rate or actually to decline. A decline in total sales of the twenty-one NCEs introduced in 1967 begins in the eighth year of NCE

43

TABLE 9

ANALYSIS OF NUMBER OF PRESCRIPTIONS WRITTEN FOR NEW CHEMICAL ENTITIES ADDED, 1967–1976
(number of prescriptions in thousands)

Year of Addition	New Chemical Entities	NCE Year of Sale										Average Year's Prescriptions of Average of Cohort
		1	2	3	4	5	6	7	8	9	10	
1967	21	180	526	787	933	1,029	1,120	1,254	1,211	1,220	1,158[a]	942
1968	9	82	148	234	344	448	598	776	1,062	1,391[a]	1,850	693
1969	8	38	297	316	347	453	465	461	477[a]	480	490	382
1970	8	311	954	1,253	1,754	2,184	1,932	1,932[a]	2,050	2,130	2,200	1,670
1971	10	430	1,105	2,053	2,510	2,674	2,866[a]	3,000	3,100	3,180	3,220	2,414
1972	9	95	382	610	741	779[a]	830	870	900	920	930	706
1973	16	104	322	361	308[a]	320	310	300	290	285	275	288
1974	15	250	1,322	1,825[a]	2,400	3,000	3,600	4,200	4,700	5,000	5,300	3,160
1975	16	102	267[a]	480	600	670	720	760	790	820	850	606
1976	7	496[a]	1,400	2,200	2,900	3,400	3,900	4,400	4,800	5,200	5,500	3,420
Total	119											
Average year's prescriptions, average NCE:												1,333

NOTE: Actual sales are set in roman type; projected sales are set in italic type.
[a] 1976 prescriptions for average NCE.
SOURCE: Compilations by the authors from IMS America data.

sales. Lower percentage rates of growth are observed or forecast for all the other years except for the NCEs introduced in 1968.

Sales observed or forecast for the tenth year vary from 275,000 prescriptions written for the sixteen NCEs introduced in 1973 to 5.5 million prescriptions forecast for the seven NCEs introduced in 1976. The wide variations observed in the absolute levels of sales and their growth rates reflect a number of influences: (1) characteristics of the therapeutic product classes represented by the group of NCEs introduced in a given year; (2) the relative commercial importance of the individual NCEs; and (3) possible errors of optimism or pessimism in the forecasts.

The prescriptions written per year per average NCE can be averaged over the ten years of sales or forecasts. The weighted (with number of NCEs) average of such averages is 1,332,546 prescriptions. If we averaged over a longer period (for example, the theoretical seventeen years of patent life), the results would not be greatly different and might even be lower, since sales after the tenth year are likely to decline in absolute terms. One cause of such a decline is the introduction of substitute products by the tenth year. This is reinforced by an average ten-year effective patent life. Although the legal patent life is seventeen years, the application for a patent is likely to be filed near the IND notice, which our earlier Hansen data suggest is about seven years before the NDA approval for marketing the new drug. Note also that the number of prescriptions for the average of the 119 NCEs in the year 1976, shown as the stair-steps data, is a lower 1,108,000. This lower estimate is an alternative estimate of an "average year's volume of an average NCE" but requires the assumption that 1976 was such an average year. We used the higher figure in our revenue estimates not only because it seems to be a better estimate, both analytically and from the probable perspective of decision makers in the expectational process, but also simply to lower the chance of biasing our revenue estimates downward.

Commentary

F. M. Scherer

My task is to discuss the Grabowski-Vernon paper. There are many nice things about the paper. The authors use data of unusually good quality, the results are plausible, and the results are also robust over several different time periods. That is all to the good.

A discussant, however, should be critical; so let me launch into the more critical parts of my comment. The chief theoretical shortcoming, it seems to me, is that, ideally, this kind of analysis ought to be done in a simultaneous equations structure, with both a supply-side equation and a demand-side equation. What Grabowski and Vernon have done, if I can make my permanent mark in the econometrics textbooks, is to estimate a reduced-form rule-of-thumb equation. Maybe that is all the situation permits, but at least I can suggest some modest improvements on what they have already accomplished.

Most of their variables deal with the supply side of pharmaceutical research and development (R&D) spending. One important variable—or, at least, one they think is important on a priori grounds—is diversification. During the past summer, I have been looking at roughly 15,000 invention patents, some 3,500 of which were organic chemical patents. What I learned is that there is very little difference between an organic chemical molecule that has pharmaceutical effects and an organic chemical molecule that may have herbicidal effects or pesticidal effects. One finds, too, that the pharmaceutical companies have learned this and have diversified into herbicides and pesticides in many cases. There are joint economies in testing particular organic molecules for effects not only of a pharmacological nature but also in various agricultural uses. It seems to me, therefore, that an appropriately defined diversification variable ought to take this sort of diversification into account. One could make the same, but a slightly weaker, argument with respect to certain organic chemical resin molecules and similar types of substances. I conclude, therefore, that Grabowski and Vernon need a broader diversification variable.

I might note further that the theoretical predictions on the sign of this diversification variable are not so clear-cut as the authors imply. If what I have said is correct, diversification reduces the average cost of finding a hit in some field, be it pharmaceutical or herbicidal or in some other area. This means that diversification has a cost-reducing effect. One might expect that to reduce the ratio of R&D expenditures to sales. On the other hand, a reduction in the average cost of a hit has a favorable effect, leading firms to conduct more R&D in real terms. On balance, it is not clear in which of these two conflicting directions the average effect of diversification on the ratio of R&D spending to sales lies.

For similar reasons, one might postulate that there are economies of scale in supporting an organic chemical research and development operation, and one might argue for a scale variable in this equation. Its sign is also not altogether clear on a priori grounds.

The most important omitted variable in the Grabowski-Vernon equation is one that reflects what various economists have called "technological opportunity." The richness of the technological opportunities facing a potential innovator is not, I think, captured by their lagged research productivity variable. The lag there is simply too long—that is to say, yesterday's successes in R&D, which are what they are capturing with their lag variable, are the result of technological opportunities that appeared on the horizon ten years or more ago. What affects today's R&D decision, however, are the opportunities that exist now as a consequence of the advance of science.

In pharmaceuticals, this may be an especially important variable. It can be argued plausibly that in the last two decades there has been growing depletion of the opportunities for coming up with really interesting new drugs, in part because the try-every-bottle-on-the-shelf approach had gone into the stage of severely diminishing returns.[1] Now, however, advances in molecular biology have opened up important new frontiers for pharmaceutical innovation. That kind of opportunity is not going to be reflected in the lagged research productivity variable of Grabowski and Vernon. I am not sure how one captures it quantitatively, but its absence from their equation is an important omission.

On the demand side of the picture, things are much tougher. Technological opportunity is relevant on the demand side, too. There may be a more or less constant menu of diseases to be cured, but what varies is the array of curable diseases, and that, of course, is affected by the advance of science. Another relevant demand-side variable is popula-

---

[1] For a recent example of this view, see "Eli Lilly: New Life in the Drug Industry," *Business Week*, October 29, 1979, pp. 134–37.

tion. This is obvious, but I suspect its inclusion would not do much good, because there is not much time series variation.

Finally, a variable that might be taken into account is access to overseas markets. Edwin Mansfield and his colleagues have found that, on average, having an overseas subsidiary enhances the sales one can get out of new product innovations sufficiently that, without such a branch, R&D expenditures might be 12 to 15 percent lower on average.[2] I hypothesize that the same kind of effect should hold in the pharmaceutical industry. If one has an overseas operation, one probably can tap the benefits of innovation more thoroughly than by simply licensing one's technology to some foreign corporation.

Let me make one final point. In their concluding section, Grabowski and Vernon note that the social returns from innovation are generally believed to exceed the private returns. This is no doubt also true in drugs. I am sure that important new drugs yield big consumers' surpluses. Social returns do not necessarily or always exceed private returns, however. Mansfield and associates found that for some innovations the social returns were actually lower than the private returns.[3] Theory shows that this can happen when some new product cannibalizes substantial surpluses from already existing products.[4]

It seems to me there may have been many such cannibalizations with the "me-too" drugs that were common during the 1950s and the early 1960s. I have the impression, however, that the situation is changing. Nowadays it is simply too expensive to develop a new drug or a new drug variant to get the relatively modest sales benefit from having a me-too follower in the market. If this is true, one might expect the ratio of social to private returns to be rising in the pharmaceutical industry. It would be interesting to try measuring such a ratio, emulating the sort of research Mansfield and associates have done for other types of products, to see just how the ratio has varied over time. This has a policy implication: the mix of innovative projects in drugs may be as important as the absolute level of spending in relation to sales.

To put the paper in perspective, let me observe again that it is a very nice paper. I like it.

---

[2] Edwin Mansfield, Anthony Romeo, and Samuel Wagner, "Foreign Trade and U.S. Research and Development," *Review of Economics and Statistics*, vol. 61 (February 1979), pp. 29–31.

[3] Edwin Mansfield, John Rapoport, Anthony Romeo, Samuel Wagner, and George Beardsley, "Social and Private Rates of Return from Industrial Innovations," *Quarterly Journal of Economics*, vol. 91 (May 1977), pp. 221–40.

[4] See F. M. Scherer, "The Welfare Economics of Product Variety: An Application to the Ready-to-Eat Cereals Industry," *Journal of Industrial Economics*, vol. 28 (December 1979), pp. 113–21.

Harry R. Woltman

The Virts-Weston paper seems to be having an identity crisis. On the basis of language in the introduction and the conclusions, one might expect a good deal of elaborate new analysis in between. What actually seems to happen, instead, is a review of the main lines of argument and evidence that have been advanced in aid of the proposition that the drug industry is overregulated, with some interesting new drug sales data thrown in. The authors have relied much on the work of Hansen, Grabowski, and others already well known to readers of AEI publications. They have presented too little, too soon, of their own contribution, which stresses the marketing side of new drug introductions in terms of patterns of sales volume, price behavior, competition, and revenues over time—or could, if it received a more liberal allocation of research and development (R&D).

The overall scheme of the paper, as described in the introduction, never really jells because the promised links between public policy and expectations about drug development costs and revenues do not materialize. The authors compare Hansen's estimation of the capitalized (fully allocated) cost of developing a marketable new chemical entity (NCE) with their own estimate of the present value of the net cash inflow expected of a marketed NCE based on a decade of experience and conclude that the relationship is unfavorable. Then they do a remarkable thing: they propose a "test" for the validity of this estimate. They look for evidence of reduced R&D intensity and various structural shifts that might follow from an unfavorable R&D climate. And lo!— they find it: reduced introduction of NCEs, declining share of NCEs in total drug sales, declining real R&D relative to real sales, a rising foreign share in the R&D expenditures of U.S. drug firms, reduced probability of innovation by independent U.S. firms, and a tendency for larger U.S. firms to become more dominant. Because these things were generally well known already, they can hardly constitute a test. The authors might more convincingly have used their "test" evidence as the basis of their hypothesis about R&D incentives and then treated their cost-revenue comparison as the test. Better yet, they could simply have offered their cost-revenue result as one more piece of evidence for the pot.

As a skeptic concerning a number of the points the authors have advanced as test evidence, I would like to respond directly to some of them, but I expect that most of us already know the standard counters. Instead, I ask the reader to look more generally at the nonutility of then-and-now, before-and-after comparisons. In the Virts-Weston paper, it is concluded that it is regulation and not market forces that is the

49

primary factor that has unfavorably shifted the returns to pharmaceutical R&D below alternative investments. Even granting for the moment the premise about returns to R&D, what can we learn from this kind of approach? What, today, is the most useful base-line comparison for appraising economic effects of drug industry regulation? Now compared with pre-1962 conditions? Or with current regulation versus now without regulation or with modified regulation? Do we know what kinds of safety, efficacy, and testing standards the industry might be voluntarily applying now (as opposed to pre-1962) with less Food and Drug Administration influence and more influence from the courts and from its own maturing social judgment? How much difference could reasonably be expected in the future (not the past) from specific modifications of the regulatory regime and industry responses to them? These are the relevant questions for analysis as 1962 fades deeper into history. Otherwise, some of us may be stuck forever on "who struck John."

To get back to the more interesting part of the paper, the authors rightly remind us that expected new product revenues are no less essential to an understanding of R&D incentives and behavior than are R&D cost expectations. They project ten-year prescription sales streams for each year's cohort within the total of 119 NCEs introduced from 1967 to 1976, average them over the ten years, convert the average to revenues with an average prescription price, and after various allowances for costs, inflation, and other manipulations, arrive at a figure for average cash inflow that converts to a present value of $43.5 million for ten years at 8 percent (1976 basis).

Considering the numerous assumptions and arbitrary procedures that go into it, the authors show considerable courage in concluding that this "estimate" compares unfavorably with Hansen's capitalized NCE R&D cost figure of $54 million (which is also laden with assumptions). It would take equal courage to conclude the opposite. Their results, as they point out, indicate that NCEs, on average, do not return sufficient revenues to earn their costs of capital. The authors' estimates do, however, indicate present values of revenues well in excess of the uncapitalized development costs. This point seems relevant because drug companies do not depend on capital markets for R&D financing but in effect write off R&D expenditures immediately against current sales. Thus, today's drug buyers are financing R&D of tomorrow's drugs. We may well identify an opportunity cost to society in this practice, but it seems a good deal less obvious that, considering taxes, the opportunity cost of this application of revenue to R&D would appear as high to a firm as the assumed discount rate of 8 percent. Even taking the authors' numbers as given, therefore, I am not compelled to the same conclusions about overall disincentives to R&D.

I also have some problems with the estimates as given. I do not want to quarrel here with the individual bits and pieces, but it does seem that a ten-year cutoff shortchanges the present value of cash inflow estimates. One would also like to know if the NCE sales and revenue data apply to the originally approved entities only or if they take in related compounds, improved formulations and dosage forms, or other follow-on products that would tend to expand and prolong the revenue stream initiated by the original entity. It would be easy to get misleading results by too narrow a treatment of the revenues associated with an NCE coupled with too broad a treatment of its development costs.

More generally, though, I wonder why the entire net income attributed to NCEs is treated as a return to R&D expenditures. There are major expenditures during the revenue-earning period of a drug for promotion and advertising, and it seems generally agreed that, especially for drugs, such expenses would warrant treatment as investments just as much as R&D. If we allow some return to this investment (and to others), the returns to R&D would presumably appear substantially lower than the authors' estimates. In that event, the burden might be on the authors to explain why drug companies are not abandoning their R&D commitments wholesale.

For my part, current upbeat reports about the increasing R&D commitments and new product development prospects of the research-intensive drug firms reinforce my skepticism about the authors' interpretation of their estimates, the estimates themselves, or both. On the other hand, I must concede the bare possibility that the data do portray the true overall state of returns to new drug R&D and that this state persists because drug firms persistently overestimate on the average the cash flows and/or success rates anticipated for their projects as they examine them individually. Perhaps they really are risk takers for whom the game is the thing.

This, in fact, may be the main trouble with aggregative approaches to expected R&D cost and expected cash flow data. Even though one knows better, one may be bemused by average R&D cost estimates on the scale of Hansen's. We can tell ourselves that drug companies *know* they do not have to see prospects of getting off a $50 million nut in order to start a project. We *know* that the main cause of the number is the 8-to-1 overall multiplier for unsuccessful NCE projects and that 8-to-1 may be meaningless for a company engaged in attaching expected values to its own portfolio of candidate chemicals. I think, though, that we still tend to apply the parameters of the general or average case to the particulars of an individual company's decisions. It seems necessary to take a more disaggregative view of costs than Hansen's and a more disaggregative view of revenues than Virts-Weston when one is essentially trying to model R&D incentives and disincentives at the only level where the decisions are made—that of the individual firm. That, I believe, would be the appropriate direction for further work in this area.

PART
TWO

The Research and Development
Process: Decision Making in a
Regulated Industry

The Pharmaceutical Research and Development Decision Process

Steven N. Wiggins

This paper presents an analysis of the research and development (R&D) decision-making process used in pharmaceutical firms. The primary motive for the paper is to determine how pharmaceutical companies change the level and allocation of research expenditures in response to changes in the stringency of federal product quality regulation. To accomplish this, however, it is also necessary to examine general pharmaceutical R&D decision making in some detail. This leads to a description of how research-intensive firms go about the R&D project selection process. Thus the current work can be viewed as a case study of how such firms make their selection decisions, for relatively little is known about this process.

It is clear that Food and Drug Administration (FDA) regulation will affect the profitability (present discounted value) of individual research projects by increasing testing costs and lowering the probability of obtaining a new product from a given research project.[1] At the margin this should affect the decision to take on research projects and thereby create an inverse relationship between regulatory stringency and the level of research spending.[2] This result implicitly depends, however, on the decision makers' ability and willingness to take this change in the profitability environment of the individual projects into account in deciding whether or not to pursue these projects. Economists are not generally troubled by such an assumption, since decision making at the margin is an inherent part of most economic analysis.

I would like to thank executives at Abbott, Ciba, Lilly, Merck, Parke-Davis, Pfizer, Roche, Schering, Searle, SmithKline, Upjohn, Warner-Lambert, and Wyeth for taking the time to answer my questions. I would also like to thank P. Joskow, D. Startz, P. Temin, and A. Werth for helpful comments. The research presented herein is from my Ph.D. dissertation at MIT.

Financial support from the Sloan Foundation through MIT for studies in public policy and from the Pharmaceutical Manufacturers Association is gratefully acknowledged.

[1] This can be demonstrated simply by noting that the FDA restricts the company's set of choices in the decision to market a new product. If the constraint is binding, profitability is lowered.

[2] This implicitly assumes that enough fewer projects are undertaken to offset the increased spending per project.

In the current context, however, such an assumption not only is unjustified but leads to significant errors in the analysis of public policy toward new pharmaceutical products.[3] The development of this result depends on the fact that pharmaceutical research scientists controlled the research decision-making apparatus in the 1960s. They explicitly considered two factors in their selection decisions: medical need and scientific feasibility. For reasons discussed in the fifth section, "An Econometric Test," it appears that this process had its own optimality properties and that it was difficult, at best, to incorporate changes in the stringency of regulation into the process. Therefore, regulation did not affect the project selection decision and did not have the supposed negative effect on research spending.

Then, in the late 1960s, nearly all major research companies took a portion of the scientists' decision-making power and gave it to others. The new decision-making process was more quantitative, and one of the results was a consideration of regulation in the project selection decision. This created the previously described inverse relationship between regulation and research spending. It is this change that permits the empirical testing of the hypothesis of no regulatory effects in the 1960s.

From another point of view, the current exercise is a contribution to our understanding of the R&D decision processes in research-intensive corporations and of the proper procedures for microeconomic policy analysis in such areas. Such organizations do not possess costless information about the profitabilities (present discounted values) of the various research projects they could undertake. Furthermore, it can be difficult and costly to develop an organizational decision-making structure that is capable of evaluating and comparing projects that differ along multidimensional lines. As the following description will indicate, this can generate the seemingly paradoxical result that a major determinant of profitability can have little effect on the decision to undertake a given research program. Presumably this is because the fixed cost of changing the decision-making process to make it capable of evaluating the factor is larger than the expected returns (in terms of better research decisions). This, in turn, makes it clear that in order to evaluate the effect of various factors (for example, the effects of regulation) on research spending, it is first necessary to understand the decision-making process of the relevant research organization.

The best way to understand this process is to question those re-

---

[3] The reader should note that this result has been developed into an empirically testable hypothesis and that the empirical results confirm the conclusion above. See S. N. Wiggins, "Product Quality Regulation and Innovation in the Pharmaceutical Industry" (Ph.D. diss., MIT, 1979), chap. 4. See also the summary regression results presented in the section "An Econometric Test."

sponsible for such decisions, and this is the approach followed in my research. The description of pharmaceutical research decision making presented here was developed from interviews with high-level executives in twelve major R&D-intensive companies. These twelve firms include eight of the fifteen largest American pharmaceutical manufacturers and four of the five largest worldwide manufacturers. From these interviews, a description is developed of how pharmaceutical companies make their R&D decisions and how this decision process has changed over time.[4] The most surprising, and possibly the most important, aspect of the interviews was the overall similarity of responses, which is particularly unusual because the interviews were conducted around open-ended questions. This leads to confidence that the information presented here is a good description of how a "representative" pharmaceutical company would make its research decisions. Furthermore, all of those interviewed reported the change in research decision making already described.

We will proceed from the general to the specific and work back to the general. In the next section there is an overview of a research project, presented to give the reader a framework for the later discussions. This is followed by a discussion of various research decisions and project control mechanisms, after which the results of this description are drawn together to develop a theory of pharmaceutical research decision making of the past fifteen to twenty years. This in turn is followed by a summary of an empirical test of that theory and the policy conclusions.

Throughout the paper, emphasis is placed on the changes that have occurred in the decision process. This is to motivate the primary theoretical result that research scientists controlled decision making in the 1960s and functioned with a very limited information set. Then, in the 1970s, a significant portion of this control was taken away, and the information set used in decision making expanded dramatically, one of the primary new factors being the stringency of FDA regulation.

Before proceeding, it is worth noting that the description presented is an abstraction from the information gathered in the interviews. The claim is that this description captures the essence of the important factors in the decision process. The result is that the review and selection process for an actual project will be more detailed than the depiction presented here. This is a necessary part of any such description, however, and all executives interviewed agreed that this description accurately characterizes the essence of the decision process.

---

[4] The research decision-making process described primarily concerns decisions to develop new chemical entities and to expand the therapeutic claims of existing products as opposed to decisions to develop new combination products or new salts and esters of existing products.

The Stages of Pharmaceutical Research

This section contains a brief description of the pharmaceutical research and development process, which is chronological from the time when the scientist first has a research idea until a product is marketed. The major decision points in the process are identified and described, as well as the kind of research that occurs between decisions. In figure 1, key decisions and different types of research are labeled. A more detailed discussion of parts of this process will be presented later in the paper.

The most important research decision of the pharmaceutical company is the initial decision to enter a new area of research, point E in figure 1. It is important because basic research is necessary to generate the leads for other research.[5] After the decision is made to enter into an area of basic research, necessary personnel will be either transferred from existing projects within the company or hired from outside sources, the former being the usual case.

Once the necessary personnel and facilities are available, basic research begins. During the usual three to six years of this basic research phase, large numbers of drug candidates are tested, using screening devices the company has developed for finding pharmacological action in a particular class of drugs. The vast majority of all chemical compounds screened will fail this test, which will end tests on such a compound (in a particular area). The screening procedure is a low-cost method of separating compounds that warrant more careful testing from toxic substances and from substances that have no observable pharmacological action.

The quality of screens varies significantly from company to company and, within a company, from area to area. It is well known, for instance, that Hoffmann-La Roche has been very successful in developing central nervous system (CNS) drugs. Part of the reason for this success is the relative quality of the Roche screens for CNS drugs. This means that the screens are relatively good at eliminating drugs that are unlikely to pass later stages of the testing procedure. Because the later testing procedures are more costly, overall research costs are held down. Good screens also eliminate few drugs that would have passed the later stages

---

[5] There are varied definitions of "basic research" in this and other industries. In this paper basic research is research that is product oriented and entails the development of screening devices, the synthesis of new compounds, and the screening of compounds for pharmacological action, as well as some biological modeling. This definition is in contrast with the National Science Foundation's definition of basic research, which excludes all product-oriented research. In the pharmaceutical area, NSF basic research, very little of which is carried out by pharmaceutical companies, is intended to elucidate the nature and development of diseases.

FIGURE 1
DECISION POINTS, DEVELOPMENT COSTS, AND TIME FOR A REPRESENTATIVE RESEARCH PROJECT

	A	B	C	D
Research activity	Basic research	Intermediate research (specific product candidates are identified and are being tested)	Developmental research	NDA review
Range of approximate annual costs	$0.5–1.0 million	$1.0–$2.0 million	$5.0 million	$1.0 million
Years project will be in stage (very approximate)	3–6	3	3–4	2

E   F   G   H   I

J   K   L

Key

A = basic research
B = intermediate research
C = developmental research
D = NDA review and approval

E = initial research decision
F = IND filing
G = major clinical studies begin
H = NDA submission

I = market introduction
J = phase I human tests
K = phase II human tests
L = phase III human tests

of the testing, for the one drug incorrectly eliminated might have been the one big "winner" from the research project.

After the screening phase is completed, the successful drugs are retested using biological models. The goal of the modeling process is the same as that of screening, but there is more accuracy and more specialization as well as a higher cost. As drugs enter this stage, project expenditures will increase substantially. Occasionally, if significant new information concerning project viability has evolved since the initial research decision, this cost increase will be accompanied by detailed project review.

After the modeling phase of animal testing, the drug is ready for testing in humans. Either just before first testing in man or just afterward, the next major decision—on whether or not the project's potential products are of sufficient quality to warrant continuation—is reached.[6] If there is a careful reevaluation before the first human tests, then there will not be a detailed review after early human testing. In some firms, however, this major decision is made after the commencement of human testing.

At this decision point, many factors are carefully recalculated for the first time since the initial research decision. At the initial stages of the research process, there is an attempt to examine the market for the product, the likelihood of success, and the project's cost. At this point, the company will want to reevaluate these factors because after this point in the research process the project will begin to constitute a substantial drain on the company's resources, approximately $5 million per year while the drug is in the phase II and phase III studies (which will be defined in a moment).[7] Therefore, if there is any information that might help the company to identify unprofitable projects, this is the appropriate time to discover and use it.

To begin human testing, the company must file an investigational new drug application (IND) with the FDA. After filing the IND, the company begins phase I human toxicology studies. These are small-scale tests on a limited number of healthy human subjects primarily to determine human toxicity. These short-term tests usually last only a few weeks, but they signify a critical point for the drug research because the company is fairly certain the drug will have *some* (possibly toxic) phar-

---

[6] The exact timing of this major review varies across companies from before filing the investigational new drug application to after preliminary phase II tests. The substance of the review is the same, however.

[7] The major jump in expenses is caused primarily by the need for larger sample populations in clinical (human) studies. These are primarily associated with the latter stages of phase II and with all of phase III testing.

macological activity. If it is determined that the drug is not toxic, a major hurdle in the discovery and development process will be passed.

If all goes well in phase I clinical studies, in phase II the drug will be introduced into progressively wider-ranging populations to determine human efficacy. These tests can run for several years and represent tremendous sums of money. If the drug is found to be efficacious, the company will begin phase III clinical studies to test for unusual side effects or those resulting from long-term use of the drug.[8] These tests are carried out on large human populations and are a major expense in the R&D process (see figure 1). If they are successful, the company will file a new drug application (NDA) with the FDA. The FDA then reviews the application and will approve the drug if it feels safety and efficacy have been proved. At times the FDA will ask for additional tests, and occasionally the FDA will simply turn down an NDA.[9]

Concurrently with phase II and III clinical studies, the company will try to ensure that it can manufacture the drug at a reasonable cost. This is usually not a significant problem; but if it is, there will be large-scale efforts to discover ways to manufacture the drug more cheaply. During this period, long-term animal toxicology studies are also carried out to demonstrate the lack of long-run side effects from continued use of the product.

The most important control the pharmaceutical company exercises over resource allocation is the basic decision to begin research in a particular area. The second most important form of control is the periodic project review. Every project that a company has will be reviewed at least annually. These project reviews are intended to eliminate unproductive projects and to funnel additional resources into projects when major breakthroughs occur.

Operationally, most projects are seeking drugs with multiple claims. The claims are that the drug will stop symptoms *X, Y,* and *Z* and have low side effects. As research progresses, the number of claims usually falls. Sometimes so many claims are dropped that a given product candidate, or even the entire project, is no longer worth pursuing. Project review is intended to identify and eliminate such problems. In addition, breakthroughs can expand claims, and in such cases project review can funnel additional resources to the project. At the earliest stages of research, project review will be annual because new information de-

---

[8] There is also extensive laboratory work occurring while phase III studies are in progress on long-term animal toxicology and other similar issues.

[9] This is area *D* in figure 1. The FDA's influence on testing costs and procedures is not limited to costs incurred at this time because FDA-firm consultations concerning which tests should be performed are present throughout the developmental phase.

velops slowly and resource expenditures are relatively small. In the later, fast-moving stages of research, the review process is more frequent.

This completes the basic framework of pharmaceutical research. In subsequent sections certain aspects will be described in more detail as needed. Now attention is turned to the changes in the basic structure of the R&D decision process that have occurred over the past fifteen years.

Changes in R&D Resource Control

There are major differences in R&D resource control in pharmaceutical companies today as compared with the 1960s. Over time there has been a lessening of scientists' control over resources and an increase in the amount of information used and the quantification of various factors.

In this section the three major forms of R&D resource control are reviewed and contrasted in the two periods (the 1960s and the 1970s). We begin with the most important form of control, the decision concerning the areas in which a company will carry out its basic research. This is most important because the leads developed in this stage determine the long-run resource allocation patterns in the company. Attention is next turned to the project review process, which affects resource allocation patterns through the mechanisms described at the end of the previous section. Finally, the major decision surrounding a product candidate's first introduction into man is reviewed. This decision process will affect resource allocation by stopping or encouraging various projects.

The story that will emerge from comparing these various forms of resource control in the two periods is that scientists had virtual autonomy in resource control in the 1960s. Their major decision criteria were medical need and scientific feasibility.[10] Noteworthy by their absence are regulatory considerations. Upon reflection, and given the system in use, this result is not surprising, as will be seen in the section "An Econometric Test." Over time, scientific domination of resource control eroded, and a variety of additional factors began to be considered in the decision process—among them, regulation.

The purpose of this discussion of R&D resource control is to develop an understanding of the factors that will affect the level of research spending in therapeutic classes. This means not only that it is necessary to understand resource control; one must also have some notion of the process that generates research ideas, because factors that affect where

---

[10] These terms are defined and discussed below.

people look for research ideas will ultimately affect resource allocation. Thus, we begin the discussion with a description of how research ideas are generated and of the factors that determine the areas in which people will search for these ideas.

Before proceeding, a definition is necessary. A research project is the basic unit of ongoing research. Research projects vary in size from one or two workers to dozens. In a large pharmaceutical company there will be from ten to twenty-five projects in progress at a given time.[11]

The Basic Research Decision. The research process is initiated when a member (if the company, as is often the case, is organized around chemist-biologist teams, it will be a pair of members) of the scientific community within the company has an idea about a possibly fruitful avenue for future research. These ideas are generated from a variety of sources but come primarily from the professional literature, from seminars, and from professional interaction of the staff. The scientist is given significant latitude in this quest for research ideas, and, according to R&D executives, he or she is driven to satisfy "medical need."[12]

After the idea is conceived, it will be informally discussed around the laboratory. This will give the scientist a good indication of the idea's validity and indicate whether it is worth pursuing. There is significant a priori information available, even at an early stage, about the basic validity and value of the insight. There may be uncertainty about *which* of a class of compounds will lead to therapeutic improvement, but there can be reasonable certainty that *one* of the class will result in significant improvement. Then, at some point, the person who has the basic idea goes to the head of his or her research unit and suggests that the idea be pursued in a formal project. This is the *primary* source of all new research projects undertaken by pharmaceutical companies.

Currently, there are other sources of new projects that could be considered; these include the management of the company, the mar-

---

[11] In a few companies, what I call a research "project" is called a research "program." In these companies projects are the research efforts surrounding a particular therapeutic compound, several of which may be ongoing in a given program at a given time.

[12] "Medical need" is a composition of various factors about the disease states of possible interest to the scientist and the state of pharmacology in the area. R&D executives, when asked how they would characterize medical need in the scientist's mind, always emphasized the disease incidence in a given area. Some said this was the *only* factor, and some referred to other factors as well. All maintained that the scientist "at the bench" never looked up the number of people suffering from a given indication, in the same way that many macroeconomists may seldom, if ever, actually look up the unemployment rate or the rate of inflation but at a given time have a pretty good grasp of the approximate size of both.

keting department, and possibly the clinical staff (which does not ordinarily get heavily involved in basic research). These sources, however, are much less usual than proposals from the basic research staff, which can always veto other project proposals if they are ill conceived. In the 1960s nonscientists did not generally have the option of suggesting basic research projects.

At this stage, potential projects will be considered at an annual meeting explicitly called for this purpose. Today, projects are evaluated in terms of a number of factors supplied by various disciplines within the company. These include the research chemist's and biologist's opinion about the technical feasibility, the clinician's opinion about the clinical feasibility and his or her rough estimates of the probable clinical cost of the project, estimates of the overall cost that such a project is likely to bear before it produces a new drug, the likelihood that the FDA will approve a drug of the type that will be produced (given the evidence the clinician thinks can be produced), the marketing department's conception of the drug's potential sales and marketability and its opinion on whether the existing marketing force will be able to handle the product without extensive retraining or expansion, the likelihood that the project can be carried out with existing research facilities and personnel and without placing undue strains on the resources of the system, and the project's synergism with existing research and product lines of the company. This sophisticated decision-making system is a development of the last ten years. Before details of this complex system are presented, however, it is worth reviewing the simpler system of the 1960s.

In the 1960s three primary criteria dominated the decision process. They included the research chemist's and biologist's opinion about the scientific feasibility of finding a drug with the attributes indicated in the area in which the project would be looking, the clinician's opinion about clinical difficulties, and the project's synergism with other activities of the company. All three considerations received some weight, though the first and last dominated the process.

The initial stages of new product discovery were basically as described above, the scientist initially conceiving an interesting research possibility and approaching R&D management. The primary difference between the system in the 1960s and the current procedure is one of degree. In the 1960s the scientist was the only possible source of new projects, and scientific opinion was virtually autocratic, whereas today nonscientists might successfully put forth a new research project. If the scientific criteria were good, there was often some attempt to discuss the project with other disciplines in the company, but the scientists made all final selection decisions because of the absence of a formal system for handling input from other groups. Even in this autocratic system, however, there was usually input from the clinician and an attempt to consider synergism.

The clinician would indicate the clinical feasibility of the proposed project, even though there was no formal attempt to estimate expected costs, number of patients, or some of the other important clinical variables. This was, in some sense, a rational approach to these decisions because clinical costs were not the dominant factor in development costs that they are today.

The final two characteristics considered in 1960s decision making were the project's synergism with existing projects and the likelihood that the firm's existing marketing team could adequately market the product. Both of these factors were informally considered by the R&D management while reviewing the project. Synergism with existing projects was relatively easy for the R&D managers to evaluate, since they were well aware of possible interproject linkages.

Companies also considered whether a potential product would be in the area of their marketing "franchise." This term, as used in several companies, implies a special relationship between the detail people of the company in question and the doctors who will prescribe heavily from a particular class of drugs. This relationship develops for several reasons. First, detail people spend a great deal of time developing a strong relationship with doctors who can, and frequently do, prescribe their company's drugs. Second, because doctors specialize, a company's reputation as a manufacturer of quality pharmaceuticals is more likely to be known within areas where it shares market leadership. Therefore, the doctors should be more receptive to the visits of the detail people from that company. Finally, there are significant economies of scale in presenting greater numbers of products to the same doctor, and if a new market is entered, which implies that there may be an entirely new set of doctors to visit, it may not be possible for the existing detailing force to cover the new market adequately. In that case it may be necessary to hire a complementary detailing force to cover the new doctors, which entails a large fixed cost. In fact, this recently happened to one major U.S. manufacturer.

Thus there are marketing incentives for a company to produce additional products in areas where it already has products. The incentives to carry out research in areas where the company possesses expertise have already been discussed. Together, these factors indicate that a company should specialize in research, and that is in fact what is observed. The incentives have not disappeared since the 1960s, and neither has this aspect of pharmaceutical R&D and market shares.

The information set used in basic research project selection has

65

changed dramatically in the last ten to fifteen years in most pharmaceutical companies. With this change there has developed a formalized system to ensure that all disciplines' inputs are considered in the project selection process. As a general rule, this has resulted in a decrease in importance of the opinion of the basic research people, the chemist and the biologist, and an overall increase in importance of many other factors. The point should not be oversold; R&D management and scientists still exercise significant control over the allocation of R&D resources, but the opinions of other professionals within the company are now used more frequently.

The chemist's and biologist's opinions, together with the judgment of the clinician, are still the most important decision criteria. This input amounts to two statements. The head of the biology unit states whether or not he or she believes the proposed project (that is, the synthesis of a certain class of compounds for investigation of the possible pharmacological effects of a particular type, or for treatment of a particular symptom of a disease) has a reasonable chance of biological success. The head of the chemistry section makes a similar statement about the technical feasibility of producing small amounts of the compounds for laboratory use and economically producing large amounts for commercial use. The chemist also indicates, where possible, the possible dosage forms, since solely injectable dosages place significant constraints on the economic market. Essentially the same information was presented by the initial proponents of the project, but the information has been verified by the heads of chemistry and biology.

If the information contained in this part of the report is highly favorable, the project will be undertaken. If it is ambiguous, then other factors become important in determining whether or not the project is taken. If the information indicates the project does not have a reasonable chance of technical success, it will not be pursued. The only factor that could discourage a project with a high probability of chemical and biological success is the opinion of the clinician about the technical feasibility of scientifically and statistically determining the presence of the desired effect.

The clinician's opinion can be divided into two separate parts. The first part concerns the feasibility of scientifically demonstrating the presence of the effect that the biologist thinks will be present. Some examples can best illustrate the difficulties that can be involved in this area.

All are aware of pain in the presence of injury or a headache or of pain associated with certain diseases. Imagine that a biologist thinks the administration of a certain compound will significantly reduce the pain associated with headache or that associated with lower backache. How is this effect measured, and how is a control group set up?

A second example provides an even clearer picture of this type of problem. It is well known that there is a strong tendency for many men and women to lose their memory and some of their mental faculties as they age (senility). It has been suggested by a research biologist that a particular class of compounds could significantly retard this process. The chemist thinks that the synthesis of the proposed compounds will be relatively easy. Measurement is a major obstacle, however, since people lose their mental faculties in different ways and at different rates. Some people lose their ability to remember recent events but retain a firm grasp on events that happened in childhood; for others it is the opposite. Some people lose their memory gradually over fifteen to twenty years, and other lose theirs essentially overnight. What is the proper control in such a situation? The attempt at statistical rigor can essentially eliminate such a research project because it is impossible to set up an accurate experiment with *enough people involved* to have any hope of good statistical evidence. This problem can plague a research project; therefore, before the project is undertaken, the clinician is called upon to give an opinion about the expected difficulties.

The clinician is also required to estimate the number of people that will be needed for the clinical experiments, the length of time that the experiments will have to run, and the type of long-term tests that will be required. These factors largely determine project costs during the years when it will represent a substantial drain on the company's resources.

In the past fifteen years these considerations have become more important for several reasons. The most important is the dramatic increase in the costs of clinical testing. Clinical testing can easily cost a company $5 million per year or more. If the chances of success are low or if this stage of the testing process is expected to last fifteen to twenty years, there is little chance that the company will find the project to be an acceptable economic investment. As costs have increased, therefore, companies have put more effort into research planning.

During project selection, overall project cost is also estimated. This cost will be influenced by several factors. First is the perceived difficulty of developing acceptable ways of determining if the hypothesized pharmacological activity is present in animals. This is important since it is impossible to test every product candidate in human beings because of the cost and morality of such experiments.

In some areas screening is relatively easy; for instance, if a particular bacterium lives in certain animals and causes disease in human beings and if a drug kills the bacterium in the animal, it is likely that it will also kill the bacterium in people. In other areas, such as arthritis or depression, it can be very difficult to develop adequate screening procedures using animal models.[13] Thus, the expected cost of developing a drug in such an area will be significantly higher.

Another element of this decision is the quality of the company's existing screens in the area. As noted earlier, for instance, Roche has good screens for central nervous system drugs. Because developing screens entails a large fixed cost, Roche would view the expected development cost of a new CNS remedy as less than would a company new to this area. The information supplied by the clinician and the costs of testing the potential products in laboratory animals are then pooled to estimate overall product development costs.

In addition, there are other economic inputs into the decision process through the marketing department. A product description is given to the marketing department, whose experts are asked to estimate the product's sales potential. These estimates are generated for a variety of product characteristics: indications the product can treat, side effects, and whether or not the product will be available in oral or injectable form. An important thing to remember about this estimate is that it is based on limited information. It amounts to an estimate of what a particular pharmaceutical market will look like in five to ten years' time and has wide confidence bounds. It is usually, however, an important means of indicating whether the marketing department feels the potential product, even if its characteristics are very attractive, can generate significant sales. As such, it is an important signaling device to discourage selection of projects with a low economic return. It is also an important device for indicating the areas and claims upon which the research project should concentrate, since the various sales estimates can be a good means of indicating the relative economic importance of various claims. Marketing considerations will also be important for potential projects with short expected development times. This will often be the case for new indications for existing products. In this case the marketing input about expected sales is much more reliable because the shorter time frame significantly increases the reliability of information concerning market characteristics.

Another consideration that enters the basic research decision-making process is the likelihood of Food and Drug Administration approval of the product. This estimation is difficult because of uncertainty about the eventual product and the nature of future regulation (at the time

---

[13] This discussion is related to the depletion of research opportunities discussed earlier. One point that is often made concerning research opportunity depletion is that pharmaceutical research is now more concerned with finding products to treat debilitating diseases closely linked to the aging process. Because these diseases are difficult to model in animals, research costs are driven up.

the drug will be submitted). In spite of this, regulation will often have a major impact. In certain cases regulation—FDA testing requirements and likelihood of approval—has had a significant observable effect on the R&D activity in a given therapeutic area. Research on new beta blockers, for instance, has been significantly reduced by the stringency of regulation and the probability of FDA approval. Another obvious area is that of oral contraceptives. Few companies have ongoing research in this area because of FDA testing requirements. In other areas the effect is less obvious, but most executives indicated that regulation will usually have some influence.

R&D executives must also consider whether existing facilities and personnel can handle the potential project. This may be a problem because of research capacity bottlenecks. If the project calls for extensive toxicology testing, for instance, and the existing testing facilities are already under strain, the project may be postponed. A possible alternative is for the company to subcontract some of this research, but many companies have an aversion to this, which will detract from the project's chances of acceptance.

Existing resources may also be inadequate because the company does not currently carry out the type of research proposed. In such a case, it might be necessary for the company to hire additional researchers. Generally, companies consider research hiring to be a major company commitment both because of hiring transactions costs and because most companies are averse to firing research personnel. To proceed with such a project usually requires the explicit approval of high-level corporate executives outside the R&D area. Thus, the company will carefully scrutinize projects requiring new hiring.

The final consideration in new project selection in the 1970s is the project's synergism with other company projects and products. These considerations were discussed in reference to the decision-making process of the 1960s and are qualitatively the same.

In conclusion, it must be reemphasized that the most important consideration is still the scientific one. If the scientific and technical side looks favorable—that is, if the scientists feel there is a real medical need and the cost and likelihood of approval are reasonable—the project will be undertaken. The other considerations (besides the issue of whether the project can be handled in existing facilities) become important only in cases where the scientific and technical picture is muddied; then all the factors listed above will be considered.

Changes in Resource Control during Basic Research and Early Development. Two potential resource allocation decisions are made once the basic research project is under way.[14] One is to increase the funding of the project, and the other is to terminate the project. There is little evidence that the former decision has changed much in the relevant past. When a significant lead is uncovered, there has always been a substantial shift of manpower into that area of research. Procedures for weeding out unproductive projects, however, have undergone major revisions through a more formal project review process.

All companies now use a formal system of project review that guarantees each project will have at least an annual review, although some are reviewed more frequently. In general, a project just getting started will be reviewed annually, and then, as leads develop and more company resources are committed, the frequency of review increases. As specific candidates are identified and animal toxicology studies are begun, annual will give way to quarterly review. Subsequently, review may change to monthly, and a high-ranking interdisciplinary committee will be set up to monitor the project; this committee will consider a wide range of factors in its decisions. In the last stages before filing the NDA, review may be weekly or biweekly. This system is designed to ensure that all segments of the company get adequate input, especially later in the process when large resources are being expended. Such a system has not always been used, however. In the 1960s only scientists sat on the review committees, and they considered only medical need and scientific feasibility and ignored such factors as changing regulatory climates and drug markets.

Another change has been the increasing use of hurdles for continued project funding. The specific form of the hurdle depends on the type of project involved. Generally the project scientists must prove that some potential products possess certain characteristics by specified dates. If the project fails, it may not be funded for the following year. This system is designed to weed out scientists' pet projects and gives an objective reason, well in advance of the imposition of the standard, for the discontinuation of the project. This system can also give R&D managers, who may be caught up in a particular project, more perspective on a project's actual progress.

Thus, companies try to cut losses on unproductive projects by identifying them as early as possible. There is a definite "art" in the process described, however. It is important to cut losses on poor investments, but it is also important to guarantee that projects are not cut too early, because one successful project can pay for many failures. Therefore, the R&D manager's experience in being able to recognize the unfruitful

---

[14] For a description of the kind of research taking place at this stage, see David Schwartzman, *Innovation in the Pharmaceutical Industry* (Baltimore: Johns Hopkins University Press, 1976), pp. 31–38, 43–47.

project is very important. This is perhaps the reason there exists such interfirm diversity in the use of hurdles for projects to clear.

Changes in Research Decisions Surrounding the Drug's Introduction into Man. Let us now turn our attention to changes in decision processes that occur much later in the R&D path of the new product. When a potential new product is introduced into man, there is a substantial jump in the project's research expenditures. This can be seen in figure 1. Annual project expenditures jump from about $1.5 million to about $5 million after the first human tests because of high human-testing costs. This jump means that to begin human testing is a major decision.

The decision can occur either just before the beginning of human tests or just after. At this point, the company tries to determine whether the product generated by the research project is of sufficient quality to warrant the investment of the resources (that is, will it generate sufficient positive cash flows—sales net of manufacturing and marketing costs?) necessary to market the product. In most companies there is a good understanding of sunk cost, and the calculations are made with respect to unexpended resources. In some companies this calculation of the return expected for the unexpended resources is formally calculated; in others the estimates are informal. A nearly universal characteristic of this decision is that it is more quantitative than the basic research decision because of the greater reliability of the quantitative techniques at this stage.[15] In many cases there is a bias on the part of the scientists to go forward with a project at this point if the technical criteria look favorable. There has been less sympathy given to this position over time, however.

In the past fifteen years there have been several significant changes in the decision-making process at this point. The basic emphasis, as above, has been in the direction of a more careful and interdisciplinary approach to the decision to enter human testing. This change has resulted largely from the realization that other disciplines within the company, besides the R&D scientists, can make valuable inputs. Once again, however, the R&D scientists' opinions are still the most valuable source of information. In looking at this stage of the decision process, it is useful to examine current decision making and then contrast that with the process existing in the 1960s.

In most companies the decision variables are basically the same as those used for the preliminary research decision, but the information about those variables has changed significantly. Furthermore, the

---

[15] Quantitative estimates of sales, development costs, and probability of regulatory approval are more reliable for a five-year planning horizon.

71

weights of various factors in this decision are remarkably similar to their weights in the initial research decision.

At this stage, the company will try to estimate the manufacturing costs of the drug. This will often be the first attempt to estimate these costs because it is the first stage at which an accurate description of the actual drug product is available. Because it is costly to estimate manufacturing costs, the company wants to expend these resources only on drugs it feels are likely to be manufactured at some point. Moreover, if the estimated costs are too high, the company can often develop cheaper manufacturing processes.

Expected sales are also reestimated at this point. This is the same variable referred to in the discussion of the preliminary research decision, but the accuracy of the estimates has increased substantially because at this stage of the research project there are one or two specific candidates (usually one) with known characteristics. Similarly, the sales predictions are for markets two or three years in the future as opposed to five to ten years for the initial decision. These combine to make the resulting estimates much more accurate.

In addition, the clinician reevaluates the number of patients necessary for the clinical tests, the length of time that each testing stage will require, the specific information that will have to be developed to prove efficacy for the compound, the likelihood that such information can be developed, and the overall and yearly expenditure estimates for the project. At this stage, the clinician will have precise information about the product and should be able to answer these questions accurately.

Another factor reconsidered at this point is the Food and Drug Administration's stance on products of the type produced and its stance on the kind of information that will be produced by the clinician. If the clinician feels a particular test is essential for a valid proof of efficacy and the FDA takes a dim view of that test, this could have a strong negative impact on the decision to proceed. Basically, if the company feels it is unlikely that the FDA will approve a drug of this type, given the existing testing technology, then it is unlikely that the company will go ahead with the particular drug. It should be emphasized that this information will be similar to information sought at the preliminary research stage, but the prospect that the current regulatory stance in the FDA will be the prevailing stance at the time that the company files its NDA is much higher than in the early stages of research. In other words, when the company started the research project, it knew that it would be at least five years before the project would generate an NDA. Thus, there was some variability in the expected regulatory environment the drug would actually face. At the later stages of the research project, there is less time for the FDA to change. This *could* cause project abandonment at this stage. In addition, a project occasionally generates a product very different from that initially expected, in which case there would be a need to evaluate regulatory possibilities in terms of the product that has actually appeared.

All of these factors are important, to some extent, in the decision at this stage. They will seldom influence decisions, however, unless radically unfavorable information comes to light in one of these areas. The project will seldom be carried forward on the strength of the information developed in these areas.

The primary motive force of projects at this stage is the scientific factor. When one considers the type of information that has been developed since the initial research decision was made, the reason for this is obvious. It rests on the fact that *most* information developed in the course of research is information about the scientific feasibility of the basic idea that was submitted before research was begun. In other words, the most important new information that has become available since the research project was begun is that, in fact, a chemical exists with such-and-such characteristics that is apparently successful at treating indication X. The belief that the drug is successful rests on the drug's having passed tests A, B, and C, which the research scientists believe have a high correlation with successful treatment of X. On the whole, if the decision makers believe that there is a favorable outlook from the scientific point of view, then the project will probably be carried forward. If they feel that the scientific outlook is unfavorable, the project will not be carried forward.

In the 1960s the decision to enter the human-testing stage was less important than it is today. The combination of lower expenses and lesser control of the research establishment by general corporate management resulted in very little nonscientific input into this decision. This is not to say that other information was not developed at this stage, but it was not used in the decision-making process. An example will best illustrate this point.

When a drug comes up for human testing, the drug is expected to have the beneficial properties being sought. The most important unknown is whether the drug has some unknown faults in addition to its beneficial characteristics. Once this issue is settled, the drug's effectiveness will have to be proved, but this can usually be done. Therefore, if phase I tests show no adverse reactions, it is often only a matter of time before the drug will be proved effective. This means that corporate management will take a great deal of interest in drugs that successfully

73

pass phase I studies because the drug will probably have a significant effect on the corporation as a whole if it should go on the market (especially on the corporate profit and cash flow pictures).

As a result, the corporate management desires detailed information about drugs that pass phase I tests. This information consists of the drug's expected manufacturing cost, price, expected sales under different prices, estimated length of time for the drug to reach the market, and development costs that are likely to be incurred between the end of phase I and marketing.

In the 1960s this information was developed but was used exclusively as a method of improving corporate planning. With the advent of the 1970s, this information has come into use as a means of making better decisions about which drugs should be taken on for further testing and which should be stopped.

Summary. This section has examined the pharmaceutical R&D resource control process. It has been shown through several different discussions that major changes in this process have taken place in the last decade and a half. In the 1960s research scientists had tight control over the allocation process, beginning with the development of basic research ideas and extending to the selection of which ideas to pursue, the control of resources allocated to existing projects, and the decision to proceed with clinical testing of products. The two primary factors that drove the scientists' interest in areas for research and the eventual decision and control processes were medical need and scientific feasibility. Noteworthy by its absence was a concern for the effects of regulatory stringency on project profitability and the likelihood of success.

Then, in the late 1960s, the resource control process changed. The degree and exact timing of the change varied across companies, but in all companies there was a lessening of scientific power over research resources. A variety of new factors came to be considered in the decision process, including expected sales, product development costs, and probability of regulatory approval. This in turn resulted in a more quantitative approach to decision making because to compare projects that differ along multidimensional lines one must translate (map) these characteristics to a common dimension. The natural common denominator is dollars, and it is necessary to use quantitative decision techniques in such a translation. The quality of the quantitative estimations (and the amount of reliance placed on them) varies across companies, and nearly all use a judgment (fudge) factor to temper the strictly quantitative results. This is similar to the way that macroeconometric modelers use shifting intercept terms in their predictions. All companies, however, currently stress the need to consider a wide range of factors in their project selection decisions.

These descriptions of decision making present several important results for public policy in this area, one of the most important of which is that regulation should not have discouraged research in various therapeutic classes in the 1960s and should therefore have had little effect on research spending.[16] With the more sophisticated decision process and wider information set of the 1970s, however, there should develop an inverse relationship between regulation and research spending. Empirical tests of these propositions will be discussed later. In addition, the results cause one to question why the decision-making process would change in the way described, and a discussion of this will follow the empirical estimations. Before turning to these issues, however, it is worthwhile to describe briefly other changes in resource control that occurred between the two periods.

Other Changes in the Research Process

There have been a number of other changes in the decision-making process since the 1960s. These changes have been separated from the others for a better presentation.

One important area of change has been in the method used to determine the size of the research and development budget. The basic approach used by most companies has undergone a radical revision much in keeping with the changes already mentioned.

In the 1960s the usual system was to give the research division 5 to 10 percent of pharmaceutical sales as its budget (in some companies this was an explicit rule of thumb, and in others it was implicit). After the research division received its budget, it was divided among existing and newly formed projects in the manner described above, the research scientists determining the final allocation with little input from other disciplines within the company.

Today the budgeting process resembles a zero-based approach. The individual project managers decide how much money their projects will need for the coming year. Their estimates are then added together, with some attempt made to use statistical averaging to get closer to an expected value for expenditures; for instance, there may be three projects entering a certain phase of animal toxicology studies that are expected

---

[16] It is not true that regulation should have had no effect on research spending, because the FDA could still require that specific tests be run for product approval. This should create a positive relationship between the "stringency of regulation" in a therapeutic area and the level of research spending.

to last six months, and, on average, only one-third of the projects that enter this stage will pass it. It may be the case that the next testing phase, after the one the projects are ready to enter, is very expensive. Because one, two, or possibly all three of the projects can be expected to fail the first test, the combined budgets will include an allocation for each project for the first stage but an allocation only large enough to fund one or two of the projects for the second stage.

After the R&D managers add up the expenditures for the individual projects, they have a total budget, which they submit to the executive committee of the corporation. The executive committee then reviews the budgetary request. Usually the request budget is too high, and the R&D division is asked to trim it. This process is then repeated to convergence.

From the viewpoint of resource allocation within the company, the current budgetary procedures are superior to those of the 1960s. The funds allocated in this manner permit the R&D managers to review the projected use of funds *before* the total amount of the budget is set. They, implicitly or explicitly, have to arrive at a ranking of projects and the value of those projects to the company, and they must justify, project by project, the total budget.

Furthermore, the corporate executives have a chance to review the projects before they allocate the R&D budget. The beneficial aspect of this is that the executive committee can increase the size of the budget if the research projects appear, as a group, to be better than those encountered in previous years and decrease it for poorer projects. Another advantage is that the research managers can fight against the budget trimming if the group of projects appears to be very good. The executive committee can use this as a signaling device. The harder the R&D people fight for more money then, *ceteris paribus,* the greater the probable value of the currently available projects.

A significant number of short-term projects are undertaken by pharmaceutical R&D establishments to obtain approval for the use of a drug for new indications. Ciba-Geigy, for instance, is currently seeking approval for one of its drugs, used in the treatment of gout, for administration to heart attack victims to prevent a recurrence. Such projects will usually be of shorter duration than the original project to gain approval for the drug because of the safety and toxicology data that have already been generated about the product. In this case the quantitative data used in project selection are much more reliable. Instead of predicting what a market will look like in ten years, for instance, marketing data are now used to predict the market structure of next year or the year after. The product profile can be established with far greater certainty, since the claims sought are very specific. This also means that surveys of doctors about the need for the new indication will be a more reliable indicator of potential sales. Manufacturing data and cost figures are not estimates but are the actual costs the company has encountered in manufacturing the product. Finally, the stiffness of regulation can be known with certainty because the company can contact the FDA and ask what kind of data would be necessary to gain approval of the product for the new indication.

Combined, these factors mean that the approach to deciding whether the project should be undertaken can be a straightforward and reliable application of the present-discounted-value formulation. There will be little uncertainty in the variables, and the rate of return can be calculated very accurately. This indicates that the quantitative approach should be relied on much more heavily for projects of this type and projects of shorter life in general.

Another interesting aspect of the current decision-making process concerning the allocation of research dollars is the way in which pharmaceutical companies respond to the behavior of competitors. In general, companies try to engage in research that is within areas of their "franchise." In other words, they prefer to bring out drugs in areas where they have an established sales force and where their company has an established reputation.

Companies also have a strong desire to be the first to market a product for a given indication. Several interviewers reported that if virtually identical products are brought out as little as three to six months apart, the product that first appears will get a large majority of the market and maintain this share indefinitely. Therefore, if a competitor markets a product in a given area that is the same as a product of another company, there is little point in the second company's continuing research. In fact, the response on the part of companies is often to drop the product under development since there are few medical or economic reasons to pursue it.

A major effect of this drive to be first is a strong incentive to be aware of the type of products that one's competitors are bringing out and of what their timetables are. Over time, information networks develop among people who are working in the same field (this does *not* refer to any form of industrial espionage). The firms already established in a given field will be a part of this information network. This creates the incentive to stay in fields where the company as a whole is aware of the state of the art. This is further incentive for the market shares in individual therapeutic areas to be concentrated in the hands of relatively few companies.

These effects combine to indicate that we should see companies specializing in given areas of research (not to mention any possible economies of scale for research in a therapeutic area).

An Econometric Test and Some Speculations about Why The Decision Process Changed

The preceding sections have shown that there was a change in pharmaceutical research decision making in the late 1960s. In this section the empirical significance of this change is examined by summarizing the author's econometric work in the area. Some speculations about why the decision process changed are also offered.

Turning to the econometric estimations, the author estimated a therapeutic class research expenditure equation of the form:

$$Res_{i,t} = \alpha_i + \beta_1 \, Sales_{i,t} + \sum_{j=1}^{n} \beta_{j+1} \, Reg_{i,t-j} + \varepsilon_{i,t}$$

where $Res_{i,t}$ = research expenditures in the ith therapeutic class in the tth period; α_i = a therapeutic class intercept dummy variable; $Sales_{i,t}$ = sales in the ith class in the tth period; and $Reg_{i,t-j}$ = regulatory stringency in the ith class in the jth lagged period.[17] The equation was estimated separately over the 1960s and 1970s. According to the interview information presented above, one would expect a zero or slightly positive effect of regulation in the 1960s and a negative effect in the 1970s. The estimated equations are:

$$Res_{i,t} = \alpha_i + \underset{(.028)}{.077} \, S_{i,t} + \underset{(.177)}{.170} \, Reg_{i,t-1}$$
$$- \underset{(.178)}{.0006} \, Reg_{i,t-2} - \underset{(.163)}{.038} \, Reg_{i,t-3} + \varepsilon_{i,t}$$

Standard error of regression $= \$6.3$ million; $t = 1965-1968$; $R^2 = .98$; n.o.b. $= 24$; $F = 64.8$; standard errors in parentheses.

$$Res_{i,t} = \alpha_i + \underset{(.019)}{.047} \, S_{i,t} - \underset{(.204)}{.486} \, Reg_{i,t-2} - \underset{(.212)}{.773} \, Reg_{i,t-3}$$
$$- \underset{(.257)}{.885} \, Reg_{i,t-4} - \underset{(.267)}{.481} \, Reg_{i,t-5} + \varepsilon_{i,t}$$

---

[17] For a discussion of the reasons behind this specification, the reader should consult Wiggins, "Product Quality Regulation," chap. 4, where the model is formally developed and consideration is given to the econometric issues and problems of estimation.

Standard error of regression = \$13.72 million; $F = 67.94$; $R^2 = .96$; n.o.b. $= 36$; $t = 1971–1976$.[18]

As can easily be seen, the estimated coefficients have the correct sign. Furthermore, one can directly test the hypothesis that the effect of regulation was the same in the two periods, the 1960s and the 1970s, in which case one rejects the hypothesis at the 5 percent level.[19] This means that the change in decision making must be recognized to estimate the effects of regulation on research spending correctly.

Now let us turn our attention to why the process changed. It is emphasized that these are speculations that appear to be valid rather than established results. We will begin with some reasons why the decision-making process of the 1960s was a good system for its time and then offer some reasons why it became outmoded, which leads into the discussion of why the changes proceeded in the direction in which they did.

To begin, the present discounted value of a pharmaceutical research project is determined by four primary factors: basic research costs, clinical development costs, the probability of getting a new drug, and the sales (net of manufacturing costs) if a new drug is obtained.[20] In the 1950s and early 1960s, the pharmaceutical research environment was characterized by relatively short development periods and relatively low development costs.[21]

Scientists considered medical need, scientific feasibility, and some aspects of project synergism in their decision processes; and if medical

---

[18] For the regressions reported here, the sum of the regulation coefficients for the 1965–1968 period was 0.27, and the standard error of the sum was 0.32. For the 1971–1976 period, the sum of the regulation coefficients was -3.00 with a standard error of 0.46.

[19] See Wiggins, "Product Quality Regulation," chap. 4, pp. 135–45. Otherwise, one would pool the 1960s observations with those of the 1970s, and the resulting equation would be biased and inconsistent.

[20] This can easily be seen by examining the present-discounted-value equation for such a project:

$$PDV = \sum_{i=1}^{n} \frac{B_t}{(1+r)^t} + \sum_{i=n+1}^{m} \frac{C_t}{(1+r)^t} + p \sum_{i=m+1}^{k} \frac{S_t}{(1+r)^t}$$

where $B_t =$ the negative of basic research costs (expended over n years); $C_t =$ the negative of clinical development costs (expended over $m - n$ years); $S_t =$ sales net of manufacturing and marketing costs if a new drug is obtained (over $k - m$ years); $p =$ the probability of obtaining a new drug if the research is undertaken.

[21] See, for example, the discussion of new product development times and costs in H. A. Clymer, "The Economic and Regulatory Climate: U.S. and Overseas Trends," in R. B. Helms, ed., *Drug Development and Marketing* (Washington, D.C.: American Enterprise Institute, 1975). The social (as opposed to private) value of a number of these products has been questioned; for example, see W. S. Comanor, "Research and Competitive Product Differentiation in the Pharmaceutical Industry in the United States," *Economica*, vol. 31 (1964), pp. 372–84.

need is highly correlated with a potential product's expected sales (which most interviewed research executives believe to be the case), the scientists' decision variables would capture most of the variation in present discounted values (PDV) across projects. This is because scientific feasibility determines the probability of success (p in the equation in note 20) and basic research costs and time (B_t and n, respectively, in the equation). Furthermore, in this era clinical costs seem to have varied relatively little across projects. Thus, one can see that the relatively simple decision framework made good sense from an economic point of view.

Another element of organizational structure in the 1960s should be noted at this point. In all companies the scientists' power to make research decisions was a carefully guarded right. Not only was the scientific decision process relatively accurate, it was considered that only scientists should be making such decisions. Scientists viewed preliminary attempts to introduce a more varied decision process in much the same way that an academic researcher would view dictates from the university administration about which topic should be the subject of his next inquiry.[22] This factor should be kept in mind as we describe the changing R&D environment of the middle to late 1960s.

Over time the pharmaceutical development process changed so as to increase the number of factors that would affect the PDV of various projects. The most obvious of these changes were those in the regulatory environment throughout the 1960s. These changes had an exogenous effect on the probability of obtaining a new drug from the research project, on clinical development costs, and on basic research costs.

In addition to regulatory changes, there were changes in the scientific environment. Before 1960 a valid way to establish the efficacy of a particular compound was to obtain a testimonial from a physician concerning the drug's quality. With the scientific revolution came a desire formally to quantify various effects and test statistically for safety and efficacy.[23] This trend was strengthened by companies' desire to protect themselves from the types of product liability settlements produced by thalidomide by stronger and more objective data to back up their claims. Unfortunately, quantitative techniques in pharmaceutical research are very expensive, and this trend sharply increased research costs.

Most of these changes occurred in the decade following the 1962

---

[22] Because the wresting of control of resource allocation from the scientists could easily make it much more difficult for a particular company to hire scientists for many years to come (because the discussion above argues implicitly that research freedom enters into the scientists' utility function), such a move entails a large fixed cost.

[23] This was reported by a large number of R&D managers interviewed.

amendments. As a result it may never be possible to separate the effects of thalidomide and changing scientific techniques on research costs from contemporaneous cost increases that resulted from regulation.[24] The interviews clearly indicate that both factors contributed to the increasing costs.

The result of these cost changes was a much more complex decision problem for R&D decision makers, because project PDVs varied not only according to the scientific factors listed above but also according to expected clinical testing costs and the difficulty of obtaining regulatory approval of a new drug. The result is that a decision process that takes account of these additional factors will do better at selecting the projects with the highest PDVs than one that does not. As a result there was an incentive to adopt a decision-making process that could take account of these factors. This appears to be the reason that R&D establishments changed their decision-making processes.

This finding raises the question why the change in decision making did not occur before the late 1960s, since most of these factors began to have some effect on the profitability of research by the mid-1960s. The reasons are varied. It is not at all clear that regulation had a major effect on research profitability until the late 1960s.[25] Furthermore, to the extent that increased quantification in science was responsible for the changes in costs, the late 1960s seem to be a plausible date for these factors to begin to affect R&D decision making. The most important reason one would expect delay in adopting the new decision-making process, however, is that it required a major change in organizational structure. The new decision-making processes required the taking of final decision-making power away from the scientists.[26]

Finally, the change in decision making required the development of significant in-house quantitative estimation and evaluation skills because decision making in the 1960s was intuitive and nonquantitative.

---

[24] It is worth noting that most of the literature that shows increasing pharmaceutical R&D costs captures both effects. Without more information than is supplied by these researchers, it is impossible to determine the relative shares of these factors in increasing research costs; see, for example, R. W. Hansen, "The Pharmaceutical Development Process: Estimates of Development Costs and Times and the Effects of Proposed Regulatory Changes," in R. I. Chien, ed., *Issues in Pharmaceutical Economics* (Lexington, Mass.: Lexington Books, 1979), and Clymer, "Economic and Regulatory Climate."

[25] For evidence that this might be the case, see Wiggins, "Product Quality Regulation," chap. 5.

[26] These problems were described earlier. The wresting of control from scientists should not be oversold. In most research organizations they still have more authority, in this area, than any other discipline. It is just that the authority is no longer absolute. The important point is that any formal system of considering nonscientific input results in a discontinuity in the decision-making process. In other words, there is a significant fixed cost associated with the change.

Furthermore, scientists had apparently developed acceptable ways of trading off medical need and scientific feasibility without quantifying either factor. When such diverse factors as regulation and clinical costs were introduced, however, it was necessary to translate this multidimensional project-profitability information to a single dimension for an adequate comparison. The natural choice was dollars, an evaluation of projects in terms of their present discounted values; but this required that such factors as scientific feasibility and medical need be quantified. This necessity also added a fixed-cost element to the change in the decision-making process, which leads to a careful consideration of whether such a change in decision making is the appropriate strategy to follow.

In summary, a plausible explanation of the change in decision making has been put forward. This explanation seems to fit the relevant data and explain the appearance of both the old decision-making process and the new one. It needs to be emphasized that several alternative explanations also exist and that the author feels they too have some validity. The most important point of this discussion is that it is probably *incorrect* to conclude that these changes were only the result of the changed regulatory environment. Rather, they resulted from a variety of factors affecting the profitability of pharmaceutical research.

Summary and Policy Conclusions

This paper has presented a careful description of the pharmaceutical R&D decision process. Two very different descriptions were presented, one for the 1960s and the other for the 1970s. In the 1960s the research scientists had nearly complete control of the decision-making apparatus. Their decision criteria were medical need and scientific feasibility, and they did not consider the stringency of government regulation. This implies that regulation should not have affected the level or allocation of research in the 1960s. As time passed, companies took some of this control away from scientists and required a more interdisciplinary approach to decision making. This resulted in a consideration of such factors as clinical development costs and regulation. It was also shown that these changes led to empirically observable differences in the way firms responded to changes in regulatory stringency in the two periods. Finally, some speculations were offered about why the decision-making process changed.

Two primary policy conclusions emerge from these findings. It has been shown that, even though a factor may have a significant effect on the profitability of research (or any other economic endeavor), it need not affect the decision to proceed. This is because one must also consider the adaptability of the relevant organization and its decision-making process to the changed environment. In the case at hand, regulation apparently did not affect pharmaceutical research spending in the 1960s because the organizational structure could not easily adapt to consider this new factor.

The second policy conclusion is that we currently face a significant trade-off between increased regulatory stringency and the level of research spending in this industry. This result does *not* imply that the current safety and efficacy regulation is too strict; it merely states that socially we face a steep decline in the number of drugs produced in exchange for increasing certainty that they do what their manufacturers claim they will do. Whether it is better to have extensive research and little product quality information or vice versa is a matter open to debate.

Bibliography

Clymer, H. A. "The Economic and Regulatory Climate: U.S. and Overseas Trends." In *Drug Development and Marketing*, edited by R. B. Helms. Washington, D.C.: American Enterprise Institute, 1975.

Comanor, W. S. "Research and Competitive Product Differentiation in the Pharmaceutical Industry in the United States." *Economica* 59 (1964): 372–84.

Faust, R. "Pharmaceutical Research Planning Strategies." *SRA Journal* (Society of National Research Administrators) (1976).

———. "Project Selection in the Pharmaceutical Industry." *Research Management* 14 (1971): 46–55.

———. "Research Planning: Perspectives and Challenges." *Drug and Cosmetic Industry* 111 (1972): 42–48, 113–19.

Hansen, R. W. "The Pharmaceutical Development Process: Estimates of Development Costs and Times and the Effects of Proposed Regulatory Changes." In *Issues in Pharmaceutical Economics*, edited by R. I. Chien. (Lexington, Mass.: Lexington Books, 1979).

Schwartzman, David. *Innovation in the Pharmaceutical Industry*. Baltimore: Johns Hopkins University Press, 1976.

Wiggins, S. N. "Product Quality Regulation and Innovation in the Pharmaceutical Industry." Ph.D. dissertation, Massachusetts Institute of Technology, 1979.

Reducing the Drug Lag: Entrepreneurship in Pharmaceutical Clinical Testing

Kenneth W. Clarkson and William C. MacLeod

The ultimate product of the U.S. pharmaceutical industry is the improved health of its customers. Because these customers also represent a constituency whose government is increasingly concerned with the same product, the industry has had to operate in two marketplaces to sell its goods. Not only must people be induced to purchase the drug firms' products, government officials must be satisfied that the goods are worthy of the people's patronage. Drugs must pass the tests of the political marketplace before they are allowed to compete for economic rewards. Drugs are complex products and are difficult to evaluate, especially without the benefit of market experience. Consequently, the nonmarket tests used to perform this evaluation have been continually revised in attempts to improve their accuracy.

Competition in the major part of the drug industry does not take the traditional form of finding a more efficient way to produce a known physical commodity and thereby outselling the competition. The sustaining business of the industrial drug makers lies in the discovery of new products that will render the competition obsolete. Although price, cost, and quality competition among different drug makers is important, the primary competitive activity of the industry leaders has been research and innovation in new and better methods of improving health with medicines.

There is no question that the introduction of the Food and Drug Administration (FDA) regulations during the past two decades has contributed to the reduction of research and innovation of pharmaceutical products.[1] Even more important, it has become apparent that the key variable linking FDA regulations to decreases in research and innovation

---

[1] See, for example, Sam Peltzman, *Regulation of Pharmaceutical Innovation: The 1962 Amendments* (Washington, D.C.: American Enterprise Institute, 1974); Martin N. Bailey, "Research and Development Costs and Returns: The U.S. Pharmaceutical Industry," *Journal of Political Economy*, vol. 80 (1972), pp. 70–85; Henry G. Grabowski, *Drug Regulation and Innovation* (Washington, D.C.: American Enterprise Institute, 1976), p. 27; William Wardell, "Introduction of New Therapeutic Drugs in the United States and

is the time involved in bringing the drug to market. Increased time delay hurts both consumers, by reducing the availability of pharmaceutical products, and producers, by lowering the net returns from investment. In this paper we investigate the relationship between the institutional constraints promulgated by the FDA beginning in the early 1960s and time. Next, we examine how differences in time influence the present value from an investment in a potential pharmaceutical product. Finally, our attention turns to industry responses in reducing the time before marketing may begin.

Pharmaceutical Research and Development under Regulation

The research and development (R&D) process that brings a new drug to market can be summarized briefly in three stages.[2] The first is chemical synthesis, in which compounds of known or suspected pharmacological activity are formulated, tested, and modified. These tests are typically conducted in vitro (in test tubes) until a specific desired reaction is achieved. Such screenings involve thousands of compounds for every one that is passed on to the next testing stage. The second stage is animal testing, primarily for precautionary reasons, to see if the drug is safe for experimentation in humans, although some pharmacological activity is monitored here as well. If the drug satisfies the standards of the animal tests, it passes on to the third and final stage—clinical (human) evaluation. Here, depending on the nature of the drug, a specific clinical program is selected to test again for safety and then for efficacy. The animal and the human testing stages overlap to some extent. Animal tests for long-term toxicity are continued beyond the commencement of the clinical phase of the investigations. The drug that survives all these stages becomes a candidate for the new drug application (NDA).

Before 1962 the emphasis and organization of the three stages were left largely to the discretion of the drug firm. Formal contact with the

---

Great Britain: An International Comparison," *Clinical Pharmacology and Therapeutics,* vol. 14 (1974), pp. 733–90, and "The Drug Lag Revisited: Comparison by Therapeutic Area of Patterns of Drugs Marketed in the United States and Great Britain from 1972 through 1976," *Clinical Pharmacology and Therapeutics,* vol. 24 (1974), p. 499; and Henry G. Grabowski, John M. Vernon, and Lacy G. Thomas, "The Effects of Regulatory Policy on the Incentives to Innovate: An International Comparative Analysis," in S.A. Mitchell and E. A. Link, eds., *Impact of Public Policy on Drug Innovation and Pricing* (Washington, D.C.: The American University, 1976), p. 47.

[2] For a more detailed description of the process, see David Schwartzman, *Innovation in the Pharmaceutical Industry* (Baltimore: Johns Hopkins University Press, 1976), pp. 57–62. For a description of the transition mechanism allowed for pre-1962 drugs, see "Drug Efficacy and the 1962 Drug Amendments," *Georgetown Law Journal,* vol. 60 (1971), p. 195.

FDA came at the end of the process, upon filing of the NDA.[3] At that point, if a firm was able to report successful results of tests for safety of the drug, the application would be approved. Shortcuts and detours, which can occur quite naturally in the serendipitous process along the way to the application, were not continually scrutinized by the FDA. In 1962 the FDA, largely independently of the congressional activity at the time, decided to restrict this flexibility by extending supervision further back in the development pipeline. The announcement came on August 10, two months before passage of the famous Kefauver amendments, in the form of proposed regulations.[4] The regulations were a modification of the required conditions for the investigational new drug (IND) exemption provided by the 1938 act.

The FDA's proposed rule making was to be overshadowed by the congressional activity that resulted in the 1962 amendments. This was unfortunate, for the fact that the FDA was acting independently has been almost overlooked in the subsequent debate over the impact of the act. The IND regulations, which were promulgated in 1963,[5] probably had a much greater immediate effect than the amendments; and these regulations had little to do with the efficacy of new drugs.

The 1938 Food, Drug, and Cosmetic Act authorized the FDA to promulgate regulations controlling the use of the exemption for investigational drugs but set no specific limits to the rule's scope.[6] For the first twenty years, the requirements were minimal, being limited to a record-keeping function for each firm. The decision to distribute investigational drugs remained with the firm. In 1962 the FDA sought to institute automatic, substantive review of this decision.

Although the proposed rules simply established the procedure of review by stages, the final rules specifically described the nature of the phases and established the points at which reports would be submitted during clinical investigations.[7] Thus, all clinical investigations after January 8, 1963, would adhere to the pattern set forth in the rule. Phase I, as the rule described it, comprised the first introductions into man. The test subjects would be limited in number and their reactions monitored primarily for purposes of determining the safety of various dosage

---

[3] The initial investigational new drug (IND) exemption did not require notice to be given to the FDA, although a firm relying on the exemption was required to maintain files that were subject to inspection by FDA personnel.

[4] *Federal Register,* vol. 27 (1962), p. 7990.

[5] Ibid., vol. 28 (1963), p. 179; codified in *Code of Federal Regulations,* title 21, section 130.3 (1964).

[6] *United States Statutes at Large,* title 52, ch. 675, section 1040 (1938); amended by *United States Code,* title 21, sections 301–92 (1964).

[7] *Federal Register*, vol. 28 (1963), p. 179; codified in *Code of Federal Regulations,* title 21, section 130.3 (1964).

forms. Phase II (which may overlap with phase I) began with the initial trial on limited numbers of patients with the disease to be treated. Reports on these two phases, along with any subsequent animal testing indicated by the results from the human tests, were to be submitted to the FDA before phase III could begin. Required in addition to the reports was a detailed description of the protocol to be observed during the phase III tests. These tests would comprise a wide distribution of the drug to hospitals and other investigators in order to observe *a large sample of patients under the drug's care.* The plan for phase III would not be acceptable unless it provided for more than one independent investigation generating an adequate number of case histories of individual patients. The records from the phase III trials were to contain, for each individual subject, adequate records pertaining to age, sex, conditions treated, and any other relevant information or observation made in the course of the investigation.

Because these regulations coincided so closely with the 1962 amendments, it is difficult to disentangle the effects of the two changes. The available evidence, however, points to the IND revisions as the more important change. Although the proposed efficacy standards were grudgingly accepted by the industry, the IND regulations met with a dramatic response. The rules were attacked by industry spokesmen as highly detrimental to drug research. Immediate effects were felt in pharmaceutical laboratories. On announcement, one lab reported that thirty projects were dropped; on enactment, thirty-seven more were abandoned—all despite favorable commercial prospects. Another firm with ninety investigations under way in August 1962 dropped all of them, and still another discontinued 30 percent of all its projects.[8] Thus, although 1962 is known as the year that efficacy requirements were added to the regulations of new drugs, it is more likely that the principal adjustments to be made at the time were in response to the more obscure changes in the IND rules—rules that would have been implemented regardless of the fortunes of the proposed legislation.

Another reason that the IND requirements probably had a greater impact than the amendments in 1962 and 1963 is that they were promulgated in reasonably specific detail. This was not true of the efficacy standards written into the 1962 amendments. In fact, nearly eight years would pass before the industry knew exactly what was required to demonstrate efficacy under the law.

The 1962 amendments gave only a very general guide to the meaning of efficacy and what would be required to demonstrate it. Substantial evidence of efficacy was defined in the amendments as follows: "the

[8] *Oil, Paint, and Drug Reports,* vol. 185 (July 1, 1975), p. 5.

term substantial evidence means evidence consisting of adequate and well-controlled investigations, including clinical investigations, . . . on the basis of which it could fairly and reasonably be concluded . . . that the drug will have the effect it purports or is represented to have."[9]

Substantial evidence speaks to the quality of evidence;[10] yet the amendments did not spell out what criteria would apply to the determination of quality. The regulations promulgated pursuant to the amendments gave no interpretation. The FDA simply copied the statutory terms verbatim in the final rules of June 20, 1963.[11] Consequently, the acquisition of knowledge of the new efficacy standards became a matter of trial and error for firms as they submitted their applications and waited for the FDA's response.

In 1966 the FDA released the first set of comprehensive formal guidelines describing the expected procedure to be followed in testing a new drug.[12] The guidelines were presented in proposed rules regarding the form of the new drug application to be submitted for marketing approval by the FDA. On June 6, 1967, the rules were promulgated as final.[13] Enforcement, again, was a simple matter. The penalty for noncompliance was a denial of financial return for the substantial investment in developing the drug. Although the experience of the prior four years under the 1962 amendments undoubtedly had established many of these standards on a gradual case-by-case basis, by 1967 the FDA erased any remaining doubt about the procedure required of all applicants.

With the IND regulations prescribing the order to be followed in conducting an investigation and the NDA regulations stipulating the kinds of tests to be administered in the process, the constraints shaping the drug development process had become quite standardized. One issue remained unresolved by the regulations, however. What would constitute "substantial evidence" of safety and efficacy? What reliability could be required of the various results of tests supporting an application? The FDA had not embellished the statutory definition of substantial evidence in its regulations. This gap would be filled in September 1969, when such regulations were published.[14]

---

[9] Drug Amendments of 1962, section 102(c), amending Federal Food, Drug, and Cosmetic Act of 1938, section 505(d); codified in *United States Code,* title 21, section 355(d)(1964).

[10] The negotiations leading to the selection of a substantial evidence standard are recounted in Richard Harris, *The Real Voice* (New York: Macmillan, 1964), pp. 204–5.

[11] *Federal Register,* vol. 28 (1963), p. 6378; codified in *Code of Federal Regulations,* title 21, section 130.4(*c*) (1964).

[12] Ibid., vol. 31 (1966), p. 13347.

[13] Ibid., vol. 32 (1967), pp. 8081, 8083; codified in *Code of Federal Regulations,* title 21, section 130.4(*d*) (1968).

[14] Ibid., vol. 34 (1969), p. 7250.

These regulations, expanding on the NDA descriptions of the tests to be conducted in the course of an investigation, modified the grounds for refusal to approve an application. Still, the standard would be a lack of substantial evidence consisting of adequate and well-controlled clinical investigations. The regulations elaborated on the meaning of such investigations, prescribing the appropriate testing methods and reporting procedures. It was made clear that studies varying from the guidelines could not provide the basis for a successful new drug application.

Thus, in the space of eight years, regulation of the pharmaceutical research and development process was completely overhauled. From a policy focusing essentially on the results of the process, the FDA brought the authority and guidance of the government into nearly every step of the process itself.

The Effects of Regulation

Complaints were heard from industrial sources as soon as the regulations of 1963 were given effect.[15] Because it was widely recognized that increased certainty in the marketing of drugs would not be costless, these protests were given little notice. By the late 1960s, more disturbing evidence was coming to light. According to a number of studies, substantial costs have been generated by the amendments of 1962: the cost of developing a new drug has risen sharply, the number of new drugs reaching the market has declined, and the United States has fallen behind its foreign competition in the search for innovation.[16] Meanwhile, the benefits have been difficult to detect. The blame for this state of affairs has usually been placed on two features of the amendments: the requirement of substantial evidence of efficacy and the IND procedure.

An alternative hypothesis is that the regulations imposed on the development of new pharmaceutical products are a product of incremental FDA decision making over a number of years rather than the promulgation of dramatically new and distinct edicts. The system of rule making in administrative law practice in the United States typically suggests the opposite procedure. Rules are first proposed, subjected to comment and criticism, and then promulgated. As promulgated, the rules constitute new constraints facing a sector of the economy. This process does not seem to have been followed in the practice of the FDA. To be sure, significant discrete changes have been generated by enactment of major legislation or by sudden policy shifts within the FDA. The 1938 Food, Drug, and Cosmetic Act and the investigational new

[15] See, for example, note 8.
[16] See note 1.

drug regulations are examples of these. During the 1960s, however, when the pharmaceutical industry began to attract wide attention, all regulatory changes came in the form of refinements and revisions of existing practice. Indeed, the most controversial regulations of the period, the 1969 "September Regulations," were prefaced with the notice that the new procedures enumerated therein were simply statements of the prevailing state of the art of drug testing. If this is generally true of FDA rules throughout the period, then comparing activity before promulgation to that after promulgation of a rule will not yield meaningful evidence of the impact of the constraints embodied in the rule.

We first check for evidence of the impact of the rules. The important years are 1963, 1967, and 1970. If the legislation of 1962 (and the IND requirements), the regulations of 1967, or those of 1970 imposed sudden additional burdens on drug makers, evidence of this would be expected to arise in the delay at the FDA between submission and approval of a new drug application. It is assumed that the delay in approving a drug is caused in part by the acceptability of the application and the quality of the tests it reports. The assumption seems reasonable in light of the FDA's comments on incomplete NDAs during the late 1960s. From 1967 through 1969, the FDA released a breakdown of reasons for incomplete NDAs. The lists showed that, on average, 25 percent of the applications were unapprovable for lack of sufficient animal safety data, 59 percent were unapprovable because of insufficient clinical safety data, and 60 percent suffered from critically deficient efficacy data.[17] One would expect, if radically different standards were imposed by new rules, that the amount of delayed NDAs would increase after the rules were announced. Table 1 gives the relevant time periods.

A rise in approval time began after 1962, but it was not a sudden rise. The longest delays were experienced in the late 1960s for drugs that were submitted, on the average, before any major rule change. In 1970, the first year in which drugs submitted under the new NDA regulations began to gain approval, the long delays began to decline. Thus, it appears that as soon as firms were operating under the new standardized procedure their efforts were judged successful by the FDA. The early 1970s, however, witnessed another increase in FDA delay, indicating perhaps that the revised definitions of substantial evidence and acceptable testing methods were causing some difficulty in compliance.

Mean development time (the period between selection of a candidate and submission of the NDA) shows the same gradual rise throughout the period. The increase mentioned earlier, from two years to nearly eight years, took place over the decade following 1962.

---

[17] U.S. Department of Health, Education and Welfare, Food and Drug Administration, *Annual Reports*, 1967–1969.

TABLE 1

APPROVAL DELAY FOR NEW DRUGS, BY CATEGORY, 1962–1976
(months of delay)

Year	Overall Average	Dermatologicals	Antiinfectives
1962	17	17	24
1963	18	18	19
1964	22	38	14
1965	25	11	13
1966	31	16	31
1967	36	21	38
1968	31	16	25
1969	44	32	38
1970	29	18	23
1971	19	16	20
1972	17	10	18
1973	29	22	10
1974	21	11	13
1975	26	35	35
1976	23	27	15

SOURCE: S. N. Wiggins, "Product Quality Regulation and Innovation in the Pharmaceutical Industry" (Ph.D. dissertation, MIT, 1979).

These movements suggest a causal relationship. If much of the information of FDA practice was revealed in a case-by-case progression, then collected and published when experience provided sufficient guidance, a measure of the impact of changing FDA policy can be determined by examining responses to individual cases. Relatively quick NDA approval by the FDA could be regarded as an indication that the agency was satisfied with current methods for a particular drug or class of drugs. Where delay times grew, the inference would arise that the FDA was modifying its policy and raising the standards for review.

Because the drug industry is a composite of many different therapeutic classes, the experience in several classes can be compared. It is assumed that the standards of review will vary from class to class. Different types of therapy call for different types of tests, some of which are more easily performed and evaluated than others. Drugs intended to treat an identifiable and measurable disease such as hypertension, for example, will yield unambiguous results after relatively short testing; antiobesity agents, on the other hand, may require more elaborate methods of evaluation. More important, standards required of producers in different classes probably do not change simultaneously. Specialization in the FDA dictates that drugs from scientifically distinct categories go through different channels of review. Comparison of delay times across categories reveals that there is significant variation among them, a variation that is not reflected in the average for all categories. Table 1 reveals some of these differences.

To what extent do these changing approval times in individual categories affect subsequent costs of development in those categories? To answer the question, a measure must be obtained for the costs incurred by drug developers. A direct measure is difficult to obtain, since cost information (to the extent the firms have gathered it) is considered highly proprietary. A reasonable proxy for this cost is available, however. We can get estimates of the time various drugs remain in the development pipeline by subtracting the patent filing date from the date of NDA submission. Patents are filed at a consistent time in the development process. When a compound is found in preliminary testing to have potentially valuable therapeutic properties, a patent application will be filed with the patent office if the drug is patentable, and the drug will begin its major preclinical tests.

The increasingly structured nature of drug development suggests that the time a candidate spends in testing will be roughly proportional to the costs of development. There certainly is some flexibility, for it would be expected that candidates with exceptionally good commercial prospects will be rushed through development as quickly as possible. Mitigating this tendency, however, is the fact that highly lucrative drugs typically represent a significant advance over existing therapy. If such drugs exhibit novel properties, or risks, they will require more careful examination, and probably more time. Similarly, once a product has been selected and placed in the pipeline, the incentive will be to move it along without undue delay, since the returns will not commence until the project is completed, and the time in the laboratory will cut into the commercial life granted by patent.

The function postulated is the following:

$$Cost_{i,t} = f(NDA_{i,\ t-1},\ X_{i,t})$$

where $Cost$ = the cost of developing a product, here approximated by time in development, in category i, year t; NDA = the time delay from application to approval for a new drug in category i, year $t - 1$; and X = vector of institutional factors, including the state of technology of the opportunities for further exploitation of a particular class in category i, year $t - 1$ (possible candidates for this variable are prior discoveries in the category, or simply an incremental variable to account for general trends in technology).

A preliminary test was run to check this relationship. Four broadly defined therapeutic categories were selected (primarily on the basis of sufficient activity to generate annual observations): cardiovasculars and diuretics, analgesics and antiinflammatory agents, psychopharmaceuticals, and antiinfectives. Delay was expressed in months. Observations over the years 1958 to 1975 yielded the following results: development time $= 22.5 + 1.8$ (NDA delay); $R^2 = .40$; $n = 37$.

From such a crude test the results are encouraging. The intercept term corresponds to the pre-1962 development time reported earlier. The coefficient of NDA delay, significant at the 95 percent level, indicates that adjustments are made in subsequent development techniques upon changes in FDA treatment of drugs in a particular category.

Simultaneity should not be a problem with this test, since costs are regressed on prior year's delays. The existence of an independent factor affecting both variables cannot be ruled out a priori, however; for example, if both development time and FDA delay respond simultaneously to news of new hazards requiring additional testing and evaluation in a particular class, the correspondence may be picked up in the lagged regression shown above. To test for this possibility, development time for year t was regressed on NDA time for the same year. No statistically significant relationship was found.

A second test for the independence of FDA time was performed. One would expect the time required for evaluation of an NDA to correspond to the manufacturer's difficulty in establishing safety and efficacy for the drug. Thus, the longer a particular drug remained in development before application, the longer would be the expected approval delay. No significant correlation was found between these two variables, however. It is possible, of course, that a longer development time results in a superior application, which the FDA can process more easily. It would seem, however, that the more important factor in the quality of an application is presentation of the tests that have been performed, a factor not as time consuming or as costly as the tests themselves.

To the extent that we can draw conclusions from this rough evidence, it seems to indicate that FDA policy, as reflected in continued enforcement, is relatively independent of the obvious factors affecting drug testing and development and is itself a significant causal factor in determining the constraints operating on the process.

Evidence that regulatory changes have had a noticeable effect on the time for and costs of developing new drugs, combined with more detailed information regarding the specific adjustments in the shaping of government policy, suggests further tests to examine their influence on the structure of the development process. Our earlier discussion of the law indicated that the FDA's emphasis on research and development gradually shifted focus during the period after the 1962 amendments. The early years of this period might be characterized as the IND years, during which the agency was refining its requirements to ensure safety in experimental drugs. Later, in the late 1960s and early 1970s, the focus shifted to standards of efficacy. Is this shift reflected in the performance of the industry?

By requiring uniform procedures to be followed in the development of a drug, the FDA limits the opportunity to substitute one resource for another. By requiring increased statistical standards, more extensive testing, and more detailed reporting at one stage, the FDA can increase the cost of that stage. In effect, regulation imposes on the producer an increasingly fixed-proportion production function, thereby decreasing the elasticity of demand for each input. This is important, for the only evidence available on the inputs to the process is indirect evidence on expenditures for those inputs. If the demand for each input is stable and highly inelastic, the unambiguous cause of an increase in expenditures on that input is an increase in its relative price. In other words, as the substitutability of resources declines, it is more likely that an increase in expenditures on one input is a result not of its becoming relatively cheaper but of its becoming relatively more expensive.

Thus, we seek evidence of the nature of expenditures over the 1960s and 1970s. The legal description suggests that increased expenditures in the early part of the period would relate to preclinical testing processes and increased expenditures on R&D later would focus on the clinical stages. Once again, direct evidence is unavailable, and the indirect evidence is highly circumstantial. What little exists, however, tends to support our predictions.

The statistical consciousness of the pharmaceutical industry experienced a great boost in the middle 1960s. Most of the more detailed records of R&D allocations are available from 1965 and later. One such series is the spending on human testing abroad by U.S. pharmaceutical firms. If our hypothesis is correct, we would expect these expenditures to rise more rapidly in the latter half of the period, when clinical testing regulations were tightened. This is what occurred. R&D spending on humans abroad (in real terms), after rising moderately through the middle 1960s, increased substantially in the early 1970s. Between 1965 and 1969, real expenditures increased at an annual rate of 9.3 percent. From 1970 to 1974, the rate was 18.6 percent, most of which was caused by the increases in 1972 and 1973, when foreign expenditures almost doubled.[18]

---

[18] Erol Caglarcan, Richard E. Faust, and Jerome E. Schnee, "Resource Allocation in Pharmaceutical Research and Development," in Mitchell and Link, *Impact of Public Policy,* p. 337.

The jump in these expenditures, coming so closely after the September and May regulations, suggests that there was still a significant adjustment to be made upon announcement of the new standards. Although, as we have posited, much of the FDA policy had been developed before that date, the information lacked full dissemination (and certainty of application) until announcement of the regulations.

Another trend that reveals a change in the structure of the R&D process is the proportion of R&D funds allocated to personnel. If early adjustments were made in the first stages of drug development, which entail more laboratory, labor-intensive research, the budget allocated to personnel would be relatively greater than when increased effort was being switched to monitoring clinical investigations. During the 1960s such an increase took place. The personnel portion of the cost per R&D dollar rose 25 percent between 1965 and 1970 but fell 15 percent from 1970 to 1975.[19]

The principal outcome of the FDA regulations instituted in the early 1960s and thereafter has been to increase significantly R&D costs and the time between the initial discovery of a new pharmaceutical product and the receipt of revenues from a successful marketing of the product. A good portion of the increase in time is directly attributable to the FDA's approach to controlling the safety and efficacy of pharmaceutical products. Rather than focus directly on the effectiveness and safety of pharmaceutical products, the FDA, like many other federal agencies, has chosen to monitor the actual production process directly. If firms differ in the amount of laboratory equipment and other capital and in the amount and skill of personnel, the lowest-cost method for determining safety and efficacy will differ among firms. The FDA regulations, however, are extremely input-specific, with detailed methods that *all* firms must follow in pursuing safety and efficacy. The movement toward standardization of proof implies that pharmaceutical firms will not be able to take advantage of special characteristics of their equipment, particular personnel, or other related resources in satisfying FDA tests.

More important, there is no a priori reason to believe that firms will necessarily have a comparative advantage in time-intensive processes. Thus, it is not surprising that we find increased specialization in the pharmaceutical industry.[20] This specialization manifests itself in

---

[19] Ibid., p. 336.

[20] In addition, we note that the size of the clinical testing market itself (which is growing rapidly) contributes to increased specialization. See George J. Stigler, "The Division of Labor Is Limited by the Extent of the Market," *Journal of Political Economy*, vol. 59, p. 185–93; reprinted in William Breit and Harold M. Hockman, eds., *Readings in Microeconomics*, 2d ed. (New York: Holt, Rinehart and Winston, 1971).

many ways, including (1) a reduction in the number of therapeutic areas in which pharmaceutical firms will invest their R&D dollars and (2) the increased use of specialized inputs provided outside the firm.[21] We have noted, for example, that the market for preclinical testing expanded significantly in the 1960s. The growth of firms specializing in this service was well documented during that time.[22] More recently, a new industry has emerged. The service it provides is wide-scale clinical testing, which still remains largely controlled by firms themselves but is gradually moving outside their private laboratories. Vertical integration is declining as the market for large-scale, standardized R&D tests grows.

Clinical Testing of New Drugs

Before we turn our attention to the costs of drug development, we recall the actual process of clinical testing—the component of drug development that entails the greatest costs.

Once a drug has been found to be reasonably safe and effective in studies with laboratory animals, the next step in the drug-testing process is to evaluate the drug in human subjects. Under FDA regulations, the sponsor may begin the clinical studies thirty days after submission of the IND unless prohibited from doing so.[23]

Most pharmaceutical companies retain investigators for these studies who are not company physicians, and some have outside laboratories do their preclinical animal studies. Private pathology/toxicology firms are often used to perform the animal tests, and the early phases of human experimentation are usually carried out by clinical researchers associated with university-affiliated hospitals.[24]

Companies have established protocols that define the procedures to be followed in the testing of the drug. The protocol prescribes the methods of testing, the drug dosage levels, and the maintenance of records and data.[25] It is the responsibility of the sponsoring company to monitor the investigators to ensure adherence to the protocol.

An important consideration in the administration of experimental drugs to humans is the choice of subjects. The principle of informed consent requires that human subjects be aware of the possible risks

---

[21] Caglarcan, Faust, and Schnee, "Resource Allocation."

[22] G. D. Searle, one of the glamour stocks of the 1960s, was one of these firms.

[23] *Code of Federal Regulations,* title 21, section 312.1(a)(2) (1979).

[24] U.S. Department of Health, Education and Welfare, Review Panel on New Drug Regulation, *Interim Report,* vol. 3 (April 25, 1977), p. 21.

[25] U.S. Congress, Senate, Subcommittee on Health and Scientific Research of the Committee on Human Resources, *Hearings on Preclinical and Clinical Testing by the Pharmaceutical Industry,* 95th Congress, 2d session, 1978.

associated with the testing of a new drug and that they voluntarily accept those risks. The FDA has suggested what should be disclosed to potential test subjects. These disclosures include an explanation of the procedures to be followed, their purposes, and their experimental status; a description of reasonably expected risks and discomforts; an outline of advantageous alternative procedures; an offer to answer any questions concerning the procedure; and an instruction that the person is free to discontinue participation in the project at any time.[26] Researchers must be aware of the special problem of obtaining consent from such persons as prisoners, children, and the mentally retarded, since obtaining their meaningful consent can be difficult.

Human testing is divided into three phases, each of which requires different considerations regarding investigators, subjects, and testing procedures. A fourth, less formal, phase may occur after the drug has been approved for sale.

Phase I generally involves a group of twenty to eighty normal, healthy adult subjects. The subjects are typically volunteers who are placed in a setting that permits close medical observation, such as a special pharmacology unit, a metabolic ward, or other hospital setting. The volunteers must be free from any abnormalities that might complicate the interpretation of the experiment.[27] Children and women who are pregnant or of childbearing age are generally excluded from phase I. The primary purpose of phase I is to test toxicity and dose ranges of the drug on a small group of human subjects to be sure that the safety parameters noted in the animal studies are applicable to humans.

The investigators in phase I studies must be skilled in the initial evaluation of a variety of compounds for both safety and pharmacological effect. In the occasional cases in which the subjects have the specific disease, the investigators should be experts in that disease and the drug effects on it.

The testing procedure begins with a physical examination of the subjects to screen out those with certain conditions and abnormalities. After this screening, drugs are administered at various dosages while the investigators study the effects on the subjects at each dosage level. Some subjects may receive a placebo because there can be a high incidence of reporting of side effects by subjects involved in any drug study. Sometimes 40 to 50 percent of the subjects taking a placebo report side effects.[28] Frequently studies are conducted double-blind, neither

---

[26] U.S. Department of Health, Education and Welfare, Food and Drug Administration, *General Considerations for the Clinical Evaluation of Drugs*, Report no. 77–3040 (September 1977), p. 2.

[27] Ibid., p. 7.

[28] Ibid., p. 8.

the person administering the drug nor the subject taking it knowing whether the subject is getting the drug or the placebo.

If the phase I study is favorable, the testing moves to phase II. The second phase of testing usually involves 100 to 200 or more subjects who have the disease the drug is meant to treat. As in phase I, the investigators in phase II are testing the safety of the drug. Because the subjects in phase II have the target disease, however, the possible effectiveness of the drug in treating the disease is carefully evaluated. The subjects should be free of other diseases and should not be receiving other therapy for the target disease. The phase II investigators should be experts in the particular disease to be treated and in the evaluation of drug effects on the disease process.

Phase II testing usually involves the use of placebos in control groups as well as double-blind administration of the drug. Drugs with established efficacy can also be used for comparison, since they are already approved. It should be noted that through phase II other tests on animals and humans continue to establish the safety of the drug, particularly over long-term use.[29]

If the information obtained in the first two phases generates reasonable assurance of safety and effectiveness or suggests that potential benefits outweigh possible risks, phase III studies may begin. Phase III clinical trials use a large group of patients to assess the drug's safety, effectiveness, and optimal dosage. The phase III study is generally less rigid than the other phases because the safety and efficacy of the drug have already been established to some degree.

Once all the clinical and animal testing has been completed, the sponsor may submit an NDA. Once the FDA has approved the NDA, the sponsor may begin marketing the drug in the United States. When the drug is marketed, clinical studies may continue in phase IV to determine, among other things, the effects of long-term use of the drug in humans and the effects of the drug on other diseases.

Cost of Regulations

By the time a new drug has reached the state of marketability, it has undergone extensive animal and human testing. The testing process, with its various phases, is extremely costly. Ronald Hansen has estimated that the average discovery costs and testing expenditures per marketed new chemical entity (NCE) in 1967 were $33.7 million when capitalized at a 10 percent rate of discount.[30] In today's (April 1979) prices, this

---

[29] Department of Health, Education and Welfare, *Interim Report,* vol. 3, p. 9.

[30] Ronald W. Hansen, "The Pharmaceutical Development Process: Estimates of Development Costs and Times and the Effects of Proposed Regulatory Changes," in R. I.

would be $72.4 million. These figures include the costs of all unsuccessful drugs as well as those that finally gain approval.

In determining the appropriate method for measuring the total costs of identifying and developing a new pharmaceutical product, we should give particular attention to those factors most likely to alter the returns from investments. These factors include but are not limited to (1) the amount of resource expenditures and period of accumulation before production begins, (2) the economic life of the resources after production begins, (3) the opportunity cost of the resources, (4) any changes in both absolute and relative prices, (5) risk (however defined), and (6) the appropriability of rewards after taxes and other liabilities.

Because it takes time for plants to gear up for new production and much longer before many research projects begin to pay off, the period of accumulation of expenditures for capital assets before output is generated is extremely important in measuring the comparative profitability of investment alternatives; and, of course, once in production, pharmaceutical products usually have a finite economic life before new products replace them. When the two periods, accumulation of capital expenditures and product life, are combined, they define the economic life cycle of the investment project.

Moreover, because resources used in any project represent alternatives forgone in other possible projects, there is an "opportunity cost" of using resources in any investment. With the average after-tax real rate of return as a base, the opportunity cost for capital is estimated to be 10 percent per year after adjustments for inflation.[31] This is the discount rate prescribed by the Office of Management and Budget for U.S. government decisions on deferred costs and benefits.[32] In addition, corrections for price changes in the level of expenditures and receipts must be made to prevent systematic biases in these measurements. Equally important, each investment project must be weighted by its corresponding risk (or the expected value of the loss must be subtracted from the present value of the investment).[33] Without weighting, riskier projects would appear to yield higher returns than less risky alternatives

---

Chien, ed., *Issues in Pharmaceutical Economics* (Lexington, Mass.: Lexington Books, 1979), p. 168.

[31] See Jacob A. Stockfisch, "The Interest Rate Applicable to Government Investment Projects," in Harley Hinrichs and Graeme Taylor, eds., *Program Budgeting and Benefit-Cost Analysis* (Pacific Palisades, Calif.: Goodyear Publishing Company, 1969), pp. 187–201.

[32] U.S. Office of Management and Budget, "Discount Rates to Be Used in Evaluating Time-Distributed Costs and Benefits," circular A–94 (March 27, 1972). This is the rate to be used after all inflation adjustments have been made.

[33] Harold Bierman and Seymour Smidt, *The Capital Budgeting Decision* (New York: Macmillan, 1966), pp. 322–25.

(or to have a positive present value when they actually have a negative value). All measurements must also be corrected for the reduction in appropriability of returns to the enterprise from tax and other financial liabilities. When rewards or benefits are not fully capturable, measurement of the returns to the organization must be corrected to reflect net benefits. Under current income tax regulation, for example, corporate enterprises can be expected to receive approximately half the net returns (defined under current accounting procedures) from new investments if the enterprise is financed by equity capital.

For investment purposes, the relationships above can be summarized in the following expression:[34]

$$PV = -\sum_{t=0}^{i-1} \frac{K_t(P_t)}{(1+r)^t} + \sum_{t+i}^{n} \frac{p(R_t - C_t)(P_t)}{(1+r)^t}(A_t)$$

where

PV = present value of an investment
t = year
K_t = investment expenditures in year t
P_t = price index for year t
r = opportunity cost of capital
R_t = gross revenues in year t
C_t = manufacturing costs in year t
p = probability of positive or favorable occurrence
A_t = appropriability of returns to enterprise
i = number of years before sales begin
n = end of the economic life for the investment

If the accumulated investment expenditure (corrected for changes in the price level and for the opportunity cost of capital) is less than expected discounted net revenues (corrected for changes in the price level and for appropriability factors), the present value of the investment will be positive, and a wealth-maximizing enterprise would undertake the project.

More important, a reduction in the time period i, the number of years before sales begin, significantly alters the present value of any investment. Consider, for example, an initial investment of $1 million that will return $1 million per year in the fourth year after the initial investment, continuing for the next twenty years. At a 10 percent rate of interest, that investment would have a net present value of $4,812,000

---

[34] Kenneth W. Clarkson, *Intangible Capital and Rates of Return* (Washington, D.C.: American Enterprise Institute, 1977), p. 31.

TABLE 2

AVERAGE TESTING COST FOR DEVELOPING NEW CHEMICAL ENTITIES BY PHASE OF TESTING, 1967 AND 1979

Testing Phase	Average Cost in 1967 Dollars (thousands)	Average Cost in 1979 Dollars (thousands)[a]
Preclinical animal	97	208
Phase I clinical	166	356
Phase II clinical	881	1,892
Phase III clinical	1,546	3,319
Long-term animal	420	902

[a] Based on producer price index for April 1979, in U.S Department of Labor, Bureau of Labor Statistics, *Monthly Labor Review*, June 1979, p. 86.
SOURCE: Hansen, "The Pharmaceutical Development Process," p. 162.

[(8.51) (0.683) − 1]. If sales began one year from the date of the initial investment and continued for twenty years, the present value at a 10 percent rate of interest is $6,736,000 [(8.51) (0.909) − 1]. Thus, the three-year earlier availability translates into a $1.9 million increase in present value. If the revenues are lower, say, $150,000 per year, the present value of the investment would be −$128,000 when revenues begin in the fourth year and continue for twenty years and $160,000 when the same revenues begin in the second year and continue for twenty years. With higher sales revenues, the differences are compounded; for example, if revenues commence in the fourth year and are $10 million for the next twenty years, the present value of the $1 million investment is $57.1 million. If, however, revenues begin in the second year, the $10 million per year revenues for twenty years yield a $76.4 million present value.

Present Value of New Drug Development

We now turn our attention to the development of a hypothetical drug and its associated costs. From Hansen's study we know that the undiscounted cost of phase I testing was $166,000 in 1967 for a successful pharmaceutical product.[35] In that same year, the average costs of phase II clinical tests were $881,000, and the costs of phase III clinical tests were $1,546,000 for successful products. In table 2 we show these costs for 1967 and, price adjusted, for 1979. Using these data, we construct a hypothetical cost profile for the development of a drug from the period

[35] Hansen, "Pharmaceutical Development Process."

TABLE 3

AVERAGE COST OF CLINICAL TESTING WITH EXISTING TECHNOLOGY AND INSTITUTIONS

Phase	Average Cost per Quarter ($ thousands)	Number of Quarters	Number of Patients	Undiscounted Cost per Patient (dollars)
I	100	3	50	6,000
II	200	8	400	4,000
III	300	11	1,100	3,000

NOTE: Data are for twenty-two quarters.
SOURCE: Calculated from authors' estimates based on industry interviews.

of IND filing to the application for a new drug. In table 3 we find the cost of drug development using existing technology and institutional arrangements. We have assumed that phase I lasts for three quarters and has an average cost of $100,000 per quarter. The undiscounted cost of testing the fifty patients in phase I is $6,000 per patient. Phases II and III are also shown in this table. The undiscounted average costs for phase II are $200,000 per quarter for a total of eight quarters. This yields an undiscounted cost of $4,000 for each of the 400 patients in the testing program. Finally, phase III, which lasts for eleven quarters, has an average cost of $300,000, or an undiscounted $3,000 unit cost for each of the 1,100 patients. Although some drugs may require larger or smaller clinical sample tests, higher or lower costs per patient, or shorter or longer periods of testing, this hypothetical pharmaceutical product is representative of the average cost of industry clinical testing programs.

In table 4 we have converted the costs of each of the quarters to present values. Thus, in the second quarter, the $100,000 has a present value of $97,600, using a 10 percent annualized rate of interest.[36]

We are now able to illustrate the effects of decreasing the period for clinical testing. If we assume that the cost per patient remains constant and that there are no increased costs from higher rates of output,[37] the average costs per quarter will increase in increasing proportion to the decrease in time.

In table 5 we have shown the cost of development for each of the phases with a new technology and no economies of scale. In our as-

[36] Office of Management and Budget, "Discount Rates."

[37] Armen A. Alchian, "Cost and Outputs," in *The Allocation of Economic Resources: Essays in Honor of Bernard Francis Haley* (Stanford, Calif.: Stanford University Press, 1959).

TABLE 4

UNDISCOUNTED EXPENDITURES AND PRESENT VALUES OF A
SUCCESSFUL NEW CHEMICAL ENTITY BY QUARTER
(thousands of dollars)

Quarter	Undiscounted Expenditures	Discount Factor	Present Value of Expenditures
1	100	1.000	100
2	100	0.976	98
3	100	0.952	95
4	200	0.929	186
5	200	0.906	181
6	200	0.884	177
7	200	0.862	173
8	200	0.841	168
9	200	0.821	164
10	200	0.801	160
11	200	0.781	156
12	300	0.762	229
13	300	0.744	223
14	300	0.725	218
15	300	0.708	212
16	300	0.690	207
17	300	0.674	202
18	300	0.657	197
19	300	0.641	192
20	300	0.626	188
21	300	0.610	183
22	300	0.595	179
Total			3,888

SOURCE: Calculated from authors' estimates based on industry interviews.

sumption we have kept the number of patients and the undiscounted costs per patient constant but decreased the total amount of time required for phases I, II, and III from twenty-two quarters to eleven quarters. Because the expenditures are higher in each quarter, the present value of the expenditures will be higher. This can be seen in table 6, which shows, for each of the quarters of clinical testing, testing expenditures and the associated present value of those expenditures at an interest rate of 10 percent. An inspection of the present value of the cost of development taken from tables 4 and 6 clearly shows that by reducing the total elapsed time from twenty-two to eleven quarters, the present value of expenditures rises by $587,000.

The increased costs of a more rapid clinical testing timetable, how-

TABLE 5

Average Cost of Clinical Testing with New Technology and Institutions

Phase	Average Cost per Quarter ($ thousands)	Number of Quarters	Number of Patients	Undiscounted Cost per Patient (dollars)
I	150	2	50	6,000
II	400	4	400	4,000
III	660	5	1,100	3,000

NOTE: Data are for eleven quarters.
SOURCE: Calculated from authors' estimates based on industry interviews.

TABLE 6

Undiscounted Expenditures and Present Values for a New Chemical Entity with No Scale Economies, by Quarter
(thousands of dollars)

Quarter	Undiscounted Expenditures	Discount Factor	Present Value of Expenditures
1	150	1.000	150
2	150	0.976	146
3	400	0.952	381
4	400	0.929	372
5	400	0.906	362
6	400	0.884	354
7	660	0.862	569
8	660	0.841	555
9	660	0.821	542
10	660	0.801	529
11	660	0.781	515
Total			4,475

SOURCE: Table 5.

ever, may be more than offset by the increase in revenues available from the earlier marketing of the pharmaceutical product. Consider, for example, an investment that yields $1 million in net revenues each quarter indefinitely. The earlier availability of revenues in the twelfth through the twenty-second quarters has a present value of $9,515,000

104

in the eleventh quarter.[38] One million dollars per quarter beginning in quarter twenty-three and continuing indefinitely has a present value of $40 million in quarter twenty-three, or $30,480 in quarter eleven. Consequently, the earlier availability of more rapid development represents an increase of 31.2 percent of the *total* present value from the drug.[39]

This result, however, probably understates the present value because earlier availability in marketing usually means a larger market share and a longer viability of the drug. Furthermore, it is unlikely that the $1 million net revenues would continue indefinitely. Thus, the earlier availability of $9,515,000 in our example represents a greater percentage of the total present value from the developed pharmaceutical product.

Of course, we must also adjust for the costs of development. In the first case, the present value of clinical testing expenditures was $3,888,000, with revenues of $1 million per quarter beginning in the twenty-third quarter and continuing at the same real level for an indefinite period. This yields a present value of $18,792,000 in the first period.[40] This can be compared with a present value of $25,455,000 for the faster clinical testing technology.[41]

In general, the benefits of increasing the present value of sales from new drug development are directly related to sales volume. In the example we have chosen, if the sales volume increases fortyfold from $0.25 million to $10 million per quarter, the present value of sales will also increase fortyfold, as shown in table 7.

New Technology for Clinical Testing

We have now seen that a significant acceleration in the development process may create substantial returns to pharmaceutical firms. Currently there are developments in the pharmaceutical industry that indicate that a significant reduction in the time required for clinical testing is possible.

Under traditional clinical testing procedures, pharmaceutical firms,

---

[38] If we assume that, of revenues collected at the end of the year, the first year's revenues are $976,000, followed by $952,000, $929,000, $906,000, $884,000, $862,000, $841,000, $821,000, $801,000, $781,000, and $762,000.

[39] ($40 million) 0.762 = $30.48 million; $9.515 million ÷ $30.48 million = 0.312.

[40] The $1 million per quarter has a present value of ($40 million) (0.567) or $22.68 million. Subtracting $3.888 million from $22.68 million yields $18.792 million.

[41] In addition to the $22.68 million (present value of revenues from the twenty-third quarter on), there is $7.25 million (present value of $1 million per quarter from the twelfth through the twenty-second quarter). Subsequently the $4.475 million (present value of clinical testing expenditures) yields $25,455,000.

TABLE 7

THE EFFECTS OF DECREASING CLINICAL TESTING TIME FOR
DIFFERENT SALES VOLUME

(millions of dollars)

Pharmaceutical Sales Volume	Cost of Clinical Testing	Present Value of Sales	Net Present Value
Low sales volume			
($0.25 million/quarter)			
Existing method (22 quarters)	3.9	5.7[a]	1.8
New technology (11 quarters)	4.5	7.5[b]	3.0
Medium sales volume			
($10 million/quarter)			
Existing method (22 quarters)	3.9	226.8[a]	222.9
New technology (11 quarters)	4.5	299.3[b]	294.8
High sales volume			
($50 million/quarter)			
Existing method (22 quarters)	3.9	1,134.0[a]	1,130.1
New technology (11 quarters)	4.5	1,496.5[b]	1,492.0

[a] Sales from twenty-third quarter on.
[b] Sales from twelfth quarter on.
SOURCE: Authors' calculations.

after establishing a protocol and a sample size, must seek patients from one of four sources. These sources include solo practitioners, medical schools and teaching hospitals, monospecialty group practices, and multispecialty group practices.

Because doctors do not usually specialize in predetermined characteristics of patients, pharmaceutical representatives must establish contact with a relatively large number of doctors to obtain a sufficient sample size of patients. When a pharmaceutical firm is prepared to engage in clinical testing, its representatives must identify physicians who are willing to participate.

The conventional method of identification of qualified and interested physician investigators is very time consuming and contributes largely to the drug lag. Even when the physician is qualified and interested in the study, other pharmaceutical representatives may have retained his services for studying a similar drug product. In an industry where numerous drug products of the same general class are commonplace, the availability of a given physician may also be a serious problem and another factor contributing to the drug lag. The new technology uses long-term physician contracts, thereby ensuring that qualified and interested investigators are available to the contract research firm and in turn to the firm's pharmaceutical client.

Traditionally, once physicians have been retained, patient characteristics must be considered in determining the appropriate sample population. The process may take many months to complete because most physicians enroll qualified patients as they visit their offices. This long enrollment period of qualified patients is one of the most significant causes of the drug lag in the United States.

Because no one firm has a substantial demand for regular clinical testing services, it is often not cost-effective for individual firms to introduce their own specialized sytems for clinical testing services. The setup costs for such a testing system are substantial. Furthermore, because these patients are geographically mobile, the clinical testing population must be continuously revised as replacements must be found for clinic dropouts. Consequently, the typical drug firm will have only a nucleus of testing physicians, which must be expanded for individual projects.

At this time, a new industry is arising that substantially reduces many of these costs;[42] it is the pharmaceutical clinical testing industry. The delivery of services in this new industry depends on the steady flow of different and simultaneous clinical testing programs. To realize the lowest costs of locating and enrolling patients, monitoring patient tests and results, and preparing data for analysis, the total patient sample population must be larger than most pharmaceutical manufacturers could realistically maintain. Lower costs can be reached by a comprehensive clinical testing firm, primarily because such firms have an established physician and patient base that is constantly maintained in all specialty areas.

The firm structure of this industry is somewhat complex but easily understood once its various elements have been defined. First, before offering clinical testing services, the clinical testing firm will approach preidentified physicians to establish long-term relationships for continuous testing. This task is often facilitated by affiliation with multispecialty group practices (clinics) where the number of staff physicians averages thirty or more and a large patient population is already available.[43] Once agreements are made, the clinical testing firm is almost immediately able to identify the characteristics of patients under the

---

[42] The information here is based in part on interviews with officers of the Institute for Biological Research and Development and members of participating clinics, including administrators, clinic research coordinators, and participating physicians.

[43] An indirect consequence of dealing with established clinics is that the patient population usually has more desirable characteristics than would be found in the normal clinical testing situations. There are, for example, fewer alcoholics, a lower turnover of patients, and an increased willingness of patients to participate in the program.

care of each physician in the clinic.[44] The procedure is repeated at clinic after clinic. The result is a population of millions of patients that far exceeds and encompasses any desired clinical sample, a population with a complete diagnostic profile. This is possible because the multispecialty group practice has an electronic data base containing all diagnostic information on the approximately 50,000 patients it cares for in an average year.

At this point, the firm is prepared to offer clinical testing services, frequently on a collaborative basis with the client. When a pharmaceutical firm has determined its protocol with specific tests, patient populations, geographic requirements, and other characteristics, the clinical testing firm can rapidly determine the potential patients and prepare rough estimates of costs for phase II and III testing. Within days, a definite commitment on costs may be obtained, contracts negotiated and executed, and testing begun.

The time and dollar savings, however, are not limited to the identification of the sample population. Because of its large volume of different clinical testing programs, the clinical testing firm is able to modify procedures and ensure better and more accurate tests, as well as improved monitoring and quality assurance procedures. The clinical testing firm will, for example, insist that a qualified individual be assigned the task of supporting these programs in the multispecialty group practice. This person is designated a clinical research coordinator (CRC) and is engaged in all the support steps of each of the clinical testing phases. The CRC is carefully trained by the firm in appropriate federal regulations, client requirements, and other important responsibilities.

In addition to participating in the initial identification of patients, the CRC schedules the patients for interviews with the physician investigator and helps the investigator in filling out the necessary forms. The CRC also coordinates the scheduling of specific tests in other clinical departments, such as ophthalmology and radiology, if required by the protocol. These individuals specialize in the creation of reliable testing procedures. The CRC also monitors all work sheets before they are transmitted to the quality assurance unit of the clinical testing firm, which in turn submits the clinical data to the pharmaceutical sponsor.

It would not be cost-effective to employ specialized persons, such as CRCs, without a large number of tasks to be completed.[45] Because the protocols for clinical testing may vary substantially among new drugs, the services of a CRC are extremely important. If additional research

---

[44] In addition to collecting information on patient characteristics, the firm may also be able to determine basic guidelines for reimbursement for different types of tests.

[45] Stigler, "Division of Labor."

data or information were needed, traditional procedures might take weeks or even months to correct the problem. This is a factor contributing to the U.S. drug lag. The CRC, however, may rapidly facilitate the submission of this critical information. In addition, access to a large volume of data permits rapid transmission of the data from the clinics to the intermediate monitoring unit and on to the pharmaceutical firms through a computer network.

It is this technology that permits the reduced time for completing clinical trials. Although the data are incomplete, it appears that the clinical testing firm is able to cut the existing time for clinical testing roughly in half. Thus, the results of our hypothetical example may actually be realized. Equally important, the institutional structure of this industry also permits a reduction of the out-of-pocket costs for clinical testing. Specialization by clinical testing firms results in substantial economies of scale, which lower average costs of developing the drug. Consider, for example, cost savings of 20 and 40 percent, savings that are potentially available to the industry. In table 8, we have shown a reduction in undiscounted costs for scale economies of 20 percent and 40 percent when compared to table 5. In table 9, we have given the present value costs and the savings for scale economies of 20 percent. With scale economies of 20 percent, the cost of clinical testing in present value terms also falls 20 percent, from $4,475,000 to $3,580,000. With 40 percent scale economy savings, there is a 40 percent reduction in present value. Table 10 shows that the costs of testing may be reduced

TABLE 8

AVERAGE COSTS OF CLINICAL TESTING WITH NEW TECHNOLOGY AND SCALE ECONOMIES

Phase	Average Cost per Quarter ($ thousands)	Number of Quarters	Number of Patients	Undiscounted Cost per Patient (dollars)
	Cost savings of 20 percent			
I	120	2	50	4,800
II	320	4	400	3,200
III	528	5	1,100	2,400
	Cost savings of 40 percent			
I	90	2	50	3,600
II	240	4	400	2,400
III	396	5	1,100	1,800

NOTE: Data are for eleven quarters.
SOURCE: Authors' calculations.

109

TABLE 9

UNDISCOUNTED EXPENDITURES AND PRESENT VALUES FOR A NEW
CHEMICAL ENTITY WITH SCALE ECONOMIES OF 20 PERCENT, BY
QUARTER
(thousands of dollars)

Quarter	Undiscounted Expenditures	Discount Factor	Present Value of Expenditures
1	120	1.000	120
2	120	0.976	117
3	320	0.952	305
4	320	0.929	297
5	320	0.906	290
6	320	0.884	283
7	528	0.862	455
8	528	0.841	444
9	528	0.821	433
10	528	0.801	423
11	528	0.781	412
Total			3,579

SOURCE: Authors' calculations.

to $2,683,000. In addition to those savings, resources can be allocated to other new pharmaceutical products under development by the client much sooner than usual, because the accelerated development and approval of the hypothetical product release these resources at the time of approval. Market entry is then favorably influenced on at least two drug products, irrespective of the development method chosen by the client for the second product, assuming it is successful.

Factors That Influence Industry Responses

At this point, one might ask why pharmaceutical firms have not completely shifted to the less expensive, faster clinical testing option. As with other new products, part of the problem may lie in the lack of information of key decision makers within these firms. In addition, there are certain economic factors that would influence the decision to provide their own clinical testing structure or seek services on the outside.

First, the firm may have a steady flow of new products for clinical tests so that the physicians may already have been contacted in an existing program. Here the fixed costs of identifying physicians and

TABLE 10

Undiscounted Expenditures and Present Values for a New
Chemical Entity with Scale Economies of 40 Percent, by
Quarter
(thousands of dollars)

Quarter	Undiscounted Expenditures	Discount Factor	Present Value of Expenditures
1	90	1.000	90
2	90	0.976	88
3	240	0.952	228
4	240	0.929	223
5	240	0.906	217
6	240	0.884	212
7	396	0.862	341
8	396	0.841	333
9	396	0.821	325
10	396	0.801	317
11	396	0.781	309
Total			2,683

Source: Authors' calculations.

signing up patients are lower than for the firms with fewer new products.[46]

Second, if the firm itself engages in a large number of simultaneous testing programs, it may be able to set up a clinical testing procedure similar to that in this new industry. It is doubtful, however, that most pharmaceutical firms have a sufficiently large number of clinical tests on line to realize significant savings.

Finally, the internal organization of the manufacturer may itself be largely responsible for not choosing the lowest-cost method of clinical testing. The internal structure of firms, even in profit-seeking enterprises, creates difficulties for maximizing the organization's wealth. Alchian, Whinston, Williamson, and others have demonstrated that, in a world with positive information costs and other transactions frictions, there will be divergences between the owner's objectives and the actual

[46] In most cases, however, these savings of fixed costs are not likely to be large. First, the same patients would probably not be used for different drugs. Thus, new patients must be identified. Second, if the physician's specialty does not include a large number of potential patients in existing programs, the cost of expanding an existing network may actually exceed the cost of starting a new one.

activities undertaken by decision makers in the institutions' various components.[47]

With larger operations and more extensive hierarchical levels, there are more losses in the reproduction of information and/or distortion of the information or instructions even when there are no conflicting objectives among the firms' agents. There are also limitations in the capacity of the central coordinator for simulating all the information necessary for decision making.

The recent research leads to the conclusion that it is virtually impossible to direct organizational units to carry out the goal of profit maximization in every decision. As an alternative to maximization, institutions have developed rules of thumb that attempt to approximate wealth-maximization behavior, but those same rules of thumb may generate inefficiencies. If, for example, research and development units are given a budget, it is in their interest to expend that budget fully on activities within their division unless the funds may be used in a future period or unless any cost savings may be shared among members of that unit. Because the decision to use outside contractors for clinical testing would significantly reduce the funds necessary for testing any new pharmaceutical product, there may be resistance to choosing outside contractors. Furthermore, outside contracting may reduce the overhead necessary to monitor clinical testing and reduce the staff of research and development divisions. Such reductions are likely to be opposed by the heads of research and development units. For these reasons, we would not expect to find an easy transition from internal clinical testing to contracting for these services with outside organizations, even when such contracting provides substantial savings to pharmaceutical firms.

Conclusions

Among other forces, the decreased level of innovation and lengthening of the drug lag in the United States have prompted congressional reforms

---

[47] Armen A. Alchian, "The Basis of Some Recent Advances in the Theory of the Management of the Firm," *Journal of Industry Economics*, vol. 14 (November 1965), pp. 30–41; Andrew Whinston, "Price Guidelines in Decentralized Organizations," in William W. Cooper, H. J. Leavitt, and M. W. Shelly II, eds., *New Perspectives in Organization Research* (New York: John Wiley, 1964); Oliver E. Williamson, "Corporate Control and the Theory of the Firm," in Henry G. Manne, ed., *Economic Policy and the Regulation of Corporate Securities* (Washington, D.C.: American Enterprise Institute, 1969), and *Corporate Control of Business Behavior: An Inquiry into the Effects of Organizational Form on Enterprise Behavior* (Englewood Cliffs, N.J.: Prentice-Hall, 1970). See Louis De Alessi, "The Economics of Property Rights: A Review of the Evidence," in Richard O. Zerbe, ed., *Research in Law and Economics* (Greenwich, Conn.: JAI Press, 1980), pp. 1–47, for a review of the literature on the effects of attenuated rights to the present value of the organization's income on managerial behavior.

of the regulations governing the pharmaceutical industry. Many policy makers are wondering if the increase in efficacy and safety requirements clearly offsets the costs of delayed introduction of new pharmaceutical products or the termination of otherwise promising avenues of research. A significant portion of these increased costs and the time delay can be directly linked to the FDA's method of carrying out congressional safety and efficacy objectives. These concerns have prompted numerous congressional bills that would substantially alter existing statutes governing the pharmaceutical industry. It has been proposed, for example, that the testing of new drugs for effectiveness be eliminated and that pharmaceutical manufacturers' reporting requirements to the FDA be substantially reduced.[48] As long as the FDA continues to promulgate and enforce regulations that are input-specific, the most promising stimulant for new pharmaceutical products appears to be the new pharmaceutical clinical testing industry.

---

[48] U.S. Congress, House, *House Report No. 54*, 96th Congress, 1st session, January 15, 1979.

Commentary

Barry M. Bloom

Professor Wiggins has indicated in his paper that the primary purpose of his study was to determine how pharmaceutical companies change the amount and allocation of their research investment in response to what he calls changes in the stringency of federal product quality regulation.

He has described his technique for collecting data as essentially a process of interviewing executives from a number of research-intensive firms. As a result of those interviews, he has offered us a characterization of the decision-making process that attempts to compare what is was like in the 1960s with what it is like today. He goes on to derive from the comparison certain conclusions that he feels have policy implications.

From my own more than twenty-seven years of involvment with drug research decision making, I conclude that a number of the elements in his characterization of the decision-making process are accurate. But I also sense that, as he tries to synthesize a global portrait of the process, he displays an understandable tendency to oversimplify and to invoke a consistency in the behavior of decision makers that does not reflect the real world. As a result, some inaccuracies creep in, and some potentially misleading conclusions are drawn. I say "potentially" because for the most part they do not appear to have affected his main conclusions. On the assumption that he is going to use this characterization in the future, however, I will comment on them anyway.

Of course we strive to be more sophisticated in our decision making than we were twenty years ago. And to a certain degree, less I fear than we might like, we succeed at it. What else would you expect? After all, we are managing much larger research organizations nowadays. Research has become substantially more expensive. We are concerned with a greater number of world markets, by far, than we used to be, and with widely differing medical cultures. The level of research competition within the industry has risen dramatically in recent years, more dramatically, I suspect, than is widely appreciated. And the stringency of regulation we must contend with has increased even more dramatically. But for all of that, I do not think that drug research decision making lends itself to being as quantitative or rigorous as Steve Wiggins implies.

The contrast between the decision-making process in the 1960s and in the 1970s is in my view nowhere near as sharp as he makes it out to be. No, budgets were not really set in the old days just by taking a percentage of sales, nor are they set nowadays by anything that appreciably resembles a zero-budgeting process. No, scientists were not absolutely in control of decision making in the early 1960s, nor did nonscientists suddenly come into the picture and wrench control away from the scientists.

Consider, if you will, the managements of the four most research-intensive U.S. pharmaceutical companies. Two of them have presidents who came out of research and medicine, as distinct from law or economics or general management. Three of them have senior research officers who serve on their boards of directors, one on the executive committee that manages the firm's day-to-day business. That simply does not jibe with some of the implications of drastic change in Steve Wiggins's characterization.

Change there has been, but evolutionary change, as you might expect. For example, it is misleading to imply that increasing regulatory stringency was not a concern of decision makers in the early 1960s. One of the first things I did, upon reading this paper, was to take from my bookshelf, more or less at random, an old annual report of Charles Pfizer and Co. (for 1960). And what did I find in it but a paragraph bemoaning, in all too familiar fashion, the difficulties that the 1958 addition to the Code of Regulations governing food additives had engendered for research on pharmaceuticals for animal health. So times have really not changed all that much.

I prefer the characterization of the research decision-making process that was drawn in a private study conducted about a year ago by the management consulting firm of Cresap, McCormick and Paget.[1] I believe it more clearly portrays the pluralism and complexity of the situation.

The Cresap study, which examined eleven research-intensive firms, seven of them American owned, also employed the interview technique. Nine of the eleven persons interviewed were the senior line research

---

[1] Cresap, McCormick and Paget, Inc., 245 Park Avenue, New York, New York 10017, *Examination of the R&D Practices of Eleven Pharmaceutical Companies* (New York, February 1979). The study was sponsored by a major pharmaceutical company, and the summary findings were made available only to those who participated in it. I was given permission by Cresap to refer to the study in these remarks. I think my comments have captured the essence of what the study found that is relevant to this discussion.

managers for their companies, and the senior interviewer had had considerable experience in industrial chemical research at an earlier stage in his career.

The study concluded that the organizations interviewed shared a common perception of the U.S. environment: increasing research costs, increasing regulatory requirements, a heightening pace of technological advance, eroding market shares, and a declining rate of major new drug discoveries. Despite this common perception, they managed their research activities in quite diverse ways, reflecting differences in corporate character or size, historical growth pattern, diversification into other businesses, current importance of foreign markets, and the personalities of their top managers.

The study also found that the research and development planning systems used by the companies interviewed ranged from informal systems that relied mainly on the perceptions of the chief research officer and his staff concerning scientific and other considerations to highly structured systems that included regular reviews of external conditions accumulated and analyzed by staff members specifically charged with this responsibility. In six of the eleven firms, the planning systems were characterized as informal.

But enough of interview findings. The more important matter before us today is the validity of Professor Wiggins's conclusions, especially those that he feels have policy implications.

From the manuscript that he sent me before this meeting, I would paraphrase his conclusions as follows: In the 1960s the scientists, who were the decision makers, were not much concerned about the impact of government regulation; so it was not a discernible factor in determining how research resources should be allocated. By the 1970s, with more sophisticated decision making, government regulation had become a matter of substantial concern and, of course, would be expected to decrease the propensity to invest in particular projects.

Other factors besides regulation, however, came along at the same time to diminish the economic viability of certain research projects, notably more rigorous techniques of clinical evaluation and a growing concern about product liability brought about by the thalidomide tragedy. Because of the concurrent emergence of these factors, Steve Wiggins feels that it may never be possible to separate the effects of thalidomide and changing scientific techniques on research costs from the increase in those costs that result from regulation.

Finally, he concluded that, although increased regulatory stringency does indeed discourage investment in certain research projects, it does not necessarily follow that current regulation is too strict, since it is debatable whether it is better to have lots of research and little product quality information, or vice versa.

Put that way, it seems to me that he ends up offering little more than a thinly veiled apology for regulation. I find it much more constructive and challenging to ponder the question of how we might optimize our regulatory system than to consider it inescapable that better product quality information inevitably means less research. Let me suggest, in the form of a few questions, what I see as critical issues:

Must our regulatory system remain so intensively adversarial? Other successful ones are not.

Is it wise to have the mandate of the FDA so narrowly drawn, or should it be broadened to include a responsibility to encourage therapeutic innovation?

Is the enormous amount of regulatory red tape that encumbers the early stages of clinical research, so critical to therapeutic innovation, really necessary for the protection of subjects? It is certainly provocative when Bill Vodra, the former FDA counsel, says that in all the years the FDA has been regulating phase I research, he cannot find an instance in which FDA intervention has made any difference to the safety of the subjects.

And, finally, just how sensible are the evidentiary standards that the FDA applies to the demonstration of efficacy, in view of their being so much greater than those of any other sophisticated country of the world?

These may not be questions that economists are uniquely equipped to ponder, but I believe they lie close to the core of the problem that should concern us all.

J. Richard Crout

A major thesis of the Clarkson and MacLeod paper is that the investigational new drug (IND) regulations promulgated by the Food and Drug Administration (FDA) in 1963, rather than the effectiveness requirement in the 1962 law, were dominant in influencing drug regulation in the 1960s. Although this thesis is plausible as a postulate if one confines oneself to an analysis of time trends as the authors have done, my impression from members of the FDA staff who were with the agency at the time is quite the opposite. I believe the effectiveness requirement was the most important of these two factors in influencing drug regulation in the 1960s.

Although the IND regulations, as the authors point out, were written before Congress passed the 1962 amendments, these regulations were written in the same political context. The great concern in the

117

Congress related to the thalidomide disaster was the distribution of thalidomide to thousands of practicing physicians before the drug was approved for marketing. The drug firm clearly was not conducting research but engaging in a practice popularly known as "seeding the marketplace." This is a standard marketing approach, and there is nothing wrong with it unless it is done as a substitute for scientific study and the product turns out to be a thalidomide.

As a result of this problem, there was considerable interest at the Kefauver hearings in the FDA's exerting greater control over the research process. The IND regulations were therefore written by the FDA in anticipation of the new law and in coordination with it.

The authors are correct in pointing out that the effectiveness requirement was almost an add-on to the 1962 amendments. It was discussed relatively little in the hearings. Support came largely from the academic community, although the drug industry also supported this requirement. The industry may not have anticipated the rigor to which it would be held in demonstrating effectiveness scientifically, but it supported the principle that drugs should be effective.

My impression is that during the 1960s relatively little attention was devoted to regulation of the research process. INDs came in, but they were, for the most part, approved rather quickly and not scrutinized with great care. The applications that were reviewed carefully were the new drug applications (NDAs). Because uncontrolled studies were the customary approach to drug evaluation at the time and because drug firms did not immediately begin doing controlled trials in response to the new law, reviewers at the FDA found themselves well into the 1960s looking at NDAs with studies that did not meet the statutory requirement for adequate and well-controlled trials. This put the FDA staff in the enormous bind of having to handle for several years good drugs that were badly studied.

Given the hard choice of upholding the high scientific standard in the new law or approving poorly evaluated drugs (no matter how valuable), many people felt obliged to respond by not approving those drugs. This led to a contentious climate that was very difficult for both the industry and the FDA. This situation was the driving force behind the agency's putting out proposed regulations on the standards for adequate and well-controlled trials in 1969 and making those regulations final in 1970.

There is a lag between the time studies are done and the time a new drug application is submitted, sometimes of several years, and so the fruits of those 1970 regulations did not begin to appear until 1973 or so. Today everyone in the industry and the FDA would agree that clinical trials are of far better quality than they used to be. We do not have nearly so many arguments over whether a recently conducted clinical trial is adequate and well controlled. I believe those regulations of 1970 were the turning point in settling down industry-FDA controversy over implementation of the effectiveness requirement.

Since then, in the 1970s, increasing FDA staff attention has been devoted to the review of INDs and of protocols for clinical studies. I agree with the authors of this paper that the IND regulations may prove in time to be an even more important factor than the effectiveness requirement in influencing the drug marketplace, but conversations with experienced members of our staff at the Bureau of Drugs do not lead me to believe that this was so in the 1960s.

Let me turn briefly to the last point made in the paper—that contract laboratories are efficient in producing data, that they are becoming an important institution in the drug development enterprise, and that the regulatory system is behind that development. I would not disagree because we are, indeed, seeing more information from contract laboratories. I do not believe, however, that the contract laboratory will turn out to be the ideal setting for research and development of the very exciting drugs, the breakthrough kinds of drugs. Those drugs are attractive to the very best academic research physicians; so research on them is likely to continue where it is now—in university medical schools under industry sponsorship. I suspect the contract laboratory is more likely to fill the societal need for documentation of safety and effectiveness of drugs that are easier to develop or are duplicates of drugs already in the marketplace.

Finally, because the theme of the paper relates to the drug lag, I would like to comment on the productivity of the drug industry over the past three decades. We now classify into an *ABC* system, for internal management purposes, all the new chemical entities that are handled by the Bureau of Drugs. *A* means an important medical advance; *B* means a gain but not as significant as one in the *A* category; *C* means the drug duplicates a drug already in the marketplace. A *C* drug, for example, would be another thiazide diuretic or another cephalosporin that basically does not add to the therapeutic armamentarium. We have now classified all the new chemical entities that have been introduced into this country since 1950. For three decades there have been about three or four *A* drugs, on the average, coming out every year, and that has continued essentially unchanged to the present. The *B* drugs also have had a fairly constant output, and today over half the new chemical entities that are approved are classified as *A* or *B*.

There are those who want to look mainly at the dark side of regulation, which is largely a matter of increasing costs in both money and time. Costs are important, but it is also important to recognize that, in spite of it all, there is a long-established record of continuing productivity of health gains by the drug industry under our regulatory system.

119

PART THREE

Competition among Drugs: The Role of
Prices and Patents

Price and Quality Competition in Drug Markets: Evidence from the United States and the Netherlands

W. Duncan Reekie

If an industry is deemed to be uncompetitive, the charge must be based on the presence of monopoly power on either or both the supply and demand sides of the market. In the former case, monopoly can be measured by the number of firms in a market or by concentration ratios. These, however, are at best poor proxies as yardsticks of monopoly power. Ease of industry entry is probably more important. If an industry is earning unreasonable profits and if entry barriers are absent, new firms will come into that industry and, to gain sales, will price at levels below the ruling rate. In the long run this will reduce both prices and profits to normal, competitive levels. This in turn will be reflected on the demand side of the market by changes in demand elasticity (or price sensitivity). The more monopolistic a market is, the less elastic is demand in that market. The more competitive it is, or becomes, then the higher is the elasticity of demand.

In the following sections I examine the structure of the Dutch pharmaceutical industry both at a point in time and over time. I then attempt to assess demand elasticities in both the short and the long runs in the Netherlands and in America. Finally, I draw conclusions about the competitiveness of the industry in both countries.

Competition in Creativity

There are very few industries in which a market can be lost as quickly as in drugs. Table 1 shows that between 1972 and 1977 only one company in the top twenty-five Dutch firms retained its original ranking by sales revenue. And even that firm (company C) suffered a market share decline from 7.01 percent to 5.34 percent of the total market. The top three and the top five firms held, in 1972, 22.64 percent and 31.44

Thanks are due to Professor van der Weijden of Erasmus University, the Netherlands, for comments and to Professor M. H. Cooper of Otago University, New Zealand, for inspiration. Neither claims any merit for the product, and I must absolve them both from blame. The author is also grateful to IMS (Intercontinental Medical Statistics), Ambler, Pennsylvania, and The Hague, the Netherlands, for access to its data.

TABLE 1

LEADING TWENTY-FIVE FIRMS, NETHERLANDS PHARMACEUTICAL
INDUSTRY: SHARE OF TOTAL MARKET AND NUMBER OF
THERAPEUTIC MARKETS DOMINATED, 1972 AND 1977

Company	Market Share		Rank		Number of Markets in Which Each Company Leads	
	1972	1977	1972	1977	1972	1977
A	8.46	4.67	1	4	9	8
B	7.17	6.93	2	1	8	8
C	7.01	5.34	3	3	3	3
D	4.87	6.11	4	2	2	3
E	3.93	3.09	5	6	2	3
F	3.90	2.49	6	11	6	8
G	3.63	2.70	7	8	2	1
H	2.95	2.05	8	14	2	1
I	2.57	3.17	9	5	4	4
J	2.46	2.44	10	12	—	1
K	2.20	2.40	11	13	1	3
L	1.97	3.02	12	7	4	3
M	1.96	1.46	13	19	1	2
N	1.92	1.20	14	23	2	—
O	1.87	1.96	15	16	4	3
P	1.55	2.53	16	10	3	3
Q	1.46	2.01	17	15	1	1
R	1.40	—	18	—	2	—
S	1.31	1.44	19	20	1	1
T	1.24	1.19	20	24	2	2
U	1.20	2.58	21	9	3	3
V	1.11	1.92	22	17	1	1
W	1.11	—	23	—	2	1
X	1.11	—	24	—	1	—
Y	1.0	1.32	25	21	1	1
Z	—	1.47	—	18	1	1
AA	—	1.29	—	22	—	4
BB	—	1.18	—	25	—	1
Total	69.36	65.96			68	70

NOTE: Merged firms counted as one company.
SOURCE: Author's computations based on data provided by IMS.

percent of the market. By 1977 these same firms accounted for 16.94
percent and 26.14 percent, respectively. In the drug industry the "top
is a very slippery place." Moreover, not only did the 1972 leaders lose
market share, the corresponding 1977 leaders held a smaller share of

the market than their counterparts did in 1972. (The three-firm and five-firm concentration ratios in 1977 were 18.38 percent and 26.22 percent.)

The reason for this volatility in market share is well known. The drug industry is highly innovative. It is continually introducing new products, and if any firm wishes to hold its place, it must also do so. No firm can rest on its laurels, content with its market lead.

In a sense, however, these figures are misleading. Firms compete with each other not within the total pharmaceutical market but rather within therapeutic submarkets between which cross-elasticity of demand is low. Within these submarkets substitutability of one product for another exists. There are around a hundred such submarkets. (It is clear, for example, that products in the laxatives market can in no way be regarded as clinical alternatives for products in the antiasthmatics market.)

Certainly, firms can spread their risks by operating in several markets simultaneously. Nevertheless, as table 2 indicates, if we look at firms alone, one-third of all markets experienced a leadership change during the six years at risk. At any time, submarkets tend to be dominated by one or a very few firms; but the domination is very short-lived. (In 73 of the 102 submarkets examined, the three-firm concentration ratio exceeded 75 percent.) This is a natural outcome of innovative competition. With high research risks, all firms depend on the emergence of better and better drugs from their laboratories. Once a drug is marketed and proves to be a major advance, it will gain acceptance, and less efficacious or more dangerous products will lose position.

At any given time, the industry may appear to be a series of oligopolistic submarkets, but these oligopolies are very short-lived. Do the top few firms in table 1 dominate many submarkets and hence have greater monopolistic control than might be evident from looking at their total market shares? Table 1 shows very little such domination. For example, companies A and B lead in only 8 or 9 of the 102 submarkets;

TABLE 2

THERAPEUTIC SUBMARKET COMPETITION, NETHERLANDS, 1972–1977

	Number
Submarkets	102
Changes in company leadership	33
Total possible ranking changes	497
Actual changes recorded	305
Firms per market (average)	10

SOURCE: Same as table 1.

and apart from A and B there appears to be little relation between numbers of markets dominated and total sales share.

To measure the competitive movement within each submarket, table 2 details the total number of possible ranking changes in the 102 groupings. Out of a possible 497, 305, or 61 percent, took place. Table 3 breaks down these 305 changes in rank: only 5 markets experienced no rank changes; conversely, 11 submarkets changed company ranking completely, and 32 experienced four ranking changes. Moreover, as the table illustrates, changes are not confined to trivial submarkets but occur across the spread of sizes.

Are company ranking movements simply the results of very small market share changes by firms with very similar sales figures? Table 4 shows the top five firms in each submarket in 1972 and in 1977. In 1977 ten firms newly dominated their submarkets, eighteen firms were newly ranked at number two, and so on. None of these firms was in the top five in 1972. Interfirm rivalry is again displayed and is again unrelated to size of submarket.

Finally, in tables 5 and 6 other measures of competition were compared. The three-firm concentration ratio, the Herfindahl index, and the rank correlation coefficients for each of the 102 markets were calculated. The H-index and the concentration ratio were fairly highly correlated, r approaching 0.8.

TABLE 3

NUMBER OF RANKING CHANGES BY FIRMS IN 102 SUBMARKETS, NETHERLANDS, 1972–1977

Number of Changes	All Markets	Number of Submarkets by % of Total Market				
		0–<0.5%	0.5–<1.0%	1.0–<3.0%	3.0–<5.0%	5.0% and over
0	5	4	1	0	0	0
1	9	4	3	1	1	0
2	22	14	2	4	2	0
3	23	9	5	7	1	1
4	32	13	10	4	3	2
5	11	6	3	2	0	0
Total	102	50[a]	24[b]	18	7	3

NOTE: Data on number of submarkets by percentage of total market are based on submarket size in 1977.

[a] In five of these markets, four rank changes were the maximum possible; in two, only three changes; in one, only two changes; and in one, only one change.

[b] In one of these markets, four rank changes were the maximum possible.

SOURCE: Same as table 1.

TABLE 4

New Entries into First Five in 102 Submarkets, Netherlands, 1977 against 1972

		Number of Firms by % of Total Market				
Entered at Number	All Markets	0– <0.5%	0.5– <1.0%	1.0– <3.0%	3.0– <5.0%	5.0% and over
1	10	4	4	1	0	1
2	18	9	5	1	1	2
3	20	10	4	3	3	0
4	28	13	7	6	2	0
5	37	21	7	6	2	1
Total	113	57	27	17	8	4

NOTE: Data on number of firms by percentage of total market are based on submarket size in 1977.
SOURCE: Same as table 1.

The rank correlation coefficient, however, did not provide similar inferences. The correlation between it and the two concentration ratios is insignificant and tiny. This is the outcome we would expect from the earlier discussion. Because of innovative competition, the ranking of firms in any given submarket is rarely the same.

The firm-turnover measure of competition is not entirely satisfactory, however. Although it is used extensively above, it is open to serious errors of interpretation. A difference of market share ranking can (but need not) be large in market share terms, for example. If it is large, some substantial economic force, such as innovation, is required to alter the ranking; but if there is any tendency for firms in a market to "bunch" together in size, then rank change measures are meaningless. Alternatively, a market can undergo changes of great economic importance but need experience no change in firm ranking. Consider, for example, a duopoly of firms A and B, where A had 51 percent of the market and B had 49 percent. This would produce a rank correlation coefficient of unity even if A's share rose to 99 percent and B's fell to 1 percent.

To overcome these difficulties, a variant of the Hymer-Pashigian instability index was applied to each submarket,[1] and the results are given in column 4 of table 5. The formula as adapted by Cocks[2] provided

[1] Stephen Hymer and Peter Pashigian, "Turnover of Firms as a Measure of Market Behavior," *Review of Economics and Statistics* (February 1962), pp. 82–87.

[2] Douglas L. Cocks, "Product Innovation and the Dynamic Elements of Competition in the Ethical Pharmaceutical Industry," in Robert B. Helms, ed., *Drug Development and Marketing* (Washington, D.C.: American Enterprise Institute, 1975), pp. 225–54.

TABLE 5

MEASURES OF COMPETITION IN 102 PHARMACEUTICAL SUBMARKETS, NETHERLANDS

Market	Three-Firm Concentration Ratio (1977)	Herfindahl Index (1977)	Rank Correlation Coefficient (1972–1977)	Hymer-Pashigian Index (1972–1977)
1	91.8	0.401	0.430	46.4
2	71.3	0.197	0.303	88.3
3	54.3	0.130	0.160	70.1
4	71.9	0.349	0.157	42.6
5	83.2	0.272	0.578	43.7
6	91.0	0.389	0.859	109.1
7	87.2	0.511	0.886	11.5
8	94.8	0.699	0.256	163.3
9	80.1	0.366	0.167	53.5
10	68.7	0.275	0.055	30.0
11	80.5	0.256	0.034	49.1
12	95.1	0.302	0.781	48.6
13	75.6	0.253	0.046	56.6
14	29.8	0.047	0.472	30.0
15	79.5	0.272	0.176	68.4
16	68.1	0.178	0.429	48.8
17	72.7	0.275	0.881	64.6
18	91.4	0.318	0.262	79.9
19	88.2	0.493	−0.234	23.2
20	100.0	1.000	1.000	0.0
21	94.5	0.433	0.048	118.3
22	64.2	0.163	0.264	72.9
23	75.7	0.219	0.516	33.0
24	58.9	0.144	−0.254	57.2
25	81.0	0.245	0.432	75.8
26	79.8	0.315	0.315	18.2
27	100.0	0.774	0.944	21.9
28	91.8	0.353	0.900	18.7
29	65.2	0.167	0.097	44.5
30	56.4	0.153	0.936	34.9
31	56.3	0.143	0.155	40.4
32	76.7	0.318	0.411	52.2
33	87.8	0.456	0.348	62.1
34	69.9	0.198	0.278	58.4
35	99.1	0.707	0.661	36.6
36	76.7	0.358	0.120	24.1

TABLE 5 (continued)

Market	Three-Firm Concentration Ratio (1977)	Herfindahl Index (1977)	Rank Correlation Coefficient (1972–1977)	Hymer-Pashigian Index (1972–1977)
37	98.5	0.422	0.134	43.6
38	92.3	0.380	0.584	65.2
39	87.2	0.356	0.064	63.0
40	100.0	0.468	0.674	23.7
41	72.5	0.183	0.841	30.5
42	58.1	0.135	0.079	59.5
43	84.3	0.307	−0.096	24.9
44	100.0	0.510	−1.000	35.8
45	75.4	0.214	−0.012	141.4
46	88.6	0.527	0.881	14.3
47	87.1	0.334	0.285	45.1
48	96.2	0.759	0.327	21.9
49	85.5	0.310	−0.463	69.9
50	73.0	0.280	0.693	53.7
51	82.1	0.287	0.440	76.6
52	81.2	0.432	0.074	46.1
53	82.3	0.309	0.124	73.4
54	98.9	0.862	0.878	19.4
55	64.1	0.168	0.063	66.2
56	82.4	0.348	0.767	50.7
57	94.7	0.488	0.828	53.6
58	99.5	0.440	−0.414	7.2
59	76.3	0.231	0.000	36.0
60	77.3	0.285	0.938	23.1
61	73.7	0.239	0.315	31.4
62	89.6	0.613	0.302	17.7
63	97.8	0.668	0.875	32.4
64	74.9	0.262	0.750	75.2
65	88.1	0.355	0.880	44.5
66	71.1	0.214	0.146	37.7
67	78.0	0.277	0.630	54.2
68	55.7	0.126	0.095	61.1
69	77.1	0.267	0.501	50.4
70	41.0	0.104	0.093	64.1
71	77.3	0.311	0.390	36.6
72	51.6	0.123	0.435	99.0
73	100.0	0.563	0.243	15.7
74	83.3	0.251	−0.087	40.4

TABLE 5 (continued)

Market	Three-Firm Concentration Ratio (1977)	Herfindahl Index (1977)	Rank Correlation Coefficient (1972–1977)	Hymer-Pashigian Index (1972–1977)
75	97.8	0.454	−0.100	12.1
76	72.9	0.202	0.379	88.4
77	71.4	0.211	−0.164	18.3
78	100.0	0.564	0.674	10.9
79	99.5	0.466	−0.871	89.2
80	89.1	0.410	0.418	16.5
81	56.6	0.167	0.018	52.4
82	85.5	0.603	−0.115	26.9
83	94.9	0.703	−0.283	24.4
84	88.2	0.416	−0.490	52.4
85	100.0	0.470	−0.500	30.3
86	99.3	0.361	0.121	64.7
87	94.6	0.527	−0.523	24.1
88	84.2	0.347	0.335	140.0
89	73.4	0.233	−0.369	48.7
90	98.5	0.440	−0.374	144.5
91	90.4	0.680	−0.192	74.5
92	80.8	0.253	0.531	53.8
93	100.0	0.802	1.000	2.1
94	72.4	0.288	−0.359	20.9
95	81.0	0.294	−0.116	36.2
96	83.0	0.241	0.227	77.5
97	90.1	0.548	−0.593	38.5
98	73.1	0.254	−0.067	28.8
99	100.0	0.606	−0.849	18.7
100	89.2	0.370	0.223	157.5
101	51.8	0.143	0.226	31.6
102	93.1	0.534	−0.018	20.6

SOURCE: Same as table 1.

the basis for the instability index:

$$\sum_{i=1}^{n} (s_{i,1977} - s_{i,1972})$$

where n = the number of firms in each submarket and s = the market share of the ith firm in 1977 or 1972. The absolute values of market

TABLE 6

CORRELATION MATRIX

	Market Concentration	Herfindahl Index	Rank Correlation	Hymer-Pashigian Index
Market concentration	1.00	0.79	0.023	−0.109
Herfindahl index	—	1.00	−0.174	−0.232
Rank correlation	—	—	1.000	−0.088
Hymer-Pashigian index	—	—	—	1.000

SOURCE: Same as table 1.

share changes for each firm were summed. As can be seen in table 6, little relationship is present between the Hymer-Pashigian index and any of the other measures of competition. The instability index takes account of all firms, even the smallest, but it is affected by them only if they grow substantially. Equally, it is sensitive to the presence of large firms only if they experience high changes in market share. To illustrate its value, consider again a duopoly where A and B exchanged ranking but simply moved from a 51:49 to a 49:51 relationship. The rank correlation coefficient would then register unity (negatively), but the Hymer-Pashigian index would register only 4. Conversely, had the market share relationship changed to 99:1, the rank correlation coefficient would equal unity (positively), implying no change, whereas the instability index would have a value of 96.0, implying a high degree of economic change.

Table 6 indicates a lack of relationship between the Hymer-Pashigian index and firm turnover as measured by the rank correlation coefficient, but the conclusions we can draw are unaltered.

Cocks discovered a value for the instability index for the U.S. drug industry of 22.8. This was close to the maximum achieved in the original study across American industries. In the Netherlands, the index was calculated for all the economic submarkets, not the industry as a whole. Thus, the results may be even more meaningful than for highly aggregated but economically unrelated industry groupings. A mean value of 50.1 was obtained. On this evidence, the Dutch drug industry is highly competitive.

Thus, irrespective of the index used, provided it is a dynamic and not a static measure of competition, it will indicate the presence of a high degree of competition on the supply side of the drug market.

COMPETITION AMONG DRUGS

Pricing Activity

In this section the demand side of the industry is studied. In the final analysis, it is an industry's pricing conduct that determines whether or not it is competitive. Industry structure may or may not determine industry conduct. It is from structure to conduct that we now turn.

All drugs identified as new chemical entities (NCEs) launched into the Dutch market between January 1970 and December 1977 were examined. (Two methods of identification were used. One was to scan the British National Economic Development Office's list of all NCEs discovered worldwide. The second was to examine the listing by the American Food and Drug Administration (FDA) of all NCEs submitted to it for marketing approval and evaluation.) Table 7 categorizes all

TABLE 7

FREQUENCY DISTRIBUTION OF RELATIVE INNOVATIVE PRICES:
PRODUCTS ANALYZED BY THERAPEUTIC VALUE

FDA Rating	Number	Price Ratio[a]		
		High	Medium	Low
Netherlands, 1970–1977				
Important[b]	23	8	3	12
Modest[c]	38	7	11	20
Little or no[d]	33	3	12	18
Total	94	18	26	50
United States, 1958–1975				
Important[b]	36	16	9	11
Modest[c]	63	6	13	44
Little or no[d]	72	7	12	53
Total	171	29	34	108

[a] Price ratio $= P_{NCE}/P_c$, where P_{NCE} = guilder or dollar sales of the NCE in terms of manufacturer's receipts, divided by the number of units sold, multiplied by the modal number of units per prescription written (that is, the modal price of a prescription for the NCE); P_c = the weighted average price of a prescription for the relevant leading competitive drugs (given the oligopolistic nature of the markets, the number of competitors examined range from three to five, and these products accounted for the bulk of the turnover not attributable to the NCE, the weights awarded being the relative sales figures of the competing products).
[b] "Important" therapeutic gain—may provide effective therapy or diagnosis not adequately provided before by any marketed drug or may provide improved efficacy or safety.
[c] "Modest" therapeutic gain—has a modest but real advantage over other available marketed drugs.
[d] "Little or no" therapeutic gain—essentially duplicates in medical importance and therapy one or more already existing drugs.
SOURCE: Price ratios for the Netherlands based on price data from IMS, The Hague, the Netherlands; for the United States, on price data from IMS, Ambler, Pennsylvania.

132

these products by price and by FDA rating criteria. Over 50 percent of the NCEs were introduced at prices less than one-fifth as high again as those of leading available substitutes. At the other extreme, eighteen NCEs were introduced at prices more than double those of competitors. Finally, inspection of the data indicates that innovations providing "important" gains tended to be priced more highly than NCEs with "modest" or "little or no" therapeutic advantages over existing products. This is illustrated by the fact that the majority of the observations lie diagonally across the table from top left to bottom right.

These findings fit well within the behavior predicted by simple price theory. If markets are composed of "effectively competitive" suppliers, if price collusion is weak, and if product demand is not inelastic, major breakthroughs will be priced above the price of older products. Consumers will be prepared to pay more for more productive new products. The demand curve for new products will be above and to the right of existing demand curves by an amount approximating the value placed by the market on the quality difference. Minor variants, however, will have to be priced close to or below the products of competitors to make a successful market entry. High-priced drugs tend to provide the market with a high degree of therapeutic novelty. Minor advances tend to provide alternative sources of supply or real price reductions.

In the United States, I discovered an even stronger association in an earlier study.[3] This was perhaps inevitable, given that in the Amerrican investigation the data base was not hybridized by using qualitative information from different countries. Only FDA ratings were compared with American market performance. These results are also provided in table 7.

Is there price flexibility over time? Do competitive forces tend to push down high initial prices? Are low prices met with competing price cuts as existing firms strive to maintain market position in the face of entry? The evidence is presented in table 8 for the Netherlands and in table 9 for the United States.

As would be expected from table 7, there is a wide dispersion of prices shown in year 1. Such dispersion, according to Stigler, "is a manifestation—and indeed it is the measure—of ignorance in the market."[4] Stigler qualified this assertion in an important way for the purpose of this study. "Dispersion is a biased measure of ignorance because there is never absolute homogeneity in the commodity. . . . But it would

---

[3] W. Duncan Reekie, "Price and Quality Competition in the United States Drug Industry," *Journal of Industrial Economics*, vol. 26 (1978), pp. 223–37.
[4] G. J. Stigler, "The Economics of Information," *Journal of Political Economy*, vol. 69, no. 3 (June 1962), pp. 213–25.

TABLE 8

THE DUTCH PHARMACEUTICAL INDUSTRY PRICE STATISTICS, 1970–1977

	Year 1	Year 2	Year 3	Year 4
Maximum	24.873	27.19	11.732	12.559
Mean	2.084	1.785	1.544	1.61
Standard deviation	3.677	2.93	1.535	1.74
Coefficient of variation	1.764	1.641	0.994	1.082
Number of observations	94	100	98	87
Variance ratios				
Years 1–2		1.255		
Years 1–3			5.738	
Years 1–4				4.466

SOURCE: Same as table 7.

TABLE 9

PRICE STATISTICS RELATING TO ALL NEW CHEMICAL ENTITIES LAUNCHED IN THE UNITED STATES, 1958–1975

	Year 1	Year 2	Year 3	Year 4
Mean	1.618	1.519	1.345	1.287
Mode	1.073	0.998	1.061	1.35
Median	1.104	1.119	1.073	1.084
Maximum	15.516	11.969	5.128	5.449
Minimum	0.251	0.368	0.371	0.402
Range	15.265	11.601	4.757	5.047
n	185	175	163	146
Variance	3.577	2.022	0.709	0.500
F-ratio		1.759	2.852	1.418
Coefficient of variation	1.169	0.936	0.626	0.549

SOURCE: Reekie, "Price and Quality Competition," p. 228.

be metaphysical and fruitless to assert that all dispersion is due to heterogeneity."

In other words, one would expect some price dispersion to persist over time because of continuing quality differences. On the other hand, to the extent that it exists because of ex ante entrepreneurial activity, one would expect it to narrow over time if the competitive process is at work. If it did not so narrow, the charges, ex post, of monopoly behavior would have some justification. The price data do remain associated with the therapeutic rating scale over each of the four served years. They also show (in tables 8 and 9) that the variance drops significantly between year 1 and year 4. High initial prices tend to fall and low prices to rise.

The reduction of spread is due more to the reduction of high than to the raising of low prices. This is evident from the large falls of the relevant maximums. Such large reductions in the extremely high values, however, highlight a danger in use of the variance. The mean real price in year 4 is lower than in year 1. Falls in the mean could be due mainly to reductions in magnitude of a few nontypical values. As a surety against being misled when a shifting mean is present, the coefficients of variation were calculated. These took account of the positions of the mean and fell by around 50 percent between years 1 and 4. Again, in the United States, where the data base was homogeneous, the results were stronger than in the Netherlands.

This movement can result from four possible (not mutually exclusive) alternatives. Since relative price

$$P = \frac{P_{NCE}}{P_c}$$

where P_{NCE} is money price of the NCE and P_c is money price of competitors, then where P is relatively low, it will tend upward toward the average, because either (1) P_{NCE} rises relatively more rapidly than P_c or (2) P_c falls relatively more rapidly than P_{NCE}; and where P is relatively high, it will tend downward toward the average because either (3) P_{NCE} falls relatively more rapidly than P_c or (4) P_c rises relatively more rapidly than P_{NCE}.

In each of these four cases, the second component in the expression may, of course, be static or moving in the opposite direction from the first.

Alternatives 2 and 3 imply the competitive responses one would expect from existing firms operating on a profit-maximizing basis as they gain and assimilate information on changing cost and demand conditions. These fit within a model of workable competition in an industry. Alternative 1 would represent the action of a firm with some degree of innovative monopoly power but one that had initially misjudged the extent to which the NCE would give it an opportunity for pricing at relatively high levels. It is difficult to think of a plausible explanation for alternative 4, other than irrationality.

Neither explanation 1 nor explanation 4 is a likely reason for the narrowing of dispersion. Moreover, both fail to fit the empirical facts. For example, indexes of Dutch family total expenditure and of ethical drug consumption show that families spend considerably less of their income on drugs now than they did in 1964. In other words, the relative price of pharmaceuticals in the economy has fallen. The same is true in America. The price index for pharmaceuticals has risen much more slowly than the wholesale price index.

In terms of our analysis, P_c (that is, a base-weighted index) is falling over time while P_{NCE} is sufficiently above P_c at launch to raise the average prescription price. This, of course, implies that the large numbers of NCEs priced near P_c do not generally achieve a high volume of sales relative to costlier NCEs. If they did, the discrepancy between the drug price index and a cost-of-living series would be even greater. None of this general evidence provides support for explanations 1 and 4. Rather, it lends support to explanations 2 and 3: that competitive price-cutting behavior is responsible for the tightening of price spread noted in tables 8 and 9. The evidence suggests that NCEs priced at high initial levels experience not only relative but also monetary price declines and that those priced toward the penetration end of the high:low launch price continuum prompt monetary price cuts in competing products.

An attempt was made to measure the elasticity of demand for NCEs by estimating a log linear function of the form:

$$\log Q_{ij} = \log a + b \log P_{ij} + e$$

where i and j denote a particular NCE and year, respectively; Q is the ratio of the number of prescriptions written in the relevant therapeutic market for the NCE to total prescriptions in that market; and P is the ratio P_{NCE}/P_c. The equation was calculated across all submarkets from 1970 to 1977 for each of years 1 to 4 of an NCE's life. This quasi-combination of time series and cross-sectional analyses, coupled with the nature of the variables, can be justified on the grounds that identification is facilitated and that many other problems involved in demand estimation are also overcome.

Over time, demand changes may be dramatic; for example, one factor that has an influence on price is the size of prescription. With Q defined in ratio form, however, we can assume that any systematic factors affecting demand, such as prescription size (or incomes), are accounted for in the equation. Second, in simple time series, index linking of prices and incomes data for purposes of comparisons of relative changes is not easy. Our definition of P (effectively an index-deflated price) and the use of a ratio for Q help to overcome this problem. Third, time series alone is not wholly appropriate, given that we wish to contrast elasticities at different stages in the product life cycle.

136

Nevertheless, cross-sectional studies are not problem free. In particular, propensities to purchase vary market by market, and cross-elasticities of demand between markets may not be zero. Differing propensities to purchase are arguably not significant in this study. Here the "consumers" are always the same group of individuals in each market: all prescribing doctors in either the Netherlands or the United States. To the extent that the prices of complements vary, the definition of Q in ratio form ensures that the impact of negative cross-elasticities is embodied in the equation. The submarkets can be regarded as separating off groups of substitutes one from the other, thus partially eliminating the problem of positive cross-elasticities. Variation in P is therefore determined largely by non-demand-related factors, and so demand is duly identified.

The results are summarized in table 10. They are not unambiguous. Nevertheless, price elasticity appears to be lowest early in the life cycle, a finding perfectly consistent with industry entry theory. Price sensitivity is relatively less in year 1 when incremental product quality is "important" and greater when the therapeutic gain is "modest." This does not confirm the view that doctors are not price conscious.

The much stronger results in America may again be due to data

TABLE 10

DEMAND ELASTICITIES ANALYZED BY FDA RATING AND PRODUCT MATURITY, UNITED STATES AND THE NETHERLANDS

	FDA Rating	
	Important therapeutic gain	Modest therapeutic gain
United States		
Year 1	−1.03	−1.11
Year 2	−1.65	−2.68
Year 3	−1.30	−1.79
Year 4	n.s.	−2.83
Netherlands		
Year 1	−0.09	−0.18
Year 2	−0.17	n.s.
Year 3	−0.35	n.s.
Year 4	−0.21	n.s.

NOTE: n.s. = not statistically significant. The poor showing of the model for NCEs of "little or no" and "modest" incremental gain can be explained by the fact that even a low price cannot obtain market success for a weak product. This is discussed in relation to table 11.
SOURCES: U.S. statistics from Reekie, "Price and Quality Competition," p. 234; Netherlands statistics computed from data made available by IMS, The Hague.

quality. Alternatively, in the American model, it was possible partially to eliminate the effect of positive cross-elasticities due to competing NCEs. In the Netherlands this could not be done because of the change in submarket definition by the data source, which made it impossible to use an identical demand equation pre- and post-1974. A third explanation for the low demand elasticities in both markets, but particularly in the Netherlands, has been suggested by Kaufer.[5] He argues that, when a market is overinsured, price elasticity is lowered and quality elasticity is raised. Insurance is generally a service purchased to guard against situations that are likely to involve an individual in exceptionally high expense relative to his total income or wealth or one whose occurrence is improbable. Given the absolutely low cost of a prescription, it is difficult to see why insurance (private or state-initiated) is required in the pharmaceutical market. The presence of a generous reimbursement scheme for purchases of drugs in the Netherlands (the Sick Fund) may explain why the elasticities calculated for the Dutch market were lower than equivalent values calculated for the largely uninsured American market.

Conclusions

The outcome of the argument in the previous two sections is that the industry is not purely competitive in the sense of static microtheory. Rather, to paraphrase Schankerman,[6] the pricing and innovative behavior of the industry suggests a competitive process with a welfare loss in the static sense but where the "monopoly rents" implied are actually the sources of funds for the research and development (R&D) that ensure new products in the future. Thus, the dynamic element must be considered, in terms of both price and market standing. The "rents" are social opportunity costs in that they partially represent what society forgoes if prices behave in the manner suggested and not in the manner predicted by standard theory. Thus, to obtain NCEs in the future, society must forgo certain benefits today, represented by product prices greater than marginal manufacturing costs. This apparent "welfare loss" is the social marginal cost of R&D. If this is added to the "production costs," the total marginal social cost may well come close to being equated with the product price. For any individual existing drug, the R&D marginal

---

[5] Erich Kaufer, "Comment," in *Medicines in the Year 2000* (London: Office of Health Economics, 1979).

[6] Mark A. Schankerman, "Common Costs in Pharmaceutical Research and Development: Implications for Direct Price Regulation," in Samuel A. Mitchell and Emery A. Link, eds., *Impact of Public Policy on Drug Innovation and Pricing* (Washington, D.C.: The American University, 1976), pp. 3–45.

social cost is transitory as prices are eroded over time; so that, for the industry as a whole, new products must be introduced on a continuum to maintain this marginal social cost in order, in turn, to provide continuing R&D activity.

Table 11 shows, moreover, that half (seventeen of thirty-four) of all minor innovations did not even obtain a market share of 7.5 percent after two years on the market. It is not from trivial innovations that the dynamic competition in creativity observed in tables 1–6 arises. On the contrary, it is major innovations that penetrate markets most successfully.

In brief, the static model of perfect competition is an inappropriate tool with which to analyze the economic performance of an innovative industry like pharmaceuticals. Even when the microeconomic model is extended to embrace oligopoly in static framework, it still fails to take account of the richness and complexity of the real-life variables that determine price and quality. A theory is required that not only is dynamic but defines marginal cost sufficiently accurately to embrace innovative expenditures. Only then can meaningful comparisons of price with marginal cost be made. When the drug industry is analyzed in this way, it is no longer obvious that accusations of monopolistic pricing by the industry and of price indifference by prescribers are valid. Either the data are wrong, or there needs to be some radical revision of orthodox opinion both about the industry and about the doctors who choose to use or to reject its products.

TABLE 11

NCEs ANALYZED BY MARKET SUCCESS AND FDA RATING,
THE NETHERLANDS, 1970–1977

FDA Rating (therapeutic gain)	No. of NCEs	Market Success		
		>20%	7.5%–20%	<7.5%
Important	19	8	8	3
Modest	30	11	10	9
Little or no	34	6	11	17
Total	83	25	29	29

NOTE: Yates's corrected chi square = 15.953 (significant at the 1% level); contingency coefficient = 0.415 (minimum value = 0.316); market success is measured by numbers of prescriptions written for the NCE as a percentage of total prescriptions written in the relevant market in year 4 of the NCE's life.
SOURCE: Same as table 1.

The Effect of Patent Expiration on the Market Position of Drugs

Meir Statman

Under the U.S. patent law, inventors are given protection from unauthorized use of their patented inventions for a period of seventeen years. The patent allows its owner to capture some of the economic benefits of the invention in return for disclosure of its nature.

A patent creates a monopoly protected by law, but it also creates an incentive to innovate. Because appropriation of information contained in an invention is difficult, the absence of patent protection might lead to less investment for innovation than is socially optimal.[1] In the determination of the socially optimal length of patent protection, the disadvantages of granting monopoly power must be balanced against the benefits to the public from increased innovation.[2] There is no general agreement that the seventeen-year patent life is indeed socially optimal.

An invention is not protected by the patent statute until a patent is issued; yet the act of marking the product "Patent Pending" will usually deter copying it during the time between the filing and the granting of the patent. We may define the nominal life of a patent as the period starting with the filing date and extending until the patent expiration date. The nominal life of a patent is always longer than seventeen years because some time is necessary for evaluation of the patent application by the U.S. Patent Office. The protection provided to an inventor by the patent statute does not become effective, however, until he or she can exploit it in the marketplace. We may define the effective life of a patent as the period starting with the market introduction of a product using the invention and ending with the patent expiration date.

Although expiration of a patent eliminates the law-protected mo-

---

[1] A comprehensive discussion is provided in Kenneth J. Arrow, "Economic Welfare and the Allocation of Resources for Invention," in R. Nelson, ed., *The Rate and Direction of Inventive Activity* (Princeton: Princeton University Press, 1962). Arrow argues that the patent system provides less than socially optimal incentive for allocation of resources to invention, because not all information contained in an invention can be appropriated.

[2] For discussion and estimates of the optimal patent life, see W. D. Nordhaus, *Invention, Growth, and Welfare: A Theoretical Treatment of Technological Change* (Cambridge, Mass.: MIT Press, 1969).

nopoly power of its owner, monopoly power is not necessarily eliminated. If sufficient brand loyalty has developed during the patent life, the patented brand may enjoy a monopoly position beyond the patent life specified by law.

The purpose of this paper is to present estimates of the changing effective patent life of drug patents and evidence on the effect of patent expiration on the market position of patented drugs.

Drug Patents

Although there are several types of patents that apply to drugs, most drug patents are product patents, for they claim as invention the chemical formula of the drug.[3] A drug is invented when a chemical compound is found to have some therapeutic utility. As a practical matter, a drug firm must apply for a patent at that point, since a delay may result in a loss of the rights for a patent if a competitor is the first to file. In general, the first to file for a patent is regarded as the inventor, and litigation to prove otherwise may be costly and sometimes futile. The invention of a drug, however, is only one step in the process that may eventually lead to commercial marketing of a drug. A chemical entity must undergo a lengthy development process and be approved by the Food and Drug Administration (FDA) before it can appear on the market and enjoy the protection provided by the patent.

The seventeen-year period provided by the patent statute has not changed since the statute was enacted. The effective period of protection for drug patents has changed considerably, however. Using a sample of 126 drugs (new single chemical entities) introduced into the U.S. market during the 1949–1975 period, the effective life of drug patents was estimated as follows:[4]

$$EP = 38.97 - 0.375 \ IN$$
$$(12.50) \quad (-7.60) \qquad R^2 = 0.32$$

where EP = the effective life of a drug patent (years), and IN = U.S. market introduction year (last two digits); t-statistics are in parentheses. We observe a continuous decline in the effective life of drug patents. The expected effective patent life of drugs introduced from 1960 to 1978 is presented in table 1.

---

[3] Edmund W. Kitch, "The Patent System and the New Drug Application," in R. L. Landay, ed., *Regulating New Drugs* (Chicago: Chicago University Press, 1973), pp. 82–107.

[4] The sample was compiled from data published in *The Generic Drug Market* (New York: Frost & Sullivan, 1972) and from a list of drugs selected randomly by Louis Leaman Co., a consulting firm.

TABLE 1

EXPECTED EFFECTIVE LIFE OF DRUG PATENTS, 1960–1978

Year of U.S. Market Introduction	Expected Effective Patent Life (years)
1960	16.5
1961	16.1
1962	15.7
1963	15.4
1964	15.0
1965	14.6
1966	14.2
1967	13.9
1968	13.5
1969	13.1
1970	12.7
1971	12.4
1972	12.0
1973	11.6
1974	11.2
1975	10.9
1976	10.5
1977	10.1
1978	9.7

SOURCE: Author's estimates (see expected-life-of-drug-patent equation).

These estimates of the effective life of drug patents are in general agreement with Schwartzman's estimate of an average effective life of 13.1 years for drugs introduced during 1966–1973.[5] They are also consistent with a study by the Center for the Study of Drug Development, University of Rochester, which found an estimated decline from 13.8 years in 1966 to 8.9 years in 1977 in the effective life of drug patents.[6]

The declining effective life of drug patents is a reflection of the increasing period needed for drug development, due in part to the increase in the amount of evidence on safety and efficacy required by the FDA before approval is granted for marketing a new drug.

[5] David Schwartzman, *Innovation in the Pharmaceutical Industry* (Baltimore: Johns Hopkins University Press, 1976), chap. 8.

[6] Unpublished report by the Center for the Study of Drug Development, University of Rochester, 1979.

Patent Expiration and Competition

The decrease in the effective life of drug patents is meaningful only if competitive pressure is exerted at the time a patent expires. If competitive pressure is increased upon expiration of a patent, we might expect a drop in sale revenues of the original drug as entering producers force the producer of the original brand either to reduce his price or to face the loss of market share.[7]

Expiration of a patent, however, does not necessarily lead to increased competition. Drugs are marketed by brand names, which are registered trademarks. Unlike patents, trademarks can be renewed indefinitely as long as they are used in interstate commerce. Producers of copies of a drug that lost its patent protection can market it under its generic name or under a new brand name, but the brand name of the original producer is protected from use by others. If the original producer created sufficient brand loyalty, expiration of the patent may result in no change in the market position of the original brand. Under such circumstances, the decline in the effective patent life is not significant because the barrier to entry of competitors in the form of a patent is simply replaced by a barrier in the form of a trademark coupled with brand loyalty.

A detailed study by Schwartzman examines competition in markets where the patent of the original drug expired.[8] Schwartzman found significant price competition in the antibiotics market, although much of it started long before patent expiration. He found little competition after patent expiration for other drugs, however.

Large drug companies argue that generic drug producers find it difficult to enter the market because generic drugs are of inferior quality. There is considerable empirical evidence to support this argument,[9] but even large drug companies with good quality control find it difficult to enter markets of drugs whose patents have expired. According to Charles T. Silloway, president of Ciba, reserpine produced by large firms met the United States Pharmacopeia (USP) standards just as Serpasil, Ciba's brand, did;[10] yet sales of Serpasil in 1973 amounted to more than $3.8 million whereas the combined sales of Raused, Reserpoid,

---

[7] A discussion of the effect of patent expiration in the polyester fibers market is presented in R. W. Shaw and S. A. Shaw, "Patent Expiry and Competition in Polyester Fibers," *Scottish Journal of Political Economy*, vol. 24 (June 1977), pp. 117–32.

[8] Schwartzman, *Innovation*, chap. 12.

[9] Ibid., chaps. 10, 11.

[10] Ibid., p. 244.

TABLE 2

Effective Wholesale Prices and Sale Revenues of Ampicillin Sold under Various Brand Names

Brand Name	Manufacturer	Year of Introduction	Price, June 1973 (250 mg/ 20 caps, in dollars)	Sale Revenues, 1973 (in thousands of dollars)
Polycillin	Bristol	1963	2.66	23,086
SK-ampicillin	SmithKline	1971	2.25	3,326
Omnipen	Wyeth	1966	1.97	10,263
Amcill	Parke-Davis	1968	1.89	6,291
Penbritin	Ayerst	1964	1.84	6,170
Totacillin	Beechem USV	1969	1.73	2,630
Principen	Squibb	1967	1.65	11,809
Pen-A	Pfizer	1972	1.42	4,747

Source: Schwartzman, *Innovation*, tables 12.5, 12.9.

and Eskaserp, brand names of reserpine by Squibb, Upjohn, and SmithKline, respectively, amounted to only $104,000.[11]

Furthermore, even in the antibiotics field, which Schwartzman cites as the field where price competition is intense, there are significant price differences. As presented in table 2, ampicillin was sold by Bristol under the brand name Polycillin for $2.66 per prescription in 1973, while the same prescription filled with Pen-A, the brand name of ampicillin by Pfizer, cost only $1.42; yet sales of Polycillin exceeded sales of Pen-A by a ratio of almost five to one.

The FDA maintains that approved drugs sharing the same generic name are bioequivalent. They suggest that the difficulties faced by manufacturers of generic drugs do not stem from quality problems. The Federal Trade Commission (FTC) provides an explanation for the continuing market dominance by the original brand, stating that "the basic problem is that the forces of competition do not work well in a market where the consumer who pays does not choose, and the physician who chooses does not pay."[12]

Until recently, the difficulties faced by entrants after patent expiration have been compounded by antisubstitution laws prohibiting a pharmacist from filling a prescription with any brand other than that prescribed by the physician. By the end of 1978, however, forty states

[11] Ibid., p. 263.
[12] Federal Trade Commission, *Drug Product Selection* (Washington, D.C., 1979), p. 2.

and the District of Columbia had repealed these laws.[13] The intent of the legislators in repealing antisubstitution laws was to encourage price competition among the original brand, generics, and other brands.

The data presented below detail the changes in the market position of twelve drugs that lost their patent protection during 1970–1976. Sales revenue and price data are available through 1978, so that any effects of competitive pressure due to the repeal of antisubstitution laws should be manifested.

Evidence on the Effect of Patent Expiration

The characteristics of the drugs in the sample are presented in table 3. Tables 4 and 5 describe the changing position of the original brands in the drugstore and hospital markets starting three years before patent expiration and continuing through 1978.

The data reveal that generic and brand-name competitors were not successful in capturing a significant market share from the original brand. In the drugstore market, reflecting physicians' prescriptions, no original drug in the sample had less than 92.4 percent of the market by 1978. The average share in 1978 of the six top-selling drugs was 96.1 percent. Generic and brand-name competitors did better in the hospital market, although in no case did the market share of the original brand decline below 81.8 percent by 1978. The average share in 1978 of the six top-selling drugs was 89.0 percent. The relative performance of generic and other brands in the drugstore and hospital markets might be the result of more incentives to economize in hospitals or of better knowledge of the alternative drugs available.

Although the overall success of generic competition is quite limited, observation of the market share of the original brand over time reveals a gradual decline in share. This suggests that such drugs will not be able to hold on to their market shares indefinitely.

The success of the original brands in maintaining their market shares was not the result of price reductions that might have deterred entry. Table 6 presents the retail prices per prescription (in drugstores) of the drugs in the sample. These prices were deflated by a prescription price index. Only four of the drugs had lower prices in 1978 than their prices three years before patent expiration.

A comparison of the vigorous price competition in antibiotics, as described by Schwartzman, and the relative lack of such competition in

---

[13] Henry Grabowski and John Vernon, "Substitution Laws and Innovations in the Pharmaceutical Industry," Center for the Study of Business Regulation, Duke University, 1979.

TABLE 3

THE SAMPLE DRUGS

Brand Name	Manufacturer	Generic Name	Therapeutic Category	Patent Number	Year of Patent Expiration
Atarax[a]	Roerig	Hydroxyzine HCl	Tranquilizers (mild)	2,899,436	1976
Compazine	SmithKline	Prochlorperazine	Tranquilizers (strong)	2,902,484	1976
Darvon	Eli Lilly	Propoxyphene HCl	Analgesics	2,728,779	1972
Diuril	Merck	Chlorothiazide	Diuretics	2,809,194	1974
Doriden	Ciba, USV	Glutethimide	Sleep inducers	2,673,205	1971
Gantanol	Roche	Sulfamethoxazole	Sulfas	2,888,455	1976
Librium	Roche	Chlordiazepoxide HCl	Tranquilizers (mild)	2,893,992	1976
Placidyl	Abbott	Ethchlorvynol	Sedatives	2,746,900	1973
Pro-Banthine	Searle	Propantheline bromide	Antispasmodics	2,659,732	1970
Robaxin	Robins	Methocarbamol	Muscle relaxants	2,770,649	1973
Tandearil	Geigy	Oxyphenbutazone	Antiarthritics	2,745,783	1973
Thorazine	SmithKline	Chlorpromazine HCl	Tranquilizers (strong)	2,645,640	1970

[a] Includes sales of Vistaril by Pfizer, the parent company of Roerig.
SOURCE: Patent data obtained from Pfizer, Inc.

TABLE 4

MARKET SHARE OF PATENTED DRUGS BEFORE AND AFTER PATENT EXPIRATION, DRUGSTORE MARKET

Brand Name	Sales in the Year before Patent Expiration ($ thousands)	Market Share in % during Years before (−) or after (+) Patent Expiration											
		−3	−2	−1	0	+1	+2	+3	+4	+5	+6	+7	+8
Atarax	16,493	100	100	100	100	99.9	99.3	—	—	—	—	—	—
Compazine	9,350	100	100	100	100	100	100	—	—	—	—	—	—
Darvon	14,581	100	100	100	100	99.8	99.2	98.8	98.2	97.0	94.4	—	—
Diuril	14,737	100	100	100	100	100	99.2	98.1	95.8	—	—	—	—
Doriden	8,790	100	100	100	100	100	100	100	100	99.3	98.4	98.0	—
Gantanol	5,088	100	100	100	100	100	100	—	—	—	—	—	—
Librium	54,690	100	100	99.5	98.3	96.8	94.5	—	—	—	—	—	—
Placidyl	4,269	100	100	100	100	100	100	100	100	100	—	—	—
Pro-Banthine	4,598	100	100	100	100	100	100	99.6	99.5	99.1	99.2	98.7	98.7
Robaxin	4,528	100	100	100	100	100	100	99.0	97.9	96.5	—	—	—
Tandearil	6,477	100	100	100	100	100	100	100	100	100	—	—	—
Thorazine	21,639	100	100	100	100	100	100	98.5	98.6	98.1	95.7	95.4	92.4

SOURCE: IMS America, *U.S. Pharmaceutical Market, Drug Stores and Hospitals* (Ambler, Penn., various years).

TABLE 5

MARKET SHARE OF PATENTED DRUGS BEFORE AND AFTER PATENT EXPIRATION, HOSPITAL MARKET

Brand Name	Sales in the Year before Patent Expiration ($ thousands)	Market Share in % during Years before (−) or after (+) Patent Expiration											
		−3	−2	−1	0	+1	+2	+3	+4	+5	+6	+7	+8
Atarax	14,203	100	100	100	100	100	100	—	—	—	—	—	—
Compazine	4,396	100	100	100	100	100	100	—	—	—	—	—	—
Darvon	3,212	100	100	100	100	94.6	93.6	95.5	84.1	83.0	82.4	—	—
Diuril	853	100	100	100	100	100	96.5	90.6	89.9	—	—	—	—
Doriden	544	100	100	100	100	100	100	100	100	98.8	99.3	98.6	—
Gantanol	533	100	100	100	100	100	100	—	—	—	—	—	—
Librium	4,492	100	100	99.5	98.9	89.4	86.5	—	—	—	—	—	—
Placidyl	360	100	100	100	100	100	100	100	100	100	—	—	—
Pro-Banthine	968	100	100	100	100	100	100	99.3	97.2	95.0	89.0	86.7	92.6
Robaxin	1,175	100	100	100	100	100	100	96.3	88.3	83.0	—	—	—
Tandearil	300	100	100	100	100	100	100	100	100	100	—	—	—
Thorazine	13,381	100	100	100	100	100	100	95.1	91.6	89.0	85.0	83.4	81.8

SOURCE: IMS America, *U.S. Pharmaceutical Market.*

TABLE 6

Retail Prices per Prescription of the Original Drugs before and after Patent Expiration

(constant dollars, 1967 = 100)

Brand Name	Retail Prices during Years before (−) or after (+) Patent Expiration												Unit
	−3	−2	−1	0	+1	+2	+3	+4	+5	+6	+7	+8	
Atarax	4.43	4.38	4.58	4.58	4.56	4.69	—	—	—	—	—	—	25mg (30 tablets)
Compazine	3.28	3.37	3.49	3.53	3.42	3.47	—	—	—	—	—	—	25mg (Rect-s, 6 units)
Darvon	3.97	3.82	3.89	3.73	3.77	3.75	3.53	3.60	3.41	3.32	—	—	65mg (30 capsules)
Diuril	3.23	3.19	3.24	3.22	3.07	3.02	2.86	2.78	—	—	—	—	500mg (30 tablets)
Doriden	2.56	2.80	3.01	2.99	3.16	3.27	3.35	3.56	3.70	3.86	4.05	—	500mg (30 tablets)
Gantanol	4.40	4.39	4.47	4.52	4.54	4.58	—	—	—	—	—	—	500mg (40 tablets)
Librium	8.91	8.50	8.14	8.19	7.76	7.73	—	—	—	—	—	—	10mg (100 capsules)
Placidyl	3.26	3.32	3.38	3.47	3.48	3.82	3.93	4.25	4.06	—	—	—	500mg (30 capsules)
Pro-Banthine	2.67	2.67	2.59	2.75	2.89	2.88	2.92	2.95	3.14	3.21	3.57	3.58	15mg (20 tablets)
Robaxin	3.86	3.94	4.03	3.92	3.98	4.02	3.90	3.72	4.17	—	—	—	500mg (30 tablets)
Tandearil	4.00	4.37	4.43	4.48	4.38	4.44	4.54	4.62	4.48	—	—	—	100mg (30 tablets)
Thorazine	9.37	9.30	8.93	7.50	6.33	6.46	6.04	5.84	5.52	5.34	5.06	4.90	25mg (100 tablets)

SOURCE: Price data are from IMS America, *NPA—Basic Data Report* (various years). Dosage chosen was the one with the highest sales revenues. The most frequent prescription size was selected within that dosage. Prices were deflated by the Firestone Index of Prescription Charges for Ethical Pharmaceuticals (Firestone's index uses a larger sample than the Bureau of Labor Statistics index. It is available from the Pharmaceutical Manufacturers Association, Washington, D.C.).

the twelve sample drugs suggests an explanation for the difference. In each of the sample drugs, only one brand of the drug was available in the market before patent expiration.[14] This provided ample time for identification of the drug with a specific brand name and the development of brand loyalty. In the antibiotics cases, in contrast, there was more than one brand name of a given drug long before patent expiration and, apparently, before there was sufficient time for the original brand to establish its market leadership. Multiple brands of a drug before patent expiration occurred through licensing or infringement on weak patents. The case of the antibiotic ampicillin is presented in table 2. Bristol-Myers started producing ampicillin under the brand name Polycillin in 1963, and Ayerst started producing it under the brand name Penbritin only one year later, both under license from Beechem. Bristol provided sublicenses to several manufacturers, and other firms entered by patent infringement. The lack of strong brand loyalty in the ampicillin market because of the short lead time of the original brand encouraged price competition as a means of gaining leadership in the market.

The length of the threshold lead time, which enables a manufacturer to develop sufficient brand loyalty to prevent price competition, has direct bearing on patent and trademark policies. Such estimates of threshold lead time are not available and should be a subject of future research. The case of ampicillin suggests that such threshold lead time may be very short. Bristol, which introduced its brand of ampicillin only one year before Ayerst, had sales in 1973 of more than double the sales of its nearest competitor while maintaining the highest price in the group.

Conclusions

The evidence presented in this paper suggests that drugs protected by a patent are able to hold on to their market positions beyond patent expiration, although, in general, generic and other name brands gradually capture an increasing share of each drug's market. There is also evidence that generic competition in the hospital market is more vigorous than in the drugstore market, even though the hospital market is much smaller. Possibly the difference is due to greater knowledge of drugs or to greater incentive to economize.

It is argued by the Federal Trade Commission that the present laws allowing substitution of drugs still make it easier for physicians to prescribe by brand name, favoring the original brand.[15] The commission

---

[14] Hydroxyzine HCl was marketed under two brand names: Vistaril by Pfizer and Atarax by Roerig, a subsidiary of Pfizer.

[15] FTC, *Drug Product Selection.*

proposed a model substitution law designed to encourage substitution. Provisions of the model law include (1) allowing pharmacists to share in the savings resulting from the difference in price between brand-name drugs and generic drugs, (2) providing pharmacists with a list of bioequivalent drugs and limiting their liability for generic drug selection, and (3) requiring physicians to write "medically necessary" on the prescription if they wish to prevent substitution.

If the commission's recommendations are made into law, it might lead to a more rapid decline in the market share of drugs after patent expiration. Such rapid loss of the market share of patented drugs is not necessarily beneficial to the consumer. As noted by Comanor, "there is a trade-off between high levels of research and high prices at one end of the spectrum and low research and prices at the other."[16]

The estimated return on drug innovation for drugs decreased from 21.7 percent for drugs introduced in 1958 to 10.3 percent for drugs introduced in 1978.[17] The cost of capital, however, increased from 11.1 percent to 12.7 percent over the period. These estimates were based on data that do not reflect the effect of the recent substitution laws. Yet the return on drug innovation in recent years is lower than the cost of capital. Observation of research and development expenditures in recent years indicates that pharmaceutical companies have reacted to the declining return by reducing the rate of growth of research and development outlays. The estimated return on drug innovation drops from 10.3 percent to 6.6 percent if a drug market life is assumed to equal the ten-year current effective life of drug patents.

A possible partial solution, which recognizes the public interest in having better drugs through research, is to extend the patent period to the original seventeen years. This could be achieved by beginning the patent life only at the approval of the drug for marketing by the FDA.

---

[16] William S. Comanor, in J. D. Cooper, ed., *The Economics of Drug Innovation* (Washington, D.C.: The American University, 1969), p. 225.

[17] Meir Statman, "Dynamic Competition in the Drug Industry: The Movement toward the Competitive Equilibrium," unpublished manuscript.

Commentary

Mark C. Hornbrook

Policy Issue: Nature and Degree of Competition

The problem of measuring and explaining the degree of competition in the pharmaceutical industry has been a perennial one for both researchers and policy makers. Much debate has occurred over whether the perceived market power in the industry and the associated welfare losses are sufficiently great to require enactment of major "procompetitive" policy measures. Such measures include compulsory patent licensing, abolition of brand names, restrictions on advertising, reduction in investigational new drug (IND) and new drug application (NDA) requirements, and so on. It is not likely, however, that an answer regarding the overall "goodness" or "badness" of the performance of the pharmaceutical industry will soon be forthcoming. The reason is that multiple policy objectives regarding drugs are often in conflict. Hence, any attempt to derive a final conclusion about whether the industry is highly competitive, and therefore should be left alone, or highly monopolistic, and therefore should be the subject of increased government intervention, is a tremendous oversimplification of the policy problem.

The policy maker is faced with the task of selecting an optimum point on a multidimensional performance feasibility frontier that specifies the trade-offs among safety, efficacy, technical progress, and efficiency. This frontier is vague and fuzzy, however; so we do not know what happens to the other performance goals if we push hard for one dimension, such as efficacy. An ultimate purpose of this volume is to define this performance frontier better.

In his paper, Professor Reekie suggests that efficiency and innovation are mutually attainable. He attempts to demonstrate a high degree of competition in the pharmaceutical industry since no one firm controls any single therapeutic market for a substantial period because of the rapid introduction of new products by competitors. He finds that major innovative products tend to be priced higher than less significant innovations and that prices of new products tend to fall, both relatively and absolutely, after introduction. He argues that this price behavior is consistent with price theory, given the presence of product quality and market information differentials. He does not, however, provide any analysis of whether consumer valuations of product quality differences are congruent with these price differentials. He concludes that accusations of monopolistic pricing by the industry are not valid.

Although it is true that drug firms must price to cover the costs of research and development (R&D), new product testing, advertising, and so on, and although it is generally accepted that drug-firm R&D produces a steady flow of desirable products, that promotion and marketing efforts produce rapid diffusion of new products, and that regulation increases the quality of drugs, the policy issue becomes one of degree. When is promotion carried to excess? When are supposedly new products trivial? When is regulation too stringent? When are new drugs rushed into use too fast? To accomplish this balance among the performance dimensions, complex models of the structure-conduct-performance interrelationships are required. Professor Reekie describes the concentration, market share instability, innovation, and pricing patterns among the various therapeutic markets, but he does not tie them together in a simultaneous model that could give us a picture of the feedback effects among these variables. An examination of table 5 in Reekie's paper shows considerable variation in concentration and market share instability across therapeutic markets. Although there is not a consistently high and stable level of oligopolistic dominance in the industry, some therapeutic markets do exhibit this structure. On the other hand, some markets are characterized by a high degree of market share instability and greater equality of market shares. Such variation in market structures is worthy of research. Reekie asserts that pricing and innovation are important determinants of therapeutic market structure, but he does not present any empirical analyses of these relationships. He shows that market penetration is a function of degree of innovation but does not link this to overall patterns of market shares in the industry. Reekie shows that new chemical entities (NCEs) tend to be priced higher than the products they are designed to replace but does not examine the competitive pricing reactions of established firms. Nowhere does he mention the impact of promotional activities on competitive structure. Thus, the principal shortcoming of Reekie's paper is what he does *not* do with the data he has in hand.

Barriers to Research

To provide more credibility to this critique of Reekie's paper, it would be appropriate to present a model of the structure-conduct interrelationships in the pharmaceutical industry. There are, however, two important obstacles to development of more complex econometric models of the industry. One is the *identification problem*. In the structure-conduct-performance paradigm of industrial organization, it is difficult to find factors in the model that can be excluded in any individual equation. The basic problem is that everything is related to everything else. To remedy this problem, we need to expand our theory to include factors unique to the pharmaceutical industry. This causes us to run into the second obstacle, *availability of data*. Anyone who has ever done research on the pharmaceutical industry can attest to the fact that we have reams of product-specific data available from the various market research services but obtaining information from the firms directly on such key variables as production costs, research and development expenditures by therapeutic category, profits by product line, and so on, is nearly impossible, except on a case-study basis. This creates some severe gaps in our efforts to model this industry.

A second-best approach is to employ the available data to estimate reduced-form models. As an illustration of this approach, this paper presents some results of a simple four-equation econometric model of market structure and conduct in the wholesale-retail sector of the U.S. pharmaceutical industry. The objective is to determine the effects of selected barriers and incentives to entry on concentration, promotional intensity, market share instability, and prices in a reduced-form model. The ultimate purpose is to indicate the directions that future research must take rather than to provide any strong conclusions regarding public policy implications. The data are not current, being for the period from 1961 to 1971, but they do provide a basis for comparison for future studies.

Structure-Conduct Interrelationships

As Reekie has indicated, the conditions of entry are the key determinants of the degree of competitiveness in an industry. Entry is assumed to be positively related to the difference between the observed and entry-limiting profit rates, given the basic behavioral postulate that drug firms are profit-maximizing:

$$ENTRY_{i,t} = e(\pi_{o_{i,t}} - \pi_i')$$

Where $\pi_{o_{i,t}}$ is the observed profit rate for market i in period t, and π_i' is the rate of profits that is equal to potential entrants' opportunity cost of capital *plus* a premium equal to the present value of the absolute cost advantages imposed by entry barriers.[1] By definition, a barrier to entry is a cost that must be borne by an entrant but not by an established firm.[2] If there are no barriers to entry, the entry-limiting profit rate equals the opportunity cost of capital. Barriers to entry allow excess profits, which, in turn, act as an incentive to entry. Potential entrants, however, must assess their expected postentry profit rate after incurring the costs of entry. In the absence of barriers, entry should act to equalize marginal rates of return across markets and within a market over time. In the presence of barriers to entry, when observed profit rates are higher than the entry-limiting rate, entry will occur until profit rates are driven down to the entry-limiting level.

The entry-limiting profit rate is postulated to be a function of the level of entry barriers. These barriers include promotional activities, concentration, patent control, governmental regulation, diversification, and product differentiation.

Two dimensions of the *observed* profit rate serve as incentives to enter: level and variation. It is assumed that drug firms are risk averters, which implies that they have a relatively high disutility for losses.[3] This means that firms face the problem of trading off between the expected profit level and the risk or variability associated with that level. Therefore, two markets that have the same observed profit levels but have different standard deviations for those rates would offer different incentives for entry.

In general, then, entry is postulated to be a function of the level of barriers to entry relative to incentives to enter. For a given level of entry barriers, the greater the incentives to enter, the greater the likelihood of entry, *ceteris paribus*. For a given set of incentives, the higher the barriers, the less the likelihood of entry, *ceteris paribus*.

Established firms are able to influence the level of entry barriers by means of promotional activities and pricing strategies in the short run.[4] These variables may be manipulated singly or in concert. Because profitability is an inverse function of entry, the problem for established firms is to set promotional expenditures and prices so as to maximize profits, subject to the condition that entry be prevented. This is the concept of an "entry-limiting" strategy. The higher the barriers to entry

---

[1] Dale Orr, "The Determinants of Entry: A Study of Canadian Manufacturing Industries," *Review of Economics and Statistics*, vol. 56 (February 1974), p. 58.

[2] George J. Stigler, *The Organization of Industry* (Homewood, Ill.: Richard D. Irwin, 1969), p. 67.

[3] Orr, "Determinants of Entry," p. 59.

[4] In the long run, patents, diversification, and product differentiation must be considered endogenous. In this study, it is assumed that the firm's stock of patents and new products is fixed and therefore exogenous.

posed by patents, product differentiation, and so on, the lower promotional expenses need to be to prevent entry; moreover, prices can be higher without incurring entry.

A Different Empirical Model

In this study, the impact of entry is assessed by two factors—concentration and market share instability. As demonstrated by Reekie, concentration by itself is a poor indicator of entry because it does not assess the dynamic shifts in firm market shares—the "slipperiness at the top." It is especially critical to assess this second dimension of market structure in the pharmaceutical industry.

The competitive behavior of new entrants and established rivals is measured by promotional intensity and average prescription price within the therapeutic market. Eight exogenous factors are included in the model. Two—market growth rate and market size—are proxy measures of the profit potential in the market, and as such they should be associated with decreased concentration and stability as entry occurs and with increased promotion and reduced prices in an attempt by established firms to forestall entry. Market size is linked to profitability by the operation of economies of scale. The minimum optimal scale of plant should constitute a lower proportion of total market output in larger markets than in smaller ones, thus allowing new entrants to operate without a cost disadvantage. To allow for potential nonlinear effects of market size, this factor is entered in quadratic form.

Increasing demand will open up new profit opportunities that may provide the necessary incentives for potential competitors to enter the market. Under conditions of continued growth in demand and recurrent lag in adjusting supply to meet that demand, profits rise, which attracts new entry.

Three barriers to entry are included in the model—patent control, product differentiation, and diversification—and they are hypothesized to lead to increased concentration and stability, decreased promotional activities, and increased prices.

Product differentiation has three aspects: first, efforts by firms to differentiate their products technically through introduction of innovative products; second, efforts by firms to capitalize on the developments of other firms through introduction of imitative products; and, third, efforts at image differentiation through the use of brand names. These differentiation efforts create barriers to entry by dividing the market into multiple submarkets in which physicians are tied more tightly to specific products through loyalty to specific brands or belief in the technical superiority of a particular salt of a given drug. Imitative

156

new product introduction is an attempt to *decrease* product differentiation. Because information on the characteristics and availability of a new product may not be uniformly distributed to all buyers, a lag may develop between the time of introduction and the time of acceptance of a new product. To allow for this circumstance, innovation and imitation are included in both current and lagged forms in the model.

Diversification is defined as the extent to which the firm produces a wide variety of different products that are sold in separate markets. In the context of this study, we are concerned with diversification across therapeutic markets. It imposes three types of barriers to entry: (1) potential for predatory promotion and pricing through the "deep pocket," that is, cross-subsidies from other markets in which the established firm operates; (2) loss of information on the profitability of operating in a given market; and (3) economies of scale in promotional and marketing activities.[5]

One other exogenous factor is included in the model—length of drug therapy. Certain types of drugs are used in the treatment of chronic diseases, with the result that the patient receives greater quantities of these drugs over a longer period of time. In this circumstance, it is much more important than in the treatment of acute conditions that the physician tailor or "fine-tune" the drug regimen to meet the medical needs of the patient. This applies to the selection of the product itself as well as to the selection of route of administration, dosage strength, and timing of administration. This means that the physician will require much more information about long-term drugs to make a selection, as compared with short-term drugs. This higher level of information on the demand side of the market can be expected to have an impact on the structure and conduct of these markets relative to short-term markets. Long-term maintenance drug markets are expected to be characterized by lower concentration, stability, and prices and higher promotional intensity than short-term markets, other things held constant.

Scope of the Study. This study is limited to prescription drug products within the wholesale-retail sector of the pharmaceutical industry. The firms in this market are termed "labelers," in the sense that it is their names that appear on the final dosage-form products. Labelers may or may not actually manufacture the ingredients in the products they sell. The products included in this study are finished dosage-form prescription drug preparations distributed through community pharmacies to patients for self-administration on an outpatient basis. These drug products have

---

[5] Stephen A. Rhoades, "The Effect of Diversification on Industry Profit Performance in 241 Manufacturing Industries, 1963," *Review of Economics and Statistics*, vol. 55 (May 1973), p. 147.

been grouped into sixty-nine therapeutic markets, representing relatively homogeneous groups in their principal therapeutic action and secondary side effects.

The wholesale-retail sector constitutes a separable submarket in the industry because of the characteristics of the ultimate transaction—the physician writing a prescription order that is filled, exactly as written,[6] at the community pharmacy—and the characteristics of the distribution channels—labeler to wholesaler or retailer. These institutional factors enable drug firms to identify a separate group of buyers—physicians— and to treat them separately without running into problems of arbitrage between markets (buyer groups), because a prescription order is non-transferable and no substitution is allowed in dispensing the prescription. Therefore, the purchasing decisions of community pharmacies are a direct reflection of the prescribing patterns of physicians in that community.

The therapeutic class is assumed to be the appropriate unit of analysis because it represents the relevant arena in which the firm makes pricing, marketing, promotional, and product strategy decisions. The substitutability, in terms of end uses, between products in different therapeutic classes is, by definition, zero. These conditions on the demand side mean that the chain of competitive relations among drug products is broken at the boundaries of the therapeutic class. Hence, the therapeutic class constitutes the product market.[7]

Measurement of the Variables. A description of the model's variables is presented below.

Concentration. The concept of concentration has two components, fewness and inequality. One index that captures both of these is the H-index, defined as the sum of squared firm market shares.

Promotional intensity. Promotional intensity is defined as the aggregate annual outlay for advertising and other promotional activities for products within a specific therapeutic market, adjusted to reflect the

---

[6] The recent trend toward repeal of drug antisubstitution laws did not begin until after the period covered by this study (1961–1971).

[7] Theoretically speaking, conditions on the supply side should also be taken into account in defining product markets. The fact that a firm is in one market may influence the probability that it will enter another market. Thus, cross-elasticities on the supply side are not as strongly separable as they are on the demand side. The assumption is made here that the degree of separability among products on the demand side is so overwhelming as to support the use of the therapeutic class as the relevant product market for the purposes of this analysis. The issue of interdependencies on the supply side across therapeutic markets must be put aside for future research.

size of the market. It is measured by the ratio of total annual promotional expenditures to total annual market sales volume.

Market share instability. To assess the dynamic changes in market structure, market share instability is defined and measured as the sum of the absolute values of the difference in firm market shares between year $t - 1$ and year t (that is, between adjacent years).

Price. To reflect the overall movement of prices in a given therapeutic market, price is defined and measured as the average price for a new prescription in year t.

Market growth rate. Market growth rate in year t is defined and measured as the ratio of the difference in total therapeutic market sales of new prescriptions between year t and year $t - 1$ to total sales of new prescriptions in year $t - 1$.

Market size. Market size in year t is defined and measured as the total dollar volume of new prescription sales in year t.

Patent control. Patent control is defined as the coverage and strength of patents on the products in a specific therapeutic market and on the processes used to produce those products. The measure of patent coverage is the proportion of total new prescription sales in a therapeutic market represented by patented drugs.

Product differentiation. Product differentiation is measured by three variables: extent of generic-name coverage, innovative new product introduction, and imitative new product introduction. Because trade names are so pervasive, the entry barrier imposed by use of trade names will be measured by its obverse, generic-name coverage. This variable is measured by the proportion of total therapeutic market sales represented by generic-name products. New product innovation in year t is defined as the introduction by a firm of a specific chemical mixture or compound that has not been available in any previous year in that specific therapeutic market. Innovative products include both new single chemical entities and new combination products. New salts of existing drugs and combination products whose ingredients have not previously appeared together in a single product, although they may have been available separately, are counted as innovations. Innovation is measured by the proportion of total market sales represented by new single chemical entities and new combination products introduced during the given year. New product imitation in year t is defined as the introduction by a firm of a specific chemical mixture or compound that has not been offered for sale in any previous year by that specific firm but has been available in the particular therapeutic market from other firms. This

159

variable is measured by the proportion of total market sales represented by duplicative products introduced in year *t*.

Diversification. Diversification is defined as the degree of heterogeneity in the total set of product offerings by a given firm, where "heterogeneity" means the number of different markets in which the firm sells its products. The index of diversification employed in this study is the total number of different therapeutic markets served by the four firms with the largest market shares in a given therapeutic market.

Length of drug therapy. This variable is measured by a dummy variable that is set equal to one if market *j* is characterized by new prescriptions with an average period of therapy of ninety days or more.

The measures for each of the variables included in this analysis are summarized in table 1.

Description of the Data. The data represent pooled time series cross-section observations on the sixty-nine therapeutic markets over the period 1961 to 1971.[8]

Market share data. The new-prescription market share data used in this study were derived from the National Prescription Audit (NPA) conducted by IMS America. The NPA is designed to measure the "retail outflow" of prescriptions—that is, drugs moving from the retail pharmacy to the consumer—and is based on a stratified random sample of prescription files in community pharmacies. Hence, it is a measure of one segment of total pharmaceutical sales, albeit the most important segment. A new prescription is defined as either a prescription, written or oral, that is newly prescribed by an authorized prescriber or a prescription given a new identification number by a pharmacist.

Promotion data. Promotional expenditure data were obtained from the National Media Audit conducted by IMS America. This survey estimates the amounts spent for detailing, journal advertising, and direct mail promotion for each drug product.

Other data sources. Data on firm subsidiaries, mergers, and acquisitions were obtained from various pharmaceutical firm directories and general corporation reports.[9] Data on the chemical composition of drug

[8] For a description of the procedures used to define therapeutic markets in this study, see Mark C. Hornbrook, "Market Domination and Promotional Intensity in the Wholesale-Retail Sector of the U.S. Pharmaceutical Industry," Technical Paper Series, National Center for Health Services Research, U.S. Department of Health, Education and Welfare, 1976.

[9] Kenneth R. Kern, *Executive Directory of the U.S. Pharmaceutical Industry*, 2d ed. (Prin-

TABLE 1

MEASURES OF THE VARIABLES

Variable	Measure
Concentration	Sum of squares of firm market shares (H-index)
Promotional intensity	Ratio of total promotional expenditures in market j in year t to total new prescription sales volume
Market share instability	Sum of absolute values of changes in firm market shares from year $t - 1$ to year t in market j
Price	Average new prescription price in year t in market j
Market growth rate	Rate of growth in annual new prescription sales in market j from year $t - 1$ to year t
Market size	Total new prescription sales volume for market j
Patent coverage	Proportion of total new prescription sales represented by patented drugs
Generic-name coverage	Proportion of total new prescription sales represented by generic drug products
Lagged innovation	Proportion of total new prescription sales represented by new single chemical entities and new combination products in year $t - 1$ in market j
Innovation	Proportion of total new prescription sales represented by new single chemical entities and new combination products in year t in market j
Lagged imitation	Proportion of total new prescription sales represented by newly introduced duplicative products in year $t - 1$ in market j
Imitation	Proportion of total new prescription sales represented by newly introduced duplicative products in year t in market j
Diversification	Total number of therapeutic markets served by top four firms in year t in market j
Long-term maintenance drug type	1 if market is characterized by prescriptions for at least ninety days' supply of the drug, 0 otherwise

SOURCE: Author.

ceton, N.J.: Chemical Economic Services, 1972); Noyes Data Corp., *Pharmaceutical and Cosmetic Firms, U.S.A.* (Park Ridge, N.J., 1964); Noyes Development Corp., *Pharmaceutical Firms, U.S.A. and Canada, 1964* (Pearl River, N.J., 1963); *Moody's Industrial Manual* (New York: Moody's Investors Services), 1961–1972 editions; *Moody's OTC Industrial Manual* (New York: Moody's Investors Services, 1970–1972); *Standard Corporation Descriptions* (New York: Standard & Poor, 1973).

products (to validate therapeutic classification) were obtained from the *National Drug Code Directory*, the *Physicians' Desk Reference*, the *American Drug Index*, and *Drug Topics Red Book*.[10] Data on drug product patents were obtained from the *Merck Index*.[11] Data on introduction of new single chemical entities and new combination products were obtained from Paul de Haen's *New Product Survey*.[12]

Results. The model estimated in this study represents the reduced-form version of a simultaneous equations model in which the endogenous variables are concentration, market share instability, promotional intensity, and average prescription price. The equations were estimated using ordinary least squares procedures. To facilitate interpretation of the statistical and policy significance of each variable, elasticities were calculated at the sample means for all explanatory variables except the annual dummies. The results are presented in table 2. Overall, the equations perform relatively well in explaining variation in the dependent variables; all are statistically significant overall; and a majority of the exogenous variables are statistically significant.

Market growth rate is positively associated with promotional intensity and market share instability, as expected. This variable represents an incentive to enter, and the positive association with instability reveals that entry does indeed occur. In reaction to this, firms attempt to raise entry barriers by increasing promotional outlays. The increased promotional activity may also be due to the efforts of new entrants to penetrate the market by extensive advertising of their own. Faster-growing markets do not tend to be less concentrated or have lower prices than mature markets.

Market size reveals the same strong quadratic effect on all the dependent variables. Larger markets tend to be more concentrated, contrary to our expectations, to be more unstable, as expected, and to have higher promotional outlays and prices than smaller markets. The higher prices may be the result of the higher costs incurred by the promotional activities, or they may reflect the higher barriers to entry

---

[10] U.S. Department of Health, Education and Welfare, Food and Drug Administration, Bureau of Drugs, Office of Scientific Coordination, *National Drug Code Directory* (Washington, D.C., 1971); *Physicians' Desk Reference to Pharmaceutical Specialties and Biologicals*, 25th ed. (Oradell, N.J.: Medical Economics, 1970); Charles D. Wilson and Tony E. Jones, *American Drug Index, 1971* (Philadelphia: J. B. Lippincott, 1971); *Drug Topics Red Book* (Oradell, N.J.: Topics Publishing Co., 1971); Arthur J. Lewis, ed., *Modern Drug Encyclopedia and Therapeutic Index*, 11th ed. (New York: Reuben H. Donnelley, 1970).

[11] Paul G. Stecher, ed., *The Merck Index*, 8th ed. (Rahway, N.J.: Merck & Co., 1968).

[12] Paul de Haen, *de Haen New Product Survey* (New York: Paul de Haen, 1971, 1972), vols. 17, 18.

TABLE 2: Elasticity Estimates

Explanatory Variable	Concentration[a]	Market Share Instability[a]	Promotional Intensity[a]	Average Rx Price[a]
Market growth rate	−0.007	0.088[b]	0.079[b]	0.003
Market size	−0.211[b]	−0.203[b]	−0.160[b]	−0.062[b]
Square of market size	0.067[b]	0.066[b]	0.054[b]	0.030[b]
Patent coverage	0.059[c]	−0.103[b]	−0.001	0.095[b]
Generic-name coverage	−0.080[b]	−0.052[b]	−0.084[b]	−0.009[b]
Innovation	0.002	0.044[b]	0.031[b]	0.004[b]
Lagged innovation	0.011[b]	0.002	−0.001	0.006[b]
Imitation	0.013[b]	0.222[b]	0.019[b]	−0.001
Lagged imitation	0.003	0.001	−0.001	0.003
Diversification	0.356[b]	−0.189[c]	−0.494[b]	0.130[b]
Long-term maintenance drug type	0.038[b]	0.012	0.091[b]	0.019[b]
Annual dummy, 1963[d]	(0.012)	(0.023)	(−0.063)	(0.039)
Annual dummy, 1964[d]	(0.012)	(−0.008)	(−0.029)	(0.069)
Annual dummy, 1965[d]	(0.003)	(−0.023)	(−0.152)	(0.098)
Annual dummy, 1966[d]	(0.013)	(−0.009)	(−0.176)	(0.176)
Annual dummy, 1967[d]	(0.024) F =	(−0.014) F =	(−0.198) F =	(0.157) F =
Annual dummy, 1968[d]	(0.029) 0.398	(−0.005) 2.145[b]	(−0.244) 7.041[b]	(0.221) 5.657[b]
Annual dummy, 1969[d]	(0.032)	(−0.040)	(−0.264)	(0.293)
Annual dummy, 1970[d]	(0.032)	(−0.033)	(−0.347)	(0.395)
Annual dummy, 1971[d]	(0.036)	(0.016)	(−0.419)	(0.449)
(Constant)[d]	(0.177)	(0.211)	(0.918)	(1.211)
$\bar{R}^2$	0.176	0.752	0.276	0.160
F	7.707[b]	96.280[b]	13.015[b]	6.985[b]
n	631	631	631	631

[a] Calculated at sample means.　[b] $p < 0.05$.　[c] $p < 0.10$.　[d] Regression coefficients reported.

163

revealed by concentration levels. This unexpected relationship between concentration and market size suggests that future research should be directed at attempting to distinguish the character of competition in very large and very small markets. One possibility is that the large, innovative drug firms concentrate their activities in the larger markets, where they are successful in creating oligopolistic structures, whereas the smaller markets are left to the smaller firms with less market power. These results are quite contrary to those presented by Reekie for the Dutch pharmaceutical industry (see Reekie's tables 3 and 4).

Patent coverage is associated with increased concentration, stability, and prices, as expected. Because nearly all patented products are sold with brand names, the generic-name-coverage variable probably picks up this effect in the promotional intensity equation. These results confirm the importance of patents in determining the structure and behavior of the pharmaceutical industry.

Generic-name coverage is associated with reduced concentration, promotion, and prices, as expected. We did not expect to find that an increased role for generics in the market leads to greater stability. Perhaps generic drugs become important only after an innovative race has cooled off and standard drugs begin to come off patents. Again, this is an issue requiring further research.

Introduction of innovative new products is associated with increased concentration, instability, promotion, and prices, as expected. In this case, even though possession of an innovation raises barriers to entry, the firm will increase promotional outlays because the innovation increases the expected returns to those outlays.[13] These results confirm the picture of "innovational" rivalry that has been used to characterize the pharmaceutical industry.

Imitation is positively associated with concentration, which leads to the question whether large firms are the successful imitators or firms select concentrated markets to embark on an imitative strategy. That such a strategy is successful is shown by its large and significant association with market share instability. It appears to have little impact on prices but is associated with an increase in promotional activity in the market.

In a somewhat surprising result, diversification turns out to be one of the most important variables in the model. It is associated with increased concentration, stability, and prices and with decreased promotional intensity. Markets characterized by large, diversified leaders tend to be more rigid and oligopolistic in structure. These results, cou-

---

[13] Marc Nerlove and Kenneth J. Arrow, "Optimal Advertising Policy under Dynamic Conditions," *Economica*, vol. 29 (May 1962), p. 141.

pled with those of Vernon and Grabowski showing that innovation is becoming concentrated in the larger firms,[14] suggest that research ought to focus specifically on the competitiveness of the largest pharmaceutical firms.

Long-term drug markets are characterized by higher promotional intensity than short-term drug markets, as expected. Long-term markets tend to have higher prices and concentration levels than short-term markets, however.

The annual dummy variables show that there has not been a statistically significant increase in concentration over time in the wholesale-retail sector. Reflecting a general inflationary trend in the economy, average prescription prices have been increasing over time. Promotional intensity reveals a downward trend from 1962 through 1971. This may reflect a decrease in the effectiveness of advertising because of greater scrutiny of the content of drug advertising by the Food and Drug Administration. Statistically significant changes in market share instability have occurred over time, but no consistent pattern emerges.

Conclusions

These results are very frustrating because they only hint at the complexity of the competitive processes in this industry. Patent coverage, generic-name coverage, innovation, imitation, and diversification should all be included as endogenous variables in the model, in order to tease out the cause-and-effect relationships. The findings presented above illustrate the need for greater complexity in our models of the pharmaceutical industry.

The strong role of diversification suggests that we should look very carefully at the nature and determinants of competition at the top of each therapeutic market, especially the larger markets.

Our model confirms the importance of innovational rivalry among drug firms, but it shows that such factors as market size and rate of growth also need to be taken into account.

We have not discussed the impact of regulation on market structure and conduct except in passing, mostly because regulation is such a difficult concept to measure. The 1962 drug amendments constituted a significant addition to the set of regulatory constraints on the industry. Their implementation has been gradual, however, and it is nearly impossible to sort out the effects of the regulations from other contemporaneous events. If there are any effects, they are probably captured

---

[14] Henry G. Grabowski and John M. Vernon, "Consumer Protection Regulation in Ethical Drugs," *American Economic Review*, vol. 67 (February 1977), pp. 359–64.

by the annual dummy variables, but there are too many difficulties in interpreting these variables as a measure of regulatory impact.

One important direction for future research is to estimate dynamic models of market shares at the individual firm level within specific therapeutic markets. These estimates, coupled with greater information on the strategies of each firm, may enable us to build a better foundation for formulating and evaluating public policy toward the drug industry.

Leonard Schifrin

Over the years, the continuing discourse on the economics of the prescription drug industry certainly has broadened and deepened our understanding of the issues involved. We have made great strides in our comprehension of the industry's operations and of the effects of many of the variables in the institutional setting on those operations. To be sure, many controversies remain, and numerous hypotheses are not yet fully tested, but we make progress. As a result, both critics and defenders of the industry find the area of agreement growing larger and firmer. As a case in point, I find myself agreeing with Professor Statman's conclusion that increases in the "effective" patent life (as opposed to the "statutory" or "nominal" patent life) of drugs, perhaps to seventeen years, would increase the returns to drug research and development (R&D), thereby stimulating R&D and, in turn, new drug innovation.

Although I am favorably inclined toward that conclusion, I do not think Professor Statman has built an acceptably strong empirical foundation in support of it. In fact, his policy proposal seems to be quite opposite to the thrust of his empirical work. He states quite strongly at one point that drugs protected by a patent are able to hold onto their market positions beyond patent expiration. If patent expiration does not erode market share, what would a longer effective patent life accomplish? What would it need to protect against or compensate for?

To reconcile this contradiction in his work, I argue that Statman's policy recommendation of a longer patent life or some alternative is plausible because he is *incorrect* in his generalization that significant postpatent market erosion does not occur. At the very least, he has failed to present suitable evidence in support of his puzzling (in view of his conclusions) contention that it does not occur; more likely, he has misread the actual experience.

Statman emphasizes that, regardless of where one looks, effective market responses to price differentials are lacking after patent expiration, as exemplified in the cases of reserpine and ampicillin. Thus, the postpatent entry of cheaper products, he contends, has little effect on product selection.

Let us take a closer look at the ampicillin data in Statman's table 2 to see if that conclusion is supported. Here we see Bristol with both the highest-priced product and the largest slice of the market for the eight brands. If we look more carefully at the data, however, particularly at those firms charging less than the midrange price, $2.04, we see that those firms below the midrange price together account for about 60–65 percent of dollar sales; and because those firms charge a lower per-unit price, their share of the market, as measured by total unit sales, is larger still. (In fact, all of Statman's market share data, based as they are on sales dollar totals rather than on physical units, overstate the relative market shares of the higher-priced product at the expense of the shares held by the lower-priced products.)

Further, the frequency of generic prescribing has increased substantially and continues to do so; yet many generic prescriptions are filled with trade-name specialty products even when multisource generics are available. Thus, market share data, even when corrected by conversion to unit terms, understate the physician's acceptance of the postpatent generic entrant. Further, Statman ignores the encroachment of any combination drugs containing the patent-expired drug.

Statman cites and accepts the contention of large firms that the continued dominance of the patented product that he observes is due to the fact that generic drugs are of inferior quality. David Schwartzman, I might add, has presented some compelling analyses in that regard.[1] As noted above, however, there are strong countercurrents challenging that position: an increasing proportion of the prescriptions of private physicians are in generic terms, and an increasing share of these prescriptions is being filled with generic products. The formulary concept, both in the hospital and in third-party payment programs, is expanding. A new category of product, the "branded generic," has become increasingly common. I find all these to constitute strong practical evidence that Statman has overstated the continuing dominance of the patented item into the postpatent period.

The third argument, or at least an expression of skepticism about Statman's empirical data, is directed toward the twelve drugs listed in his table 3. The data in his tables 4 and 5 show the postpatent share change for these twelve drugs in the drugstore market and in the hospital market, respectively. These are the essential data of the study; I have indicated earlier, however, that they are seriously flawed at the outset

---

[1] David Schwartzman, *Innovation in the Pharmaceutical Industry* (Baltimore: Johns Hopkins University Press, 1976), chap. 11.

because they use dollar sales rather than unit sales as measures of market share. Here, I would like to raise some questions about these data and the lack of market-entry impact they display.

1. For all twelve drugs, was entry accessible upon the expiration of the single patent listed for each in Statman's table 3? In my reading about drug patents, I find that rarely does only one patent control the market gateway. For this to be so, and for all twelve listed, seems not quite plausible. Perhaps, then, the expiration of one patent was not sufficient to generate market entry.

2. To what extent does a drug lag, at this point, work to the advantage of the original patent holder by delaying the firms seeking to market a follow-on product? Admittedly, it may not be a long lag, but I think we might include it in the consideration. In other words, is Statman using too brief a postpatent time period to test the market entry thesis?

3. In the same vein, to what extent is there a practical introduction lag for follow-on drugs resulting from the need to make the products widely available in the distributional system, from the need to inform institutional purchasers and retailers of their availability, or from the delays in purchases due to the existence of contracts for year-long requirements? These are questions that need answers before we can assign meaning to the postpatent market share data, even after their correction to unit sales.

Even with all the impediments to effective market entry, we do see some evidence even in Statman's data that the expected market effects occur. We see market erosion in years 2 and 3 in the hospital market for Librium and Darvon. By implication, we would expect to see similar responses whenever the constraints against price sensitivity and product selection are weakened, particularly for those drugs that represent large outlays by purchasers. Thus, it is clear from my remarks that Statman's evidence can be read in ways that support a different interpretation than he has given it, yet one compatible with his conclusions. I suggest that, taking into account the qualifications above, there is enough of an observed response to patent expiration to warrant the inference that this response is strong and is likely to continue to grow considerably and to accelerate dramatically if certain institutional changes are made in the drug selection, distribution, and payment systems.

Further, we must recognize that the factors contributing to a shorter effective patent life include more than the Food and Drug Administration (FDA) regulations. To the extent the Patent Office improves the efficiency of processing patent applications, the drug industry is hurt, since more of the patent life is used up while the FDA clearance process is under way. Neil Pettinga of Eli Lilly has spoken of the development of new tests for drug effects, tests that did not exist before and that drug developers, even in the absence of requirements to do so, would pursue.[2] Steven Wiggins's comments herein reinforce Pettinga's earlier observations.[3]

Lags, to the extent that they affect follow-on drugs, extend the effective patent life. Delays in the FDA approval process, expedience in the Patent Office, and advances in testing methods shorten it. In many cases, the dynamism of discovery and the product turnover it creates make the length of the patent life irrelevant. We need to know the extent of all these qualifications before we can say with accuracy what the effects would be of the Federal Trade Commission's model substitution law or of any other institutional change in the prescription setting. Nonetheless, there is ample evidence to support Statman's contention that the effective patent life of drugs has declined, although I have contended that his own postpatent evidence seems to argue somewhat against the acceptance of that conclusion. I think that it is more plausible to hold that the effective patent life has declined because an increasing proportion of that life has expired before the drug comes to market, and the firm *cannot* extend it beyond patent expiration, Statman's evidence notwithstanding.

To prevent the curtailment of R&D that may result, I would protect the patent period from such erosion and even extend it, but I would not lose sight of the fact that the opportunities for price competition do not necessarily have to be sacrificed to protect the potential returns to R&D.

These opportunities for competition loom large and would be socially beneficial if developed. I suggest, as I have before, that a rational policy alternative would be to implement a protected patent life of two parts: first, a fairly short postintroductory period, permitting exclusive patent utilization, followed by a second, rather long period of continuing patent protection but with compulsory licensing at a profitable royalty rate. This policy would be particularly beneficial to consumers when combined with strong efforts to provide useful information about alternative products and to ensure product quality in the marketplace.

This dual-phase patent can easily be envisioned as simultaneously generating lower market prices for drug products, beginning in the second stage of the patent, and higher total returns to industry-financed R&D. I will not go into the rate-of-return issue raised by Statman—it is very complex, and much has been said about it—but that rate of

---

[2] Neil Pettinga's discussion in Joseph D. Cooper, ed., *Regulation, Economics, and Pharmaceutical Innovation*, Proceedings of the Second Seminar on Pharmaceutical Public Policy Issues (Washington, D.C.: The American University, 1976), p. 288.

[3] Steven N. Wiggins, "The Pharmaceutical Research and Development Decision Process," herein. See also the comments by Louis Lasagna in the discussion in part 6.

return, whatever it is, may well be raised by the policy recommendations I suggest here. I believe that the goals of more competitive prices and increased R&D profitability are compatible. There may possibly be trade-offs between them when we are choosing among different optimal solutions, but we can, at this point, come closer to both these goals by moving from our decidedly suboptimal position in the direction of optimality.

PART
FOUR

The Economics of Drug Choice

Physician Prescribing Behavior: Is There Learning by Doing?

Peter Temin

Despite the importance of prescribing patterns by physicans, surprisingly little is known about them. Miller's extensive survey of the literature dealt almost entirely with articles describing how doctors reported gathering information or how doctors evaluated the prescribing patterns of others.[1] The main study that discussed actual behavior of physicians dealt only with the diffusion of a new drug.[2] This paper uses market data from IMS America to describe some important aspects of actual prescribing behavior.

Method

The data are drawn from two samples of physicians' behavior collected by IMS America. The first sample is IMS's Audatrex: "A panel of approximately 700 physicians across the nation provides IMS with actual copies of each prescription written."[3] The sample includes doctors from six specialties: general or family practitioners, internists, obstetricians/gynecologists, pediatricians, psychiatrists, and dermatologists. Data from only the first four specialties are used here.

The sample includes doctors from varied locations within the United States and doctors who exhibit a wide variety of prescribing frequency (see figure 1). It is hard to know whether the sample is random with respect to the variable analyzed here because the physicians' willingness to be included in the sample may be correlated with this aspect of their behavior. There is no reason to expect such a correlation and no comparable body of data collected on an alternative basis with which to test for its presence.

This research was supported by a grant from the Sloan Foundation to the Department of Economics, MIT. The market statistics appearing in tables 1–4 are copyrighted by IMS America (1976).

[1] R. R. Miller, "Prescribing Habits of Physicians: A Review of Studies on Prescribing of Drugs, Parts I–VIII," *Drug Intelligence and Clinical Pharmacology*, vol. 7 (1973), pp. 492–500, 557–64; vol. 8 (1974), pp. 81–91.

[2] J. S. Coleman, E. Katz, and H. Menzel, *Medical Innovation: A Diffusion Study* (Indianapolis: Bobbs-Merrill, 1966).

[3] IMS America, Audatrex, 1976.

FIGURE 1
DISTRIBUTION OF DOCTORS BY NUMBER OF DRUG PRODUCTS USED,
JULY 1975–JUNE 1976

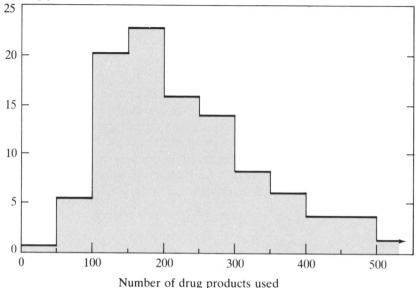

Number of drug products used

IMS was able to group the data collected from 491 doctors in the first four specialties listed above into the categories shown in table 1, where a drug product refers either to a brand of a drug or to a generic drug. That is, Achromycin and tetracycline are separate drug products, but Achromycin 250 and Achromycin 500 are not. The first column of table 1 shows the proportion of doctors in the sample who fell into each category during the year ending June 30, 1976. This frequency distribution is graphed in figure 1. The second column of table 1, also reported by IMS, shows the average number of new prescriptions (as opposed to refills) per doctor. That is, it shows the total number of new prescriptions written by doctors in the appropriate class divided by the number of doctors in that class. Unfortunately, the number of new prescriptions written is not available on an individual basis.

From these data, I derived the average number of new prescriptions of each drug product per doctor shown in column 3 of table 1 as follows. The average number of new prescriptions per doctor in each class needed to be divided by the average number of different drug products used by doctors in that class. Without direct observation of the latter data, such data had to be estimated. The method was to approximate the discrete distribution shown in figure 1 by a continuous distribution by minimizing

TABLE 1

AVERAGE NUMBER OF DRUG PRODUCTS USED AND NEW
PRESCRIPTIONS WRITTEN PER DOCTOR,
(JULY 1975 THROUGH JUNE 1976)

Number of Drug Products Used	Percentage of Doctors Using This Number of Drug Products (1)	Average Number of New Prescriptions per Doctor (2)	Average Number of New Prescriptions of Each Drug Product per Doctor (3)	Possible Range of Average in Column (3) (4)
1–50	0.8	305	8	—
51–100	5.7	832	10	8–16
101–150	20.4	1,500	12	10–15
151–200	23.0	1,664	10	8–11
201–250	16.1	2,240	10	9–11
251–300	14.1	3,226	12	11–13
301–350	8.4	3,692	11	11–12
351–400	6.3	5,299	14	13–15
401–500	3.9	5,924	13	12–15
501+	1.4	11,095	20	—

SOURCE: IMS America.

the sum of squared deviations between the observed distribution (shown in figure 1) and a hypothesized gamma distribution. Given the parameters of the best-fitting gamma distribution, conditional means of this distribution were derived for each interval shown in table 1. Then the entries in column 2 of table 1 were divided by these conditional means to get column 3.

The same data are shown in table 2, where doctors are grouped by specialty rather than prescribing frequency. (The final entry in table 2 is the weighted average of the entries in column 3 of table 1). Various subsets of these data are shown in table 3, which was derived by the same methods as the preceding tables.

The second sample is IMS's National Disease and Therapeutic Index (NDTI). These data are drawn from a representative sample of over 1,500 physicians who report four times a year on a forty-eight-hour period of their practice. The panel includes doctors from forty-eight states and from all physician specialties engaged primarily in private, office-based practice. The information collected includes both a diagnosis and a report of any drug used in each case. The primary use, of course, is in prescriptions, but the data also include hospital orders of

TABLE 2

USE OF SINGLE DRUG PRODUCTS PER DOCTOR, BY TYPE OF
MEDICAL SPECIALTY, 1976

Specialty	Size of Sample	Times/Year
General practice	187	12
Internal medicine	140	7
Obstetrics/gynecology	98	10
Pediatrics	66	18
Dermatology	55	23
Psychiatry	51	10
Total[a]	491	11

[a] Excluding dermatology and psychiatry.
SOURCE: IMS America, Audatrex, 1976.

TABLE 3

USE OF VARIOUS TYPES OF SINGLE DRUG PRODUCTS PER DOCTOR,
BY DRUG AND MEDICAL SPECIALTY, 1976

Drug	Medical Specialty	Size of Sample	Times/Year
Tetracyclines	All doctors	505	34
Antigout	All doctors	340	4[a]
Oral diabetics	General practitioners	181	7
Oral diabetics	Internists	132	5
Antidepressants	Psychiatrists	46	17
Antidepressants	General practitioners	186	9
Antidepressants	Internists	140	7
Antidepressants	Obstetricians/gynecologists	79	4
Antidepressants	Pediatricians	59	7

NOTE: The frequency of use is for doctors who used the drug type listed at least once during the year.
[a] 1974.
SOURCE: IMS America, Audatrex, 1974, 1976.

privately practicing physicians in office-based practice, office adminis-
trations, dispensation by doctors, and doctors' recommendations. The
data shown in table 4 were taken from a computer sort of the NDTI
data for 1976 by IMS.

Results

The Audatrex data show that doctors average only about a dozen new
prescriptions a year for each drug product used (see column 3 of table

TABLE 4
SHARE OF VARIOUS DRUGS DESIGNATED FOR THE SAME DISEASE, 1976
(percent)

Disease	Tetracyclines	Chloramphenicols	Cephalosporins	Erythromycins	Ampicillins	Amoxicillins	Other Broad-Spectrum Antibiotics	Streptomycin	Aminoglycosides	Other Broad- to Medium-Spectrum Antibiotics	Penicillins V and VK	Penicillins G	Antistaph. Penicillins	Other Penicillins	Total
Respiratory disorders	23	a	6	17	16	5	a	a	1	2	13	16	a	—	100
Diseases of central nervous system/ sensory organs	8	1	5	12	31	12	a	a	1	1	15	13	1	—	100
Special conditions without sickness	19	2	34	5	16	1	2	a	9	3	2	4	4	—	100
Diseases of skin-cellular tissue	38	a	7	16	9	2	a	a	2	5	6	7	7	—	100
Genitourinary disorders	37	a	19	2	26	4	2	a	7	1	1	5	1	—	100
Infective/parasitic disorders	14	1	3	12	9	2	a	2	3	2	22	30	1	a	100
Digestive disorders	25	1	20	6	16	3	a	1	9	4	4	11	1	—	100
Circulatory disorders	15	a	9	12	14	2	1	1	2	1	15	24	3	—	100
Accidents and injuries	17	1	20	10	16	3	1	—	3	1	10	15	4	—	100

a Less than 1 percent.
SOURCE: IMS America, National Disease and Therapeutic Index (NDTI), 1976.

1). Doctors avail themselves of the wide variety of drugs available; they do not restrict themselves to a small number of drug products.

This conclusion does not depend on the method of estimation used. The process described above was used to avoid the assumption that the true frequency distribution approximated by the histogram of figure 1 was linear within the intervals shown. In that case, the conditional means are simply the midpoints of the intervals. Using that assumption yields the same estimates as those shown in column 3 of table 1, except for the first two rows and the final row (where the midpoint was not defined). In both cases where using the midpoint makes a difference, the estimated average number of new prescriptions per drug is brought closer to twelve.

The possible ranges of the estimates in column 3 of table 1 are given in column 4. They were derived by assuming alternately that all the doctors in each category were at one and then at the other end point of the relevant interval. With the exception of the first two ranges shown, the ranges of possible values are quite small. The overall range for all the estimates is only from eight to sixteen.

Doctors who used between 50 and 100 drug products in the year ending June 1976 wrote an average of 830 new prescriptions during the year. This is an average of only three new prescriptions (as opposed to refills) for each of 250 working days; these doctors prescribed far below the average of their colleagues. They also wrote an average of only ten new prescriptions per drug. At the other end of the spectrum, doctors who used between 400 and 500 different drug products wrote an average of almost 6,000 new prescriptions during the year, or an average of just under 24 new prescriptions on each of 250 working days. But they wrote on average only thirteen new prescriptions per drug during the year. Despite the difference in the volume of prescriptions between the two groups, the frequency with which they used any single drug product was remarkably constant. Table 1 shows that this constancy was preserved throughout almost the full range of doctors.

Although the rate of a dozen prescriptions a year is only average, deviations on one side are matched by deviations on the other. A doctor may have more extensive experience with some of the drugs he uses, but, if so, he must also have even less experience with some others. To see how this might work, consider a doctor who used 200 different drug products and wrote 2,000 new prescriptions in a year. (He was near the median doctor in table 1.) If he used 30 drugs most of the time, say, once a week, he would have used these 30 drugs in 1,500 of his new prescriptions. This would have left 500 other new prescriptions spread among 170 other drugs. Each of these other drugs therefore would have been used an average of only *three times a year*.

Tables 2 and 3 show that the results shown in table 1 are not simply a reflection of the way that table was derived. Doctors in different specialties exhibit similar patterns, although dermatologists tend to use each drug product more often and psychiatrists less often than the average. Subsets of the data also reveal the same behavior as the whole data set (see table 3).

Although tables 1 through 3 demonstrate how infrequently a doctor uses any single drug product, table 4 shows how many different drugs doctors use in similar circumstances. It shows the variety of antibiotics used in 1976 in the treatment of the diseases shown. The diseases listed are all those for which more than 1.5 percent of antibiotics were used, and no more than 5 percent of any single antibiotic class was used for a disease not listed here. The 23 in the upper left-hand corner of the table, for example, shows that tetracyclines were used 23 percent of the times when drugs were used for respiratory disorders. In the table as a whole, no single drug class contains over half the drug uses for a given disease.

The diversity revealed by table 4 is not the result of aggregation. Each classification of table 4 contains several diseases, and the diversity of that table might be the result of lumping together diseases for which different drugs are used. Such is not the case, however. No matter how finely the diseases are divided, doctors still use a wide variety of drugs for each one.

These data cannot distinguish between two types of diversity. There is no way to know if the same doctor is using different drugs for the same diseases—so that the tables reproduce the behavior of each doctor sampled—or if different doctors consistently use different drugs for the same disease. In the first case, if each doctor varies his treatment, doctors *may* be responding to differences among patients or diagnoses not shown in these tables; for example, since antibiotics are organism-specific, the dispersion of table 4 may reflect the dispersion of disease-causing microorganisms. The data do not exist to test this hypothesis or even to show if cultures were made in each case to identify the disease-causing organism.

Discussion

These results show that doctors use each different drug product (different drug or different brand of drug) an average of less than twelve times a year, or approximately once a month. They also demonstrate the variety of drugs used to treat similar diseases.

The infrequency with which doctors use each drug product means that they cannot learn about the relative merits of competing drugs and competing brands of the same drug by using them. Even if they had complete enough records to separate the patients to whom each different drug or brand of a drug had been given, it would take a very long time to accumulate a large enough sample to show significant differences. In addition, if the drugs or brands to be compared were not prescribed randomly, the results of even a large sample would be impossible to interpret.

This is not to say that doctors prescribe irrationally. If doctors cannot learn about the relative merits of competing drugs by prescribing them, it is irrational for them to try. Even if they could learn about these relative merits through use, it might not be the most efficient way of getting that information. The question is not whether doctors are or are not rational; it is how they act.

Given, then, that doctors do not learn about the relative merits of competing drugs through use, how do they choose which drug to prescribe? The data in table 4 are consistent with the view that most doctors choose drugs by adherence to medical custom. In other words, they try to replicate the customs of an appropriate reference group, as opposed to considering the possible effects of alternative actions. The diversity of prescribing patterns reveals the absence of any tight controls or indications on which drugs should be used in any given circumstances. It shows, on the one hand, that doctors have not all solved the same analytic problem and obtained the same result and, on the other hand, that no central authority has mandated a unique choice of drugs.

Again, this does not say that doctors act irrationally. Customary behavior may be the best mode of action possible under the circumstances. Where information on outcomes is hard to come by, it may be efficient to design decision processes that do not call for frequent use of these hard-to-acquire data. Customary patterns may be the best way to communicate current medical knowledge to medical practitioners in the field.

The results shown above and the inference that doctors follow customary patterns in prescribing drugs are consistent with the views expressed by other authors. The literature on the evaluation of prescribing habits, for example, emphasizes the customary nature of these habits by concentrating on the prescriptions themselves, not by asking whether the patient got well or was treated at the lowest cost. In some studies, panels of experts reviewed the medical records and ranked the prescriptions according to whether they would have acted similarly. These studies did not measure the health of the patients; they convened a "council of elders" to evaluate adherence to the group's norms, that is, to medical custom. In other studies, the doctors were ranked by the extent to which they prescribed chloramphenicol. Again, no evaluation of risks and benefits was made; doctors were ranked by their adherence to the custom of not using chloramphenicol. Both tests used data on the prescriptions themselves, not on their effects.[4]

Similarly, the classic study of new-drug adoption by Coleman, Katz, and Menzel examined the diffusion of an unnamed drug without relating this diffusion to the effectiveness of the drug.[5] No comparison with other drugs was attempted. No data were collected, therefore, that could show the impact of differential effectiveness on the rate of adoption. The authors found that the new drug diffused according to two quite distinct patterns among physicians who were and were not members of a professional community. The rate at which the new drug diffused through the relevant medical population decreased steadily when isolated doctors were examined but was maintained or even increased during the first six months among doctors integrated into a medical community. The authors explained this by reference to two processes. One involved a constant rate of adoption for each person, leading to a decreased rate for the population as a whole as fewer and fewer doctors were left to make the change. The other was analogous to an epidemic, where the risk of "infection" spread according to both who was at risk and how many "carriers" were around. The authors did not attempt to delineate the precise nature of the infection in this model.

Even if the infection consisted solely of information, the presence of this infection confirms the dominance of customary behavior in two ways. First, published information of all sorts was equally available to integrated and to unintegrated doctors. The contagion model assumes, however, that only information from colleagues increased the probability of adopting the new drug. No other information that became available increased the probability that a given doctor would adopt the new drug. Personal communication within the medical community was all-important. Second, the time period involved—six months for the epidemic model—was too short for any serious evaluation of relative therapeutic effects and drawbacks. The information being transmitted must have been about the custom itself—"I use this new drug"—and about short-term effects. Even if practicing doctors were engaged in the business of testing the relative therapeutic effects of new drugs, which

---

[4] M. H. Becker et al., "Differential Education Concerning Therapeutics and Resultant Physician Prescribing Patterns," *Journal of Medical Education*, vol. 47 (1972), pp. 118–27, and "Correlates of Physicians' Prescribing Behavior," *Inquiry*, vol. 9 (1972), pp. 30–42; T. W. Meade, "Prescribing of Chloramphenicol in General Practice," *British Medical Journal*, vol. 1 (1967), pp. 671–74; C. Muller, "Medical Review of Prescribing," *Journal of Chronic Diseases*, vol. 18 (1965), pp. 689–96; and P. D. Stolley et al., "The Relationship between Physician Characteristics and Prescribing Appropriateness," *Medical Care*, vol. 10 (1972), pp. 17–28.
[5] Coleman, Katz, and Menzel, *Medical Innovation*.

they are not, there was not enough time for them to have obtained a reasonably complete description of the drug. In particular, they could not have known whether the new drug was better or worse than its older competitors or whether it posed any long-range dangers.

The drug studied by Coleman, Katz, and Menzel was not identified, but it probably was Achromycin (tetracycline). Although Achromycin is an important drug, the benefits of switching to it from one of the two previously existing competitors noted by Coleman, Katz, and Menzel (probably Aureomycin and Terramycin) are minor in most cases.

This important study thus confirms the customary nature of prescribing habits, both by the way it formulated the question to avoid interdrug comparisons and in the conclusions it reached. The role of the medical community is critical in altering prescribing habits.

Government regulatory policy therefore must acknowledge the important function of medical customs if it is to be effective. It must take account of how customs are transmitted and how doctors are kept in touch with advances in research knowledge.

This model suggests, for example, that professional standards review organizations (PSROs) may be dysfunctional. Their method of operation is to look at the physician's behavior itself, in keeping with the customary nature of these actions. But they will tighten the hold of existing custom on medical activity, reducing its flexibility and the rapidity with which new customs can be diffused throughout the community. A more effective means of control would be to improve and verify the educational base of prescribing physicians, while leaving the doctor the freedom in any given circumstance to follow the most advanced customs of his or her community.

The Market for Research and Development: Physician Demand and Drug Company Supply

Lester G. Telser

The purpose of this paper is to explain the economic forces affecting the market for research and development of prescription drugs. This market is implicit in the more general market for pharmaceutical products, which is in turn implicit in a still more general market—the market for health. The demand for health care, recovery, and maintenance is met by various sources of supply. The demand is not absolute regardless of price; like any other economic good, the quantity of health care demanded varies inversely with its price. The willingness of buyers to pay for the care of their health furnishes an incentive for various kinds of supply response. Our society permits many ways of satisfying this demand, and these include a sector that operates in response to a profit motive—the companies that make pharmaceutical products and the distributors of these products. In addition, physicians themselves may be regarded as entrepreneurs who operate small firms motivated by the desire to maximize their net return. The health industry includes other kinds of organizations that are subject to various legal constraints and governmental controls. Many hospitals are nonprofit enterprises, though privately run, and various government agencies own and operate health care institutions.

Some would emphasize other peculiar or special aspects of the health care industry in addition to its mixed private-public nature. Third-party payment is important. The user of health services, the patient, often does not pay for them directly. Private insurance companies or government agencies may pay for some or all of the costs of health care. This aspect of the health market would seem to weaken the economic forces that govern the outcome when the buyer pays directly for the goods or services. Does the man whose dinner will be paid for through his expense account pay as much attention to its cost as the one who pays for his own dinner? Similarly, does the physician who prescribes the drugs for which he does not pay care as much about their prices as he would about the price of drugs to treat himself and for which he must pay himself?

Still other special circumstances seem to apply to the health industry. Pharmaceutical companies seek new knowledge about drugs. In general, the search for new knowledge raises some difficult problems about the nature of property rights, because it is often cheaper to copy new knowledge than to bear the cost of finding it. Thus, those who discover new knowledge may be unable to obtain remuneration for the expenses of their search. This tends to reduce the resources allocated to the search for new knowledge to the extent that the search depends on a desire for profit and not on other motives. That is to say that one who finds new knowledge cannot always regard it as a property on which he can obtain a return. A prudent person anticipating this difficulty may well decide to make his investments in areas where it is easier to protect his property. Hence, there may be less expenditure on research than society as a whole would find desirable.

We can see various ways of dealing with the economic problems of research. One way is to give the discoverer of new knowledge a temporary monopoly in the form of a patent, which confers the legal right to prevent others from using one's knowledge unless they satisfy (reasonable) demands for payment. The purpose of a patent is to restore an economic incentive as a means of remuneration to those who bear the costs of research. Simultaneously, the law requires the patent owner to make public the nature of his discovery; the intent of the law is to encourage the widespread dissemination of new knowledge while giving others an incentive to incur the costs of research.

Our society has other and different means of obtaining knowledge outside the profit-seeking business world. Nonprofit research laboratories in universities, government, and foundations are the leading examples. It is not entirely clear to me why this has come about. Some believe that this arrangement is necessary for basic research—that is, research with a very broad range of application—because the laboratory of a profit-seeking pharmaceutical company restricts its activities to a narrower range and confines itself to areas with shorter-term goals. It is also possible that pharmaceutical companies are content to have others do what they would have to do and pay for themselves. The point is that some laboratories in profit-seeking corporations are very highly regarded in the scientific world because of the high quality of their research. Hence, even on the basis of a purely pragmatic approach, it seems possible to have basic research in a business environment.

This brief survey shows that the health care industry has many entities that operate under incentives other than profit maximization. It is likely that government regulation, control, and operation in this industry will increase. The government will finance a larger share of health care costs, and a smaller share of the health insurance industry will remain in the private sector. Physicians may find themselves the employees of the government, as they are in many countries at this time. Many prescription drugs now have price ceilings, and there are more to come. One must be aware of these trends to form a valid judgment about an economic analysis of the health industry that emphasizes the ways in which it closely resembles other industries. I shall focus on those traits that the health industry has in common with other industries.

Economic theory can apply to the health care industry without the necessity of invoking special assumptions about its peculiar nature. As we shall see, such an analysis, drawing on propositions of general validity, reveals much about the economic aspects of the health care market. This paper has a narrower focus, for it concentrates on pharmaceutical drugs and studies the derived demand and supply for research and development with respect to the market for these prescription drugs.

Economic Environment of a Drug Company

The prices of drugs are the resultants of pressures in the marketplace. No drug company can choose its prices arbitrarily without regard to these market pressures and expect to survive; it must accept the prices that are appropriate for its manner of doing business. The drug prices of all companies that have an active research program are the resultant of the laws of market equilibrium. Because these companies constantly find new knowledge that results in new applications and uses of established drugs and in the introduction of new drugs better than the old ones, which, as a consequence, tend to disappear from the market, there is a constant need to furnish physicians with new information. Therefore, the drug companies create, maintain, and increase a stock of intangible capital in the form of promotional and research capital. These forms of capital do not appear among the tangible assets listed on a company's balance sheet. Of at least equal importance is intangible capital in the form of firm-specific human capital. "Firm-specific human capital" is the term used to describe the cost of training and the cost of the acquisition of knowledge in the minds of the employees of the company that is of specific value to that company. This capital cannot be transferred from one company to another. Every company has a stock of it, which is the result of accumulations of knowledge over many years. The accumulation and maintenance of this capital are costly, and the company will not incur the expense unless it expects a return large enough to compete with alternative forms of investment available to it.

The constant search for new drugs and for new ways of treating

185

illness and of maintaining health means that no established drug has a secure market. There is always the chance that a new and better therapy will replace an existing drug, no matter how successful it has been.

Research is an exploration of the unknown. By definition, the outcome is not known in advance. Consequently, it is not subject to control to the same extent as an ordinary activity. Serendipity is often important in research. People do not always find what they were looking for, and sometimes what they do find far exceeds their expectations. Failure is more common than success. The laws of probability aid our understanding of this mysterious process, but they do not explain the reasons for success and failure. These laws are compatible with differences in the skills of different researchers and with differences in the quality of the research laboratories of different companies. Calculations based on the theory of probability can aid the rational allocation of resources, but they do not explain the mechanism of research. Individual researchers need all the skill (and luck) they can command to recognize the importance of their findings and to proceed, step by step, to new discoveries. Even the best scientist cannot predict the outcome of the current search for new knowledge.

These considerations strongly affect the economics of research in the pharmaceutical industry. The successes must pay for the failures. Thus, on average over the long run, the investors in the pharmaceutical companies, the owners of these companies, can expect to receive a return commensurate with their alternative opportunities. It makes as little sense to calculate the rate of return on a successful drug as to calculate the rate of return on a winning lottery ticket.

Being able to identify its products so that the physician can recognize the brand name and the identity of the company making the drug furnishes an inducement to the drug company to invest in intangible capital. People want progress in the treatment of illness. The greater the improvement in the methods of treatment, the more they are willing to pay for the new methods. Physicians must be able to recognize and identify those companies that have successful products, so that they can prescribe the products of those companies in the belief that they are superior to those of companies that have been less successful in their research. Nor is this all. A physician may well have greater confidence in a drug made by a company with an active research program than in one that is a mere drug maker.

The product of a drug company is not merely the physical drug. It is a joint product consisting of a number of attributes, all of which the physician has come to recognize and appraise. He has definite preferences among the various drugs, based on his experience. His confidence in the drug also depends on his experience with other drugs made by the same company. This argument leads to a very important implication. Unless physicians can recognize the company with which they are dealing, which branding makes possible, they cannot use the knowledge about various drugs and drug makers that results from their practice— their experience in treating patients.

Branding is important because it protects the property rights in the intangible capital of a drug company. This intangible capital rests on a foundation of knowledge that is costly to acquire and to maintain. The presence of intangible capital does not imply the absence of competition in the pharmaceutical industry. On the contrary, the ability to identify the products of a drug company fosters competition with respect to the search for new products. The company can then provide physicians and their patients with the types of products they want. Competition has many dimensions. Competition with respect to price for a set of homogeneous products is only one special and simple form, more a convenience for the writer of elementary textbooks in economics than a useful description of what happens in reality. Designing a product that people will want and are willing to buy is also an important avenue of competition. Identification of a company's product enables a demand to express itself for the intangible capital of the company.

A drug company chooses what kind of company it wants to be and what kinds of products it wants to offer. This choice involves not only the physical attributes of the product but also the research and promotional capital per unit of the product. Once the company has made its decision in view of its comparative advantages, its special skills, and its previous experience, market forces determine the prices of its products. This is because there are many companies that can make similar choices and because physicians can choose among them according to which gives the greatest benefit per dollar. We may expect that prices are higher, the larger the quantity of research and promotional capital that is furnished jointly with the physical product. This is a special case of the more general problem of overhead cost. The price that any customer of a firm pays for the product includes a contribution to the overhead cost of the firm. This overhead cost is common to all units of the product that the firm makes, and it does not depend on the actual quantity that a given customer happens to buy. In a sense this overhead cost resembles a semiprivate good because all who buy the products of the firm obtain a benefit of this semiprivate good that may be independent of how many units they buy. These fixed inputs yield a benefit to the customers; for instance, they include machines that enable production to occur at a lower total cost. It is not merely the actual materials in the physical product—their cost does depend on the number of units bought—that affects the equilibrium price; all customers share the overhead cost of the firm.

The research and promotion capital is not specific to a given therapeutic category. There is a derived demand for research. Costs alone do not determine the price. The equilibrium price is a resultant of the forces of both demand and supply. Costs affect the supply conditions, which are part of the total picture. The demand for drugs, which is derived from the demand for health, gives the other blade of the scissors determining the equilibrium price. The theory of derived demand asserts that the quantity demanded of a product is such that the value of its marginal product equals the price of the product. In this case, the marginal product of a drug is its contribution to the health of the patient. The standard theory of derived demand illuminates the nature of the factors that affect the shape of the demand for drugs. This theory, in conjunction with those considerations that are pertinent to the market for pharmaceutical drugs, furnishes a framework of analysis with which to study the equilibrium prices of drugs.

The Market for Prescription Drugs

The prices of drugs depend on the same kinds of factors that determine prices of all goods in the economy, namely, supply and demand. The supply factors represent the behavior of the sellers, and the demand factors the behavior of the buyers. This section examines in detail how these factors determine the prices of prescription drugs.

Participants in the market and, sometimes, outside observers cannot always see how the laws of economics can explain what happens. To the participants in the market, the direct determinants of prices seem to be tested rules of thumb, aphorisms, old customs, and special features of their industry. Economic analysis looks at things differently and sometimes can give a coherent explanation of the determinants of prices that seems at odds with the direct, "common-sense" explanations.

The marketing of prescription drugs is a good example of this. The patient does not determine what drugs to buy. It is the physician who chooses the treatment and the drugs. This seems to differ from the usual situation where the customer decides for himself what to buy. Therefore, the case of prescription drugs seems to pose a special problem for economic theory because it does not resemble what many people would regard as the typical market situation. On the contrary, there are more points of similarity than of contrast between the market for prescription drugs and the market for most economic goods. It is generally true that buyers are often in the position of a doctor's patient. Buyers choose among complex products made of many components. When they select among the various products, they express a demand for the components making up the good. Often they do not know what those components are, and yet choosing among alternative goods determines a derived demand for the components. An automobile, for example, is a complicated product made of thousands of parts. The buyer of the car does not determine how it should be made. It is nevertheless possible to derive the demand for piston rings, crankshaft bearings, spark plugs, and steering wheels, which are all parts of an automobile. There is also a derived demand for all kinds of specialized workers who make these parts. There is even a derived demand for the machine tools that make the tools that make the auto parts. Economic theory can furnish a reliable guide toward understanding the properties of the derived demand for all these factors that go into making an automobile. Although the buyer of an automobile does not tell the manufacturer how to make cars or what parts to use, it is still possible to infer the properties of the demand for all the inputs going into the final product, an automobile.

The demand for drugs is related to the demand for the more general good health in the same way that the demand for automobile parts is related to the demand for automobiles. The demand for nurses is related to the demand for health in the same way that the demand for auto workers is related to the demand for autos. This is not to say that the demand for automobiles is the same as the demand for health; the two are obviously different things. The point is this: the laws of economics apply equally well to both goods. It is the theory of derived demand, describing the properties of the relation between the demand for final products and the demand for their components, that is the same in both cases. The laws of derived demand serve the useful purpose of giving a systematic description of the important factors determining the properties of the derived demands.

Economic theory has four laws of derived demand originating with Alfred Marshall and modified by Sir John Hicks. These are as follows:

I. The demand for anything is likely to be more elastic, the more readily substitutes for that thing can be obtained.
II. The demand for anything is likely to be more elastic, the more elastic is the supply of cooperative agents of production.
III. The demand for anything is likely to be more elastic, the more elastic is the demand for any further thing which it contributes to produce.
IV. The demand for anything is likely to be less elastic, the less important is the part played by the cost of that thing in the total cost of some other thing, in the production of which

it is employed, provided it is easier to substitute among final products than among inputs.[1]

Let us see how these laws of derived demand help explain the factors that affect the elasticity of demand for prescription drugs. Health is the final product. The demand for health relates the quantity of health demanded to the price per unit of health and to other factors, notably the wealth of the demanders. There is also a production function relating health as an output to quantities of the various inputs that help to recover, maintain, or improve health. We may regard this production function as a technological relation between the variables that affect health and the state of health. A person can directly control the inputs of some of these, such as his consumption of alcoholic beverages, tobacco products, and harmful addictive drugs; the nature and quantity of his food consumption; the nature of his work, how long he works, and how much he rests; the nature of his recreations; and so on. The individual cannot directly control certain other inputs, such as contact with harmful bacteria or viruses causing illness, his genetic composition, and other factors responsible for chronic bad health. The input of physicians' services is under the partial control of the consumer because he can determine to some extent how often he will visit a physician. Some inputs that affect his health and that are controllable are left by the patient to the discretion of the physician. Once a person chooses a physician, when this is possible, the amount of services of this physician and the other inputs under the control of the physician follow automatically. Certain inputs in the technical relation giving health as a function of the inputs are complements to inputs over which the patient has no control. For example, a strep infection may be thought of as a bad input in the health production function. An antibiotic is an input complementary to the strep input. If there is such a thing as a drug of choice in this case, the elasticity of substitution between the drug of choice and other drugs is very low. Hence, the law of derived demand asserts that the elasticity of the derived demand for the antibiotic that is the drug of choice for the strep infection is likely to be low. Although this is true for the class of antibiotics including the drugs of choice, it does not follow that the elasticity of demand for a given branded antibiotic of a given drug company will also be low. It may be that the elasticity of substitution among the different drugs in a given class is high. If so, the elasticity of the derived demand for any one of them will also be high. To say that there are close substitutes among certain drugs means there is a high elasticity of substitution among these drugs,

---

[1] Sir John R. Hicks, *The Theory of Wages* (London: Macmillan, 1932), p. 242.

and, consequently, the elasticity of the derived demand for one of these is likely to be high.

The second law of derived demand asserts that the more elastic is the supply of cooperative agents, the more elastic is the demand for the given thing. In the case of drugs, this means that the elasticity of demand for a given drug is higher, the more elastic the supply of the complementary inputs. The complementary inputs are those inputs that work together with the given drug in the treatment of the condition for which the drug is being used. The critical point, therefore, is that complementary input for which the supply is the least elastic. To give an extreme example, suppose there is some drug that is used in conjunction with a kidney machine and that the elasticity of supply of kidney machines is very low. It would follow that the elasticity of the derived demand for the drug that is complementary to the kidney machine would also be low. More generally, if there is some specialized health input that has an inelastic supply and that is used to treat some illness, the elasticity of demand for the inputs complementary to this specialized input will also tend to be low.

The third law of derived demand relates the demand for the final product, health, to the demand for the input to which it contributes, the drug. The less elastic is the demand for health, the less elastic are the demands for the inputs going into the production of good health. The elasticity of demand for health is a common factor, however, entering as a determinant of the elasticity of demand for all drugs and for all inputs in the production function of health as an output. Therefore, the size of the elasticity of demand for health does not explain differences among the elasticities of the derived demand for various drugs. At best, it might explain why the elasticities of derived demands for drugs are lower than the elasticities of derived demands for a whole class of other products unrelated to health.

The fourth law of derived demand is well known and most acceptable to "common sense." It requires a careful qualification. Everyone assumes that, if the total amount spent on a given input constitutes a small proportion of the total outlay on the good, the demand for that input must be inelastic. That is, the demand is inelastic for any input that is unimportant in the sense that it is a small part of the total cost of the final commodity. This assertion is incorrect for two reasons. First, although a small amount may be spent on some input, it may have close substitutes. Hence, the derived demand elasticity may nevertheless be high. Stigler gives an amusing example.[2] Suppose we classify carpenters

---

[2] George J. Stigler, *The Theory of Price* (New York: Macmillan, 1966), p. 244.

on a construction project according to their paternal grandfathers' countries of origin, so that we would have Polish carpenters, Lithuanian carpenters, Latvian carpenters, Estonian carpenters, Russian carpenters, and Finnish carpenters. The amount spent on each type of carpenter would be very small. It does not follow that the derived elasticity of demand for each type of carpenter is also small. Presumably, there is a high elasticity of substitution between, say, Estonian and Russian carpenters, so that the derived elasticity of demand for Estonian and Russian carpenters is high despite the relative unimportance of each type.

The second complication in the analysis of the effect of being unimportant is more subtle. It relates to the difference between the elasticity of demand for the final product and the elasticity of substitution among the inputs. If the elasticity of substitution among the inputs is bigger than the absolute value of the elasticity of demand for the final product, then it may well be that unimportant factors have a more elastic demand, the less important they are. This is because substitution among inputs may be easier than substitution between the final product and other final products. In fact, if the elasticity of demand for health is low, and if the elasticity of substitution among inputs is even moderately high, say on the order of 0.4, then "unimportant" drugs may have more elastic demands than "more important" drugs.

The preceding analysis concentrates on the factors that determine the shape of the derived demand for a drug. Of at least equal importance are the factors that determine the level of demand for a drug. The theory of derived demand also illuminates the factors that affect the level of demand. The derived demand for an input relies on the postulate that a given quantity and a given quality of health care are obtained by the consumer at the least total cost. Therefore, it follows that the quantity demanded of an input is at a level where the value of the marginal product of that input equals its price. Hence, given the real price of a prescription drug, the quantity demanded is higher, the higher is the value of its marginal product as a contributor to health. One implication is this: the total quantity demanded is larger, the greater the number of individuals with the condition that the drug is supposed to treat.

It is not an implication of this analysis that the price of a given drug is higher, the greater is its marginal productivity. The equilibrium price depends on both supply and demand. The marginal product of a drug affects the demand conditions. Although the marginal effectiveness of a drug may be high, the elasticity of demand for the drug facing a given producer of it may also be high. This elasticity, which takes into account competing suppliers, is more pertinent in determining the price of a drug for a given company than is the level of the marginal productivity of the drug. It is also true that the marginal productivity is generally a decreasing function of quantity. Hence a very useful drug may have a low marginal productivity in equilibrium because a large quantity of it is being used in treatment. Indeed, the decreasing marginal productivity of a drug with respect to increases in its quantity gives one of the reasons for an inverse relation between price and the quantity demanded. Given the price and the factors determining the shape of the derived demand for the drug, a manufacturer chooses an appropriate strategy.

The preceding material describes the determinants of the shape and the level of the derived demand for drugs. Two other aspects of this demand deserve attention: the identification of drugs by brand name and uncertainty about the life span of a given drug.

The use of brand names is pervasive in the economy and is hardly unique to prescription drugs. It is, accordingly, easier to understand the general theory of brand names and to apply it to drugs than to regard prescription drugs as some kind of special case. Virtually all economic goods are a bundle or a combination of attributes of which the physical attributes form only part. Even a quart of milk includes many more relevant aspects than the mere physical commodity. A buyer has no testing laboratory and so must acquire confidence in the reliability of the seller. A bad experience with one brand of milk may lead the buyer to shun it thereafter, whereas favorable experience will result in repeated purchases. Brand names help one to avoid buying the bad and to identify the good. The brand name permits easy association between the commodity and the buyer's experience with it. It is even more important when there is continuous introduction of new products and continuous disappearance of old ones. In this case, the user must acquire and store knowledge about the makers of the various goods that individually have short lives. Everyone is familiar with this phenomenon. Consider the example of books. The buyer of books learns which books give him pleasure by knowing the names of the authors and the publishers. Thus, a potential customer reasons by association. He assumes the unknown attributes of a new product are like its known attributes in the same way that the two sets of attributes are associated in the old products. For books this means that a reader who likes a book written by some author and published by some publisher has reason to believe that he will also like a new book written by the same author and published by the same firm.

This mode of reasoning, illustrated by books, is widespread. It applies to almost all economic goods, including prescription drugs. It is pertinent information for a physician to learn the name of the company making a new drug in addition to the therapeutic properties of that drug. The physician accumulates a stock of knowledge about various drug manufacturers from what he has learned in his practice. He draws inferences about the new on the basis of this past knowledge. A drug company is aware of this. It does more than furnish a physical product. It must give the physician information about itself and its past record, as well as information about the new drug. A drug is an economic good that together with its physical attributes includes a stock of knowledge by virtue of its associations. The cost of creating, maintaining, and increasing this stock of knowledge enters into the determination of the equilibrium prices of drugs.

An established drug has an uncertain life. Someone may find a better drug or a better therapy that replaces the given drug. Because some drugs may not long survive on the market or may fail soon after their introduction, whereas others may be very successful, a company relies on the laws of probability and the skill of its employees so that there is a large enough return on the successes to compensate for the loss on the failures. In equilibrium, the average return over all products and over a long period of time must give the owners of the concern a rate of return commensurate with their alternative opportunities. Otherwise, the supply will adjust until an equilibrium results. If the return is too low, the quantity supplied will contract, and prices will rise until there is a new equilibrium.

A successful drug company that currently sells widely accepted drugs knows that rival firms are eagerly searching for new products to replace the current best sellers. Therefore, no firm, no matter how great its current success, can remain secure with its present array of products. A drug company wishing to survive must compete in the search for new products to replace the old ones whose markets disappear. For this reason many pharmaceutical companies have research laboratories staffed by scientists who seek new pharmaceutical products and new therapies. These concerns invest in the acquisition of new knowledge. It is costly to acquire such new knowledge, and the firm will not bear the cost without the expectation of at least a competitive rate of return.

A convenient analogy illustrating some but not all of the pertinent issues is a lottery. The search for a successful new drug requires an outlay analogous to the purchase of a lottery ticket. Only a few tickets win prizes. It is nonsense to calculate the rate of return on a winning ticket. The relevant calculation is the expected return on a lottery ticket before the outcome is known. This expected return to a buyer of lottery tickets influences his decision about how many, if any, lottery tickets he will buy. The lower the probability of success, the larger is the size of the prize necessary to induce a purchase of the ticket. Somewhat similar considerations motivate the research outlays of the drug companies. There are, however, important differences between the purchase of lottery tickets with its attendant risks and the costs and outcomes of pharmaceutical research. The search for new knowledge is not a blind gamble. The chance of success depends on the skill of the researcher as well as on the amount spent on research. It would be useful to construct a formal theory of this process, but this task is outside the scope of the present paper.

The stock of knowledge about a pharmaceutical company—its past record, its reliability, the kinds of products it sells, their properties, and the cost of informing physicians—is a form of capital that is costly to create and maintain. The stock of knowledge is lodged in the minds of the physicians who are now in practice. New physicians begin to practice, and old ones retire. Hence, this stock of knowledge is subject to depreciation. The cost of this stock of knowledge constitutes part of the capital of the company. Its relevance for pricing lies in a different direction. This knowledge is a valuable property of the company. The brand names of the company's products identify the company in the minds of the physicians and enable them to associate their complex and varied experience with the company, its representatives, and its products. Even if two companies make the same drug with respect to physical, chemical, or biological properties, physicians may, with good reason, prefer the pharmaceutical products of one company over another because of the many attributes of the company that they associate with the drug. These attributes together with the physical product constitute the economic goods among which the physicians make their choices; for instance, physicians may have greater confidence in the quality of the controls exercised over production by a company that has an active research program. There is a presumption that the company that does more research for new drugs also makes better and more reliable existing drugs.

Costs and Prices

The preceding analysis describes some of the factors underlying the supply of and demand for prescription drugs. The demand for drugs is derived from the demand for the recovery and maintenance of health. The standard theory of derived demand yields several propositions relevant to the derived demand for prescription drugs. There is also the important point that drug companies finance research to find new ways of treating, controlling, and preventing illness. The search for new knowledge and the dissemination of new knowledge about therapeutic discoveries require an appropriate theory of equilibrium drug prices, taking these considerations into account. The task of this and the next section is to furnish such a theory.

195

At the outset there are two rival points of view about the determination of prices that require some attention. The first asserts that costs determine prices. The second asserts that the prices of competing drugs determine the price that a company can obtain for its product. Neither proposition is correct. Before we give the correct explanation, it is necessary to examine the error in these two positions.

The assertion that costs determine prices has two possible interpretations: that costs do in fact determine prices or that they should determine prices. To argue that costs do determine prices differs from the proposition that price equals unit cost or marginal cost. The equilibrium price of a given drug depends on both demand and cost conditions. According to the theory of derived demand, the quantity demanded of a given drug is such that the value of the marginal product of that drug equals its price. The marginal product depends on the nature of competing therapies and their effectiveness, complementary inputs, and all the other considerations described in the preceding section. The theory of derived demand is especially useful for explaining the determinants of demand for a new drug for which the closest competitors may not be drugs at all. Both demand and cost factors determine the equilibrium price. The equilibrium price cannot be found from a simple calculation based on cost or on a standard markup.

Some would urge that the product price should equal marginal cost because this is supposed to give the outcome under perfect competition; but the standard models of perfect competition apply under well-defined conditions that do not exist in the real world where it is costly to obtain information, so that the optimal stock of information requires an optimal amount of ignorance as well. Perfect competition assumes and requires that all participants have complete information. Equivalently, information is a free good and is therefore in abundant supply. Once the theory incorporates the effects of costly information, it must abandon one of the main premises of the standard model of perfect competition. This is especially pertinent in studying the economics of research outlays, which differ from the kind of good that is the subject matter of most theories of perfect competition. Theories of perfect competition assume given demand conditions, depending on given tastes and wealth and a given set of commodities. If old commodities disappear and new ones appear, old knowledge becomes obsolete and new knowledge is in constant demand.[3] Those responsible for treating illness, the physicians, must constantly acquire new knowledge about new pharmaceutical prod-

---

[3] For a discussion of conditions of perfect competition, see Frank H. Knight, *Risk, Uncertainty, and Profit* (Boston: Houghton Mifflin, 1921), pp. 76–81. See also Edward H. Chamberlin, *The Theory of Monopolistic Competition* (Cambridge: Harvard University Press, 1933), chaps. 1 and 2.

ucts. This learning is costly for both the physicians and the drug companies who wish to transmit the information. For all these reasons, the standard theory of perfect competition is no useful guide to understanding the determination of equilibrium prices in the pharmaceutical industry.

Although the standard model of perfect competition fails as a useful theory of equilibrium prices in the pharmaceutical industry, the theory of monopoly is neither a better guide nor the only alternative. Competition works in the pharmaceutical industry partly by the search for and supply of new drugs. Some forms of competition in the industry do approach the kind that is the center of attention in the neoclassical theory of perfect competition. Thus, once a drug becomes well established and widely accepted, there are firms willing to make it at a price close to the marginal cost of manufacture. In some therapeutic categories it may also be true that the demand for new knowledge is small and the cost of maintaining the stock of knowledge correspondingly small. This conjunction of conditions may lead to an equilibrium price for these drugs similar to the equilibrium price of a homogeneous, well-established commodity such as copper. In other categories the demand for new knowledge may be large, and the cost of creating and maintaining a stock of knowledge is correspondingly large. In these cases the equilibrium price will reflect these factors.

None of this is to say that there is necessarily a close connection between ongoing research in a given therapeutic area and the ratio of price to unit manufacturing cost for existing drugs in this area. More subtle and complex relations are possible. A company can acquire a following of physicians willing to encourage its research. Even if some of the company's drugs are in therapeutic categories where there is little research and for which there is a small cost of maintaining knowledge, physicians may prefer and prescribe that company's drugs in this category because of their confidence in the value of the company's research. Some physicians may choose to prescribe somewhat more expensive drugs offered by some companies in a given category although cheaper versions are available from other companies because these physicians believe that the more expensive drugs represent a better economic good than the cheaper drugs. This is to say that there is a demand for a joint product consisting of the given drug itself and of all of the other services, including research and promotion, furnished by the pharmaceutical company.

This argument seems to overlook the possibility of freeloaders. The research outlays of a drug company do not directly relate to the quantity of drugs it produces. These outlays are part of its overhead cost. Similarly, much of its plant and equipment does not directly relate to its current rate of production; it is also part of its overhead cost. It would be possible for buyers to drive a hard bargain with a company when overall demand is low such that the price covers short-run marginal cost and is high enough to recover short-run variable cost, thereby leaving the company with little or no contribution to its overhead cost. A company cannot survive under these conditions unless its price is substantially above average variable cost during times of high levels of demand so that on average it obtains enough revenue to cover total cost. It is an implication of this process that prices would vary and would be sharply higher when demand is high and lower when demand is low. In this case one may describe the situation by saying that the drug price is like a spot price for a commodity that moves up and down in accord with short-run conditions and on average is consistent with a long-run equilibrium.

Another mode of attaining an equilibrium is possible that will lead to a price equal to long-run marginal cost and high enough to support an equilibrium rate of output. This price corresponds to a long-term contract between the drug company and the physicians such that the price does not rise when the demand increases or fall when the demand decreases. This price may be lower than the average of the spot prices that would prevail if there were frequent adjustment to short-term conditions. Without such a policy of setting a price consistent with long-term conditions, it may not be possible to support an equilibrium that will lead to total production at the least total cost and to outlays in research and development.

Provided there are enough physicians who are aware of the long-run implications of a company's research and development strategy, it will be possible to have an equilibrium with a stable price. Such an equilibrium represents an outcome consistent with rational expectations by the physicians because they know that the purchase of the cheapest drugs, when temporary conditions allow it, may extinguish the alternative of having new drugs in the long run that are the fruit of research and development. Although buying the lower-priced drugs gives a temporary gain with respect to the more expensive varieties, the present value of the benefit to the physicians and their patients is higher if they buy the higher-priced drugs of the companies who have active research and development programs. The validity of this argument does not depend on altruism on the part of physicians. It depends on their selfish interest and on the assumption that they are intelligent enough to recognize the outcome that is best for themselves and their patients in the long run.

The long-run marginal cost of a research-oriented pharmaceutical company is difficult to calculate ex ante. The component of total cost depending on manufacturing is more readily estimated. Some costs vary with changes in the current output rate; they include the costs of raw materials and some of the labor cost. Other costs vary closely with long-term output rates and only slightly with current output rates. Research and development costs affect the long-term output of a research-oriented company because it does not produce a given set of products. It produces new products that result from its search for new knowledge. Based on this expectation, there is a demand for its current products at a price that covers the cost of its long-term strategy as a property of equilibrium.

A company must accept and cannot affect the equilibrium price, which depends on the kind of joint product that it offers. The success and the very survival of the company depend on how well it responds to market forces. The prices of all drugs are jointly the result of a common set of forces. Hence, they may change in response to these common forces. This, however, is not the same as saying that the prices of the products of one company depend on the prices of other companies' products. It may seem to the management of a company that its prices must depend on the prices of competing products. The relations among prices of competing products, however, depend on the underlying cost and demand factors. It is not possible for one company to choose its prices arbitrarily or to set arbitrarily the relation between its prices and the prices of competing drugs. The price relations among the drugs are the outcome of market forces. One company cannot simultaneously choose its prices and the quantities that it wishes to sell. The topic of the next section is an account of the theory of equilibrium prices under these conditions.

A Formal Theory of Equilibrium Prices

To give precision to the preceding arguments requires a formal theory on the basis of optimal outlays on research and promotion. One of the important features of this theory is to show how such outlays are consistent with competition. This is a consequence of the nature of the demand facing a research-oriented company that makes, promotes, and sells prescription drugs. To simplify the argument and without loss of generality, we may assume that the company makes and sells two kinds of drugs.

We begin with a preliminary statement about those aspects of research outlays that are relevant for our purposes. Research often takes a long time before the outcome becomes known. It is not only the current outlays on research that are pertinent. It is also the accumulation of knowledge that is a form of economic capital resulting from a long-term program of research. The validity of this view is well established by the empirical work of many economists on research outlays and on other forms of intangible capital that finance an accumulation of knowledge for the firm.[4] This intangible capital results from promotional outlays and from the training and experience of the company's employees. The research capital of the firm, the accumulation of its knowledge about pharmacology, indirectly affects the nature of the demand for the products of the company. This holds even if only the current outlay on research affects demand; that is, the argument applies even if there is a 100 percent rate of depreciation of research capital. The true rate of depreciation is probably far below 100 percent, and it is plausible to believe that it is on the order of 5–10 percent. These estimates rely on the proposition that the stock of knowledge depreciates at a rate that is related to the separation rates of certain classes of a company's employees. In the first instance, research knowledge comes from the minds of the research workers. Some of this knowledge disappears when the research worker leaves the company. Some research findings are forgotten. Some findings are in error or become obsolete. There can be no complete record available to the company of all of the pertinent knowledge in the mind of a scientist who acquires this knowledge by his direct experience. It is necessary to communicate knowledge from the discoverer to others, which is an imperfect process. On occasion it is literally true that previous findings are forgotten or lost and are rediscovered independently later. This is true, for instance, of DDT. Some knowledge becomes obsolete owing to new findings, and some old knowledge becomes more valuable for the same reason. With rapid scientific progress, with forgetting, and with the departure of scientists, there is some loss of knowledge. This is why there is a rate of depreciation of the stock of knowledge.

One type of estimate of the cost of accumulated knowledge resulting from outlays on research and development assumes a constant rate of retention, δ, so that $1 - \delta$ is the rate of depreciation. If the research capital did not depreciate, the retention rate would be 1. If there were no retention, the depreciation rate would be 1, so that δ would be 0. Let r_t denote the outlays on research and development during year t. The capital resulting from these outlays is given by the expression that follows:

$$R_t = \Sigma_{i=0}^{i=\infty} \delta^i r_{t-i} \qquad (1)$$

---

[4] See Kenneth W. Clarkson, *Intangible Capital and Rates of Return* (Washington, D.C.: American Enterprise Institute, 1977), and the references cited therein. Implications of the capital aspects of promotional capital and their effects on entry are discussed in Lester G. Telser et al., "The Theory of Supply with Applications to the Ethical Pharmaceutical Industry," *Journal of Law and Economics*, vol. 18 (October 1975), pp. 449–78.

This expression is equivalent to the simpler version, as follows:

$$R_t = r_t + \delta R_{t-1} \tag{2}$$

The research capital at the end of period t equals the outlay on research during that period, which is r_t, plus the research capital retained from the preceding period, which is the fraction δ of the total research capital of the preceding period. It is an immediate implication of equation (2) that $R_t = r_t$ if $\delta = 0$. With $\delta = 1$, R_t would have no upper bound for any bounded sequence $[r_t]$. The subscript t serves as a reminder that the research capital can change over time. For our purposes, we may ignore this possibility and work instead with the long-run optimal stock of research capital denoted by R.

Next, consider the demand conditions. Let q_1 and q_2 denote the rate of sales of the two drug products that are the subjects of the analysis. Let p_1 and p_2 denote their respective unit prices. These are the unit prices received by the drug company that makes the two drugs. Hence, they represent the wholesale prices to the trade. The retail prices depend positively on the wholesale prices, but the drug manufacturer has no control over the retail prices. Some drug companies may suggest retail drug prices to their distributors, who are free to ignore these suggestions if they please. Retail prices of a given branded drug show considerable variation among different retail outlets. The reasons for this are outside the scope of this analysis. The wholesale price of a drug plainly exerts an indirect effect at least on the mean of the distribution of retail prices of the drug. Our present concern is with the determination of the equilibrium wholesale prices.

The use of some simple algebra is indispensable for the description of the model. The demand for drugs is a relation between the price of the drug and the quantities demanded. We may represent these by means of the two equations that follow:

$$p_1 = f_1(q_1, q_2, R) \tag{3}$$

$$p_2 = f_2(q_1, q_2, R) \tag{4}$$

The theory of derived demand for drugs gives the implication that the price of a given drug and the quantity demanded of that drug vary inversely. Therefore, p_1 and q_1 vary inversely, and so too p_2 and q_2 vary inversely. If the two drugs were substitutes, an increase in the quantity demanded of one of them would lower the quantity demanded of the other, assuming a given price of the first drug. Hence, if the two drugs were substitutes, p_1 would vary inversely with q_2, and p_2 would vary inversely with q_1. If the two drugs were complements, a rise in the quantity demanded of one drug would raise the quantity demand of the other, given the price of the first. Hence, for complements, p_1 and q_2 would vary in the same direction, and so too would p_2 and q_1. The theory is valid for both complements and substitutes. It is also possible to have independence between the two drugs, so that a change in the quantity demanded of one has no effect on the quantity demanded of the other, given the price of the first. This possibility is also consistent with and allowed by the formulation given by equations (3) and (4).

In accordance with the preceding discussion, the research capital enters as an element in the derived demand for the two prescription drugs. For given rates of sale—that is, for given values of q_1 and q_2— the argument asserts that demanders are willing to pay a higher price, the larger is the research capital of the company. Equivalently, holding prices constant, the quantities sold are increasing functions of the research capital. This does not assume that the research is necessarily directed at the same therapeutic categories containing the two products. It does not necessarily assume that the demand for research is equally strong by the physicians who prescribe these two products. Perhaps the physicians who prescribe one of them confer a greater value on research through the derived demand for the given drug than the physicians who prescribe the second. It is also possible that the derived demand for research is weak for both drugs. The formal model imposes no restrictions on these. It is an empirical and not a theoretical question to measure the effect of research capital on the demand for drugs. This model explores the consequences of the hypothesis that such a derived demand exists. Some empirical implications of the existence of such a demand, which are described below, seem consistent with the facts. This increases confidence in the theory.

So far the assumptions about the demand relations are general. The assumption that the firm is in a competitive environment places restrictions on the nature of the demand it faces. Nor is this all. The theory must also accommodate the firm's choice of what kind of product it wishes to make. Hence, the demand function must represent the twin constraints that the firm can choose what to make and yet, given this choice, the product price does not depend on how much of the product it sells.[5] The product price depends on the nature of the product, and it does not depend on the firm's rate of sales. There is a unique solution of this problem. The demand function facing the firm must be homogeneous of degree zero in the q's and in R. This means that proportional

[5] See Lester G. Telser, "Advertising and Competition," *Journal of Political Economy*, vol. 62 (December 1964), pp. 537–62; and Harold Demsetz, "Do Competition and Monopolistic Competition Differ?" *Journal of Political Economy*, vol. 76 (January/February 1968), pp. 146–48.

increases in q_1, q_2, and R do not affect the prices at which the firm can sell its products. It follows that the price per unit of the product depends on the research capital per unit. Formally, let q_1, q_2, and R increase by a positive factor α. This hypothesis about the nature of the demand facing the firm asserts that

$$p_1 = f_1(\alpha q_1, \alpha q_2, \alpha R) = f_1(q_1, q_2, R) \tag{5}$$

$$p_2 = f_2(\alpha q_1, \alpha q_2, \alpha R) = f_2(q_1, q_2, R) \tag{6}$$

Therefore, a proportional increase in q_1, q_2, and R does not affect the unit prices that demanders are willing to pay for the products. This does not say that the research capital per unit of the product is the same for all products. The ratios q_1/R and q_2/R may be different for the two products. Given these ratios, however, if it is true that these ratios remain constant as q_1 and q_2 change, it also follows that the prices p_1 and p_2 will remain constant. The demanders in this theory are assumed to want research in general and not necessarily research specifically directed at the illnesses treated by the two products in question. They are willing to pay for this research jointly with the physical products. Mathematically, we represent this assumption about the nature of their demand with functions that are homogeneous of degree zero in the q's and in R. If the company reduces its research capital per unit of product, it follows from this theory that it cannot maintain the same rate of sales of its products without lowering the prices of the products.

These assumptions about the properties of the demand relations have several additional implications. First, it follows from equations (5) and (6) that the prices of the products depend on the ratio of the research capital to the quantities sold. There is a simple way to verify this. Equations (5) and (6) are valid for all values of α. In particular, they are valid for the choice of $\alpha = 1/R$. For this choice of α, we find

$$p_1 = f_1(q_1/R, q_2/R, 1) = f_1(q_1, q_2, R) \tag{7}$$

$$p_2 = f_2(q_1/R, q_2/R, 1) = f_2(q_1, q_2, R) \tag{8}$$

Therefore, as claimed, the prices are functions of the ratios q_1/R and q_2/R. The prices do not depend on the actual quantities that the company sells. Once the company chooses the research capital per unit quantity of its products, it determines the character of its economic products, and it no longer controls its prices.

We are now in a position to appreciate the economic implications of these demand relations. They represent the demand conditions facing a firm in a competitive market in which it is free to choose the nature of the commodities that it wishes to furnish its customers. More to the point, the demand conditions represent a competitive market if and only if the demand functions facing a firm are homogeneous of degree zero in the quantities and in the research capital. Below we shall see how to incorporate the effects of promotional capital on the demand functions facing a firm.

This model has another important implication. The products of the company cannot be anonymous. The customers of the company must be capable of identifying its products. Here "customer" refers to the physicians who are the ones to decide the choice of drugs. Physicians are assumed to have preferences among different companies' products. They are not indifferent among chemically similar products that are available from different companies, even if we assume that different companies do offer chemically similar products. They want an economic good from a drug company that is a bundle of many characteristics. To gratify their demand, the company needs the power to label its product so as to distinguish it from those available from its rivals. Therefore, a competitive equilibrium requires branded drugs.[6]

A second set of important implications of this theory of demand derives from the consequences of changes in quantities and in the research capital. If the demand relations satisfy equations (5) and (6), the maintenance of a constant real price of the products requires the maintenance of a constant amount of research capital per unit quantity. This requires equality between the percentage change in research capital and the percentage change in quantity. If the percentage change in research capital is smaller than the percentage change in the quantity sold, then the price must fall. A company cannot maintain a constant real price per unit and a constant rate of sales unless it also maintains a constant amount of research capital per unit.

The preceding argument gives an empirical test of the theory. We should observe a tendency for companies to maintain their research outlays at a constant percentage of sales if prices remain constant and if the rate of depreciation of their research capital remains constant. There does seem to be a tendency for research outlays per dollar of sales to remain constant over time. This can be taken in support of the theory if it is also true that the rate of depreciation of research capital is constant over time. It would seem desirable to subject this theory to empirical testing by studying the relations among prices, quantities, and research capital over time by company.

For a company to maintain its position as a supplier of research and to maintain constant real prices for its products, it is compelled to keep

---

[6] Telser, "Advertising and Competition."

a position of balanced growth between the quantities it sells and its research capital.

It is an implication of the theory of demand given here that such behavior by the pharmaceutical companies results from the forces of competition in the industry. Once a company chooses its research posture in terms of its research capital per unit, it also determines the prices of its products. These prices do not depend on the quantities sold by the company. They do depend on the kind of products sold by the company. Once the company chooses what kinds of economic products it wishes to offer, it implicitly accepts a niche in the market and the equilibrium prices corresponding to it. A company, therefore, does not control the prices of its products. It controls the nature of its products. The equilibrium prices are an inevitable consequence of its choice of product type.

This theory has another important implication. If a company wishes to maintain a constant real price for one of its products and it chooses the policy appropriate for this goal, it also must accept the real prices of its other products for which the demands are related to that of the given product. The choice of a research posture by a company implies a set of equilibrium prices for all of its products that are related in demand and not merely for one of them. Nor is this all. The prices of these related products are the resultant of the company policy with respect to its research capital per unit of quantity. This is not to say that the same research capital per unit applies to all its products. It is perfectly consistent with this theory for the company to have different amounts of research capital per unit of product for different products. Once it chooses its various ratios of research capital per unit of product, it does implicitly accept the equilibrium prices consistent with its choice of product type. As we shall see, a similar consideration pertains to its promotional capital.

The optimal policy of a firm depends not only on the demand conditions facing it but also on the cost conditions. Given the cost conditions and the demand conditions, the company chooses its optimal quantities (a mathematical appendix gives the details). If the firm chooses well, this determines its research capital per unit of quantity, and in the resulting equilibrium it obtains a competitive return. This holds although the demand functions facing the firm are *not* infinitely elastic with respect to quantities. The hypothesis that the demand functions are homogeneous of degree zero in quantities and in the research capital does imply that the equilibrium prices are functions of the ratios q_1/R and q_2/R. These prices do not depend on the actual quantities sold, provided the ratios q_1/R and q_2/R remain constant. It is consistent with a competitive equilibrium to have prices vary inversely with quantities sold by a firm, whereas prices do not depend on quantities if the firm chooses constant ratios between q_i and R. The optimal firm policy becomes one of choosing what kinds of products it wishes to offer.

The theory embraces promotional outlays in the same way as research capital. Physicians want information about drugs. They obtain information from various sources, including the field force of the company, advertising in medical journals, direct mail from pharmaceutical companies, seminars, colleagues, and other avenues of communication through which a company sends messages to physicians. Therefore, the demand for the products of a company is an increasing function of its promotional capital. This is the capital that results from current outlays on promotion, and it is subject to depreciation as a result of changes in various conditions.

The formal analysis of promotional capital resembles that for research capital. A sequence of promotional outlays creates a component of the company's intangible capital corresponding to the stock of knowledge about its products in the minds of physicians. Because people forget, information becomes obsolete, old physicians retire, and new ones start to practice, the capital resulting from outlays on promotion is subject to decay and deterioration. Let a_t denote the outlay on promotion during period t, and let A_t denote the accumulated promotional capital at the end of period t. If the retention rate of promotional capital is δ_a, so that the depreciation rate is $1 - \delta_a$, then the promotional capital satisfies the following equation:

$$A_t = \Sigma_{i=0}^{i=\infty} \delta_a^i a_{t-i} \tag{9}$$

which is of the same form as R_t in equation (1). Also, corresponding to equation (2), there is:

$$A_t = a_t + \delta_a A_{t-1} \tag{10}$$

The demand relations incorporating both promotional and research capital become:

$$p_1 = f_1(q_1, q_2, R, A) \tag{11}$$

$$p_2 = f_2(q_1, q_2, R, A) \tag{12}$$

Let proportional changes in q_1, q_2, R, and A leave prices constant. This means that the demand functions given by equations (11) and (12) are homogeneous of degree zero in q_1, q_2, R, and A. Formally,

$$p_1 = f_1(\alpha q_1, \alpha q_2, \alpha R, \alpha A) = f_1(q_1, q_2, R, A)$$

$$p_2 = f_2(\alpha q_1, \alpha q_2, \alpha R, \alpha A) = f_2(q_1, q_2, R, A)$$

The choice of $\alpha = 1/R$, shows that the equilibrium prices facing the firm depend only on the ratios q_1/R, q_2/R, and A/R.

$$p_1 = f_1(q_1/R, q_2/R, 1, A/R) \tag{13}$$

$$p_2 = f_2(q_1/R, q_2/R, 1, A/R) \tag{14}$$

We see that the prices do not depend on the absolute quantities sold by the firm, provided the firm maintains constancy of the ratios appearing as arguments on the right-hand side of equations (13) and (14). Nevertheless, it is also true that if these ratios do not remain constant, p_i varies inversely with q_i. Once the firm chooses the ratios q_1/R, q_2/R, and A/R, the values of the prices that satisfy equations (13) and (14) are determined. The company chooses what kinds of goods it wishes to offer in terms of these ratios and has no additional degrees of freedom. It can maintain constant real prices only by maintaining constant values of these ratios. If promotional or research capital fails to keep pace with quantity sold, prices must fall. The introduction of promotional capital into the theory does not change the main conclusions of the simpler theory that considers only the effects of research capital.

This theory solves an old puzzle. Some economists claim that advertising and research allow a firm to differentiate its product, thereby creating a monopoly return.[7] Such an argument takes promotional and research outlays as prima facie evidence of monopoly. The theory of monopolistic competition is one of the formal versions of this type of argument; although it asserts that the return is competitive, it claims that there is a loss of real income owing to these attempts at product differentiation. It is not necessary to invoke monopoly to have a theory with firms that offer different products;[8] nor need there be a departure from the efficient use of economic resources in an economy with firms that offer distinguishable products. Promotional and research capital are not sources of monopoly return. Any company can offer an economic good that is a combination of research, promotion, and its physical attributes. Competition is present by means of choices of what kind of product to offer.

---

[7] The best-known exponent of these views is Bain. See Joe S. Bain, *Barriers to New Competition* (Cambridge: Harvard University Press, 1956).

[8] See Sherwin Rosen, "Hedonic Prices and Implicit Markets: Product Differentiation in Pure Competition," *Journal of Political Economy*, vol. 82 (January/February 1974), pp. 34–55.

Retail Price Data for Some Prescription Drugs No Longer on Patent

The preceding theory implies that, even in a therapeutic category where the drugs no longer have patent protection, the prices of drugs made by manufacturers with substantial research and development expenditures will exceed the prices of manufacturers that do little or no research. Such price differentials could not persist unless physicians were willing to prescribe the higher-priced drugs so that the manufacturers of these drugs could sell them in large enough quantities to cover their costs. Because it is desirable to confine attention to those prescription drugs that are now without patent protection or that never had patent protection, the sample is necessarily restricted almost entirely to antibiotics. As time passes, it will be possible to expand the sample and include other therapeutic categories, such as diuretics and ataractics. The source of the data is the price catalog of Osco, which is a chain of drugstores owned and operated by the Jewel Companies. Hence, the prices are genuine offers to sell and do not suffer from the objections that would be raised to the use of list prices. The Osco chain is a leading one in the Chicago area. Together with Walgreen's, it accounts for a substantial portion of all sales of prescription drugs in this market. The data come from catalogs available in 1974 and 1975. Hence, they precede the period when the government imposed restrictions on the prices it would pay as reimbursement to those on Medicare and similar programs. All these points should be kept in mind when studying the figures in tables 1–9. Since the data in these tables are retail, not wholesale, prices, however, they represent the effects of the price policies of Osco as well as the wholesale prices charged by the manufacturers of these drugs. In particular, because the pharmacist normally transfers the medicine from larger containers to the smaller containers required by the prescription, some of the price differentials for a given drug across prescriptions of different sizes reflect the pricing policies of the retailer, Osco, and not those of the manufacturers.

The figures in tables 1–9 speak for themselves. Observe in particular that penicillin-G, which never had patent protection, shows a large price differential between the generic and the branded items. Similar differentials exist for the other drugs. The only drug in the tables that is not an antibiotic is reserpine (table 9). Here, too, we observe a large difference between the price of the generic and the price of the branded item, which is made by Ciba, the original patent holder.

These price data are not peculiar or special. Similar price differentials appear in Schwartzman.[9] Using data from other sources, he also

[9] David Schwartzman, *Innovation in the Pharmaceutical Industry* (Baltimore: Johns Hopkins University Press, 1976), chap. 12.

TABLE 1

DIFFERENCES BETWEEN BRAND NAME AND BASE PRICES FOR
TETRACYCLINE HYDROCHLORIDE, SEPTEMBER 30, 1974
(patent expired 1972)

	Quantity at 250 mg/Capsule							
Brand	12	18	24	36	48	50	60	100
Generic (base price)	$0.89	$0.89	$0.89	$1.08	$1.44	$1.50	$1.79	$2.99
Squibb (P)	0	0	0.30	0.70	0.94	0.98	1.18	1.96
Lederle (P)	0	0.19	0.55	1.08	1.44	1.50	1.81	3.01
Robins	0.40	0.85	1.04	1.44	1.47	1.48	1.51	1.91
Roerig	0.40	0.85	1.04	1.44	1.47	1.48	1.51	1.91
Bristol (P)	0.46	0.93	1.15	1.61	1.70	1.81	1.89	2.38
Upjohn (P)	0.48	0.97	1.21	1.69	1.80	1.82	2.02	2.60

	Quantity at 500 mg/Capsule							
	12	18	24	36	48	50	60	100
Robins (base price)	$1.93	$2.52	$2.91	$3.79	$4.77	$4.90	$5.55	$8.45
Bristol	0.18	0.27	0.36	0.53	0.71	0.74	1.19	1.48
Lederle	−0.15	−0.36	−0.03	0.53	0.82	1.15	1.32	2.10

	Quantity (oz) at 125 mg/5cc Syrup							
	2	3	4	5	6	8	12	16
Generic (base price)	$1.35	$1.83	$2.05	$2.48	$2.70	$3.15	$4.15	$5.25
Roerig	0.39	0.21	0.49	0.35	0.43	0.68	1.06	1.45
Robins	0.42	0.25	0.54	0.42	0.51	0.78	1.21	1.65
Lederle	1.07	1.12	1.54	1.64	2.15	3.07	4.21	5.64
Bristol	1.19	1.31	1.79	1.95	2.53	3.58	4.96	6.65

NOTE: P = original patent holder.
SOURCE: Osco Drug, Inc., price catalog, September 30, 1974.

finds price differentials of magnitude approximately equal to those in tables 1–9, although his data refer to a broad sample of retail drugstores instead of to a single chain, and he also reports wholesale prices.

This evidence supports the belief that prices of drugs made by manufacturers who have substantial research and development programs exceed the prices of those who do not have such programs even in therapeutic categories where there never was or no longer is patent protection. This evidence is consistent with the hypothesis that there is a demand for research and development coming from the physicians and furnished by the pharmaceutical manufacturers.

TABLE 2

DIFFERENCES BETWEEN BRAND NAME AND BASE PRICES FOR TETRACYCLINE HYDROCHLORIDE, JANUARY 1975
(patent expired 1972)

Brand	Quantity at 250 mg/Capsule							
	12	18	24	36	48	50	60	100
Generic (base price)	$0.89	$0.89	$0.89	$1.08	$1.44	$1.50	$1.79	$2.99
Squibb (P)	0	0	0.30	0.70	0.94	0.98	1.18	1.96
Lederle (P)	0	0.19	0.55	1.08	1.44	1.50	1.81	3.01
Robins	0.40	0.85	1.04	1.44	1.47	1.48	1.51	1.91
Roerig	0.40	0.85	1.04	1.44	1.47	1.48	1.51	1.91
Upjohn (P)	0.48	0.97	1.21	1.69	1.80	1.82	2.02	2.60
Bristol (P)	0.77	1.03	1.49	1.81	2.07	2.10	2.23	3.25

	Quantity at 500 mg/Capsule							
	12	18	24	36	48	50	60	100
Robins (base price)	$1.93	$2.52	$2.91	$3.79	$4.77	$4.90	$5.55	$8.45
Lederle (P)	−0.15	−0.36	−0.03	0.53	0.82	1.15	1.32	2.10
Bristol (P)	0.52	0.48	0.74	1.16	1.59	1.64	1.91	3.08

	Quantity (oz) at 125 mg/5cc Syrup							
	2	3	4	5	6	8	12	16
Generic (base price)	$1.35	$1.83	$2.05	$2.48	$2.70	$3.15	$4.15	$5.25
Robins	0.42	0.25	0.54	0.42	0.51	0.78	1.21	1.65
Roerig	0.42	0.25	0.54	0.42	0.51	0.78	1.21	1.65
Lederle (P)	1.07	1.12	1.54	1.64	2.15	3.07	4.21	5.64
Bristol (P)	1.45	1.80	2.30	2.80	3.60	4.60	6.90	8.70

NOTE: P = original patent holder.
SOURCE: Osco Drug, Inc., price catalog, January 1975.

Mathematical Appendix

The n-vector $t = \langle t_1, \ldots, t_n \rangle$ describes the characteristics of a good such that q units of the good contain an amount qt of these characteristics. In this formulation q is a scalar to represent the quantity of good t. Thus, q units of the good have a total amount $x_i = qt_i$ of characteristic i.

According to this model there is a variety of products only if the users have different preferences, regardless of whether or not the producers have different cost functions for producing the same product t. The simplest hypothesis to represent the differences among the users

TABLE 3

DIFFERENCES BETWEEN BRAND NAME AND BASE PRICES FOR PENICILLIN-G POTASSIUM, SEPTEMBER 30, 1974
(unpatented)

Brand	Quantity at 200,000 Units per Tablet							
	12	18	24	36	48	50	60	100
Generic (base price)	$0.89	$0.89	$0.89	$1.08	$1.44	$1.50	$1.79	$2.99
Pfizer	0	0	0	0	0	0	0	0
Squibb	0	0.41	0.84	1.51	2.02	2.10	2.53	4.21

	Quantity at 250,000 Units per Tablet							
	12	18	24	36	48	50	60	100
Generic (base price)	$0.89	$0.89	$0.89	$1.08	$1.44	$1.50	$1.79	$2.99
Pfizer	0	0	0	0	0	0	0	0

	Quantity at 400,000 Units per Tablet							
	12	18	24	36	48	50	60	100
Generic (base price)	$0.89	$0.89	$0.89	$1.08	$1.44	$1.50	$1.79	$2.99
Pfizer	0	0	0	0	0	0	0	0
Squibb	0.37	1.00	1.63	2.70	3.60	3.75	4.51	7.51

	Quantity at 800,000 Units per Tablet							
	12	18	24	36	48	50	60	100
Squibb (base price)	$2.87	$3.73	$4.69	$6.51	$8.04	$8.29	$9.56	$15.03

	mg per 5 cc	Quantity (cc) of Syrups				
		60	80	100	150	200
Upjohn	125	$1.81				
Squibb	200			$2.49		$3.70
Upjohn	250		2.43	$2.70	$3.70	
Squibb	400			2.59		4.30
Pfizer	400			2.77		3.80

SOURCE: Osco Drug, Inc., price catalog, September 30, 1974.

introduces a continuous variable σ to describe a given user. The benefit function is given as follows:

$$b = B(x, q, \sigma) \tag{1}$$

According to this formulation, for each value of σ there is a benefit b that depends on the values of x and q.

TABLE 4

DIFFERENCES BETWEEN BRAND NAME AND BASE PRICES FOR PENICILLIN-G POTASSIUM, JANUARY 1975

(unpatented)

Brand	Quantity at 200,000 Units per Tablet							
	12	18	24	36	48	50	60	100
Generic (base price)	$0.89	$0.89	$0.89	$1.08	$1.44	$1.50	$1.79	$2.99
Pfizer	0	0	0	0	0	0	0	0
Squibb	0	0.41	0.84	1.51	2.02	2.10	2.53	4.21

	Quantity at 250,000 Units per Tablet							
	12	18	24	36	48	50	60	100
Generic (base price)	$0.89	$0.89	$0.89	$1.08	$1.44	$1.50	$1.79	$2.99
Pfizer	0	0	0	0	0	0	0	0

	Quantity at 400,000 Units per Tablet							
	12	18	24	36	48	50	60	100
Generic (base price)	$0.89	$0.89	$0.89	$1.08	$1.44	$1.50	$1.79	$2.99
Pfizer	0	0	0	0	0	0	0	0
Squibb	0.37	1.00	1.63	2.70	3.60	3.75	4.51	7.51

	Quantity at 800,000 Units per Tablet							
	12	18	24	36	48	50	60	100
Squibb (base price)	$2.87	$3.73	$4.69	$6.51	$8.04	$8.29	$9.56	$15.03

	Units per 5 cc	Quantity (cc) of Syrups				
		60	80	100	150	200
Upjohn	125,000	$1.81	—	—	—	—
Squibb	200,000	—	—	$2.49	—	$3.70
Upjohn	250,000	2.43	$2.70	—	$3.70	—
Squibb	400,000	—	—	2.59	—	4.30
Pfizer	400,000	—	—	2.77	—	3.84

SOURCE: Osco Drug, Inc., price catalog, January 1975.

Write the total cost function as follows:

$$c = C(x, q) \qquad (2)$$

This assumes that the total cost does not depend directly on σ. Instead, it depends on the amounts x and q.

TABLE 5

DIFFERENCES BETWEEN BRAND NAME AND BASE PRICES FOR
PENICILLIN-VK, POTASSIUM PHENOXYMETHYL PENICILLIN,
SEPTEMBER 30, 1974
(patent expired July 31, 1968)

Brand	Quantity at 125 mg per Tablet							
	12	18	24	36	48	50	60	100
Ross (base price)	$1.79	$2.12	$2.64	$3.28	$4.03	$4.14	$4.87	$7.32
Wyeth	0.07	0.29	0.12	0.29	0.25	0.26	0.31	0.52

	Quantity at 250 mg per Tablet							
	12	18	24	36	48	50	60	100
Lilly (base price)	$1.38	$2.07	$2.76	$4.14	$5.52	$5.75	$6.90	$11.50
Squibb	0.98	0.80	0.72	0.55	0.49	0.43	0.12	−0.70
Wyeth	1.04	0.88	0.83	0.71	0.70	0.65	0.39	−0.25
Ross	1.04	0.89	0.84	0.73	0.73	0.68	0.42	−0.20

	Quantity at 500 mg per Tablet							
	12	18	24	36	48	50	60	100
Squibb (base price)	$3.18	$4.19	$5.30	$7.43	$9.26	$9.56	$11.48	$17.57
Lilly	0.30	0.51	0.71	0.61	1.22	1.26	1.03	1.71
Ross	0.37	0.61	0.85	0.82	1.49	1.54	1.37	2.28
Wyeth	0.49	0.79	1.09	1.19	1.98	2.05	1.98	3.30

	Quantity (cc) at 125 mg/5cc Solution				
	40	80	100	150	200
Lilly } (base price) Ross }	$1.87 —	— $2.45	$1.99 —	— $2.78	$3.30 —
Lilly	0	—	0	0.42	0
Squibb	—	—	0.66	—	0.40
Wyeth	—	—	0.68	—	0.43

	Quantity (cc) at 250 mg/5cc Solution				
	40	80	100	150	200
Ross } (base price) Squibb }	— —	$3.01 —	— $3.03	$3.66 —	— $4.30
Wyeth	—	—	−.02	—	0.10
Lilly	—	—	0.30	0.54	0.10

SOURCE: Osco Drug, Inc., price catalog, September 30, 1974.

213

TABLE 6

DIFFERENCES BETWEEN BRAND NAME AND BASE PRICES FOR PENICILLIN-VK, POTASSIUM PHENOXYMETHYL PENICILLIN, JANUARY 1975
(patent expired July 31, 1968)

Brand	Quantity at 125 mg/Tablet							
	12	18	24	36	48	50	60	100
Ross (base price)	$1.79	$2.12	$2.64	$3.28	$4.03	$4.14	$4.87	$7.32
Wyeth (P)	0.07	0.29	0.12	0.29	0.25	0.26	0.31	0.52

	Quantity at 250 mg/Tablet							
	12	18	24	36	48	50	60	100
Lilly (P) (base price)	$1.38	$2.07	$2.76	$4.14	$5.52	$5.75	$6.90	$11.50
Squibb	0.98	0.80	0.72	0.55	0.49	0.43	0.12	−0.70
Wyeth (P)	1.04	0.88	0.83	0.71	0.70	0.65	0.39	−0.25
Ross	1.04	0.89	0.84	0.73	0.73	0.68	0.42	−0.20

	Quantity at 500 mg/Tablet							
	12	18	24	36	48	50	60	100
Squibb (base price)	$3.18	$4.19	$5.30	$7.43	$9.26	$9.56	$11.48	$17.57
Lilly (P)	0.34	0.57	0.79	0.74	1.38	1.43	1.23	2.05
Ross	0.37	0.61	0.85	0.82	1.49	1.54	1.37	2.28
Wyeth (P)	0.49	0.79	1.09	1.19	1.98	2.05	1.98	3.30

	Quantity (cc) at 125 mg/5cc Solution			
	40	100	150	200
Lilly (P) (base price)	$1.99	$2.19	$3.58	$3.71
Ross	—	0.46	−0.80	—
Squibb	—	0.46	—	−0.01
Wyeth (P)	—	0.48	—	0.02

	Quantity (cc) at 250 mg/5cc Solution		
	100	150	200
Squibb } (base price)	$3.03	—	$4.30
Ross }	—	$3.66	—
Ross	0.17	0	—
Wyeth (P)	0.30	—	0.10
Lilly (P)	0.71	1.17	0.76

NOTE: P = original patent holder.
SOURCE: Osco Drug, Inc., price catalog, January 1975.

TABLE 7

DIFFERENCES BETWEEN BRAND NAME AND BASE PRICES FOR ERYTHROMYCIN, JANUARY 1975
(patent expired September 29, 1970)

	Quantity at 250 mg/Tablet							
Brand	12	18	24	36	48	50	60	100
Generic (base price)	$2.40	$2.93	$3.55	$4.80	$6.15	$6.33	$7.20	$11.10
Upjohn (P)	0.55	0.92	1.30	1.96	2.21	2.30	3.16	4.60

NOTE: P = original patent holder.
SOURCE: Osco Drug, Inc., price catalog, January 1975.

TABLE 8

PRICES OF TABLETS BY ABBOTT, ERYTHROMYCIN STEREATE
(unspecified patent expired September 29, 1970)

	Quantity of Tablets							
mg/tablet	12	18	24	36	48	50	60	100
125	$2.43	$2.97	$3.61	$4.88	$6.26	$6.44	$ 7.34	$11.33
250	2.40	3.60	4.80	7.20	9.15	9.45	11.34	17.34

SOURCE: Osco Drug, Inc., price catalog, January 1975.

TABLE 9

DIFFERENCES BETWEEN BRAND NAME AND BASE PRICES FOR ANTIHYPERTENSIVE RESERPINE, JANUARY 1975
(patent expired June 26, 1973)

	Quantity at 0.25 mg/Tablet							
Brand	12	18	24	36	48	50	60	100
Generic (base price)	$0.89	$0.89	$0.89	$0.89	$0.89	$0.89	$0.89	$0.99
Ciba (P)	0	0	0.16	0.69	1.21	1.30	1.74	3.39
	Quantity at 0.1 mg/Tablet							
	12	18	24	36	48	50	60	100
Ciba (P) (base price)	$0.89	$0.89	$0.99	$1.48	$1.98	$2.06	$2.47	$4.12

NOTE: P = original patent holder.
SOURCE: Osco Drug, Inc., price catalog, January 1975.

The net benefit function, denoted by $H(x, q, \sigma)$, is defined as follows:

$$H(x, q, \sigma) = B(x, q, \sigma) - C(x, q) \tag{3}$$

The necessary conditions for a maximum of $H(.)$ with respect to x and q are that

$$H_x = 0 \text{ and } H_q = 0 \tag{4}$$

Therefore, these expressions define x and q as implicit functions of σ. Among the interesting questions that this theory addresses is whether there is a one-to-one correspondence between σ, the type of user, and t, the type of product. Stated differently, this asks whether there is a unique t for each σ and a unique σ for each t. There may be a continuum of product types compatible with the equilibrium conditions given by equation (4). It is also possible to have a finite number of product types consistent with equation (4), although there is a continuum of user types.

There is an alternative way of writing the model that illuminates some of its properties. Observe that

$$x = qt \tag{5}$$

so that we may replace x by qt in both the benefit and cost functions and use the fact that

$$dx = t\, dq + q\, dt$$
$$dH = H_x\, dx + H_q\, dq = H_x\, (t\, dq + q\, dt) + H_q\, dq$$
$$= (H_x\, t + H_q)\, dq + q\, H_x\, dt$$

Necessary conditions for a maximum may be written in the following form:

$$H_x\, t + H_q \le 0 \text{ and } q\, H_x \le 0 \tag{6}$$

if we impose a nonnegativity requirement on t and q. The inequalities in equation (6) are equivalent to

$$B_x\, t + B_q \le C_x\, t + C_q \tag{7}$$

$$q\, B_x \le q\, C_x \tag{8}$$

There is equality in any one of these expressions for which the optimal value of the component is strictly positive. This assertion is a consequence of complementary slackness. (Complementary slackness means that $q[H_x\, t + H_q] = 0$ and $q\, H_x\, t = 0$. In these expressions, recall that

216

x and t are n-vectors whereas q is a scalar. Hence, $B_x t$, for instance, is a scalar product.) Now, the term $C_x t + C_q$ gives the marginal cost of producing a good of type t, and the term $B_x t + B_q$ gives the marginal benefit of q units of type t. If it is optimal to have a positive amount of type t, then there is equality in equation (7). Nor is this all. For each positive quantity of x that is actually present in the good of type t, it follows from equation (8) that $B_x = C_x$.

An important special case is where $C(x, q)$ is homogenous of degree one.

$$c = \Sigma x_i C_{x_i} + q C_q \tag{9}$$

is an implication of Euler's Theorem in this case. Divide through by q and obtain

$$c/q = \Sigma t_i C_{x_i} + C_q \tag{10}$$

This expression gives the average cost. According to equation (7), it is also the marginal cost with respect to q. This result has the interpretation that the supply schedule for a product of type t is infinitely elastic. This does not mean that an individual firm has constant returns to scale. The cost function refers to all the producers, not just to a single one. If a positive quantity of a type t good is produced and sold, then its price, call it p, satisfies

$$p = c/q = dC/dq, \text{ given } t$$

Hence,

$$p = \Sigma t_i C_{x_i} + C_q \tag{11}$$

We also obtain the familiar result that every good that is actually made available on the market does not yield its producers a positive return, and all those goods not made available would impose losses on their producers. The observable price relation for the different types of products depends only on the cost conditions. Price differentials among products of different types equal the marginal cost of the characteristics by which they differ.

The neoclassical theory of perfect competition requires that the output of an individual firm does not affect the price that it can get for its product. We now wish to see how to reconcile this postulate with the theory of product variety. Write the demand function facing an individual firm j as follows:

$$p = \phi (x^j, q^j) \tag{12}$$

217

where x^j denotes the quantities of the characteristics that it makes available and q^j denotes the number of units that it makes. Now, q^j does not affect p for a given product type t if and only if the function $\phi(x^j, q^j)$ is homogeneous of degree zero. If so, one may rewrite $\phi(.)$ in equation (12) as follows:

$$p = \phi(t, 1) \tag{13}$$

Observe that according to equation (13), every firm faces exactly the same demand conditions. The objective of the firm is a choice of product types and scales of operation for the product types that will give it a maximum net return. In equilibrium, for all product types actually available on the market,

$$p = \Sigma B_{x_i} t_i + B_q = \Sigma C_{x_i} t_i + C_q \tag{14}$$

Therefore, in equilibrium

$$\phi_{t_i} = B_{x_i} = C_{x_i} \qquad \text{for all } t_i \text{ and } q > 0$$

In an alternative approach, there is product variety although all consumers are alike because each product serves a different purpose or function. Consequently, the number of available products does not exceed the number of functions or purposes. The observation that there is only a finite number of products actually available is explained by the postulate that each person has a finite number of basic purposes that a product would serve. In this approach, associated with Becker, Lancaster, and others, we assume that utility derives from the inputs of some basic goods.[10] The basic goods are in turn produced by various combinations of physical commodities available in the market. If in fact the consumers have the same preferences and if all consumers face the same market opportunities, then the finding that all consumers do not buy the same commodities can be explained by differences with respect to their initial endowments (wealth). If we find, however, that consumers with the same initial endowments do not buy the same commodities, then we seem driven to abandon the postulate that they all have the same preferences. One can, of course, combine a theory that basic goods enter the utility function with a theory of different consumer preferences. The theory of basic goods is most useful in explaining the relations

---

[10] Gary Becker, *Economic Approach to Human Behavior* (Chicago: University of Chicago Press, 1976), pt. 4; and Kelvin Lancaster, "A New Approach to Consumer Theory," *Journal of Political Economy*, vol. 74 (April 1966), pp. 132–57.

among commodities rather than as an explanation of differences among consumer tastes.

We now wish to study how x and q vary with σ. The purpose is to see how much product variety is consistent with the theory. Consider figure 1. In the first graph, AA_1 shows the equilibrium curve relating the product type t to σ. In this case there is a one-to-one relation between the two. In the second graph, AA_1 is not single valued. For a given value of t, there are several types of consumers. Stated differently, in the second graph the same product type t is used by consumers with

FIGURE 1

RELATION BETWEEN PRODUCT TYPE AND CONSUMER TYPE

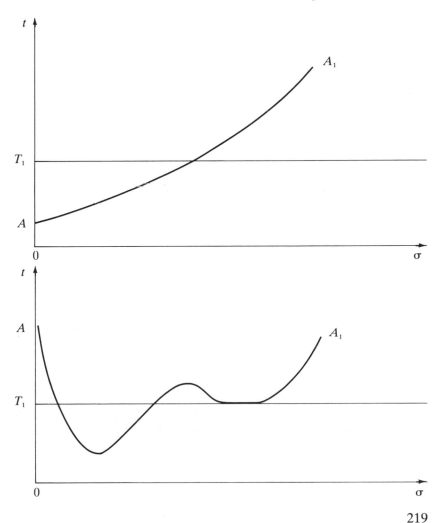

different σ. Plainly, if and only if x or t is a monotonic function of σ do we find a one-to-one correspondence between x or t and σ. We now study these problems.

Differentiate equation (4) with respect to σ and obtain

$$\begin{bmatrix} H_{xx} & H_{xq} \\ H_{xq} & H_{qq} \end{bmatrix} \begin{bmatrix} x_\sigma \\ q_\sigma \end{bmatrix} = - \begin{bmatrix} B_{x\sigma} \\ B_{q\sigma} \end{bmatrix} \tag{15}$$

As a consequence of strong concavity of the net benefit function, the matrix of second-order partials is negative definite so that

$$B_{x\sigma}\, x_\sigma + B_{q\sigma}\, q_\sigma > 0 \tag{16}$$

Since $x_\sigma = q\, t_\sigma + t\, q_\sigma$, we may replace equation (16) with the following expression:

$$(B_{x\sigma}\, t + B_{q\sigma})\, q_\sigma + q\, B_{\sigma x}\, t_\sigma > 0 \tag{17}$$

According to equation (14), the equilibrium price satisfies $p = B_x\, t + B_q$. Therefore, $p_\sigma = B_{x\sigma}\, t + B_{q\sigma} + B_x\, t_\sigma$, and, instead of equation (17), we may write $p_\sigma\, q_\sigma + t_\sigma\, [q\, B_{\sigma x} - B_x\, q_\sigma] > 0$.

An important case has t a periodic function of σ. This occurs if plants have fixed costs and convex increasing variable costs. In this case there is no longer a one-to-one correspondence between product and user type. A given product variety will be used by all of the consumers in a neighborhood of a given point. There will be fewer product types than consumer types.

Bibliography

Bain, Joe S. *Barriers to New Competition.* Cambridge: Harvard University Press, 1956.

Becker, Gary. *Economic Approach to Human Behavior.* Chicago: University of Chicago Press, 1976.

Chamberlin, Edward H. *The Theory of Monopolistic Competition.* Cambridge: Harvard University Press, 1933.

Clarkson, Kenneth W. *Intangible Capital and Rates of Return.* Washington, D.C.: American Enterprise Institute, 1977.

Demsetz, Harold. "Do Competition and Monopolistic Competition Differ?" *Journal of Political Economy* 76 (January/February 1968): 146–48.

Hicks, Sir John R. *The Theory of Wages.* London: Macmillan, 1932.

Knight, Frank H. *Risk, Uncertainty, and Profit.* Boston: Houghton Mifflin, 1921.

Lancaster, Kelvin. "A New Approach to Consumer Theory." *Journal of Political Economy* 74 (April 1964): 132–57.

Rosen, Sherwin. "Hedonic Prices and Implicit Markets: Product Differentiation in Pure Competition." *Journal of Political Economy* 82 (January/February 1974): 34–55.

Schwartzman, David. *Innovation in the Pharmaceutical Industry*. Baltimore: Johns Hopkins University Press, 1976.

Telser, Lester G. "Advertising and Competition." *Journal of Political Economy* 62 (December 1964): 537–62.

Telser, Lester G., et al. "The Theory of Supply with Applications to the Ethical Pharmaceutical Industry." *Journal of Law and Economics* 18 (October 1975): 449–78.

Commentary

Michael Halberstam, M.D.

I think Professor Temin himself realizes that his very original analysis is a construct and that, as he said, more data are needed. One very important bit of information comes through, however, that, as a physician, I find very surprising. That is his conclusion that even heavy prescribers do not become particularly dependent on one or two groups of drugs in each class; instead, they not only write a large number of prescriptions but write a large variety of prescriptions.

The reason this is quite surprising to me is because of the heavy prescribers whom I personally know. It is often said, "You can't go into so-and-so's office without coming out with a prescription for Elavil." Everybody gets Elavil or everybody gets Valium or everybody gets tetracycline.

It has been my experience that heavy prescribers tend to rely on one or two drugs in each class, and therefore when I first saw Temin's tables I was really astounded. I thought to myself, "Well, these very heavy prescribers with 5,000 new prescriptions per year certainly will have a much higher frequency per individual drug than those who are low prescribers." I think his figures are consistent all the way through, and we will have to accept that. To a certain degree, this will also fit the construct that the doctor who writes many prescriptions is easily susceptible to advertising, to word of mouth, and does not stick with any one drug particularly faithfully.

Let me in my comments try to give an empiric model of two separate problems. (I believe they have to be considered two separate problems.) The first is the adoption of new items by the physician, and the second is the continuing prescription of certain items by the physician.

One must realize that there are strong antiinnovative feelings in the medical community about drugs. I know it was true in my medical school days, and I am sure it is true now, that in every medical school in the United States, the professor of pharmacology teaches the students two general guidelines. First, because they are faced with a bewildering array of drugs, they should, in each category of medication, learn one or two medicines, learn those well, and forget about the others. Second, I think an eighteenth-century couplet is still dominant and is probably still taught to students: "Be not the first by whom the new is tried or yet the last to put the old aside."

These two guidelines place a strongly antiinnovative burden on the physician. The physician is, to a certain degree, taught to be skeptical and, to another degree, *must* be skeptical and must limit his or her choices among a bewildering array of pharmaceuticals. Therefore, the use of a new medication is something that the physician tries only under certain circumstances, most clearly when the patient is dissatisfied with the current therapy or when the physician is dissatisfied with the current therapy. Change may also occur when there are indications that, even if the current therapy is adequate, new therapy might be even better. The models here are different for each of these two actions on the part of the physician, the innovative use or the continuing use.

The Coleman study that Temin discusses is very interesting,[1] and yet I think it is limited by the fact that it was done in the 1950s and in a particular community. Innovation in the use of pharmaceuticals in a medical community—I should like to talk about the "diffusion" rather than the "epidemic spread" of the use of a new medication—clearly depends on the type of medical community that one is talking about. No two communities are identical, but clearly, since 1955, many things have changed in the practice of medicine in the United States.

The isolated general practitioner, who was used as one of the models in the Coleman study, probably no longer exists. He or she is a legend. That kind of physician does not exist because communication has improved, group practice has spread (not necessarily prepaid group practice but either single-specialty group practice or multispecialty group practice, particularly in the western United States), and specialty practice itself has increased since that time.

Certainly the situation between 1955 and 1965 differed from that between 1970 and 1972, when the United States had the lowest percentage of people identifying themselves as general practitioners or family practitioners in its history. In 1970 I believe the three Boston medical schools graduated only three physicians who said that they intended to become general practitioners or family practitioners. Certainly the percentage of primary-care physicians in training has increased since then, even in Boston.

Another profound change has come through the ascendance of

---

[1] J. S. Coleman, E. Katz, and H. Menzel, *Medical Innovation: A Diffusion Study* (Indianapolis: Bobbs-Merrill, 1966).

Continuing Medical Education. This has dramatically changed the way that physicians acquire knowledge, and certainly it has changed their approach to new medication.

When a physician is contemplating the use of a new medication, I think he or she goes by what I call the service-station-owner model—that is, I may not know very much about my automobile, but if Charlie Windsor, who owns the Amoco station on the corner, says that Pennzoil is better than all other oils, then I do not care what I read or what I hear; I trust Charlie Windsor, and I will put Pennzoil in my car. Similarly, if Charlie Windsor says that all these oils are the same, that I should just buy the cheapest one, no amount of advertising is going to change my behavior on that point.

So it goes with physicians. I am an internist, I have a subspecialty in cardiology, I see patients with gastroenterologic disease, but if my gastroenterologist, the one I use for consultation when I have difficult patients, says, "Well, we are now using cimetidine for all our ulcer patients," then I will start using cimetidine. If my respiratory disease consultant says, "We are using Theodur," I say, "What was that again?" He says, "Theodur," and I write it down, and I look it up. I may not ask him what it is, because I do not want to sound too ignorant—but I will look it up and I will start using it, because if it is good enough for Harold Silver or if it is good enough for Don O'Kieffe, then it is good enough for me.

I am different, in one regard, from the average physician, in that I am the editor of a magazine that goes to physicians and carries a lot of drug advertising. I often write about medications. No matter what I read, however, I am most profoundly influenced by the people who are my colleagues and who are active in subspecialties other than my own. I believe that this is the most important factor in the innovative use of medications by physicians.

In the continuing use of medication, different factors obtain, and in this area I disagree with Peter Temin. The physician, like almost everybody else, wants to decrease dissonance and noise in his life. If I prescribe a medication for a patient, I only want to hear the patient say, "Dr. Halberstam, that new medicine really helped my pain. That really was marvelous." I do not want to get a phone call reporting, "That new medicine has just torn me up inside. I've been vomiting, and I've just been ripped apart by it." I do not need to hear that.

When the patient comes back and I ask how the new medicine is working, I also do not want to hear, "Oh, well, it's not really doing very much," or "Doctor, that new pill isn't helping much." I would like to feel that I am helping the patient, and I would certainly like to feel that I am not hurting the patient. Therefore, like other physicians, I believe,

I operate on what I might call a hot-stove basis; that is, having been burned once, I am reluctant to return to the area of that stove.

If a patient has a bad reaction to a medication, I say, "Well, that happens sometimes. It's been reported. It's not serious; but we'll stop the medicine, and we'll try something else." If the second patient or the third says the same thing, however, I say to myself, "Gee, I don't need that any more." I do not want to be called, I do not want to be complained to, I do not want to have any additional unhappy voices on the phone, reproaching me for prescribing something. Even though Harold Silver and Don O'Kieffe may have said the medication is marvelous, I am no longer convinced that it is.

Physicians do look for this kind of feedback from their patients. I hate the use of the word "feedback," but I think it is about the only word that is appropriate. A doctor prescribes a new medication, and when the patient comes back for the scheduled follow-up visit, in many cases the results are quite clear. People who have arthritis, for example, have the same pain day in and day out for years; they know their pain very well, and they have tried a dozen different medications. If such patients report that the new medicine really helped, I believe that it is not a placebo effect, because these people have been given placebos before to no effect, and I trust this particular patient's perception of his own pain. I feel good, the patient feels good, and I am tempted to use the medication again, even in the face of an occasional adverse reaction.

If I am treating a hypertensive with a new medication and the blood pressure has not budged, I am less than enthusiastic about the medication. If I have started a new medication in a hypertensive patient and the patient reports that it works but his sex life has gone to nothing, I make a mental note right there and say, "Well, you know, that happens sometimes, but we'll try something else."

There is, I think, a constant refining of knowledge—of common knowledge of these medications among physicians—and the informal network that Temin referred to and that Coleman and his colleagues referred to does, indeed, exist. The enthusiasm or lack of enthusiasm of one physician is, in fact, communicable to his or her colleagues.

I, for example, almost never use ampicillin. I know that it is a very widely prescribed medication, but 15 or 20 percent of the people for whom I have prescribed it call me up and say, "Gee, Doc, my sinuses are better, but I just have this terrible diarrhea. Can you prescribe something for that?" That is an example of the kind of noise and dissonance that I do not need.

Clearly, the situation is different when one is faced with a life-threatening disease. That usually occurs in a hospital situation, and the ground rules are quite different there. In the outpatient situation, in the office situation, where the majority of oral medications are prescribed, these I believe are the constraints.

It is clear that we lack an enormous amount of knowledge. I thought that I had something in my files, in addition to the studies mentioned by Temin, about diffusion of innovation—pharmaceutical innovation within the medical community—but I do not. Both Professor Telser and Professor Temin have pointed out the need for more knowledge.

Let me suggest some models that the economists and the social scientists among us might use. There is a model of a single specialty. It would be very interesting to study a small, well-defined specialty, such as neurosurgery or pediatric ophthalmology, where the numbers of physicians involved are comparatively small, 2,000–4,000, where the annual meeting is a meeting at which everybody gets together, where the level of knowledge is very high, and where academic affiliation is almost universal.

It would be very interesting to see how new medication diffuses in a community like that. I would guess that the annual meeting of such a society is a tremendously powerful force in diffusing new knowledge. It is, indeed, *the* convention of that society, and everybody goes, whereas in fields like surgery or internal medicine the national meetings are important but lack the ripple effect of smaller medical subspecialties.

It would be interesting to go again into a specific community, as Coleman and his colleagues did, and see how a new medication is adopted. I think that their study has to be repeated because medical practice and the medical community have changed so much.

I take various Continuing Medical Education courses; as a physician, I sometimes speak at these courses, and I am always profoundly affected by the eager audience out there. I recently spoke at a meeting in North Carolina of the American College of Cardiology. The program was put on by an old friend of mine, Dr. Leonard Gettes of the University of North Carolina, and he asked me before the meeting, "What are we doing here? Here I have all of my hotshot residents and fellows, I have the researchers from the dog lab, I have Boris Surawicz up from Kentucky, I have William Parmley in from the University of California; we are giving all this heavy stuff, and these doctors in the audience are nice, but they are never going to be able to handle all this stuff. They are good guys, but what are they going to be able to do with it?"

Of course, he was right to a certain extent, and yet I think that it is very touching that physicians go to these meetings, trying to hear the latest word, trying to upgrade themselves, trying to get the brownie points that are necessary. Besides, Dr. Gettes's bright young fellows may be attending—not giving—such courses in ten years, when some of them are out in practice.

Such meetings have a genuine effect; again, they promote the diffusion of knowledge much more rapidly, particularly the diffusion of practical and pharmaceutical knowledge. When the researcher from the dog lab has gone through all his stuff about how to prevent ventricular arrhythmias in dogs who are given heart attacks in the laboratory, the first question from the audience is, "What drugs seem to prevent it the most?"

The researcher says, "Well, we have had something from Russia called ethmosin; it is not available here."

What are the drugs that *are* available in this country? What was most effective? That is what everybody writes down, and that is what they carry home. I think that that kind of diffusion of knowledge is very real, and very profound. Again, if the physician goes home and starts the new drug back in Blowing Rock, North Carolina, and the first five patients to use it all come up with severe diarrhea, he is probably going to stop using it.

The scientific background and the genuine research impetus do exist, however. By focusing on these various models—a single community, a single medical subspecialty, or a single new drug—one can provide hard evidence about physicians' prescribing patterns.

In my office recently I had a very bright patient with hypertension, and he said, "I'm a new patient. I've been taking this medicine and this medicine and this medicine. We've tried a whole bunch of things, but they don't work particularly well. I read in the *Wall Street Journal* about Captoril, and I want you to tell me about it, and I want to see if you can get me some, and I also want you to see if I need it."

If we have a patient population that is that informed—and it *is* becoming increasingly informed, remember—then we have another force for innovation. It is a patient-directed innovative force, which did not exist, I think, thirty or forty years ago.

All these forces can be isolated; they can be studied in a small model. The need for doing that is imperative.

David F. Lean

It is a pleasure to offer comment on what is yet another thought-provoking piece by Professor Telser. My general reaction is that he presents an idea that has merit, but in deriving its implications I fear that he strays, perhaps, in the wrong direction. I find much in his paper with

David F. Lean's remarks represent only his personal views and should not be construed as representative of the views of any other members of the Federal Trade Commission staff or of individual commissioners.

which I agree, but there are some basic and important aspects with which I must disagree. Some of my disagreement is based on the assumptions of his demand model, some of it is based on his perceptions of the pharmaceutical industry as a competitive industry, and some of it has to do with intellectual leaps from abstraction to policy. Let me start by briefly reviewing what I think are the central elements of his theory of demand.

Of great merit is his incorporation into a demand model of the notion that physicians base their selection of drug products in part on their perceptions of firms as providers of "quality" products. He argues that these perceptions are largely influenced by the research and promotional activities of the firm, activities by which the firm acquires a quality reputation described as its stock of intangible capital. In turn, this "capital" image is a prime determinant of the long-run equilibrium prices of drugs. The capital image may be cultivated by increased effort in research and development (R&D) and in the new drugs generated by that process and by promotional effort. Firms that differentiate themselves successfully to enjoy a superior quality image will earn higher prices for products than those that fail or do not even try. A side proposition is that physicians serve their own interests better by prescribing the products of firms that engage in R&D and promotion. Another essential ingredient in this process is the clear identification of manufacturers' products through some form of branding or labeling. From these arguments, we have a message that firms engaged in R&D and promotion are socially productive and good to have around. Firms that do not try but simply offer old products at "competitive" prices are not. Finally, the model implies an industry in the future made up only of firms that engage in R&D and promotion.

Telser attempts to formalize certain of these propositions in his model. Note, however, some inferences contained in the scenario I just described: (1) If physicians prescribe according to an overall capital "image" of the firm, it implies that they may not be very discriminating with respect to the selection of particular drugs for a particular ailment, behavior that would bother me terribly as a consumer. One might concede that a firm X is a "quality" firm and know that it has a good drug for use against illness A, but without other knowledge one cannot infer that illness B can be given superior treatment with another of the company's drugs. (2) The model and other notions in the paper suggest that firms can spend themselves to riches by devoting more effort to R&D and promotion. Clearly, this is not possible for all firms. In generating new products or in cultivating new images, some firms may be more successful than others. How does one explain this? Even if two firms are endowed with and are perceived to have the same intangible stock of research and advertising capital, the rate of sales of their respective products may differ. How do we explain this? These questions suggest that other things are going on and are influential in affecting relative outputs and prices.

Perhaps here I should look at the formal model itself. We have been given an assumed competitive environment and a homogeneous demand function of degree zero for a single firm offering two different drugs. The stock of intangible research and advertising capital associated with the firm as a whole (not the individual products) is incorporated with the respective drug quantities to explain a long-run equilibrium price. Relationships between the variables are postulated, including one that depicts a positive relationship between the research (R)—and advertising (A)—capital factor and the quantities of the drugs, (the q_i's), given the prices of the drugs. The model generates a result that prices depend on the research capital per unit of the product, as denoted by the ratio q_i/R. For each product, q_i/R is permitted to be different, but we have no good explanation of why this may occur. Because the R (or A) factor in the denominator is the same, differences in the q_i/R's must arise in the quantities sold (the q_i's). It is not clear how these differences will arise within a firm. They must surely not stem from physicians' assigning different R values to different products in the same firm. The model then appears to suggest that the firm selects a research-capital-per-unit ratio for a given drug, apparently by manipulating the quantity sold; yet in the long run the firm has no control over quantities sold. Telser's "competitive" equilibrium commands firms to have no control over price or output. The firm is presumed to select the research capital per unit of product and accept a long-run equilibrium price as dictated by market forces. What seems puzzling, then, is the nature of the relation between the quantities sold of each product and the research (or advertising) capital of the firm, and my questions suggest that the model may be oversimplified. These same issues appear to arise if the model is extended to more than one firm, each firm having equivalent R values.

Research conducted by Ronald Bond of the Federal Trade Commission and I on drug product sales and promotion in two therapeutic markets suggests that there is more to the prescribing behavior or demand for drugs than is represented in the Telser model.[1] Differentiating characteristics associated with the timing of entry and the therapeutic merit of a drug itself appear to exert a strong influence on both sales and promotional levels of drugs independent of the influence of any

---

[1] R. S. Bond and D. F. Lean, "Sales, Promotion, and Product Differentiation in Two Prescription Drug Markets," staff report to the Federal Trade Commission, February 1977.

overall firm research and promotional "capital" characteristic. Indeed, through these differentiating properties, firms do appear to have discretionary control over the prices they exact in the market. The evidence we gathered also showed that prestigious firms, with perhaps an equally high performance level in bringing new products to market (we shall assume an equal Telser capital image factor), fared significantly differently: the market share of identical drugs differed significantly by virtue of different market introduction dates. Attempts to offset a late-entry disadvantage by offering lower prices and by intense promotion were unsuccessful. Together these findings suggest that physicians as a group make purchasing (ordering) decisions on other bases in addition to that postulated by Professor Telser. Of interest for further research, then, is to learn a great deal more about physicians' prescribing patterns and what influences them. With a recent gradual move toward product selection by pharmacists, it will become important to study their selection bases as well.

If the Telser image factor is important—and I concede it does have relevance—it does indeed follow that a manufacturer's drugs should be identified in such a way that the prescriber knows who the manufacturer is. He suggests that brands are the appropriate vehicle for such identification, although he does not specify the form a brand should take. Currently, trademarked brand names rarely reveal in form the name of the manufacturer. The SmithKline so-called branded generics are an exception, but generally Valium as a name does not look or sound like Hoffmann–La Roche, Darvon does not look or sound like Lilly, and Hydrodiuril does not look or sound like Merck. Although physicians probably know who produces the leading trademarked, brand-name drugs, I doubt that they could get high grades on a match-the-firm-and-drug test that covered a large number of items. The logic of the Telser argument suggests that trademarked brand names are, shall I say, superfluous in this industry, a point with which I have considerable sympathy. If, indeed, a firm's research capital is important to the prescribing and dispensing function and if, indeed, the firm must be recognized, then let the firm be recognized in the drug labeling itself. The logic suggests that Valium should be known as Roche-diazepam, Darvon as Lilly-propoxyphene, and Hydrodiuril as Merck-hydrochlorothiazide. Perhaps Professor Telser would stay with the established system of nomenclature. I point out simply what I see to be the most relevant form of identification.

Let me close with some thoughts about future research and the future of the industry, thoughts stimulated by my own work and by Telser's. We need to know more about the factors that influence physicians' prescribing patterns. Furthermore, we need to know whether long-term survival in pharmaceutical manufacture requires an active role in research. Also, how will product equivalency guarantees affect physicians' perceptions of the research and advertising image factor embodied in a firm? A situation may exist, moreover, in which a firm has a lackluster image yet markets a high-quality drug used to treat a particular ailment. If physicians do indeed spurn this drug because the firm has a low capital image, how then do we raise the competitive status of that drug?

Finally, the model raises questions about the future structure of the pharmaceutical industry, an issue of importance because we need to ensure the flow of beneficial drugs but, at the same time, ensure that competitive forces are such that prices are kept in reasonable relationship to costs. The model predicts a world of R&D-active firms that have no control over prices: market forces control price after the firm decides its research capital per unit. What does this reveal about the future structure of the market and the size distribution of firms? This aspect remains unclear. Will the structure be such that competitive problems are generated? A highly skewed size distribution of firms and high concentration, should they prevail, would indeed create conditions favorable to firms' having discretionary control over their prices. Whether this situation is desirable depends in part on the performance of the industry in generating new and improved products. Although the end result is not clear, Telser's paper may spark some fresh thinking about this issue.

PART FIVE

The Social Returns to Pharmaceutical
Research and Development

Some Economic Consequences of Technological Advance in Medical Care: The Case of a New Drug

John F. Geweke and Burton A. Weisbrod

Introduction

How should a technological change be evaluated? Conceptually, we would like to know whether the present value of its discounted future net benefits is or is not greater than zero. An innovation that imposes increased social costs compared with the counterfactual is not ipso facto inefficient. Neither is an innovation necessarily efficient if it imposes decreased social costs. Both costs and benefits, and their time streams, must be examined.

The technology of medical care encompasses such labor and capital inputs as surgeons and surgical capital, equipment for diagnoses and treatment, and drugs. Given the variety of input combinations available and their expansion over time, the development of expensive new types of inputs, and the widespread use of public and private "insurance" arrangements that provide incentives for inefficient choice, it is understandable that concern is growing about the rate of increase of medical care expenditures. Whether that concern reflects implicit recognition of allocative inefficiency or of the income redistributions occurring through the governmental tax-transfer system, the facts of political and economic pressure to reduce expenditures on health care are clear.

Thus, notwithstanding the economist's social perspective that treats costs and benefits evenhandedly, government policy makers have become increasingly concerned about the effects of innovations on costs alone; this is especially so in the medical care area. It has become a matter of considerable concern that the percentage of gross national product (GNP) devoted to medical care has continued to rise, from 3.5 percent in 1929 to 5.3 percent in 1960 and to 9.1 percent in 1978 (table 1). Numerous mechanisms have been discussed and used for the express purpose of "cost control": deductibles and copayment in health insur-

Research support and access to data were provided by Pracon, Inc. We wish to thank Don Roden, vice-president of Pracon, for his cooperation and Steven Edison and Bernd Luedecke for research assistance. We are solely responsible for views expressed and for any errors.

TABLE 1

HEALTH CARE EXPENDITURES IN THE UNITED STATES, 1929–1978

Year	Percentage of GNP	Dollar Amounts (in billions)
1929	3.5	4
1950	4.5	13
1960	5.3	27
1970	7.6	75
1975	8.6	131
1978	9.1	192

SOURCE: U.S. Department of Commerce, Bureau of the Census, *Statistical Abstract of the United States, 1979*, p. 97.

ance, prepaid group practice (health maintenance organizations—HMOs) and regional hospital planning councils in the organization of health care delivery, and prospective reimbursement and second surgical opinions to induce efficiency in the face of health insurance that frequently confronts physicians and patients with zero private marginal costs of care. Recently the Carter administration sought to impose a "cap"—a constraint on the rate of increase in each hospital's total annual expenditures. Somehow, rising total expenditures have come to be regarded as bad, irrespective of the (admittedly hard to measure) benefits. For decades, the percentage of GNP devoted to automobiles, by contrast, has grown, but this never came to be perceived as a problem, let alone a reflection of allocative inefficiency.

This paper seeks to accomplish two goals: (1) to develop a methodology for examining the consequences of any new medical care technology and (2) to apply that methodology to the case of a new drug. The selection of a drug rather than some other health care input, and of the one specific drug that we consider, was determined by the availability of data. With small modifications, however, the data could be exploited to examine the expenditure consequences of other (drug and nondrug) medical innovations.

The question whether a particular medical input—drug or other—causes expenditures to increase or decrease has obvious policy relevance, given the current political emphasis on "expenditure containment." Individual states makes decisions, for example, on whether to approve payments for particular drugs and other specific health resources used by Medicaid patients; and the approval process involves consideration of the aggregate expenditure effects.

Our methodology, dictated by the twin desires to be conceptually correct and to be operationally relevant, is a simplification of the benefit-cost framework, in which benefits from a new technology consist only of reductions in costs and, indeed, reductions in only those costs that are reflected in explicit payments for health resources.

Measuring net benefits by reductions in costs results in biased estimates of net benefits, but in general we cannot determine the direction of bias. If, for example, a new medical technology were to be both more effective in enhancing good health and also less costly than the technology it replaced, a focus on costs alone would understate the net social benefits of the new technology. Similarly, if the new technology were more effective but also more costly, then disregard of the increased effectiveness would lead to the false conclusion that the new technology brought negative net social benefits. If, on the other hand, the new technology were both less effective and less costly, then measuring its net benefits by the reduction in cost would overstate the net benefits.

Measurement of increased effectiveness is fraught with complexity. If a medical care innovation reduces pain and suffering, we would have a difficult time valuing those benefits. If the innovation led to a strengthening of the body's defense mechanisms so that there were subsequent improvements in health status, this would also be difficult to assess; under some circumstances, however, such benefits would appear as reductions in medical care expenditures and thus would be captured by the cost-based approach. What will be overlooked is the value that the affected persons place on their improved health or longevity; reduced medical care expenditures are generally an underestimate of this value.

In the preceding paragraphs we have used the terms "costs" and "expenditures" synonymously. In some contexts this produces misleading conclusions, as in discussions of "inflation" of medical care "costs," which confuse increases in total expenditures on medical care with increases in the prices of a constant-quality set of inputs. To some extent this confusion of costs with expenditures is present in the operational model we set forth here. Ideally, we would measure changes in both benefits and costs. Insofar as we omit some forms of benefits, we are in effect estimating changes in expenditures on a commodity, health status, that is of varying quality, not the cost of producing a commodity of constant quality. This is another way of seeing the possible bias resulting from the systematic omission of those benefits that are not captured by reductions in expenditures. Any observed changes in *expenditures*, in short, do not necessarily imply a change in the *cost* of purchasing a given level of health.

Another variable in the present-value formulation (V) is the "lifetime" of the innovation. Determination of its magnitude is complicated, for it depends on future research and innovation; the length of life of an innovation will be a function of when some other medical advance will make that innovation economically obsolete. Though difficult to determine, this variable is likely to be of critical importance. An innovation that would be initially more costly than another may be far less costly, as well as more beneficial, in later years; the number of those "later years" can be crucial to a determination of the present value of the prospective innovation.

The other key variable in the computation of present value is the discount rate. For a long-lived innovation, the value selected for the discount rate can have a great effect on the present value.[1]

As we proceed with our examination of the effect of a new medical input on expenditures, note that: (1) as pointed out above, a change in expenditures is not equivalent to a change in net costs (costs minus benefits); (2) the change in expenditures bears no particular relationship to a change in real production costs for the producers involved or to the profits of the firm or firms that developed or produce the good involved.

In our application the innovation is the use of cimetidine, a drug that was granted a conditional-use permit by the Food and Drug Administration (FDA) in September 1977 for use in the treatment of duodenal ulcer. It is fundamentally different from antacids, the most commonly used medical treatment for duodenal ulcer, and from an older group of drugs known as anticholinergics. Further details are provided in appendix B.

The outline of this paper is as follows. Having set the stage in the section above—that is, having presented a structure for evaluating a new or proposed medical care technology—we turn in the next section to survey previous research that estimates social costs of ulcers and the change in social costs resulting from the use of cimetidine. The third, fourth, and fifth sections present, respectively, our methodology for measuring the change in social costs resulting from the new drug, the data base, and our findings. A concluding section summarizes, and appendixes describe the medical nature and treatment of duodenal ulcers.

Social Costs of Duodenal Ulcer Disease

There is a substantial literature devoted to the estimation of the social costs of various diseases and to ulcers and duodenal ulcers (DU) in particular. Much less attention has been given to the effect of changes in medical technology on these costs, the question to which this paper is ultimately addressed. Before describing our approach to this question, we summarize what is known about the social costs of DU and briefly

---

[1] A sensitivity analysis of the importance of r, N, and related variables can be found in Burton A. Weisbrod, "Costs and Benefits of Medical Research: A Case Study of Poliomyelitis," *Journal of Political Economy*, vol. 79 (1971), pp. 527–44.

describe a preliminary estimate of the likely effect of cimetidine on those costs.

Traditionally, social costs associated with any disease have been classified as direct and indirect. Direct costs are the uses in medical care of the disease of resources that have been diverted from other uses. They include hospital care, physicians' services, drug therapy, nursing home expenses, etc. Indirect costs are those resulting from the loss of current and future productivity due to disability and mortality caused by the disease. Measurement of indirect costs is fraught with well-known conceptual problems relating to the valuation of human life and non-market activities and to the forecasting of future productivity and interest rates. None of these conventional measures includes the pain, discomfort, and suffering incurred by the patient and his family and associates, which are social costs but very difficult to quantify and even more difficult to value.[2]

A number of social cost estimates have been undertaken for peptic ulcers, which include all ulcer diseases of the digestive system, rather than for duodenal ulcers alone. Robinson has estimated that 68 percent of peptic ulcer social costs should be ascribed to duodenal ulcer;[3] this figure permits at least some rough inferences about social costs of duodenal ulcer disease from social cost studies of peptic ulcers.

The results of earlier studies are reviewed and updated by von Haunalter and Chandler.[4] They estimate that, in 1975, 4 million U.S. residents suffered from some form of ulcer disease. There were 6,840 deaths attributed to ulcer in that year, and 77,000 persons were disabled. Their total social cost estimate for 1975 is $2.6 billion. Of this total, direct costs account for slightly less than half but are increasing at a faster rate than indirect costs. The largest single cost component is morbidity, divided fairly evenly between those disabled by ulcer and those temporarily absent from work. The reduced productivity of those ulcer sufferers who work at a slower pace is not included because of the near impossibility of measuring this loss.

The only effort to date to evaluate the likely impact of the introduction of cimetidine on the social costs attributed to duodenal ulcer is contained in a study by Robinson Associates commissioned by Smith

---

[2] For a recent attempt to measure these "intangible" effects, in the context of a randomized experiment in treating the mentally ill, see Burton A. Weisbrod, "A Guide to Benefit-Cost Analysis, as Seen through a Controlled Experiment in Treating the Mentally Ill," Discussion Paper 559–79, University of Wisconsin Institute for Research on Poverty, 1979.

[3] Robinson Associates, Inc., *The Impact of Cimetidine on the National Cost of Duodenal Ulcers* (Bryn Mawr, Pa., 1978).

[4] George von Haunalter and Virginia V. Chandler, *Cost of Ulcer Disease in the United States* (Menlo Park, Calif.: Stanford Research Institute, 1977).

Kline & French Laboratories. In that study, twenty-three of the physicians who conducted clinical trials of cimetidine for the Food and Drug Administration were asked to describe in detail their drug treatment regimens for various types of DU patients with and without the availability of cimetidine. They were asked to evaluate both regimens according to the criteria of frequency of repeat episodes, frequency of patient visits to physician, likelihood and frequency of hospitalization, likelihood of surgery, frequency of diagnostic X-rays and endoscopies, amount of missed work, and likelihood of death from ulcer complications. These estimates were then combined with secondary source information on indirect costs and costs of various forms of treatment to compute cost reductions due to the availability of cimetidine for each type of DU patient. The physicians were also asked to estimate a penetration rate for cimetidine—that is, the proportion of each type of patient that would be treated with cimetidine when the drug was being used by most of the physicians in the United States who would eventually do so.

The findings of this study are summarized in table 2. At the average estimated penetration rate of 80 percent, a reduction of $645 million, or 29 percent, in health care costs for DU was estimated. The drug cost component was estimated to increase by 40 percent, but decreases in all other components were estimated. The authors of the study claim that because the sample of twenty-three physicians constituted a carefully selected group of experienced respondents offering highly technical information on a subject with which they were more familiar than any other physicians in the United States, a high degree of confidence may be placed in their assessments. The study provides no quantitative assessment of the confidence that can be placed in these estimates, however. They do imply that the 40 percent increase in "drug therapy" costs associated with usage of cimetidine (table 2) are offset by an enormously greater decrease in every other form of direct and indirect cost of ulcers.

Methodology

The problem addressed in our study is measurement of the socioeconomic costs and benefits of the introduction of a new drug. The methodology developed here is general enough to be used in the evaluation of any new drug, although we focus specifically on the use of cimetidine in the treatment of duodenal ulcers. In the introduction of any new drug, it is all but impossible to evaluate economic and social effects—as distinguished from medical effects—within a controlled-experiment framework. Besides inherent political and ethical problems, the costs of designing and monitoring such an experiment plus the cost of intro-

TABLE 2

Costs of Duodenal Ulcers, Computed for 80 Percent Cimetidine Usage, 1977

Cost Component	National Costs (in millions)		National Per-Patient Costs (in dollars)		
	DU costs	Reduction	DU costs	Reduction	Percentage Reduction
Direct costs					
Hospital care	474	258	225	123	35
Physicians and related	139	47	66	23	26
Drug therapy	119	− 34	57	− 16	− 40
Nursing home	11	—	5	—	0
Other professional	2	—	1	—	0
Total direct costs	745	271	351	130	27
Indirect costs					
Mortality	201	44	96	21	18
Morbidity	602	329	286	156	35
Absenteeism	307	148	146	70	33
Long-term disability	295	181	140	86	38
Total indirect costs	803	373	381	177	32
Total	1,547	645	732	307	29

Source: Robinson Associates, *Impact of Cimetidine*, pp. 2–3.

ducing yet another delay in the introduction of new drugs are apt to be prohibitive. For the foreseeable future, inferences about socioeconomic effects must therefore be drawn in nonexperimental settings, often using data bases that were not constructed for the purpose of making such inferences. These problems are paramount in the evaluation of cimetidine, and we believe that they are likely to be of overriding concern in the introduction of other drugs and medical techniques as well. The methodology devised here to cope with the problems of non-experimental design should be applicable in other cases.

A Hypothetical Experiment. To highlight the difficulties in making inferences about socioeconomic effects in nonexperimental settings, imagine that a controlled experiment could be constructed in which duodenal ulcer patients and providers were randomly assigned to three groups: group 1, in which the key treatment variable, cimetidine, was not available; group 2, in which cimetidine was used mandatorily; and group 3, in which cimetidine was available but its use was not mandatory. Group 1 might be termed the control group, C; groups 2 and 3, the experiment

FIGURE 1
HYPOTHETICAL COSTS PER PATIENT, EXPERIMENTAL AND CONTROL GROUPS

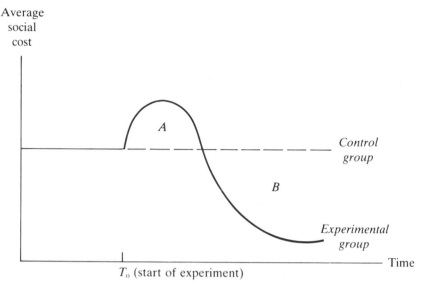

groups, E_1 and E_2. In many controlled experiments in the health area, only groups C and E_1 are compared. This approach can be quite misleading if the most effective therapy is to use the experimental variable (cimetidine in this case) only some of the time. Our group E_2 patients would use or not use cimetidine, depending on provider judgments. Clearly, the more interesting experiment is a comparison of groups C and E_2.[5]

The social costs associated with each of the two groups, C and E_2, would be monitored over a period of time. One possible relationship of the social-cost paths of the two groups is illustrated in figure 1. During the preexperimental period, social costs for the two randomly chosen groups are the same, because of the controlled nature of the experiment. Early in the experimental period, some patients in E_2 would be treated with cimetidine and perhaps other therapies as well. Because cimetidine treatment normally lasts about eight weeks, drug therapy costs per patient for the experimental group might be expected to be higher early in the experimental period. As the experiment proceeds, however, it

---

[5] Even E_2, however, is subject to shortcomings as a model of reality. In reality, not all DU patients for whom cimetidine is the medically preferred therapy will obtain it—because of physicians' misdiagnoses, failure of the patient to seek medical advice, or failure to heed the advice. Similarly, some patients will actually receive cimetidine even though it is not the medically preferred therapy for their particular set of problems.

could be hypothesized that the social costs associated with the E_2 group would be lower than those of the control group. In the case of a chronic disease like DU, complete measurement of social costs might well require an experimental period of many years. The net social cost saving from the introduction of cimetidine would simply be the difference between the area marked B and that marked A in figure 1 after appropriate discounting for passage of time.

This hypothetical experiment has two attractive features in common with any well-designed experiment, one of which is absent in nonexperimental situations and one of which is likely to be absent. The first is that the "fairness" of the trial is guaranteed by random assignment of patients and providers. In the actual introduction of any new drug, assignment is made by the actors themselves—primarily providers but, to varying degrees, the patients as well. There are two problems here. First, we have no practical way of knowing whether those providers and patients who use the new technology differ in important ways from those who do not use it. It could be that as soon as the new drug is approved for conditional use by the FDA, all providers have access to the drug and are fully aware of how it should be used in conjunction with other treatments; but this case is rather implausible. It might also be that in the new technology all patients receive the drug just introduced; but this case is also unlikely. If neither of these polar cases prevails, systematic differences between the experimental and control groups are likely to exist. In particular, patients whose social costs are higher may well be proportionately more important in one group than in the other. The obvious bias that this nonproportional representation introduces in measurements of the type illustrated in figure 1 is an example of the selectivity bias that can exist whenever inferences are made in nonexperimental settings under the (erroneous) assumption of random assignment.

The second attractive feature of our hypothetical experiment is that extensive measures of socioeconomic well-being may be made, provided the control and experimental groups are kept small enough that the costs of measurement are not prohibitive. In nonexperimental situations this is usually not the case, although it could be: intensive measurements on a randomly selected subpopulation could be made, as is done for the general population by the Bureau of the Census and the Bureau of Labor statistics each month. In fact, however, most of the measures are those made of the entire population. Like the data discussed in the previous section, they have insufficient coverage and detail because they are collected for other purposes.

Making Inferences from Nonexperimental Data. It seems unlikely that

TABLE 3

DISTRIBUTION OF CIMETIDINE PRESCRIPTIONS, SEPTEMBER 1977–JUNE 1978

(sample size = 530)

September 1977	0.057	February 1978	0.160
October 1977	0.100	March 1978	0.075
November 1977	0.098	April 1978	0.087
December 1977	0.134	May 1978	0.094
January 1978	0.098	June 1978	0.096
		Total	1.000

SOURCE: Authors.

either of the two polar cases just discussed would prevail in practice, and in the introduction of cimetidine there is some evidence that they did not. The FDA certified effectiveness of the new drug only in the case of DU and some hypersecretory conditions that are rare by comparison. In our sample, however, we were able to associate only about one of every fourteen prescriptions of cimetidine with a DU diagnosis. It is clear that providers' behavior and the FDA certification restrictions cannot both reflect optimal use of the drug, thus ruling out the first case.[6] In the other polar case, in which all DU patients receive cimetidine, the penetration rate should increase toward unity, and the ratio of DU patients treated with cimetidine to those not treated should increase without bound. Tables 3 and 4 show, however, that this was decidedly not the case for the Texas Medicaid sample.

The Medicaid data, being nonexperimental, do not permit separate analyses of the E_1 and E_2 groups discussed above. We know only that some providers prescribed cimetidine to some patients, and so we have an approximation to group E_2. There is no group E_1, for which cimetidine therapy was mandatory. (It is also notable that we can distinguish between those cimetidine users for whom duodenal ulcers were diagnosed and other users of the drug.)

We identify all duodenal ulcer patients who received cimetidine between September 1, 1977, and June 30, 1978, as the T group, all other patients who received treatment (but not cimetidine) for duodenal ulcer during that period as the F group, and control for selectivity bias within

---

[6] We might further expect that if the FDA proscription on use of the drug beyond an initial eight-week period reflected the consensus of practitioners, the number of cimetidine prescriptions would eventually decline, as the stock of patients with DU at the time of the drug's introduction was treated once and only those with new ulcers were treated with cimetidine. Certainly there is no evidence that this occurred in the ten months for which we have data (table 3), although such a decline might occur beyond the sample period.

TABLE 4

RATIO OF PATIENTS TREATED WITH CIMETIDINE TO NEW DUODENAL
ULCER PATIENTS NOT TREATED WITH CIMETIDINE, SEPTEMBER
1977–JUNE 1978
(sample size = 1,206)

September 1977	0.698	February 1978	1.308
October 1977	0.946	March 1978	0.571
November 1977	1.182	April 1978	0.719
December 1977	1.164	May 1978	0.667
January 1978	0.839	June 1978	0.375

NOTE: A "new" DU patient is one whose first indication of DU in the period September
1977–June 1978 occurred in the month indicated.
SOURCE: Authors.

the limitations imposed by the data base. With a sufficiently large sample, this strategy would be implemented as follows. We restrict our attention to those patients with indications of an "active ulcer" diagnosis in the period P, September 1, 1977, to June 30, 1978; a patient is assumed to have an active ulcer problem if any treatment is provided for duodenal ulcer as a primary or secondary diagnosis, or if he or she is treated with an antiulcer drug and has a past (preceding year) diagnosis of DU. The time of incidence of any indicator of socioeconomic cost for each patient is measured with reference to the first indication of an active ulcer problem within the sample period for those in group F and with reference to the prescription of cimetidine for those in group T. The "point of reference" is the analogue of the start of the experiment in a controlled environment and corresponds to the point T_0 in figure 1. For group F the point of reference is chosen to be the first indication of ulcer rather than September 1, because the latter choice could cause to be included in F some patients with no active ulcer problem at the reference point, whereas all patients in T do have an active ulcer problem at the time cimetidine is prescribed; presumably there would then be a downward bias in the measurement of social costs for group F relative to group T and a resulting upward bias in the estimated cost-reducing effects of cimetidine.

Samples F and T are then subdivided to control for all measured factors that might affect real treatment costs. The divisions are made conditional on two groups of variables.

The variables in the first group are demographic: the sex, race, and age of each patient are known, and our subsample may be further divided conditionally on these variables. There is an obvious and large potential for selectivity bias if demographic factors are ignored. (As we shall see,

245

even if all demographic groups were identical with respect to the relevant medical factors and proportioned in the same way between F and T, there would still be reason to separate these groups for the purpose of assessing social medical care costs.)

The second group of variables consists of those associated with the "severity" of a given disease. It is important to recognize that we can never adequately measure all those factors that would be controlled implicitly in a randomized experiment. Even in the experiment contemplated above, providers may (even subconsciously) take into account unmeasured or unmeasurable dimensions of a patient's health in deciding whether or not to prescribe cimetidine. There is no way to account for nonrandom factors that affect assignment to groups F and T but are uncorrelated with measured variables. The best that one can do is to account adequately for the variables that are measured.

In the present study, there are available four specific variables that, it is reasonable to assume, are associated with potentially nonrandom assignment factors and that, in turn, are related to social costs: first, the number of indications of sickness in a prespecified period before the reference point, which we shall call the "presample period"; second, expenditures on health care in that same period; third, days hospitalized in that period; and fourth, indications of other disease over that period. Each is important because it may be positively correlated with medical care costs over the presample period *and over the sample period*, whether cimetidine was prescribed or not. Failure to account for these variables could introduce a potentially very large source of selectivity bias: one has only to conjecture polar situations in which providers prescribe cimetidine only to patients at death's door or, alternatively, those in which cimetidine is given only to those who are relatively healthy or are on no other medication and consequently unlikely to suffer complications.

In principle, selectivity bias would be minimized by evaluating treatment costs while controlling for each of these factors, using a very fine categorization, but this can lead to more cells than observations. We tested for the existence of selectivity bias for each of seven dimensions (sex, race, age, indications of sickness, expenditures on health care, days of hospitalization, and indications of other disease) by testing the hypothesis that the proportion receiving cimetidine is unaffected by variations in that dimension in the presample period. We control for selectivity bias through subdivision of the sample only in those cases where such bias appeared to be substantively and statistically significant. Once this initial subdivision was made, tests for selectivity bias were undertaken within each subsample, and further subdivisions were pursued only where there was evidence within a subsample of selectivity bias conditional on another dimension. The subsamples so selected are the populations within which treatment costs associated with the new technology, incorporating cimetidine, and the old are compared.

Measurement of Social Cost Variables. Having subdivided our sample in this way, we have now approximated the conditions of controlled experiments undertaken on each of a number of groups of patients. The proportion of patients in each subsample receiving cimetidine is in general not the same, which is what necessitated the subdivision of the original sample to reduce selectivity bias. Within each group, we monitor indicators of social cost in the fashion anticipated in figure 1, the subdivisions and testing procedures outlined above providing some assurance that the paths of measurable treatment cost variables in the presample period are about the same for the F and T groups in each subsample, as they would be expected to be in a randomized experimental design.

At this point, further division of the sample may be desirable. Tests for selectivity bias, for example, may indicate no need to dissociate young males from older females, but it is quite conceivable that the differential response of the two groups to cimetidine- and non-cimetidine-based treatments in the sample period might be great. Since the socioeconomic implications of the ability to control a chronic disease indefinitely are very different for the two groups, they would be analyzed separately. In the interests of manageability, however, we treat groups separately only if separation is necessary to reduce (and, it is hoped, to eliminate) selection bias or if it is desirable because of statistically significant different behavior in the sample period for groups with different socioeconomic characteristics.

For each group, we estimate the mean and standard deviations of paths of the form shown in figure 1. For continuous variables like health care expenditure, the quantity estimated is the expected value for a patient in the group at a particular time relative to the reference point. For categorical variables like "no days hospitalized," the estimated quantity is a probability. From the nature of our sample, it is obvious that the position of the path is estimated with less accuracy as one moves to the right of the reference point, especially for group T, because the sample becomes thinner. Means and probabilities for the entire ten-month sample period are also estimated. Appropriate weighting by the numerical importance of each group treated separately then provides estimates of magnitudes associated with treatment costs.

Data Base

All the data used in this study are taken from Medicaid claims in the state of Texas for the period September 1976 through June 1978. The data were collected originally for accounting purposes and were made available to us by Pracon, Inc., of Fairfax, Virginia, an independent consulting firm. Pracon and SysteMetrics, Inc., of Santa Barbara, California, converted the data from their original form to a format more suitable for studying the health care experience of individual patients.

The basic organizational unit from which our files were constructed is the claim. A claim is a bill submitted to the state of Texas for a medical service or drug. In some cases, claims are amended after their original submission, in which case the amended claim was used. Associated with each claim are a patient identification number; an identification number for the provider (for example, a physician or pharmacy); a primary and, in some cases, a secondary diagnosis if the claim is for hospital, physician, or nursing home services; the date of the claim; the date on which the service was rendered; the nature of the service performed by the physician (for example, surgery or consultation); the length of stay for hospital and nursing home claims; the amount filled, in the case of drug claims; and the size of the claim. Demographic information—sex, race, and age—about each patient is provided, as is detailed information about the provider: for example, the specialty of physicians and whether a hospital is profit, nonprofit, or a unit of an institution.

Perhaps the most attractive feature of this data base relative to others that might have been used is the availability of detailed medical information about the period in which health care costs are incurred as well as the time at which they are billed. Together with the availability of patient identification numbers, this information makes possible a detailed reconstruction of that portion of a patient's health care history that was paid for by the state. Although we believe that this data set constitutes the best nonexperimental evidence yet assembled for the evaluation of innovations in medical technology, it is not without its shortcomings. We shall briefly discuss those that are most important in limiting the kinds of questions that can be addressed or in evaluating the results presented here:

- The only aspects of patients' experiences that are known to us are those that entail a claim. In particular, there is no direct information on morbidity outside institutions, which might have been obtained had the purpose of data collection been research rather than accounting. At most, we can make rough guesses about the implications for work experience of days hospitalized and various diagnoses and drug prescriptions.

- Only those direct costs billable to the state Medicaid system are known. In general, there is no way of knowing the nature or magnitude of health care costs not publicly paid. For patients over sixty-five, the

248

problem is significant, because many of their health care costs are paid by Medicare. For those under sixty-five, Medicaid generally pays all health care bills when the recipient is eligible.

• In the case of DU, there is little information available about the severity of the illness. Diagnoses are recorded using the International Classification of Diseases, which provides eight gradations of severity for DU, but most providers use the code for a ninth classification in which severity is unspecified. Hence, we have little information about a potentially important source of selectivity bias.

• Drug claims have no associated diagnosis and are not itemized for inpatients. Hence the drug therapy component of direct costs may be compared only for drugs prescribed on an outpatient basis, and in each case the associated diagnosis must be inferred from the patient's prior health care history.

• Deaths are not recorded in our data set. If patients in one group had higher mortality experience, we would observe lower expenditures on medical care for that group.

It should also be noted that our data are limited to Medicaid patients, and although we do not believe that they constitute a biased sample of the entire DU population in terms of the expenditure effects of cimetidine, we cannot be certain. If, for example, cimetidine treatment was more effective than alternative therapies, so that cimetidine patients were more able to obtain and sustain employment, their increased incomes might cause them to be dropped from Medicaid and, hence, from our sample (which includes only persons covered by Medicaid for the entire period of the study, as described below). The result would be a downward bias in the estimated effect of cimetidine.

From the original file of about 12 million claims, the sample S described in the previous section was constructed. This sample is restricted to those individuals who were eligible for the Medicaid program during the entire period September 1976 through June 1978. Sample T is composed of the individuals in S with a DU diagnosis on some claim during the period September 1976 through June 1978 who also had a claim for cimetidine in the period September 1977 through June 1978. Sample F is composed of the individuals in S with a DU diagnosis on some claim during the period September 1976 through June 1978 who had either a claim with a DU diagnosis or a claim for an ulcer prescription (but not cimetidine) during that period. For the latter group, "ulcer prescription" is defined by the National Drug Commission codes, and base dating begins with the first such claim or prescription in the September 1977 through June 1978 period. There are 1,206 persons in sample S, of whom 530 are in sample T.

Unfortunately, only outpatient prescriptions for cimetidine are recorded. Some hospitalized patients doubtless received cimetidine; so the "noncimetidine" F group includes some persons who should have been in T. To the extent that those patients are similar to those who were included in T, measured differences between the T and F groups have been biased downward. To the extent that hospitalization reflects more serious health care problems, however, measured costs will be biased upward for the F sample and downward for T.

Findings

In this section we report our estimates of the changes in certain public expenditures and other measures of costs that may be ascribed to the introduction of the new medical technology that incorporates cimetidine. After briefly discussing selectivity biases evident in the data, we treat total health care expenditures, hospital and physician expenditures for duodenal ulcer, and days of hospitalization. All three measures can be disaggregated in various ways, but a careful discussion at this level of detail is beyond the scope of this paper.

By any number of measures, it appears that the new drug has been administered to patients who exhibited more illness in the preceding twelve months than did those patients who were treated using older therapies. As shown in table 5, patients treated with cimetidine were hospitalized almost 50 percent more days than those who were not in the preceding twelve months—7.46 days compared to 5.14—and their total health care expenditures for this period were significantly higher, $1,506 compared to $1,293.

A close examination of monthly expenditure and hospitalization records reveals that much of the difference between the two groups' presample history occurs in the single month immediately preceding the base date. This difference may be accounted for by the environment in which cimetidine is prescribed and by our definition of the base date. For patients who receive cimetidine, any immediately preceding duodenal ulcer therapy is by definition in the presample period, whereas for patients who do not receive cimetidine the construction of our sample is such that there can be no duodenal ulcer therapy in the immediately preceding month—only therapy with other diagnoses—unless the treatment occurred during September 1977. There is, however, a selectivity bias problem that exists independently of the problem of how the first presample month should be treated. For the first eleven months of the presample period, cimetidine patients still exhibited greater health problems in the seven dimensions exhibited in table 5, although the differences are arithmetically smaller than when the first presample month

250

TABLE 5

Tests for Selectivity Bias

Variable	Sample T (n = 676)		Sample F (n = 530)		t-values
	Mean	St. dev.	Mean	St. dev.	
Days hospitalized, −12/−1	7.46	111.0	5.14	9.57	−3.84[a]
Total expenditures, −12/−1	$1,506.0	$2,224	$1,293.0	$1,945	−1.72[c]
Drugs	125.0	110	111.0	109	−2.18[b]
Outpatient	74.8	181	44.9	118	−3.28[a]
Hospital	674.0	1,314	499.0	1,096	−2.45[b]
Physicians	278.0	1,476	231.0	370	−1.88[c]
Physician and hospital expenditures with DU diagnosis, −12/−1	117.0	376	60.5	219	−3.07
Days hospitalized, −12/−2	5.33	9.57	4.44	8.51	−1.69[c]
Total expenditures, −12/−2	$1,280.0	$2,104	$1,138.0	$1,826	−1.26
Drugs	113.0	102	100.0	100	−2.20[b]
Outpatient	65.6	162	38.2	100	−3.41[a]
Hospital	542.0	1,177	434.0	1,005	−1.68[c]
Physicians	241.0	431	203.0	338	−1.63
Physician and hospital expenditures with DU diagnosis, −12/−2	61.5	316	54.7	212	−0.42

[a] Significant at 1 percent level.
[b] Significant at 5 percent level.
[c] Significant at 10 percent level.
Source: Authors.

is included and are significantly different at the 10 percent level in only four instances.

Examination of demographic variables turned up no significant differences between the two groups. Expenditures associated with the treatment of duodenal ulcer in the first eleven months of the presample period averaged only a few dollars per month per patient and were not significantly different for the *T* and *F* samples. Both health care expenditures and days of hospitalization in the presample period affected the probability that a given patient would be treated with cimetidine. Because of the size of the sample, stratification was attempted only on total health care expenditures in the first eleven months of the presample period.

Because of the special behavior of the history of health care in the first presample month in the T and F samples, we have treated this month in two different ways in reporting our results. In essence, the question is whether treatment received immediately before a cimetidine prescription is an integral part of the new technology that incorporates cimetidine. If it is, then expenditures incurred in the first presample month should be associated with cimetidine, and comparing expenditures for the T and F samples beginning with the base date would lead to a downward bias in the expenditure estimate for the T sample. If it is not, then this kind of comparison is the correct one to make. In all likelihood, expenditures in the first month of the presample are part of the new technology for some patients treated with cimetidine—for example, those whose newly diagnosed ulcer was confirmed by an endoscopy—but are not for others—for example, those for whom the new technology was used after other methods failed. In the estimates reported below, we compare samples T and F for three months, -1 through $+2$, for the two months -1 and $+1$, and for the single month $+1$. The cost of the treatment with therapy incorporating cimetidine relative to that not incorporating cimetidine is probably overstated for the first two groups of months and understated for the last.

In tables 6, 7, and 8 we report mean total health care expenditures, hospital and physician expenditures on persons with a diagnosis of duodenal ulcer, and days of hospitalization for several interesting subperiods of the presample and postsample periods. In all cases we eliminated from the sample patients over sixty-five, since expenditure records for patients eligible for Medicare are incomplete. In each table the sample has been stratified by those patients with less than $300 total health care expenditures in the first eleven months of the presample period (referred to as group A), those with $300 to $1,000 expenditures (group B), and those with more than $1,000 (group C). All groups and samples show high levels of mean expenditures and mean days of hospitalization immediately after the base date, followed by a decrease that is sometimes sharp but does not usually return to presample levels. See, for example, figures 2–5 in the case of expenditures. In the first month or two of the sample period, almost all patients exhibit levels of expenditures that are high relative to their presample expenditures, but in the latter months of the sample period a few patients have high expenditures and many (in some instances, most) have no expenditures at all in a given month, as reflected in standard deviations greater than the mean for all but one

TABLE 6

HEALTH CARE EXPENDITURES

Control Group[a]	Month	No.	T Sample Mean ($)	St. dev. ($)	No.	F Sample Mean ($)	St. dev. ($)	t-values
A	−12/−2	149	113	93.5	206	95.3	90.1	−1.83[d]
	−1/+1	149	504	781	206	745	1,460	2.00[c]
	+1	149	325	658	206	663	1,404	3.01[b]
	−1/+2	139	569	781	190	835	1,432	2.15[c]
	+2/+4	116	316	580	151	313	772	−0.02
	+5/+7	57	264	570	81	154	337	−1.30
	+8/+10	10	79.6	68.7	31	202	434	1.51
B	−12/−2	97	543	184	127	594	196	1.99[c]
	−1/+1	97	449	709	127	481	866	0.31
	+1	97	305	593	127	359	711	0.61
	−1/+2	92	587	770	119	576	889	−0.09
	+2/+4	65	335	540	95	383	719	0.48
	+5/+7	37	205	383	64	459	790	2.16[c]
	+8/+10	16	150	215	18	511	806	1.82[d]
C	−12/−2	132	3,432	2,581	149	2,951	2,265	−1.65
	−1/+1	132	900	1,204	149	736	938	−1.25
	+1	132	511	913	149	423	678	−0.90
	−1/+2	125	1,114	1,316	140	1,068	1,292	0.78
	+2/+4	101	878	1,272	117	863	1,170	−0.08
	+5/+7	44	694	1,109	76	598	832	−0.49
	+8/+10	10	929	1,088	33	691	1,432	−0.55

[a] Patients under sixty-five with less than $300 total health care expenditures in months −12/−2 of the presample period constitute group A; $300 to $1,000, group B; over $1,000, group C.
[b] Significant at 1 percent level.
[c] Significant at 5 percent level.
[d] Significant at 10 percent level.
SOURCE: Authors.

entry for the months +2/+4, +5/+7, and +8/+10 in tables 6 and 7. As discussed above, the data on which table 7 is based are less reliable than those for tables 6 and 8, because diagnostic information is often not reported.

Systematic and significant differences emerge only early in the sample period and only for the groups with low expenditures in the presample period. For this group, expenditures and days of hospitalization are significantly lower for the T sample than for the F sample in the months +1 and −1/+2. The estimated reduction in hospital and physician expenditures for persons with a diagnosis of duodenal ulcer is

TABLE 7

HOSPITAL AND PHYSICIAN EXPENDITURES FOR DUODENAL ULCERS

			T Sample			F Sample		
Control Group[a]	Month	No.	Mean ($)	St. dev. ($)	No.	Mean ($)	St. dev. ($)	t-values
A	−12/−2	149	4.39	22.6	206	355	14.9	−0.39
	−1/+1	149	173	514	206	447	1,257	2.81[b]
	+1	149	108	445	206	438	1,258	3.47[b]
	−1/+2	139	196	533	190	439	1,261	2.37[c]
	+2/+4	116	51.2	170	151	36.3	217	−0.62
	+5/+7	57	95.2	357	81	7.91	45.1	−1.83[d]
	+8/+10	10	0	0	31	23.6	116	1.12
B	−12/−2	97	47.7	127	127	61.7	142	0.77
	−1/+1	97	124	293	127	146	435	0.43
	+1	97	98.0	271	127	144	435	0.98
	−1/+2	92	139	304	119	136	364	−0.06
	+2/+4	65	51.5	207	95	23.2	104	−1.01
	+5/+7	37	4.93	22.6	64	14.5	79.0	0.90
	+8/+10	16	0.849	3.39	18	25.8	109	0.96
C	−12/−2	132	166	603	149	143	409	−0.35
	−1/+1	132	167	918	149	197	505	0.55
	+1	132	97.4	339	149	187	498	1.79[d]
	−1/+2	125	167	386	140	211	517	0.78
	+2/+4	101	60.2	228	117	42.2	241	−0.56
	+5/+7	44	29.2	170	76	63.6	364	0.70
	+8/+10	10	0	0	33	8.90	35.6	1.43

[a] Patients under sixty-five with less than $300 total health care expenditures in months −12/−2 of the presample period constitute group A; $300 to $1,000, group B; over $1,000, group C.
[b] Significant at 1 percent level.
[c] Significant at 5 percent level.
[d] Significant at 10 percent level.
SOURCE: Authors.

between 55 percent and 75 percent, depending on how the first presample month is treated. In the latter months of the sample period, differences in expenditures and hospitalization for the two samples are for the most part statistically insignificant. Because these differences are small arithmetically as well, it does not appear that this result is simply the consequence of the smaller portion of the sample for which longer periods beyond the base date may be observed.

For the two groups with higher presample-period health care expenditures, groups B and C, differences between the T and F samples during the sample period are mostly statistically insignificant. It could

TABLE 8

DAYS OF HOSPITALIZATION

Control Group[a]	Month	T Sample			F Sample			
		No.	Mean	St. dev.	No.	Mean	St. dev.	t-values
A	−12/−2	149	0.19	0.12	216	0.14	1.06	−0.34
	−1/+1	149	2.41	3.99	206	4.02	6.18	2.97[b]
	+1	149	1.49	3.39	206	3.68	5.48	4.36[b]
	−1/+2	139	2.51	3.74	190	4.50	6.61	3.45[b]
	+2/+4	116	1.18	2.92	151	1.31	3.54	0.32
	+5/+7	57	1.22	3.37	81	0.703	2.15	−1.03
	+8/+10	10	0	0.00	31	0.806	2.18	2.06[c]
B	−12/−2	97	2.04	5.38	127	2.21	2.75	0.28
	−1/+1	97	2.23	4.02	127	2.64	5.06	0.67
	+1	97	1.36	3.26	127	2.00	4.21	1.28
	−1/+2	92	2.86	4.32	119	3.48	6.86	0.79
	+2/+4	65	2.35	6.06	95	2.30	6.13	−0.04
	+5/+7	37	0.70	2.41	64	1.89	3.97	1.86[d]
	+8/+10	16	0	0	18	3.00	7.12	1.78[d]
C	−12/−2	132	14.4	12.1	149	13.2	11.9	−0.81
	−1/+1	132	4.71	6.33	149	3.47	5.99	−1.68[d]
	+1	132	2.59	4.74	149	2.10	4.12	−0.92
	−1/+2	125	5.69	6.79	140	4.65	7.05	−1.22
	+2/+4	101	3.82	6.54	117	3.25	6.03	0.65
	+5/+7	44	3.77	7.50	76	1.73	3.34	−1.70[d]
	+8/+10	10	3.90	6.75	33	1.48	3.34	−1.09

[a] Patients under sixty-five with less than $300 total health care expenditures in months −12/−2 of the presample period constitute group A; $300 to $1,000, group B; over $1,000, group C.
[b] Significant at 1 percent level.
[c] Significant at 5 percent level.
[d] Significant at 10 percent level.
SOURCE: Authors.

be the case that the technology that incorporates cimetidine does not, in fact, reduce health care costs for those patients with more severe health problems. On the other hand, the proportionate reduction in total health care expenditures would be less to the extent that "more severe health problems" imply afflictions other than duodenal ulcer, and hospital and physician expenditures associated with the treatment of duodenal ulcer may be difficult to define or may be recorded less reliably in this case as well. There is some evidence of the latter problem here: total health care expenditures for the groups with high presample expenditures are about the same as or higher in the sample period than those for the groups with lower presample expenditures (table 6), but

255

FIGURE 2

AVERAGE TOTAL HEALTH CARE EXPENDITURES, PERSONS UNDER
SIXTY-FIVE, $0–$300 EXPENDITURES IN PRESAMPLE

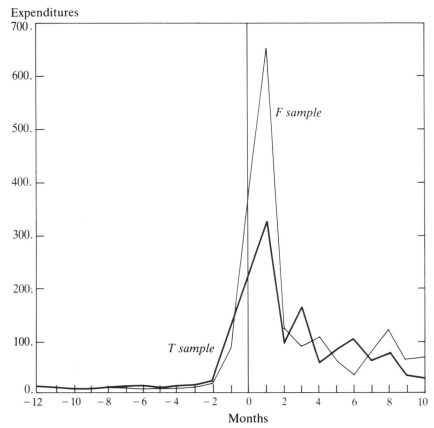

their recorded expenditures for hospital and physician treatments associated with diagnoses of duodenal ulcer are about the same (table 8).

An alternative presentation of our findings is provided in table 9, where we have controlled for presample health care expenditures by regression on total health care expenditures in the $-12/-2$ period rather than stratification. Significant differences between the T and F samples again emerge early in the sample period, most strikingly in the first month. In each case the new technology seems to have the most favorable impact for those patients with the lowest presample total health care expenditures, as shown by comparison of estimated intercepts; for example, total health care expenditures in the first month are $212 less for the T sample ($211) than for the F sample ($423) among patients with no health care expenditures in the presample period. This differential declines as presample total health care expenditures increase and

FIGURE 3

AVERAGE TOTAL HEALTH CARE EXPENDITURES, PERSONS UNDER
SIXTY-FIVE, $300–$1,000 EXPENDITURES IN PRESAMPLE

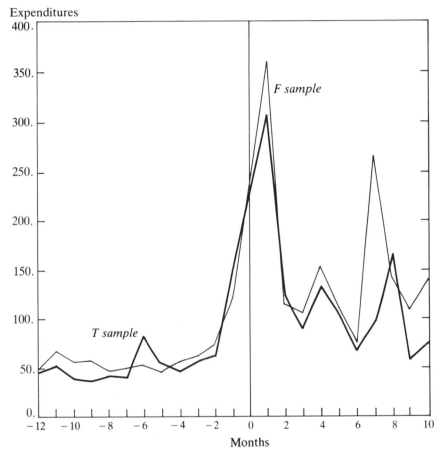

becomes negative when these expenditures exceed $2,700, which is well above the mean expenditure level of $1,200. For hospital and physician expenditures associated with the treatment of duodenal ulcer, the estimated "break-even" point is $20,000, well outside the range of our sample, and for days of hospitalization it is $4,700, which is exceeded only for a few observations in the entire sample.

For later months in the sample period, there are some interesting and significant differences in expenditures between the T and F samples (table 9, *HCE* and *DU HCE* dependent variables). In most cases the cimetidine-based technology is relatively more advantageous for patients with low presample expenditures. The only exception worthy of note is total health care expenditures in the $+2/+4$ period, in which the

FIGURE 4

AVERAGE TOTAL HEALTH CARE EXPENDITURES, PERSONS UNDER
SIXTY-FIVE, $1,000+ EXPENDITURES IN PRESAMPLE

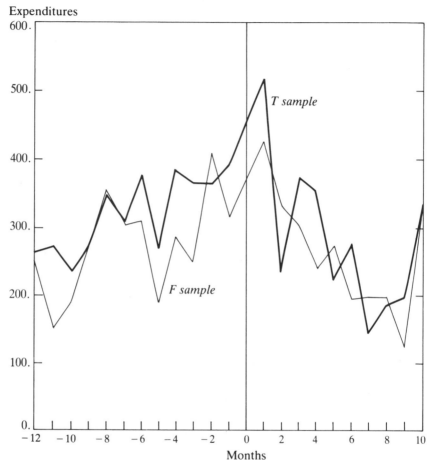

entire regression and the slope coefficients alone are significantly different and the situation is reversed; the "break-even" level of presample expenditures here is $1,200. Days hospitalized are directly related to health care expenditures in the presample period for both samples, and the incremental effect is once again greater for the T sample than for the F sample in the periods $+5/+7$ and $+8/+10$. In both cases, however, days hospitalized tend to be lower for the F than for the T sample, even when presample health care expenditures are set to zero—that is, the intercept for T is larger than for F. The pattern for days of hospitalization shown in table 9 is consistent with the interpretation that the

258

FIGURE 5
AVERAGE TOTAL HEALTH CARE EXPENDITURES,
PERSONS UNDER SIXTY-FIVE

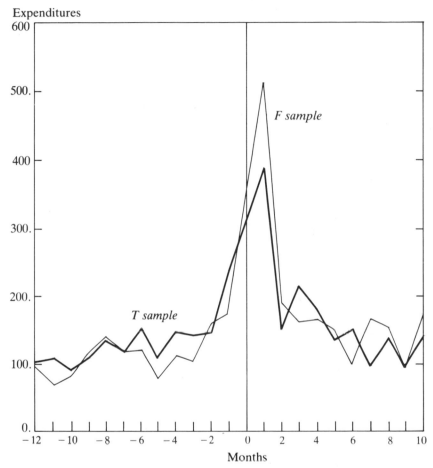

NOTE: Total health care expenditures are obtained from figures 2, 3, and 4 by weighting each group by its proportionate representation in the portion of sample S under sixty-five.

cimetidine technology provides a substitute for surgery in many cases,[7] whereas in some others it merely postpones surgery to a later date.[8]

---

[7] J. D. Elashoff and M. I. Grossman, "Trends in Hospital Admissions and Death Rates for Peptic Ulcer in the United States from 1970 to 1978," *Gastroenterology*, in press.

[8] More detail on this point is provided in another paper by the authors now in progress.

TABLE 9
Cost Measures Controlling for Prior Health Care Expenditures by Regression

Dependent Variable[a]	Months	T Sample			F Sample			"F"[c]
		No.	Intercept	Slope[b]	No.	Intercept	Slope[b]	
HCE	−1/+2	500	407 (9.47)	236 (13.2)	633	516 (9.58)	213 (8.65)	1.16
	+1	530	211 (6.33)	106 (7.65)	676	423 (9.33)	27 (1.31)	7.31[d]
	+2/+4	395	276 (6.09)	160 (8.71)	533	199 (5.22)	222 (12.6)	3.07[e]
	+5/+7	187	203 (3.73)	140 (6.17)	345	205 (5.21)	158 (8.44)	0.30
	+8/+10	51	116 (1.32)	220 (3.90)	136	170 (2.03)	187 (5.92)	0.08
DU HCE	−1/+2	500	161 (8.13)	−2.56 (0.31)	633	269 (6.64)	−8.28 (0.44)	3.01[e]
	+1	530	43.1 (5.63)	−1.85 (0.26)	676	266 (6.78)	−10.6 (0.58)	8.52[d]
	+2/+4	345	47.5 (4.62)	.080 (0.02)	533	28.3 (3.24)	−.661 (0.16)	1.57
	+5/+7	187	34.4 (1.86)	6.82 (0.88)	345	23.0 (2.00)	−.171 (0.03)	0.94
	+8/+10	51	.375 (1.14)	−.096 (0.45)	136	14.5 (1.95)	−1.36 (0.48)	0.82
DH	−1/+2	520	3.98 (12.6)	.634 (4.84)	633	4.52 (13.4)	.260 (1.68)	1.34

+1	530	1.73	.266	676	3.62	−.136	14.42[d]
		(8.15)	(2.94)		(13.6)	(1.10)	
+2/+4	345	1.87	.380	533	1.25	.478	1.37
		(6.32)	(3.16)		(5.14)	(4.25)	
+5/+7	187	1.65	.334	345	1.28	.059	2.82[f]
		(3.69)	(1.82)		(5.92)	(0.60)	
+8/+10	51	1.49	1.08	156	1.09	.075	3.55[e]
		(1.43)	(1.62)		(2.81)	(0.51)	

NOTE: Ratios of coefficients to standard errors (*t*-statistics) are reported in parentheses. The control variable is total health care expenditures in the −12/−2 period, measured in dollars.
[a] *HCE* denotes total health care expenditures; *DU HCE*, hospital and physician expenditures for DU; *DH*, days hospitalized.
[b] Coefficients have been scaled by a factor of 1,000.
[c] For a test of the hypothesis that intercept and slope coefficients for the *T* and *F* samples are the same.
[d] Significant at 1 percent level.
[e] Significant at 5 percent level.
[f] Significant at 10 percent level.
SOURCE: Authors.

Conclusion

We have set out a methodology for assessing the effect on total health care expenditures of a change in medical technology, and we have applied the methodology to a new drug, cimetidine. Governments at all levels—federal, state, local—are increasingly concerned with rising medical care expenditures, and thus they are often preoccupied with the effect on those expenditures of any change in the health care system, whether it be a change in technology, administrative arrangements, input prices, or anything else. At the same time, as we emphasized in the introduction to this paper, identification of the effect of some activity on expenditures is not generally equivalent to determination of whether it would or would not pass a social benefit-cost test of economic efficiency, let alone a test of its net contribution to social welfare.

In our estimation work we relied on Medicaid records for the state of Texas as the basis for determining the expenditure effects of cimetidine, recently approved by the Food and Drug Administration for treating duodenal ulcers. Medicaid is available largely to the poor; thus, our data all apply to this population. We are aware of no reason to believe that findings for this population cannot be generalized to the nonpoor population, but we cannot be certain that the two populations are essentially identical in the expenditure effects of the new drug.

We have found that the introduction of cimetidine resulted in a large and statistically significant decrease in hospital and physician expenditures for the treatment of duodenal ulcers for a substantial portion of our sample and smaller but insignificant decreases for the other portion. Whether the new technology is more or less efficacious than the old and whether it has affected morbidity and mortality rates are questions that cannot be addressed using our data base. Whether or not it affects public expenditures for the treatment of this chronic disease over longer periods of time is a question that could be answered with more data of the type used here.

In this study we concentrated on the impact of cimetidine on three broad measures of resources devoted directly to health care: total health care expenditures, hospital and physician expenditures for duodenal ulcers, and days hospitalized. These measures can be disaggregated to provide more detail on the composition of expenditures under the old technology and the new. In tables 10 and 11, we provide examples of this decomposition for that part of the sample and that period for which differences in the two technologies seem to be the greatest: patients with low presample total health care expenditures in the period immediately surrounding their treatment for duodenal ulcer. As discussed

TABLE 10

DECOMPOSITION OF HEALTH CARE EXPENDITURES, CONTROL
GROUP A, MONTH + 1

	T Sample (n = 149)		F Sample (n = 206)		Percentage Reduction,	
	Mean	St. dev.	Mean	St. dev.	T over F[a]	t-values
Total expenditures	325.80	658	663.42	1,406	57	3.02[b]
Hospital	140.60	520	512.36	1,308	63	3.19[b]
Physician	80.41	145	117.95	195	32	2.08[c]
Drugs	29.66	12.9	11.32	8.37	− 162	− 15.19[b]
Outpatient	15.80	40.7	15.02	36.5	—	− 0.18
Nursing home	4.05	49.4	0.32	4.62	—	− 0.91
Other	5.26	17.4	6.43	20.0	—	0.58
DU expenditures	108.63	445	438.32	1,258	75	3.47[b]
Hospital	84.81	402	404.18	1,225	79	3.49[b]
Physician	23.81	65.8	34.14	116	—	1.06

[a] Provided only where reduction is statistically significant at the 10 percent level.
[b] Significant at 1 percent level.
[c] Significant at 5 percent level.
SOURCE: Authors.

earlier, expenditure differentials for the first sample month alone (disaggregated in table 10) probably overstate the short-term impact of cimetidine, whereas those for the last month of the presample and the first two months of the sample period (disaggregated in table 11) probably understate it. Whichever estimates are used, however, the same conclusions emerge about the way in which expenditures are reduced by the new technology. The reduction in mean (per capita) total health care expenditures for persons treated with cimetidine—between $265 (table 11) and $338 (table 10)—is accounted for almost entirely by a reduction in those hospital expenditures resulting from the treatment of duodenal ulcer, between $242 and $330. By contrast, the difference in drug costs between the two groups, between $18 and $27, is trivial. This decomposition suggests the conjecture that cimetidine has been a substitute for surgery in many cases. If this conjecture is correct, then morbidity and mortality due to treatment, and the accompanying pain and suffering of patients, relatives, and others, are very probably lower in the new technology than in the old. At the same time, we cannot rule out the possibility that use of cimetidine serves primarily to postpone surgery beyond the ten-month sample period covered by this research rather than to eliminate it.

TABLE 11

DECOMPOSITION OF HEALTH CARE EXPENDITURES, CONTROL
GROUP A, MONTHS $-1/+2$

	T Sample (n = 149)		F Sample (n = 206)		Percentage Reduction, T over F[a]	t-values
	Mean	St. dev.	Mean	St. dev.		
Total expenditures	569.76	781	835.22	1,432	35	2.15[c]
Hospital	336.03	601	602.81	1,322	44	2.45[c]
Physician	129.68	165	165.41	213	22	1.70[d]
Drugs	50.50	27.3	23.18	18.3	−118	−10.20[b]
Outpatient	28.99	54.2	26.97	101	—	−0.23
Nursing home	8.83	104	0.34	4.81	—	−0.95
Other	15.70	47.1	16.47	47.1	—	0.14
DU expenditures	196.95	533	439.26	1,261	55	2.37[c]
Hospital	164.12	495	402.28	1,242	59	2.39[c]
Physician	32.83	66.7	36.97	101	—	0.44

[a] Provided only where reduction is statistically significant at the 10 percent level.
[b] Significant at 1 percent level.
[c] Significant at 5 percent level.
[d] Significant at 10 percent level.
SOURCE: Authors.

This new medical care technology, cimetidine, has substitutes in the forms of both surgery and conventional antacids. From a narrow viewpoint of government expenditure minimization, the question is, Which alternative or combination involves the lowest level of expenditure? We have not compared all possible treatment combinations, but what we have found is that using cimetidine does appear to reduce expenditures on treatment of duodenal ulcers compared with the average of other treatment technologies not employing cimetidine.

It would be tempting to conclude that cimetidine is "cost effective" compared with non-cimetidine-using alternatives. It is likely that this is a correct conclusion—subject to two qualifications: (1) longitudinal extension of our data—now in progress—might show a reversal of the cost advantage in favor of the cimetidine therapy, and (2) the efficacy (or, more generally, the benefits) of the various treatment modes and the accompanying health states—morbidity, mortality, pain and suffering—have not been measured explicitly in our *in vivo* study (as distinct from a laboratory setting); thus we cannot be certain that the efficacy of the cimetidine technology is at least as great as that of the others.

It seems inappropriate, however, to end on a note of reservation. Regarding point 1, above, our evidence is that the cost advantage in favor of the cimetidine therapy is not likely to be reversed, particularly for persons who were "healthier" in the presample year. Regarding point 2, it seems likely that a therapy that produces a decrease in hospitalization and in medical care is also bringing about an improvement in the state of patients' health, both because treatment is itself productive of discomfort and disruption of normal work and leisure activities and because people who experience a decrease in involvement with the medical care system may be presumed to have improved their health status.

In short, the apparent expenditure-reducing effect of cimetidine therapy, though measuring only (average) resource *costs*, seems to reflect a favorable *benefit-cost* relationship. In general, a change in expenditures on a commodity is of dubious worth as an index of the net benefits. Reduced expenditures on medical care and specifically on duodenal ulcer therapy, however, reflect both savings in resource costs and increases in social benefits resulting from improved health and the decreased demand for medical attention.

The work reported here is now being replicated with data for the state of Michigan. Since the quality of those data is better than that for Texas—largely because the diagnostic information is far more complete—more confident conclusions may emerge from the Michigan study.

Appendix A. The Nature of Duodenal Ulcer

A duodenal ulcer (DU) is any tissue death that results in a crater on the mucous membrane of the duodenum, which is the first ten to twelve inches of the small intestine. The disease appears to result from the acidity of the gastric juices, which in effect digest the mucous membrane in the same way they process food, until a cavity is formed. In comparison with other persons, DU patients typically secrete more acid from cells in the stomach and duodenum during the digestive process, maintain this high acid level longer, and secrete less of the hormone secretin that stimulates the pancreas to release alkaline pancreatic juice.

The cause of DU in unknown. Failure of the processes that regulate gastric acidity may be a cause, either through hypersecretion of gastric juice (mainly water, hydrochloric acid, mucus, and various enzymes) or through inadequacy of the mechanisms that secrete alkaline substances to neutralize gastric acid. Alternatively, DU may be caused by a change in the structure or chemistry of the cells and tissues of the mucous membrane, so that its resistance is reduced and it becomes eroded by gastric juices. In some cases DU arises in response to other maladies. It may be a by-product of biliary disease or a nearly spontaneous reaction to severe stress, for example, from external burns or advanced alcoholism.

DU is a chronic, recurrent disease characterized by sporadic episodes of acute symptoms. Pain due to DU is usually not localized, being in the general area of the stomach and upper abdomen, and may be described as "a burn," "a knot," "a pressure" or be said to resemble hunger cramps. Depending on the patient's eating habits, rhythmic distress (pain occurring every day in a regular manner) may indicate DU. Episodes of pain may also be periodic, lasting for seven to ten days followed by periods of no pain. Pain due to any ulcer is often relieved by eating food and intensified in periods of increased psychosocial stress or excessive alcohol or caffeine intake. In all cases the pain seems to be caused by gastric acid coming into contact with the base of the ulcer crater. A commonly used analogy is that acid dripping on an open ulcer is like boiling water being poured onto a burn.

In diagnosing DU, the practitioner usually considers whether pain abates after a meal; whether fatty foods increase the pain; whether the patient has been awakened at night; and the extent to which DU symptoms have been alleviated by any nonprescription antacids that may have been used by the patient. To confirm an initial diagnosis of DU, the doctor may refer the patient for X-ray, chemical analysis of the gastric juice, and measurement of the capacity of the stomach and duodenum to secrete under various stimuli. An X-ray that shows a swollen duodenum together with a consistently high level of gastric acid secretion indicates active DU. Using fiberoptic endoscopy, the physician may examine the inside of the stomach and duodenum with a flexible tube and light source that is swallowed by the patient and manipulated by the operator to yield very clear views and even color photographs. Fiberoptic endoscopy is considered accurate in identifying DU, particularly when X-ray and gastric analysis are nonreinforcing or ambiguous. On the other hand, the technique is expensive, unpleasant for the patient, and time consuming.

In the treatment of DU, the patient is "managed" through symptomatic relief while the ulcer, it is hoped, heals itself, usually in six to eight weeks. Although most DU patients respond well without surgery, recurrence of the disease for those patients is common. Only about 25 percent of patients with newly diagnosed DU will eventually require surgery and, of these, only 10 to 25 percent will experience permanent remission of all symptoms. The primary aims of medical management are the relief of pain and the encouragement of healing; secondary goals are preventing complications and reducing recurrence. The primary aims are achieved by decreasing the amount of acid secreted in the gastric system and neutralizing that which is secreted. More frequent, smaller meals diminish acid secretion. Antacids are usually prescribed liberally, with the dosage adjusted according to the severity of the symptoms. Even if the treatment seems effective and the symptoms abate, the sporadic and recurrent nature of ulcer pain requires that the patient be monitored over a considerable period of time to determine whether the ulcer is dormant or has indeed healed.

An important social characteristic of DU is that it seems to be a "life-style" disease. That is, certain ways of living and kinds of activities may increase the overall occurrence of DU in the population. (Lung cancer, coronary disease, and obesity are other examples of life-style diseases.) Although they no longer consider the characterization of the "ulcer personality" as hard-driving, ambitious, overachieving, and competitive to be accurate, psychiatrists have observed that many ulcer patients need to be dependent but fight that need. Hence, if the doctor allows the patient to become dependent on him in an acceptable way through a good doctor-patient relationship, this may help to avoid exacerbations of the disease. The avoidance of "life crises" or other psychosocial problems can also avoid irritation of an already active ulcer.

A pattern of regular living with few emotional upsets is therefore a key factor in the long-term management of DU patients. This pattern may, of course, be more difficult to bring about than the desired regularity and frequency of food intake. An additional complication is that eating habits and life style are often closely linked: for example, the socially condoned activities of smoking and drinking in combination tend to irritate an active ulcer, particularly if the stomach is empty at the time. Mild depression and ulcer symptoms can alternate in neurotic personalities. Some doctors prescribe sedatives and tranquilizers in the management of acute ulcers, since gastric secretion is known to rise if the anxiety level increases.

Ulcers that refuse to heal may eventually lead to various complications. Minor bleeding from the ulcer crater is common, and massive bleeding due to the ulcer's eroding a major blood vessel may also occur. The mortality rate for bleeding from a DU is about 10 percent; for massive bleeding it is 14 to 25 percent. Perforation of the mucous membrane (literally, a hole in the wall of the stomach or duodenum) and obstruction of the opening from the lower end of the stomach into the duodenum (the pylorus) are further possible complications.

If these conditions develop, hospitalization of the patient is invariably required, and frequently surgery is necessary. There are other reasons, however, why a provider may hospitalize a DU patient: a long history of DU that is not responsive to medical management; a home environment unlikely to reinforce compliance with a therapeutic regimen; or a job that makes therapeutic compliance a practical impossibility. For the hospitalized patient, surgery is indicated by failure of a fair trial of sound medical management, uncontrollable or repeated bleeding, perforation, or obstruction.

Appendix B. The Chemical Behavior of Cimetidine

The chemical histamine occurs in the human body wherever tissue is damaged or irritated. It stimulates visceral muscles, dilates capillaries, and encourages salivary, pancreatic, and gastric secretion. Because ulcer is a form of tissue damage, histamine is present in the stomach and duodenum of DU patients. Even in healthy individuals, the normal processes of digestion release the hormone gastrin, which in turn stimulates the production of histamine to stimulate the parietal (acid-producing) cells in the gastric mucosa. Cimetidine "blocks" the effect of histamine on the mucosa.

For over forty years the antihistamine group of drugs has been used to act as antagonists to the action of histamine. Although these drugs are effective in antagonizing the action of histamine in certain allergic conditions, such as hay fever, they are not capable of antagonizing the action of histamine in the gastric mucosa. Ash and Schild suggested an explanation for this seeming anomaly,[9] which centers on the behavior of receptors—sites in body tissue at which physiological substances interact with cells to produce their characteristic responses. Although different tissues may respond to the same physiological substances, the cellular receptors in these tissues may not necessarily be identical. The significance of this observation is that, whereas a physiological substance is capable of producing its effects at all its receptor sites, an agonist or antagonist drug may be capable of interacting with only some of them. Ash and Schild proposed that there was more than one type of histamine receptor. They postulated that, although histamine itself was capable of binding to and eliciting physiological responses in all types of histamine receptors, the "classical" antihistamines were capable of binding to only one type of receptor—which they termed H_1. This would explain the ability of these drugs to counteract such effects of histamine release as urticaria and hay fever and their inability to affect certain other histamine-mediated processes, such as gastric acid secretion. On this basis, the classical antihistamines could be reclassified as H_1 receptor antagonists. Histamine receptors at which these antihistamines are ineffective are termed H_2 receptors.

Empirical evidence for the existence of the H_2 receptor emerged

---

[9] A. S. F. Ash and H. O. Schild, "Receptors Mediating Some Actions of Histamine," *British Journal of Pharmacology*, vol. 27 (1966), pp. 427–39.

from synthetic modification of the histamine molecule undertaken by Smith Kline & French Laboratories. This work led to the synthesis of burimamide, a chemical of low potency in inhibiting gastric acid secretion and relatively ineffective when given orally, and metiamide, which is highly effective but seriously reduces the number of white blood cells in the peripheral blood circulation, leading to infections. The compound that combines the effectiveness of metiamide with the innocuousness of burimamide is named cimetidine and is marketed by Smith Kline & French Laboratories under the brand name Tagamet. Cimetidine blocks the action of histamine only at the H_2 receptor sites; it has no effect at the H_1 sites. By contrast, the anticholinergics block the effect on gastric acid secretion of acetylcholine, another stimulant. To attain inhibition of gastric acid secretion, however, near-toxic doses are required, which invariably lead to adverse reactions, such as dry mouth, blurred vision, and urinary retention.

The manufacturer claims that cimetidine inhibits the gastric acid secretion produced by all common stimulants, promoting rapid ulcer healing and effective symptom relief, and that this is done to a degree unparalleled by clinically acceptable doses of other currently available drugs. The first claim, at least, seems to be borne out by independent pharmacological studies. Richardson and Winship concluded the following from their clinical studies.[10]

- Cimetidine inhibits basal and nocturnal acid secretion and acid secretion stimulated by histamine, pentagastrin, caffeine, insulin, sham feeding, and food.
- Cimetidine (300 mg) inhibits basal acid secretion in DU patients by 95 percent for at least five hours.
- When taken at bedtime, cimetidine inhibits nocturnal acid secretion by greater than 80 percent for most of the night.
- Cimetidine markedly inhibits food-stimulated acid secretion and is more effective than anticholinergic drugs. There is also evidence that the effects of H_2 receptor antagonists (in the experiment, metiamide was used rather than cimetidine) and anticholinergics (isopropamide was used) are additive; that is, a combination of these drugs suppresses gastric acid secretion to a greater extent than either drug given alone.
- To get adequate suppression of food-stimulated acid secretion throughout the day, cimetidine should be given with each meal.

---

[10] Charles T. Richardson, "Effect of H_2-Receptor Antagonists on Gastric Acid Secretion and Serum Gastrin Concentration," *Gastroenterology*, vol. 74 (November 1978), pp. 366–70; and Daniel H. Winship, "Cimetidine in the Treatment of Duodenal Ulcer," *Gastroenterology*, vol. 74 (November 1978), pp. 402–6.

- Cimetidine has no effect on nocturnal serum gastrin concentration (that is, on the concentration in the bloodstream of gastrin—a hormone that induces secretion of gastric juices), but, when stimulated by food, serum gastrin concentration is higher after cimetidine than after placebo.
- In eight prospective, randomized, double-blind, placebo-controlled studies (where neither the doctor nor the patient knows whether the drug currently being administered is cimetidine or a placebo), cimetidine was administered to 348 DU patients with an incidence of endoscopically verified healing of 71 percent compared with a healing incidence of 37 percent in 300 placebo-treated patients.
- Healing rates were similar in patients receiving cimetidine in doses ranging from 0.8 to 2.0 grams per day.
- It appears that at least three to four weeks of cimetidine therapy are needed to achieve healing rates of about 70 percent.
- In most trials, cimetidine was superior to placebos in achieving symptom relief in patients with DU.
- The drug has not been shown to result in acid rebound (a higher-than-previous level of gastric acid secretion) or any changes in the parietal cell ultrastructure after cessation of therapy.
- There are no published prospective studies on the question of whether or not treatment with cimetidine results in increased ulcer recurrence when the drug is discontinued.
- Although more data are required for an assessment of long-term therapy with cimetidine, the drug appears to be effective in the short-term treatment of DU.

Adherence to the prescribed dosage has been found to be essential if the patient is to realize the greatest benefits of the drug. Disappearance of symptoms after a few days may lead some patients to feel that further medication is unnecessary. Although symptoms may subside and healing may occur within the first week or two, treatment with cimetidine should be continued for four to six weeks. Under the conditions of its approval by the Food and Drug Administration, treatment periods are not to exceed eight weeks. Few side effects in excess of those found with placebos have been reported in clinical trials. Studies of acute toxicity in rats indicate that doses from nine to fifty-six times the recommended human dose are required to induce cell tumors and eventually death. Because cimetidine is relatively innocuous, it is not necessary to confirm the presence of DU endoscopically before prescription. Sufficient indication for its use is the presence of DU based on a thorough physical examination of the patient and the considered professional opinion of the examining physician.

Tagamet is generally more expensive than other currently available drugs in the treatment of DU. In price per dose, Tagamet is about three times as expensive as anticholinergics, fifteen times the cost of sedatives, and thirty times that of antidepressants. One week of therapy using Tagamet costs $8.40, at $0.30 per 300-mg tablet. In terms of effectiveness, however, it is less clear that Tagamet is more costly; thus, it appears that the cost of the recommended daily dosage of Tagamet is similar to the cost of a quantity of antacid that has approximately the same short-term effect.

Pharmaceutical Innovation, Product Imitation, and Public Policy

S. Y. Wu

Innovations yield producer's as well as consumer's benefits. In a market economy, it is the profit-seeking entrepreneur who decides where to allocate his innovative efforts. In making these decisions, the entrepreneur is not primarily concerned with the issue of whether his efforts will ultimately benefit society in an essential way. Society as a whole, however, is interested in appropriating the fruits of innovation to all of its members. The crucial question is, Does market allocation of innovative activities through profit-seeking entrepreneurs yield a result consistent with the society's welfare?

If the economy is perfectly competitive and property rights are appropriately defined, then it seems reasonable to take the position that there is not a special need for public policy toward innovations or public concern over the size of the social benefits derived from them. Suppose, first, that the product mix in the economy is given. If the economy is perfectly competitive, then every equilibrium is Pareto optimal. This is to say that every state of equilibrium is consistent with profit-maximizing choices of the producers and utility-maximizing choices of the consumers. The market thus acts to reconcile the diverse interests of the individuals with the interest of the society at large.

Innovation, by its nature, however, represents a disruption to the state of an equilibrium. Its social consequence, thus, cannot be assessed by the implications derived from an equilibrium analysis. In a competitive economy, however, disruption to equilibrium by innovative activities is strictly transitory. The producer, in an attempt to augment his profit, may endeavor either to introduce new products or to reduce the cost of producing existing products. Excess profit derived from innovation is, however, short-lived. Profit accruing to an innovator attracts imitation, causing itself to dissipate. Because disruption caused by innovative activities is temporary, the economy, thus, has the propensity of gravitating toward a new competitive equilibrium. Because compet-

In writing this paper, the author benefited greatly from discussions with Michael Balch, Yale Brozen, and Timothy McGuire. Financial support from National Science Foundation PRA/76–18777 is also gratefully acknowledged. The views expressed in this paper are strictly my own and do not reflect those of the National Science Foundation.

272

itive equilibrium implies that the society's welfare is maximized in the Pareto sense, the consumer is therefore the ultimate benefactor of innovation. He is first benefited by the availability of a new or an improved product, and he is subsequently benefited by a lower price through product imitation.[1] The effort to compute social benefits derived from innovation under these circumstances would appear to be redundant.

Casual observation reveals that innovative activities often take place in nonperfect markets. Schumpeter conjectured that monopoly profit is the most important source for financing innovative activities and concluded that innovation is most likely to take place among firms in monopolistic industries.[2] The presence of market imperfections, or imperfection in property rights, however, causes a divergence between private and social interests. Public policies are, therefore, needed to bring private interests in line with social welfare. Information on social and private benefits is especially relevant because it is possible that some high-profit innovations are associated with high social rates of returns, and some low-profit innovations are associated with low social rates of returns. Under these circumstances, measures of social benefits become indispensable for both the formulation and the execution of public policies.

The role of public policy is to supplement the market and to bring about a maximum improvement in social welfare through innovative activities. As was stated above, innovation benefits the consumer in two stages: first, it offers the consumer a new or an improved product and, second, through product imitation, it subsequently provides the consumer with a lower price. Public policy, thus, must be directed (1) to creating a market environment conducive to innovative activities, (2) to channeling innovative activities to areas where the greatest benefits are yielded to the society, and (3) to disseminating as rapidly as possible the fruits of innovation to the consumers.

Obviously, many public policies will ultimately have some effect on innovative activities. Our concerns in this paper are limited to those policies that are designed explicitly to influence innovative activities. These include patent policy and policies that affect the rate of product imitation. Public policies affecting the rate of imitation are especially

---

[1] Clemens and Cocks suggest that the two-tier benefit derived from innovation is a natural consequence of the Schumpeterian innovation process. Eli W. Clemens, "Price Discrimination and the Monopoly Firm," in Richard Heflebower and George W. Stocking, eds., *Readings in Industrial Organization and Public Policy* (Homewood, Ill.: Richard D. Irwin, 1958), pp. 262–76; Douglas L. Cocks, "Product Innovation and the Dynamic Elements of Competition in the Ethical Pharmaceutical Industry," in R. B. Helms, ed., *Drug Development and Marketing* (Washington, D.C.: American Enterprise Institute, 1975), pp. 225–54.

[2] Joseph A. Schumpeter, *The Theory of Economic Development* (Cambridge: Harvard University Press, 1934), chap. 2, and *Capitalism, Socialism, and Democracy*, 3d ed. (New York: Harper, 1950), pp. 100–110.

relevant because imitation determines both the profitability of innovations and the diffusion of the benefits derived from these innovations. The choice of public policy thus influences (1) the incentives of firms to innovate, and (2) the size and distribution of the total benefits derived from innovations between firms and consumers. Although less interventionist policies may encourage innovation, they also prevent the fruits of innovation from being quickly passed on to consumers. A more interventionist policy, on the other hand, will cause the benefits of innovations to be diffused rapidly but may at the same time dampen the incentives for innovation to take place. An optimal policy would provide just enough incentive for the innovator to perform his service and disseminate the fruit of innovation to the public at a maximum speed.

This paper is concerned with public policy issues relating to optimum imitation in pharmaceutical products. Longstanding controversy over the relationship between profitability and innovative efforts in the pharmaceutical industry makes this case especially interesting to study.[3] Because imitation in pharmaceutical products may take place by introducing either a brand-name substitute (a product with different chemical composition and hence a differentiated product) or a generic substitute (a product with identical chemical composition and hence a homogeneous product), the market consequence and the public policy issues are different between these cases. We will in this paper concentrate our efforts on the issues associated with the latter type of imitation.

This paper is divided into three sections. The first presents a method that can be used to measure social benefits derived from imitation by generic substitutes. The second section introduces an analytical framework whereby the nature of the trade-off between the incentive to innovate and the diffusion of benefits to the society can be investigated. Finally, some relevant public policy issues are discussed.

Social Benefits Derived from Imitation

To estimate the social benefits derived from imitation by generic drugs, we borrow a technique introduced recently by Mansfield and his collaborators.[4] The original purpose of Mansfield and his colleagues was

---

[3] Harry Bloch, "True Profitability Measures for Pharmaceutical Firms," in J. D. Cooper, ed., *Regulation, Economics, and Pharmaceutical Innovation* (Washington, D.C.: The American University, 1976), pp. 147–57; Leonard G. Schifrin, "The Ethical Drug Industry: The Case for Compulsory Patent Licensing," *Antitrust Bulletin,* vol. 12 (Fall 1967), pp. 893–915; and David Schwartzman, "Pharmaceutical R&D Expenditures and Rates of Return," in Helms, *Drug Development,* pp. 63–80.

[4] Edwin Mansfield, John Rapoport, Anthony Romeo, Samuel Wagner, and George Beardsley, "Social and Private Rates of Return from Industrial Innovations," *Quarterly Journal of Economics,* vol. 91 (May 1977), pp. 221–40.

to study the social rate of return to innovation in seventeen manufacturing industries. This study calculates the social benefits as the consumer's surplus derived from lowering the prices of the products following an innovation, plus the value of the resources saved (producer's surplus). The latter is equivalent to the profits of the innovator plus the profits of the imitators, less the profits that would have been made if innovation had not taken place. This technique is valid only for innovations that do not appreciably change the nature of the product. For this reason, it is difficult to apply the Mansfield technique to situations where innovation has altered the product in an essential way. Because the two types of drugs are chemically equivalent and the unit of quantity measurement is the same, the Mansfield technique is, therefore, especially suitable for computing the social benefits derived from substituting a generic product for the corresponding brand-name drug.

In order to apply the Mansfield technique to the problem at hand, we need to characterize the market demand function for a family of drugs (both the brand-name and the generic product). Because of factors such as advertising and promotional efforts, physicians' and pharmacists' judgments, and consumers' bias toward the generic drug, the demand for the brand-name drug and the generic product differ. Let Q_b, Q_g, P_b, and P_g denote the quantities and prices of the brand-name and the generic drug, respectively. We assume that the demand for the brand-name drug and for the generic drug is a function of both prices. Furthermore, we also assume that the brand-name drug is preferred by all and that the generic drug is demanded only if its price is less than that of the brand-name drug. The relationship between the demand for the brand-name drug and the demand for the generic drug is presented in figure 1. Let the curve D represent the demand curve for the brand-name drug before the generic drug was introduced to the market. Assume that the generic drug is brought to the market at a price P_2. The curve AmD now represents the demand curve for the brand-name drug. The shape of AmD reflects the fact that, if $P_b \leq P_g$, then no generic drug is demanded. As P_b rises above P_g, the quantity demanded for the brand-name drug will decrease, and the quantity demanded for the generic drug will increase. On the basis of this characterization of the market demand for a family of drugs, we now turn to compute social benefits derived from generic drug imitation à la Mansfield.

Assume that before the introduction of the generic product, Q_0 units of the innovator's brand-name drug were demanded at the price P_0. The appearance of a generic product causes the price of the brand-name drug to be reduced from P_0 to P_1 and the quantity to be reduced from Q_0 to q_1. Let the price of the generic drug be P_2 and the quantity sold be q_2; $q_1 + q_2 = Q_1$. In addition, let MC_1 and MC_2 be the marginal

FIGURE 1
THE DEMAND FOR A BRAND NAME AND A GENERIC DRUG

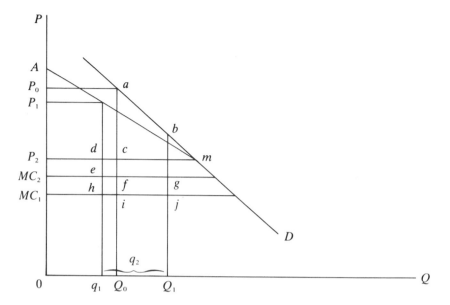

costs of production for the innovator and the imitator, respectively; we
assume $MC_2 \geq MC_1$ and that they are both constants. The net social
benefit derived from imitation in period t, denoted by ΔB_t, is equal to
the change in the consumer's surplus in that period, ΔS_t, plus the net
change in the producers' profits in that period, $\Delta \pi_t$. ΔS_t is equal to the
total dollar value that the consumer is willing to spend on the additional
drug in period t after the imitation has taken place, less the change in
the consumer's expenditure in that period—that is, $[abQ_1Q_0 - (P_1q_1
+ P_2q_2 - P_0Q_0)]$. $\Delta \pi_t$ is equal to $[(P_1 - MC_1)q_1 + (P_2 - MC_2)q_2 -
(P_0 - MC_1)Q_0]$. $\Delta B_t = abQ_1Q_0 - MC_1(Q_1 - Q_0) - (MC_2 - MC_1)q_2$
and thus is represented by the area $(abgf - efih)$ in figure 1.

Inspecting figure 1, we see that the introduction of the generic drug
not only offers a low price alternative for the consumer but also causes
a reduction in the price or the quantity or both of the brand-name drug
sold. These results, in turn, induce a transfer of profit from the innovator
to the imitators and a transfer of the producer's surplus to the consumer's
surplus. Imitation in this case yields two effects in opposite directions:
(1) an increase in net social benefits B_t, and (2) a reduction in the
innovator's profit π_t^F. This phenomenon serves as the basis for designing
a public policy for generic drug imitation.

Analytical Framework

The nature of a generic imitation of a brand-name drug can be characterized by the date at which the first generic product appears in the market and the rate of change of the market share of the generic product. Let θ_t denote the percentage of the generic drug sold in period t. The time path $(\theta_0, \theta_1, \ldots, \theta_t, \ldots)$ describes the whole process of imitation. Typically, we will have $\theta_t = 0$ for all $t < t_I$, where t_I is the date at which imitators first enter the market. In general, θ_t's will follow a path, such as θ^1, shown in figure 2. It is convenient, however, to take a linear approximation of this path, such as θ^2. Along a linear path, the rate of imitation $d\theta/dt \equiv k$ is a constant, so that the imitation process is completely described by the pair (t_I, k). We shall hereafter assume that imitation can be described in this manner.

Let $\pi_t^F(t_I, k)$ denote the innovator's profit and let B_t (t_I, k) denote the social benefits derived from imitation in period t. We observe that $\pi_t^F(t_I, k)$ increases with t_I, and decreases with k, while B_t (t_I, k) decreases with t_I and increases with k. Because t_I and k affect π_t^F and B_t in opposite directions, public policy can be used to influence t_I and k and to guide the allocation of resources in a more desirable way.

Under the present institutional arrangement, there are both public and private determinants of t_I and k. The date at which imitation first begins is determined to a large extent by the length of the patent pro-

FIGURE 2
TIME PATH OF GENERIC DRUG IMITATION

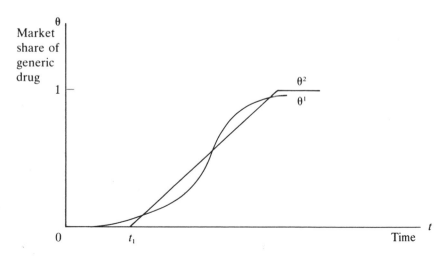

NOTE: Market share of generic drug is 100 percent when $\theta_t = 1$.

tection. The rate of imitation is determined by the nature of the product and the market structure, as well as by public policies.

Although patent policy is a primary determinant of t_I, the actual number of years during which the product is protected may differ from the nominal seventeen-year patent period. In many instances, competitors are deterred from imitation once it is known that an application for a patent has been filed; the effective period of protection may thereby be lengthened by several years. On the other hand, in the pharmaceutical industry a patent application is ordinarily filed for a new chemical compound as soon as its potential therapeutic value is recognized. Because it is time consuming to complete clinical testing and to obtain approval from the Food and Drug Administration (FDA) for marketing the drug, a substantial portion of the period of patent protection may have expired before the drug ever reaches the market. The effective patent protection period is, thus, reduced.

Although the FDA regulation has a tendency to reduce the length of effective patent protection, in some instances it may increase the length of protection. Under the new drug approval procedure adopted by the FDA after the 1962 drug amendments, firms must file a new drug application (NDA) before marketing the drug. Because the approval of the NDA depends on the results of extensive tests and because these results are not entirely in the public domain, any firm that wishes to market a chemically identical drug must engage in clinical tests sufficient to support its own NDA. Because the testing period is lengthy, the NDA has been estimated to provide protection for the innovator for a period of four to eight years.[5] Thus, the net effect of FDA regulation on the length of patent protection is, at best, ambiguous. In any event, although patent policy nominally determines the date at which imitation begins, the NDA approval process modifies the period of protection.

Public policy not only can affect the date at which imitation begins (t_I) but can also affect the rate of imitation (k). When a pharmacist fills a prescription for a Medicare-Medicaid patient, for example, he is required to substitute a lower-priced generic product for a brand-name drug prescribed by a physician. Likewise, many states (for example, Iowa, Michigan) have passed laws that permit druggists to make similar substitutions for all prescriptions. These policies undoubtedly will affect the rate of imitation.

Not only public policies but also market structure and competitors' behavior affect the time and rate of imitation; for example, entry conditions, advertising, and pricing policy affect the rate of imitation. Pri-

---

[5] Harold A. Clymer, "The Changing Cost and Risks of Pharmaceutical Innovation," in Joseph D. Cooper, ed., *The Economics of Drug Innovation* (Washington, D.C.: The American University, 1970), pp. 111–24.

vate influence on t_l and k weakens the impact of public policy and causes the outcome of a given policy to be less predictable. These facts must be kept in mind when selecting and designing appropriate public policies.

Suppose for the moment that the policy maker has sole control over t_l and k and has perfect knowledge regarding the functions $B_t (t_l,k)$ and $\pi_t^F(t_l,k)$. Our purpose, in this section, is to propose a theoretical framework capable of assisting us in characterizing the nature of an optimal public policy regarding product imitation. In this section, we arrive at the notion of an optimal public policy by examining the returns to research and development (R&D) investment from the point of view of both the firm and the society.

There is an enormous time lag between the R&D outlays and the cash flow. Thus, in evaluating the desirability of any investment prospect, consideration must be given not only to the magnitude of the net revenue flow but also to the timing of these receipts or benefits. The reason is that a dollar expended (received) today is not the same as a dollar expended (received) tomorrow as long as there exists an alternative to earn a positive return on the dollar during the interim. To take account of this opportunity cost, economists employ the time discount measures of returns to evaluate investment opportunities. One such measure is the net present value, and the other is the internal rate of return. For convenience, we employ net present value to measure the returns to the firm and internal rate of return to measure the returns to the society.

The net present value of the innovator's R&D investment, denoted by π^F, is defined as:

$$\pi^F = \sum_{t=1}^{T} \frac{\pi_t^F (t_l,k) - R_t}{(1+r_m)^t} \tag{1}$$

where R_t denotes the R&D expenditures incurred in period t, and r_m is the market interest rate faced by the innovator. π^F obviously depends upon t_l and k. This dependence is in part due to the fact that π^F depends on $\pi_t^F(t_l,k)$ and in part due to the fact that t_l and k affect the life of the innovative product because the life of the innovative product increases with the length of patent protection and decreases with the rate of imitation. The internal rate of return to the society, denoted by r_s, on the other hand, is defined as the discount rate that equates the present value of the stream of the net social benefits with the discounted R&D outlays—that is, r_s satisfies the equation

$$\sum_{t=1}^{T} \frac{B_t (t_l,k) - R_t}{(1+r_s)^t} = 0 \tag{2}$$

279

It is obvious that r_s is also a function of t_I and k.

Just as changes in t_I and k affect the values of π_t^F and B_t in opposite directions, they also affect π^F and r_s in the same manner. Thus, an optimal public policy toward imitation must mean that, through public policy's influence on t_I and k, the largest social internal rate of return can be realized without discouraging the innovator's activities. Technically, an optimal public policy toward imitation can be derived by solving a mathematical problem that maximizes r_s subject to the constraints $\pi^F \geq 0$ and the identity represented by equation (2).

In order to understand the nature of this maximization problem, let us first examine the property of the set of points in the (t_I, k)-plane over which $\pi^F \geq 0$, in particular, the set of boundary points represented by the curve $\pi^F = 0$. Referring to figure 3, suppose initially $\pi^F = 0$ at (t_I^0, k^0). Now let $t_I' > t_I^0$. At k^0, the innovator's profit has increased because the number of periods under patent protection has increased. To offset this increase in profit, k must increase during the post–patent protection periods. An increase in k not only reduces the profit in each period but also shortens the product life after the expiration of the

FIGURE 3
RELATIONSHIP BETWEEN PATENT PROTECTION AND RATE OF IMITATION

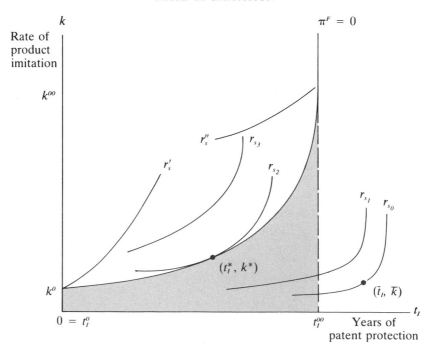

280

patent. Suppose there exists a k' such that the reduction in profit caused by an increase in the rate of imitation from k^0 to k' just offsets the increase in profit caused by an increase in the patent protection from t_l^0 to t_l'; then π^F again equals zero at (t_l',k'). It is reasonable to assume that, as t_l increases, k must increase at an increasing rate to offset the increase in profit caused by a marginal increase in the length of patent protection. Because an increase in k also shortens the product life after the expiration of the patent, there exists a t_l'' beyond which it is no longer possible to offset the increase in profit derived from an additional year of patent protection even with an infinite rate of imitation. The product life after t_l'' is already too short; the elimination of the remaining life will not affect the innovator's profit in an essential way. The discussion above suggests that $\pi^F = 0$ is convex to the horizontal axis and is asymptotic to the line $t_l = t_l^{00}$, where t_l^{00} lies just a little to the right of t_l''. A typical $\pi^F = 0$ curve is shown in figure 3.

In order to understand the nature of the maximization problem, we also need to examine the curvature of the social-rate-of-return-level curves r_s. As t_l increases, B_t will decrease. To offset this decrease in B_t, an increase in k is needed. An increase in k implies that a greater proportion of the product is sold under a lower price, thus benefiting society more. Because P_g is assumed to be fixed, each increase in k reduces its impact on B_t. This phenomenon again suggests that r_s curves are convex to the horizontal axis. A set of social-rate-of-return-level curves is shown in figure 3. The social rate of return increases as the r_s curve moves in the northwesterly direction, for example, $r_{s1} < r_{s2} < r_{s3}$.

As both $\pi^F = 0$ and r_s curves are convex to the horizontal axis in figure 3, optimal public policy depends on the relative curvature between the $\pi^F = 0$ and the r_s curves. If the r_s curves, for instance, are more convex than the $\pi^F = 0$ curve, the optimal policy is achieved at (t_l^*,k^*) when the social-rate-of-return-level curve r_{s2} is tangent to the $\pi^F = 0$ curve. If the r_s curves are less convex than the $\pi^F = 0$ curve, however, the optimal policy is represented by (t_l^0,k^0) if the social-rate-of-return-level curves belong to the family of curves represented by r_s'; it is represented by (t_l^{00},k^{00}) if the social-rate-of-return-level curves belong to the family of curves represented by r_s''. We identify (t_l^{00},k^{00}) as the optimal policy in the latter case because there exists an upper bound for the social rate of returns as $k \to \infty$. This upper bound is assumed to be represented by the curve r_s'' in figure 3.

Public Policy Options

The preceding section indicated that, if the public authority knows the level curves r_s and the location of the curve $\pi^F = 0$ with certainty and has sole control over t_l and k, there exists an optimum public policy

concerning innovation and imitation. In other words, under these conditions the agent could pursue a policy that offers the innovator t_I years
of patent protection and then allows the imitators to increase their
market share at k percent per annum. In this way the society derives
the maximum benefit from innovation.

Thus depicted, the selection of public policy appears to be simple.
The problem confronting the policy maker never presents itself in this
ideal form, however. In the first place, public policy must be formulated
and implemented at a time when the public authority does not have
complete knowledge of the level curves r_s and the location of the curve
$\pi^F = 0$. Moreover, public authority does not have a firm control over
t_I and k. Under these circumstances, public policy cannot be decided
solely on the basis of objective calculations; rather, it involves considerable judgment. In the subsections "Incomplete Knowledge" and "Incomplete Control by the Public Agent," we will discuss the judgmental
nature of the policy selection. We will first examine the case where the
public authority does not know r_s and $\pi^F = 0$ curves with certainty and
then examine the case where the authority does not have full control
over t_I and k.

Incomplete Knowledge. Because an enormous time lag exists between
R&D activities and the marketing of the final product, the effect of a
given public policy designed to influence innovative activities cannot be
observed without a similar time lag. Because policy must be selected
and implemented long before its effectiveness is known, a great deal of
risk exists with each policy selection. In addition, ex post realization
may deviate significantly from ex ante expectation. Under these circumstances, judgment and risk attitude of the public authority are essential
ingredients of any public policy revision.

Once a public policy is implemented, the outcome of this policy can
be described by the location of the 2-tuple (t_I, k) in the (t_I, k)-plane. It
is important to note that the outcome of the current policy can fall into
one of the four regions, as shown in figure 4. The location of the current
outcome is important because it determines the directions toward which
the public policy must adjust in order to bring about an improvement
over the current policy. In other words, the location of the current
outcome determines the public authority's policy option. Inspecting figure 4, we see that:

- The policy revision is simplest when the current public policy yields
  an outcome in region IV. A movement toward the potential optimum policy requires a simultaneous increase in k and decrease in
  t_I.
- If the current policy yields an outcome in region I, one cannot

FIGURE 4

POLICY ADJUSTMENT TO MOVE TOWARD A SOCIAL OPTIMUM

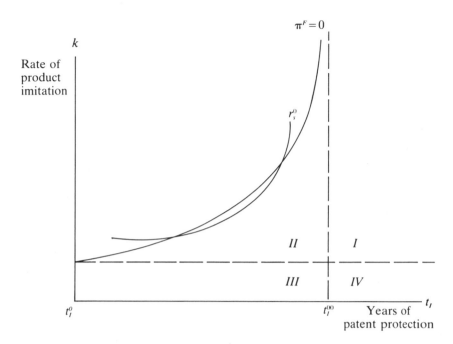

follow the strategy of either an increase in t_I or a change in k or both. To bring it to a potential optimum, a movement toward the potential optimum must include a reduction in t_I.

- If the current policy yields an outcome in region II, one cannot follow the strategy of either a change in t_I or a decrease in k or both. A movement toward the potential optimum must include an increase in k.

- Policy revision is most complex when the current policy yields an outcome in region III. All we can say is that an increase in t_I or a decrease in k alone or a simultaneous increase in t_I and decrease in k would lead to unfavorable consequences. The impact of a change in public policy in other directions cannot be ascertained a priori; it depends upon the precise location of the current outcome.

Policy adjustment is often complicated by the fact that, because of a lack of information, the public authority cannot ascertain the precise location of π^F and r_s curves ex post and hence the location of the current policy outcome. Thus, the lack of knowledge about the r_s and $\pi^F = 0$ curves not only prevents the public authority from selecting the optimal

283

policy at the outset but also obscures the options that may be available to him after the policy has been implemented and thus prevents him from making efficient adjustment of the existing policy. Decision making under this environment is again judgmental.

Although thus far our analysis does not yield a practical decision rule to guide policy adjustments, it does shed some light on two important issues. First, there exists a maximum period of patent protection beyond which any increment in the length of protection will not provide additional incentive for the innovator. Suppose we can empirically establish the fact that the shape and the location of the $\pi^F = 0$ curve associated with innovations in certain industries are similar and that they, in turn, are different from those of other industries; our analysis then suggests that the length of patent protection should be different among these industrial groups. The estimated value of t_I^{00} associated with each industrial group can serve as a guide to determine the maximum length of patent protection for that industrial group.[6]

Second, when the r_s curves are shaped like those shown in figure 3 and when the current policy yields an outcome at a location such as $(\bar{t_I}, \bar{k})$, changing k alone will not be effective in promoting greater social rates of returns. The maximum increase in the social rate of return derived from any increase in k in this case is from r_{s_0} to r_{s_1}. A better result could always be achieved by a reduction in t_I and a simultaneous increase in k.

Incomplete Control by Public Agent. As a rule, the public agent does not have absolute control over t_I and k. Whenever the innovator can choose his own policy instruments to offset the effect of public policy on t_I and k, the $\pi^F = 0$ and r_s curves will shift. These shifts render the outcome of the public policy uncertain and cause policy adjustments to be ineffective.

There are two possible alternatives that the public authority may choose to cope with this difficulty. First, in selecting his policy, the authority may formally incorporate into his analysis the interaction between himself and the innovator. Second, he can consciously select a strategy that minimizes the degree of conjectural variation between his policy and that of the innovator. To avoid expositional cumbersomeness,

---

[6] Nordhaus and Scherer analyze optimal patent protection under a different framework. F. M. Scherer, "Nordhaus' Theory of Optimal Patent Life: A Geometric Reinterpretation," *American Economic Review*, vol. 62 (June 1972), pp. 422–27; W. D. Nordhaus, "The Optimal Life of a Patent: Reply," *American Economic Review*, vol. 62 (June 1972), pp. 428–31.

we assume in this section that, instead of the net present value criterion, the innovator also bases his decision on the internal rate of return to R&D investments.

One way of capturing the interaction between public policy and the innovator's response is by casting the present problem in a game-theoretic framework. The crucial characteristic of the present problem is that the social internal rate of return depends not only on the government-controlled variables that influence t_I and k but also on firm-controlled variables, such as pricing policy and promotional expenditures. Likewise, the firm's internal rate of return to R&D also depends on variables controlled by both the firm and the government.

Let us denote the government-controlled variables by A_1 and the firm-controlled variables by A_2. Thus, $r_s = r_s(A_1, \acute{A}_2)$, and $r_F = r_F(A_1, A_2)$, where r_F denotes the firm's internal rate of returns to R&D expenditures. Suppose each party assumes that the other will react to his choice of a policy in accordance with a subjectively perceived probability distribution pattern. Thus, the authority will choose an A_1, which is the best against this perceived distribution, and, likewise, the innovator will choose a best A_2. Neither the authority nor the innovator, however, can ignore the possibility that his adversary will attempt to profit by deviating from what was expected of him. Thus, both parties will adjust their choice of strategies accordingly. Consequently, the very fact that each party postulates an a priori distribution for his rival's response to his own policy will inevitably produce a force that causes a revision of his own initial choice of that policy. This conjectural variation in policies among rivals thus generates a pair of reaction functions. Under suitable assumptions, an equilibrium (t_I^{**}, k^{**}) and hence (r_s^{**}, r_F^{**}) will emerge. It is interesting to note that because the innovator can modify the impact of the authority's policy on his profit, (t_I^{**}, k^{**}) will lie interior to the $\pi^F = 0$ curve. The outcome (t_I^{**}, k^{**}) will move farther into the interior if the public authority and the innovator are risk averse.[7]

We have now cast our problem in a game-theoretic framework. This approach, though illuminating, does not provide much insight for guiding the practical formulation and execution of the public policy. This motivates us to examine the following alternative.

As we have seen, the difficulty associated with the selection and the adjustment of a public policy stems from the fact that the π^F (or r_F) and r_s curves shift if the firm revises its behavior in response to a change in public policy. Suppose we assume that the degree of the firm's reaction

---

[7] The difference between r_F^{**} and the market interest rate can be interpreted as the risk premium that is required to induce the firms to stay in business.

to an adjustment in public policy depends on the extent of this adjustment and that a small movement away from the existing policy does not induce a change in the firm's behavior. Unless the outcome of the current policy is known to be grossly nonoptimal and requires a major correction, it seems reasonable to assume that the public authority, in order to avoid the uncertainty created by the firm's reaction to his policy adjustments, would prefer a strategy of seeking marginal improvement with small policy adjustment.[8] The likelihood that the authority will adopt a small adjustment strategy is greater if he faces a greater uncertainty caused by the firm's reaction to his policy and if he is more risk averse. In the following paragraphs we examine the implications of the small adjustment strategy.

Let a policy be represented by the 2-tuple (t_I, k). Two policies that give the same (t_I, k) will be treated as equivalent. Given (t_I, k), we note first that estimates of social and private internal rates of returns r_s and r_F can be obtained by solving, respectively, the following equations:

$$\sum_t \frac{B_t\,(t_I,\,k)\,-\,R_t}{(1\,+\,r_s)^t} = 0$$

and

$$\sum_t \frac{\pi_t^F(t_I,\,k)\,-\,R_t}{(1\,+\,r_F)^t} = 0$$

Let $r_s(t_I^0, k^0) = r_s^0$, $r_s(t_I', k') = r_s'$, $r_F(t_I^0, k^0) = r_F^0$ and $r_F(t_I', k') = r_F'$. Suppose that an innovation is profitable under the existing policy environment, that is, $r_F^0 \geq r_m$. An alternative policy (t_I', k') is said to be feasible if it yields the result $r_F' \geq r_m$. A policy (t_I'', k'') causing $r_F'' < r_m$ is not feasible because it discourages potential innovations and retards the implementation of existing innovations—a result clearly contrary to the expressed goal of all public policies. A feasible policy (t_I', k') may still be socially undesirable, however, if it should yield the result $r_s' <$

---

[8] There are two sources of uncertainties: (1) that generated exogenously and viewed by the decision maker as the state of the world, and (2) that generated endogenously by the decision maker's attempt to exercise some conditional influence over his environment or from the interrelatedness of human behavior in a particular interactive setting. A decision maker, as a rule, finds it most difficult to cope with uncertainty of the second type and is, therefore, anxious to avoid it. In the present context, a small policy adjustment strategy is plausible and may even be socially desirable because conjectural variations in policies could endogenously generate a sufficient amount of uncertainty to produce serious antisocial consequences. For a more detailed analysis of uncertainty, see M. Balch and S. Wu, "Some Introductory Remarks on Behavior under Uncertainty," in M. Balch, D. McFadden, and S. Wu, eds., *Essays on Economic Behavior under Uncertainty* (Amsterdam: North-Holland, 1974), pp. 1–22.

r_s^0. A viable public policy thus must be both feasible and socially desirable. Among the feasible and socially desirable policy alternatives, there are two subclasses: (1) $r_F' > r_F^0 > r_m$; and (2) $r_F^0 > r_F' > r_m$. It is interesting to note that (1) under the present circumstances a departure from the current policy may benefit both the innovator and the society, and (2) given that the public agent is anxious to avoid triggering the firm into revising its behavior, there is a propensity for the agent to negotiate a policy settlement with the innovator whereby a gain is realized by both the innovator and the society.

To clarify the proposition stated in the preceding paragraph, let us illustrate it with our familiar diagram. Suppose under the existing public policy environment (t_I^0, k^0) the social rate of return is r_s^0 and the firm's discounted present value of the returns to R&D expenditure is $\pi^F 0$. The outcome of this current public policy is represented by the point A in figure 5. Suppose further that a slight change in public policy does not materially affect the r_s and π_F curves. Let the new policy yield a result (t_I', k') falling in the neighborhood (within the circle) of the point A. Because the circle lies in the region $\pi^F > 0$, the new policy is feasible. Among the feasible policies, however, some are not socially desirable. The undesirable policies include those (t_I, k) whose coordinates fall in

FIGURE 5

CHOOSING POLICIES AMONG FEASIBLE ALTERNATIVES

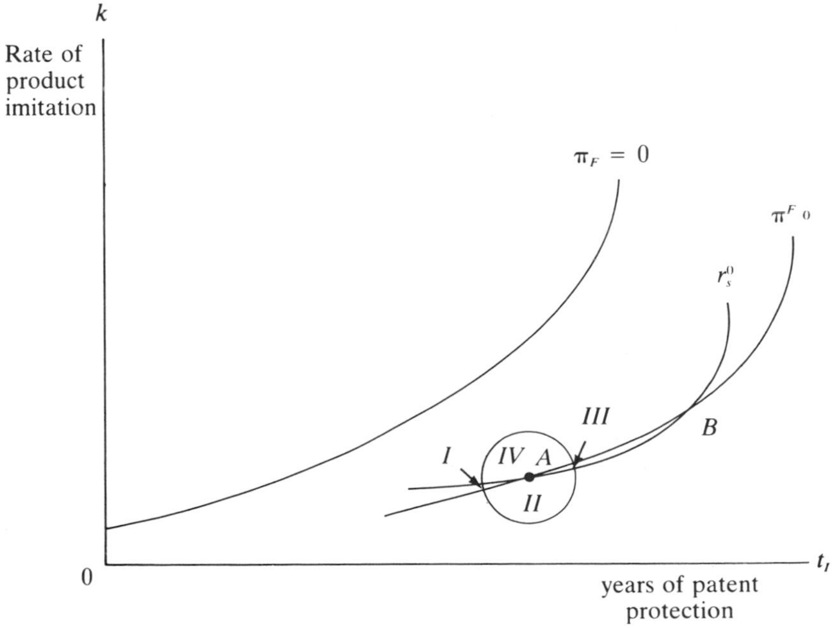

the regions I and II around A. Among the socially desirable policies, those that fall in region IV make the innovators worse off, and those policies that fall in region III make both the firm and the society better off. We conjecture that when a high degree of interdependence between public and private policies exists, the likelihood is that the public policy will tend to move from the point A to a point in region III.[9]

The tendency for the public agent to adjust public policy in the manner above yields profound welfare consequences. Although each move in public policy constitutes an improvement from both the innovator's and the society's points of view, a sequence of such movements does not bring the public policy closer to the one that is socially optimal. Moreover, the maximum improvement that can be brought forth by adjusting public policy in this manner is limited by the current policy. In this sense, policy options available to the public authority are path-dependent; our future depends on our past, and history does matter.

Summary and Conclusions

This paper proposes a framework that can be used to evaluate social benefits derived from pharmaceutical innovations and public policy regarding generic product imitation. Imitation by generic products will reduce the demand and the price of the innovator's product. It thus reduces the rate of return to the innovator and at the same time increases the consumer welfare.

Public policy is a relevant issue in this context because it affects both the length of the patent protection and the rate of imitation; and these factors, in turn, determine the incentive to innovate and the size and distribution of benefits derived from innovation between the innovator and the consumer. An optimal public policy is one that provides just enough incentive for the innovator but manages to pass the fruit of innovation rapidly to the consumer.

Public authority does not have complete knowledge of the innovator's profit function and the social-rate-of-return function. In addition, it does not have full control over either the effective length of patent protection or the rate of imitation. For these reasons, public policy cannot be relied upon as sole determinant of social benefits and the innovator's profits. Under these circumstances, whenever the result of the current policy is not desirable, it may not be possible or realistic for the public authority to set a goal to move immediately to an objectively

---

[9] Note that when point A represents the outcome of the current policy, a small increase in both t_l and k increases both innovator's profit and social welfare. If point B should represent the outcome of the current public policy, however, in order to obtain the same result, policy would have to be changed in exactly the opposite direction.

defined "optimal situation." Instead, a sensible alternative is to seek marginal improvements.

Seeking marginal improvements often leads the decision maker to adopt moves that simultaneously benefit both the innovator and the consumer. Such public policy adjustment, in general, does not lead to a convergence to the optimal social policy. This manner of adjustment is, therefore, inconsistent with the society's ultimate objective. Although this conclusion is disturbing, unfortunately, given the market environment, there does not appear to exist a natural mechanism that will enable us to break away from this tendency.

Commentary

Michael A. Riddiough

Research such as Geweke and Weisbrod's must pass at least two levels of review in the real world of technology assessment. At one level, its technical content will be scrutinized by peer researchers, technocrats, and policy analysts. This group collectively will judge the value of the work on the basis of the model, method, data sources, and data analyses used. At another level, the work will be reviewed by policy makers and politicians. This latter group of reviewers will not be interested in models and data sources; rather, they want to know the bottom line: Do the results of this analysis mean anything to me or my programs? If so, what? Can I use the results favorably? If so, how and where?

I will address Geweke and Weisbrod's paper from three perspectives. First, I will comment on federal health policy makers' general acceptance of formal economic analysis. Second, I will discuss a specific potential application of Geweke and Weisbrod's work. Third, I will comment briefly on some technical aspects of their paper.

General Policy Perspectives about Formal Economic Analyses in Federal Health Policy

Some students of federal health policy believe that the goal of reducing the rate of rise in medical care expenditures has replaced all other objectives of federal health legislation and regulation. Although the current focus on cost containment often appears to overshadow issues such as the quality of health care and the safety and efficacy of medical technologies, these latter issues still attract much regulatory and legislative attention.

One result of the federal government's concern about rising medical care expenditures is that formal economic analysis of the benefits, risks, and costs of medical technologies has moved out of its limited traditional role as solely an academic exercise into a fledgling but potentially relevant role as a tool for health policy analysis and decision making. An

290

example of such a movement is the establishment by Congress of the National Center for Health Care Technology (NCHCT) of the Department of Health and Human Services. A major function of this center is to submit selected medical technologies to a variety of analyses and to make reimbursement recommendations regarding the use of these technologies to the Health Care Financing Administration (HCFA). One of the types of analysis that NCHCT plans to use is cost-effectiveness analysis (CEA).

Further, at the request of two Senate health subcommittees, the Office of Technology Assessment has studied the potential applications and implications of using CEA in the evaluation of medical technologies. Although the direct impact of this assessment cannot be evaluated at this time, it indicates increasing congressional interest in the topic of CEA. We recently completed a CEA of vaccination against pneumococcal pneumonia. The results of this analysis helped stimulate legislation in both chambers of Congress to modify the Medicare law to permit payment for pneumococcal vaccinations among the elderly.

Issues in certain areas of federal health policy, however, are not likely to be resolved through the use of formal economic analysis. Many congressional decisions in areas such as drug regulation, for example, are based on political, personal, and social values, rather than on quantitative analysis of data. Congress has, for example, mandated the use of stringent safety and efficacy standards in the drug-marketing approval process, in spite of arguments about drug lags and economic burdens on pharmaceutical companies. One must assume from Congress's posture on this issue that it places a higher priority on drug safety than on the costs associated with regulating pharmaceutical research and development (R&D).

Specific Application of Formal Analyses in the Evaluation of Medical Technologies

I believe that at least for the immediate future the use of formal economic analyses to evaluate medical technologies will be limited to postmarketing evaluations and possibly to the selection of specific technologies for reimbursement by health insurance programs. Certain analyses might be used to select for payment one type of intervention over another to diagnose, prevent, or treat a given medical problem. In addition, benefit-cost analysis or cost-effectiveness analysis might be used either (1) to select specific medical problems on which intervention programs might be focused or (2) to identify selected populations in which a particular type of intervention is likely to be most beneficial or most cost-effective.

In the policy framework that I described, Geweke and Weisbrod's research has a somewhat narrow application, that is, to compare the potential economic impacts of selecting one drug regimen versus another in the treatment of duodenal ulcer. Their model could be expanded upon, however, to help address larger issues. The inclusion of some measurement of health effects is essential; by itself, the measurement of changes in costs is of very limited value. Reliance on the assumption that, by itself, a decrease in treatment costs signifies an improvement in health status requires a substantial leap in faith.

If Geweke and Weisbrod's model included an assessment of health effects, it might be used, for example, by those responsible for selecting one therapeutic agent over another for inclusion in a drug formulary at the hospital, state, or—perhaps in the future—national level.

The use of formal economic analysis to select benefits under either publicly or privately financed health insurance could—in turn—lead pharmaceutical companies to use such analyses to help direct their R&D efforts. If the marketplace for drugs is substantially affected by government reimbursement policies, such as the use of a drug formulary, and if economic criteria, such as cost-effectiveness, are used to establish such reimbursement policies, it seems likely that drug developers would—at least in part—direct their research efforts in accordance with such criteria and policies.

Economic criteria and analysis apparently are not used in the Food and Drug Administration (FDA) marketing approval processes. Although economic criteria are used in marketing approval processes for drugs in some other countries, I suspect the FDA will not use economic criteria for drug approval in this country in the near future.

Specific Comments on Methods, the Model, and Data

This type of analysis needs to quantify health effects associated with the use of the experimental intervention. Side effects of the experimental technology should also be included.

As pointed out by the authors, from the preliminary analysis of data presented here, *a cause-and-effect relationship between use of the drug and decline in medical care costs* cannot be readily established. Three primary reasons for this are:

• The number of study subjects for which data have been analyzed is too small.

• The correlation between assumed diagnosis and prescribed therapy needs to be better validated. Cimetidine is used to treat gastrointestinal problems other than duodenal ulcer, for example, Zollinger-Ellison syndrome, benign gastric ulcer, gastrointestinal hemorrhage, and pancreatic insufficiency. I would also like to see a better explanation of how patients were—or were not—matched for the number, type, and severity of their medical problems, including duodenal ulcer. Differences in medical expenditures between the experimental and control groups both during the twelve-month pretreatment period and during the ten-month observation period could be due to differences in medical problems other than duodenal ulcers.

• Better controls need to be incorporated to ensure that the decline in expenditures is associated solely with the prescribing of the experimental drug, rather than with a mixture of factors such as changes in life style and dietary habits. Patients' compliance rates with prescribed treatments should also be assessed.

Formal economic analysis has several pragmatic limitations. Cost-effectiveness analyses, for example, usually lack considerations of equity, distribution, social values, and political realities. Geweke and Weisbrod's research illustrates two problems that face those investigators who use formal economic analysis: (1) insufficient data bases require researchers to develop a list of qualifiers, assumptions, and caveats that often is longer than the list of their results, and (2) methods currently used for economic analysis vary so substantially that interstudy results can seldom be compared. These problems certainly are not insurmountable; however, their resolution will require a strong commitment—probably from the federal government—to develop respectable data sources and standardized methods. Until economic researchers and policy analysts agree to use uniform models and research methods, the results of singularly and unilaterally developed formal economic analyses will be of limited help to decision makers attempting to formulate comprehensive health policy. The National Center for Health Care Technology will be forced to address problems related to poor data and varying methods; perhaps its efforts will help direct some standardization.

My bottom-line assessment of this study is this: I think the research represents an innovative approach to using Medicaid claims data to assess the potential economic impact of a new drug. If changes in health status are worked into the model and better controls are added, this type of analysis could become quite useful to policy analysts in government and possibly to R&D analysts in industry.

I strongly encourage Drs. Geweke and Weisbrod to continue to improve and broaden the scope—and hence the utility—of their model.

Ronald W. Hansen

In his paper, Professor Wu addresses the timely but difficult problem of how to compensate innovators adequately at the lowest social cost.

293

To encourage innovation, public policies offer rewards to innovators, often in the form of exclusive or preferred marketing rights for the innovative product. The conferring of these rights, however, usually results in a reduction in the application of the new innovation, in part because of the high prices that the innovator, as exclusive marketer, can charge. Thus, we are faced with the problem that the method by which the innovator is rewarded may reduce the potential gains to the community from the innovation.

One should note at the outset that Professor Wu does not explore radically different alternative reward schemes, such as a government-sponsored payment to innovators coupled with free access to the marketing of the invention. Most such schemes, which can be made to appear very appealling in theoretical models that abstract from information and transaction costs, are potential nightmares if put into practice. Depending on the specifics of the scheme, great operational difficulty could be expected to arise in the assessment of the value of the innovation and in the prevention of excessive claims for reward. This paper was wisely restricted to considering rewards for innovation based on market processes. The question the paper seeks to answer is thus: If we try to promote innovation through exclusive or preferred marketing rights, what are the socially optimal policies with regard to the length of the preferential period and the encouragement or discouragement of imitative products?

In my discussion of Wu's paper I shall begin with a criticism of the measurement of social benefits of innovation, describe the implications of these criticisms for the social optimization model he presents, and then discuss the difficulties of establishing policies to maximize the social gains from innovative activities.

In order to estimate the social value of an innovation or an imitative product, Wu relies on a market-determined assessment of the value of pharmaceutical products. Some critics would object to the use of a market demand schedule to measure the value of a prescription drug because of several alleged distortions in this market, such as the selection of products by physicians rather than patients and some third-party reimbursements. Although it is the case that consumers' preferences are translated into market demand in a less direct manner in this market, I would be willing to place a greater reliance on the market demand schedule as a measure of the consumer evaluation of prescription drugs than on any nonmarket assessments made by a party not involved in the transaction.

Although I agree with his use of market measures of value, I believe the manner in which Wu calculates the value of introducing imitative products is inappropriate. Wu states that his model is similar to that used by Mansfield and his colleagues in their article addressing the social benefits of innovation.[1] Although this model is appropriate for the problem addressed by Mansfield and the others, it is not appropriate for the problem addressed by Wu. Mansfield's group is concerned with measuring the benefits of new technology, which makes it possible to produce the same final product at a lower cost per unit. Because the characteristics of the final product are unchanged, they can use a single demand schedule to analyze the effects of a change in production cost and to estimate changes in consumer surplus and profits to producers.

The problem addressed by Wu is to measure the social benefits of introducing a generic imitation of a single-source brand-name product. Wu claims that this is analogous to the problem addressed by Mansfield because the generic and brand-name products are chemically equivalent and the unit of quantity measurement is the same. He later states, however, that "we also assume that the brand-name drug is preferred by all and that the generic drug is demanded only if its price is less than that of the brand-name drug." Thus, even though the products may be chemically the same, consumers view the products as not being equivalent. One cannot, therefore, measure the consumer valuation of both of the drugs by the original demand schedule for the brand-name product, as is done by Wu. To analyze the effect of introducing a generic product properly under these conditions, one should treat the generic as a separate product that is a close but not identical substitute for the brand-name product.

Measuring the benefits of introducing a substitute good in the presence of externalities has been discussed by Arnold Harberger, E. J. Mishan, and others.[2] To demonstrate the technique for measuring this social gain, we will consider the following scenario. Let aD in figure 1 be the demand schedule for the brand-name product before the introduction of the generic and P_1 be the price of the brand-name product. Let $a'D'$ in figure 2 be the demand schedule for a generic substitute, assuming that the price of the brand-name product is held at P_1. If the generic is introduced at a price P', q_0' units of the generic would be purchased, the demand schedule for the brand-name product would be reduced to gmD, and its sales would decline to q_1. So long as there is no change in the price of the brand-name product, the consumers' surplus resulting from the introduction of the generic would be measured by the area $a'b'd'$. It is not necessary to subtract any consumers' surplus loss due to the shift in demand for the brand-name product, since the

[1] Edwin Mansfield, John Rapoport, Anthony Romeo, Samuel Wagner, and George Beardsley, "Social and Private Rates of Return from Industrial Innovations," *Quarterly Journal of Economics*, vol. 91 (May 1977), pp. 221–40.

[2] Arnold C. Harberger, *Project Evaluation* (Chicago: Markham Publishing Co., 1973); and E. J. Mishan, *Cost Benefit Analysis: An Introduction* (New York: Praeger, 1971).

FIGURE 1
DEMAND FOR BRAND-NAME PRODUCT WITH AND WITHOUT GENERIC SUBSTITUTE

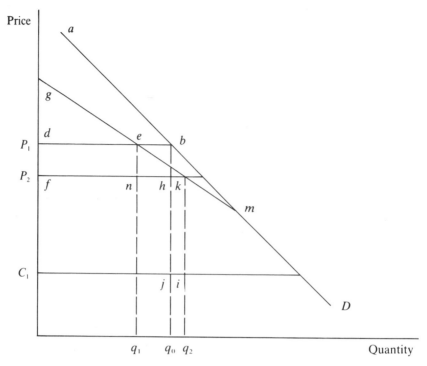

consumers' evaluations of their potential net surplus from using the brand-name product are incorporated in the generic demand schedule.

If the producer of the brand-name product changes the price of his product in response to the introduction of the generic, then there will be additional gains or losses to consumers. If, for example, he lowers his price to P_2, then consumers will demand q_2 units of the brand-name product, the demand schedule for the generic will shift to $g'c'D''$, and at an unchanged price for the generic its sales will fall to q_1'.[3] The increase in consumers' surplus arising from both a reduction in the cost of the previously purchased quantity of the brand-name product and from the increase in brand-name purchases is *dekf*. The fact that the generic

---

[3] Wu asserts that the brand-name producer will have lower sales after the introduction of the substitute. If the demand schedule for the branded product rotates around a point n as described by Wu and reproduced in my figure 1 and if point n lies above the marginal cost line, then the profit-maximizing output for the monopolist selling the branded product increases.

FIGURE 2
Demand for a Generic Substitute

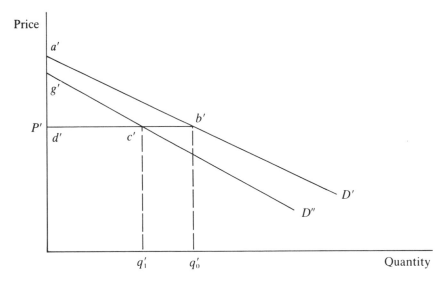

demand schedule has shifted inward does not necessitate a subtraction of previously measured consumers' surplus.

The total increase in consumers' surplus resulting from the introduction of the generic at a price P' and the decline in the price of the brand-name product is $a'b'd'$ plus $dekf$. To compute the total social benefits, we must add in the gain or loss in profits of the brand-name and generic producers. We would expect the profits of the brand-name producer to decline as a result of the competition from the generic supplies. If the brand-name producer's marginal cost is C_1, in figure 1, his profit has decreased by $dbhf - kijh$ as a result of the entry of the generic product. If the generic producer prices at marginal cost, the total social gain is $a'b'd'$ plus $dekf$ minus $dbhf$ plus $kijh$. This expression is not as simple as one that would be derived if consumers treated the two products as identical.

So far, our analysis and that presented by Wu have proceeded in the absence of an evaluation of any cost of entry on the part of the generic producer. The imitator may have to invest a substantial sum in research and development or in plant and equipment before entering the market. The fixed cost of entry may not be large enough to prevent imitation but may be substantial enough to make the net social gains from imitation negative. To illustrate this most easily, we will assume that the consumers treat the product of both producers as identical so

297

that we can work with a single demand schedule DD in figure 3. The marginal production cost for both producers will be assumed to be identical and equal to C. If P_1 is the price when there is only one producer and P_2 the price after the entry of the second producer, then total producer profits have fallen by the difference between P_1beC and P_2dfC or by $P_1bgP_2 - gdfe$. Because consumers' surplus increased by P_1bdP_2, the net gain per period after entry is $bdfe$. If this net gain is less than the second producer's share in total profits, we can construct cases in which the investment necessary to enter the market could be economically profitable to the entrant but the net social gain is negative. This result is hardly startling: it is the basis for justifying natural monopolies in utilities, for example. One could even construct cases in which the original innovation has positive private returns and negative social returns; however, I would judge this to be a less likely occurrence. The possibility of positive private but negative social returns is important to note here, however, because in Wu's paper and many other discussions of innovation and imitation, there is a presumption that the social benefit exceeds the private benefit (except where imitation discourages future innovation).

FIGURE 3
NET GAIN TO CONSUMERS AFTER ENTRY OF A NEW FIRM

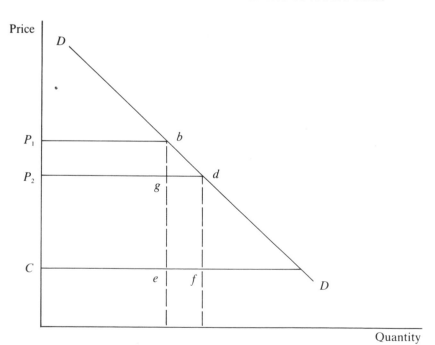

In the context of Wu's model, the possibility of positive private but negative social returns to innovation or imitation requires an expansion of the dimensions of his analytical framework. For some products the relationship between levels of social benefit and the policy variables may be reversed.

In his model Wu uses two policy parameters, the time of first imitation t_I and the rate of imitation k, and calculates the combination of the two variables that would maximize social benefits consistent with innovation's being sufficiently profitable to be forthcoming. When the policy maker has complete control over the variables, the socially optimizing combination he derives lies on the innovator's zero-profit line. This result follows from measures of the social benefits of imitations used by Wu in which he obtains only positive returns to imitation. Once we allow for the possibility of negative social benefits to imitation, we are no longer necessarily driven to the zero-profit frontier.

More important, there is not a single zero-profit frontier for all innovations. Although Wu recognizes that differences may exist across industries, he states that these can be handled by having industry-specific policies. Even within an industry, however, there is likely to be considerable difference in the location and shape of the zero-profit frontier. As long as we are able to have only one policy for a set of different innovations, we are likely to discourage some potentially beneficial innovation while also having greater than zero profits for other innovations. To attempt to adjust the policy variables case by case would impose a potentially costly burden of obtaining the necessary case-by-case information, require monitoring of the public representative, and involve the game-theoretic problems that Wu demonstrates so well at the end of his paper.

Because we are likely to settle on one set of rules for a wide range of innovative projects, we should frame the rule selection problem in terms of trade-offs between the forgone innovation and specific product market distortions. A critical area for future research in this regard is the estimation of the supply response of innovation to changes in policy parameters. Until we have better estimates of the effect of policies on innovative activity, it is presumptuous to try to formulate optimal public policies. Unfortunately, this estimation process is likely to be very difficult, particularly for pharmaceutical innovation.

Although my remarks have focused on several specific points of disagreement with Wu's paper, I am in general agreement with the approach of considering the social costs and benefits of the interactive effects of innovation and imitation. Many insights and elements of the model that Wu has given us in his paper will be useful in future assessments of alternative policy proposals.

PART
SIX

Drugs and Health: What Research
Agenda for Public Policy?
A Panel Discussion

Introduction

Robert B. Helms

The purpose of this discussion is to present several views about the direction policy research related to drugs should take. In selecting the panel, I have attempted to obtain the views of those who have been active in various aspects of either drug regulation or economics of regulation in a broader sense. That is, I have selected people who have done research related to pharmaceuticals as well as people who have also studied regulatory policy issues in other industries. It is my hope that the introductory statements by the four panelists plus the ensuing discussion will be of use to all those concerned about the future of drug policy and especially to those engaged in this research.

Let me briefly say a few words about each of the panelists. Professor Yale Brozen, as an adjunct scholar of the American Enterprise Institute, is in charge of its Evaluative Studies series. In this capacity, he has been a critical reviewer of all of the AEI studies dealing with drug regulation and has contributed forewords to several of these volumes.[1] As is evident in any of his writings on pharmaceutical regulation, he has definite ideas about what kinds of research projects should be undertaken.

Dr. William S. Comanor has been writing about pharmaceutical economics since he finished his dissertation on that topic at Harvard in 1963.[2] On leave from the University of California, Santa Barbara, he is now director of the Bureau of Economics at the Federal Trade Commission, an agency that has taken considerable interest in the perform-

---

[1] Yale Brozen, forward to Sam Peltzman, *Regulation of Pharmaceutical Innovation: The 1962 Amendments* (Washington, D.C.: American Enterprise Institute, 1974), pp. 1–3, and foreword to Kenneth W. Clarkson, *Intangible Capital and Rates of Return* (Washington, D.C.: American Enterprise Institute, 1977), pp. 1–17; see also his *The American Drug Industry: Private Enterprise or Public Utility?* (Washington, D.C.: American Enterprise Institute, 1977), reprint no. 79.

[2] William S. Comanor, "The Economics of Research and Development in the Pharmaceutical Industry" (Ph.D. diss., Harvard University, 1973); see also his "Research and Competitive Product Differentiation in the Pharmaceutical Industry in the United States," *Economica*, vol. 31 (November 1964), pp. 372–84, "Research and Technical Change in the Pharmaceutical Industry," *Review of Economics and Statistics*, vol. 47 (May 1965), pp. 182–90, and "Competition in the Pharmaceutical Industry," in Robert I. Chien, ed., *Issues in Pharmaceutical Economics* (Lexington, Mass.: Lexington Books, 1979), chap. 4, pp. 63–68.

ance of the pharmaceutical industry. He also has some definite ideas about this research.

Dr. George Eads is now a member of the president's Council of Economic Advisers, a position that puts him in the thick of the regulatory reform debate in Washington. He brings both academic and government experience to this debate, having taught economics at George Washington University and served as director of regulatory studies at the Rand Corporation and as a senior staff economist at the Council on Wage and Price Stability. He has done academic research on airline regulation and remains an active participant in the ongoing assessment of airline and other deregulation.[3] In addition to his broad interest in all types of regulatory issues, he is familiar with the body of literature relating to the economics of pharmaceuticals and the effects of drug regulation.[4] Having him on the panel is my attempt to bring some of the lessons learned from the regulation (and deregulation) of other industries into this discussion about the future agenda for policy-related research in pharmaceuticals.

Dr. Louis Lasagna, a well-known pharmacologist, writer, and proponent of responsible medical research, is included to keep the economists honest. To say the least, he has been a major participant in the ongoing debate about the effects of drug regulation on medical research and the practice of medicine. In addition to his writings on these topics,[5] he was a member of the Dripps Committee when it functioned in 1973–1974, and he founded the Center for the Study of Drug Development at the University of Rochester, a center that has the distinction of collecting and analyzing almost all the factual information about drug regulation now available outside the Food and Drug Administration. Dr. Lasagna was also instrumental in founding the Center for Health Policy Research at AEI and has served on its advisory committee since its inception. He is currently chairman of the Department of Pharmacology and professor of medicine at the University of Rochester Medical Center.

---

[3] George C. Eads, *The Local Service Airline Experiment* (Washington, D.C.: Brookings Institution, 1972), and "Railroad Diversification: Where Lies the Public Interest?" *Bell Journal of Economics and Management Science,* vol. 5, no. 2 (Autumn 1974), pp. 595–613.

[4] George C. Eads, "Economist versus Regulators," in James C. Miller III, ed., *Perspectives on Federal Transportation Policy* (Washington, D.C.: American Enterprise Institute, 1975), pp. 101–9, "Chemicals as a Regulated Industry: Implications for Research and Product Development," Rand Corporation working paper P–6198, February 1979, and "The Benefits of Better Benefits Estimation," Rand Corporation working paper P–6261, December 1978.

[5] William M. Wardell and Louis Lasagna, *Regulation and Drug Development* (Washington, D.C.: American Enterprise Institute, 1975), *International Drug Regulation* (Rochester, N.Y.: University of Rochester Medical Center, publication no. 7704, 1977), and "Who Will Adopt the Orphan Drugs?" *Regulation* (November/December 1979), pp. 27–32.

Statements

Yale Brozen

In considering a research agenda for evaluating public policy toward pharmaceuticals, one fact should be kept stage center: drugs are our most cost-effective input in supplying the demand for health. A ten-dollar prescription is frequently a substitute for $2,000 worth of hospital services—a substitute that produces a positive outcome with much higher frequency than hospital care.

There is, at present, a long list of ailments that still require costly and frequently ineffective treatments and for which there is no low-cost drug substitute. Our progress in the past in producing drug substitutes for such procedures and the developments on the horizon indicate that pharmaceutical innovations could contain the cost explosion in the health industry. If we are serious about minimizing costs, our best bet is to increase the number of drug innovations. "It should be clearly recognized that existing drugs are inadequate to deal with most of the diseases we face."[1] I would suggest, then, that the foremost item on any agenda is to learn as much as we can about what factors affect the size and productivity of the pharmaceutical research effort. There is much that can and should be done to increase research productivity, particularly in view of its marked decline since 1962.[2]

Because drugs are cost-effective in producing health, I tend to lose patience when I see so much effort devoted to finding a monopoly explanation for pricing in the drug industry. It has been demonstrated that what some investigators blame on monopoly is usually a disequilibrium phenomenon in a competitive market[3] or a consequence of ar-

---

[1] William M. Wardell, *Regulation and Drug Development* (Washington, D.C.: American Enterprise Institute, 1975), p. 144.

[2] Henry Grabowski, *Drug Regulation and Innovation* (Washington, D.C.: American Enterprise Institute, 1976), pp. 36, 54. Apparently, productivity of pharmaceutical research is now about one-sixth of what it was before 1962.

[3] Yale Brozen, "The Antitrust Task Force Deconcentration Recommendation," *Journal of Law and Economics*, vol. 13, no. 2 (October 1970), pp. 279–92.

bitrary or governmentally required accounting conventions.[4] If we want to investigate pricing, let us find out why the prices of drugs are so low relative to their value when that value is measured relative to nondrug alternatives. Why is it that drug prices have consistently fallen relative to the consumer price index?

A high-priority item for the research agenda is a measurement of the benefits of drugs. If they are a great bargain, as the evidence so far suggests, we need to make that obvious. We need to revive memories of the day when drugs were referred to as *miracle* drugs. Apparently, the drug industry has fallen to the state of the senator who, after reminding his constituents of the projects he had obtained for his state ten years before, was asked, "So what have you done for us lately?"

The importance of measuring explicitly the value of the medical innovations produced by the drug industry should not be underestimated. My reason for believing this is that attitudes in the making of policy are colored by notions of "me-too" chemical entities, as if research efforts were and are being devoted to reruns that serve no useful purpose. The me-too propaganda has been exposed,[5] but its influence lingers. Policy-making and regulatory attitudes are also colored by notions that the industry can promote any chemicals, no matter how lacking in efficacy, into multimillion-dollar moneymakers by bribing physicians with samples and prizes.[6] It is this sort of attitude that leads some Food and Drug Administration (FDA) officers to demand such absurdities as comparative efficacy studies and to demand repeated efficacy studies to replicate what the efficacy studies have already proved.

Attitudes are also colored by the belief that the drug industry makes so much money that we might as well "stick it to them" by demanding costly efforts, no matter how little the value of duplicative efforts or how much delay is suffered in drug introductions. Commissioner Kennedy, testifying in the 1979 House drug innovation hearings, argued that drug firms are doing magnificently in financial terms and that they can afford to pay for whatever nonsense is demanded by the FDA without stinting on their research effort.[7] It is time that the Kennedys were told

---

[4] Kenneth W. Clarkson, *Intangible Capital and Rates of Return* (Washington, D.C.: American Enterprise Institute, 1977); Robert Ayanian, "The Profit Rates and Economic Performance of Drug Firms," and T. R. Stauffer, "Profitability Measures in the Pharmaceutical Industry," in Robert B. Helms, ed., *Drug Development and Marketing* (Washington, D.C.: American Enterprise Institute, 1975).

[5] Larry L. Deutsch, "Research Performance in the Ethical Drug Industry," *Marquette Business Review*, vol. 17 (Fall 1973), pp. 129–43.

[6] S.1075 contains a provision prohibiting promotional gifts to physicians whose value exceeds ten dollars.

[7] U.S. Congress, House, *Drug Innovation Hearings,* 96th Congress, 1st session, June 21, 1979, transcript, p. 46. Cited in American Enterprise Institute Legislative Analysis, *Proposals to Reform Drug Regulation Laws* (Washington, D.C., 1979), p. 37.

that real resources are being consumed in FDA-demanded boondoggles—resources that could be producing lifesaving innovations that are not being produced.

We need to demonstrate just how competitive the drug industry is. A showing of how low drugs are priced relative to their value would help in that endeavor. We also need to demonstrate just how profitable research is—apparently it is no longer very profitable[8]—to end the demand for boondoggles.

Some of the research needed is conceptual rather than empirical. It seems to many economists that drug prices are high relative to marginal cost—which means to them that the industry is not competitive—but their notion of the relationship of price to marginal cost is based on a primitive conception of marginal cost. Professor Telser has demonstrated that marginal cost is a bit more complicated than the usual economist's notion of this concept.[9] His work needs extension and elaboration in language and examples from the pharmaceutical industry that can be comprehended by minds less subtle than his.

While we are clarifying some of the primitive notions we use when introducing innocent students to economics in order to make these notions into operational concepts appropriate for research use, we should also remove some of the obfuscation resulting from the use of the structure-conduct-performance paradigm. Perhaps the boxes are useful, but the arrows from structure to performance point in the wrong direction.[10] Instead of automatically accepting the notion that structure determines conduct, which determines performance, we should recognize that it is performance and conduct that determine structure.[11] The efficient and innovative firm that behaves competitively wins the market. A concentrated structure and a variety of products result from such good performance. Concentration and product variety are a proof of competitive conduct and good performance,[12] not a cause of bad conduct and poor performance.

I would suggest that we apply an upended structure-conduct-per-

---

[8] Meir Statman, *Returns on Pharmaceutical Research and the Competitive Equilibrium* (Washington, D.C.: American Enterprise Institute, forthcoming); David Schwartzman, *The Expected Return from Pharmaceutical Research: Sources of New Drugs and the Profitability of R&D Investment* (Washington, D.C.: American Enterprise Institute, 1975).

[9] Lester G. Telser, "The Market for Research and Development: Physician Demand and Drug Company Supply," herein.

[10] Yale Brozen, *Industrial Concentration and Public Policy* (New York: Macmillan, forthcoming).

[11] Almarin Phillips, "Structure, Conduct, and Performance—and Performance, Conduct, and Structure?" in J. W. Markham and G. F. Papanek, eds., *Industrial Organization and Economic Development* (Cambridge: Harvard University Press, 1970).

[12] George J. Stigler, appendix to "A Theory of Oligopoly," *Journal of Political Economy*, vol. 72, no. 1 (February 1964), pp. 44–61. Reprinted in Stigler, *The Organization of Industry* (Homewood, Ill.: Richard D. Irwin, 1968), pp. 60–62.

formance paradigm to an analysis of the history of innovation and industrial structure in each of the various therapeutic categories. We need to analyze the benefits of innovations as they appear and the benefits of new product varieties. I believe we would find that we should be praising concentration and product variety, then, as evidence of good performance and competitive conduct. Product "differentiation" is a virtue, not a sin.

On our research agenda, we should also be looking into what proof of efficacy there is of the investigational new drug (IND) requirement and of the proposed monitoring of animal studies. The IND requirement presumably was installed to make sure that animal toxicology studies were adequate and that no harm would be done in human trials. Has the harm done to patients in clinical studies been reduced by the IND requirement? Since practically zero harm was done in clinical studies before the IND requirement was installed, I believe that the efficacy of the requirement is nonexistent. Let us apply the same standards of efficacy to such requirements as the FDA applies to new chemical entities. If the efficacy of the IND requirement cannot be demonstrated, then there are grounds for discarding it—for removing it from the regulation panoply.

Let us also examine the efficacy of the efficacy requirement. There is some evidence indicating that it is not effective.[13] Let us apply the efficacy requirement standard to efficacy demonstration requirements. I think a double-blind test here will demonstrate that there is not even a placebo effect.

The whole regulatory mechanism may be a gigantic sham with enormous costs and no benefits. If it is a charade, we should go about the task of unmasking the charade. If it is not, let us prove it is not. If some parts are valuable and some are not, let us sort them out. It is time to get on with this task, above all others.

William S. Comanor

There are really two literatures on the economics of the pharmaceutical industry. These two literatures focus on different positions and come to different conclusions for public policy. In this comment, I briefly examine both these literatures and how they relate to each other, for it appears that they frequently pass as ships in the night and do not really confront each other on the relevant issues.

The first literature is perhaps the more conventional. It follows the

---

[13] Sam Peltzman, *Regulation of Pharmaceutical Innovation: The 1962 Amendments* (Washington, D.C.: American Enterprise Institute, 1974).

traditional industrial organization paradigm of structure-conduct-performance. There is little need to review here this methodological approach. I should emphasize, however, that dynamic efficiency or progressiveness is as important a dimension of performance in this paradigm as is static efficiency.

Many of the studies included in this literature have called attention to the relatively high prices and profits earned in this industry and have sought an explanation. One explanation is that we have measured costs incorrectly, but there are other explanations as well. Whatever the implications of these studies for static efficiency, it is clear that they provide no evidence on progressiveness as an independent dimension of performance.

In this approach to industrial organization, there is an element of asymmetry in the relationship between competition and these two dimensions of performance. Competition is traditionally defined by the extent to which the behavior of firms is similar to what would be enforced under the purely competitive model with the same demand and cost conditions. This definition, however, focuses on the extent to which actual market conditions depart from those expected under competitive conditions with the same exogenous factors present.

Although the purely competitive model provides a necessary benchmark by which to appraise actual states of competition in this industry and in others, its use creates some analytical problems. Foremost among them is that the competitive model, though fairly precise regarding certain variables, provides little information on others. It is known that the competitive price equals marginal cost, but there is no similar assistance in defining competitive levels of advertising or research. This definition of competition, therefore, requires us to focus on such variables as prices or outputs, on which the competitive model is fairly explicit, rather than on such variables as advertising or research, where there is no apparent way of determining competitive norms.

The degree of competition, therefore, is defined largely in terms of prices and quantities, which are closely related to the norms for static efficiency. As a result, there is always the possibility that competition may be inversely related to progressiveness, which is defined on other grounds. The prospect is raised that higher degrees of competition may be associated with reduced progressiveness.

This point is not new. Indeed, the essence of the Schumpeterian hypothesis is that the most rapid rate of innovation may not be served by the maximum degree of competition. As a result, there can be conflict between static and dynamic efficiency.

What this means for purposes of public policy is that a finding of monopoly, or of reduced competition, in the pharmaceutical industry, or indeed in any other, does not necessarily mean that policy measures are required to correct for the monopoly observed. Monopoly power represents a concept in positive rather than normative economics, and additional factors must be considered before taking the additional step of recommending policy measures. In this regard, I agree that policy recommendations are not necessarily implied from a finding of the lack of competition alone.

As suggested above, there is a second literature that deals with the economics of the pharmaceutical industry. In many respects, it is a more recent literature, and it emphasizes the dynamic competition provided by the entry of new firms and the development of new products.

How different are these studies from those that follow the more traditional approach? Some parts of this new literature use market-share turnover to measure dynamic competition. By this measure, the pharmaceutical industry appears highly competitive, and it is argued that this variable, or a similar one, is a more accurate index of competition in this industry than the more conventional measures of concentration or profitability.

These new measures, however, are not better or worse than the more conventional ones; rather they are different. They reflect a different facet of industry behavior, which may bear little relationship to what is measured by concentration or profitability. *The question is not which is a better measure of competition but rather what it is that each variable measures.*

A rapid pace of new product introduction may be the primary reason for the high level of market-share instability in the pharmaceutical industry, which has been pointed out by others. In this case, substantial dynamic competition may be quite compatible with high degrees of monopoly power, as defined by the relationship between prices and marginal costs. Rapid innovation is not inconsistent with the exercise of monopoly power.

Although consumer welfare may be improved by rapid product innovation, it may also be reduced by prices that exceed costs because of limited competitive pressures. The dilemma posed by the Schumpeterian hypothesis is that rapid innovation may indeed be at the expense of substantial price competition. Whether or not this is the case in the pharmaceutical industry is a major research question before us, with important implications for public policy.

During the past dozen years or so, large numbers of economic studies have appeared, dealing with various facets of the pharmaceutical industry. For the most part, these studies have examined specific features of this industry. What is primarily needed at this time is a framework of analysis to consider how the results obtained fit together. Many of the existing studies seem to point in diametrically opposite directions. Searching for the common ground among them represents a major task before us.

George Eads

When Bob Helms asked me to speak at this conference and at this session, I told him that I have never performed any research on pharmaceutical innovation. He reminded me of research I had done for a paper entitled "Chemicals as a Regulated Industry." What I was trying to learn in that search was whether the various studies of the relationship between regulation and innovation that had been done in pharmaceuticals might tell me anything useful about the impact of regulation elsewhere, in particular, in chemicals. In the paper I ultimately wrote, and delivered at the American Chemical Society meetings in the fall of 1978, I contended that the drug experience was of somewhat limited relevance. I should like to go through that argument here.

The point I was making was that one must consider the particular purpose and type of regulation before deciding whether the experience in drugs is relevant. There are certain types of regulation whose avowed purpose is to alter the rate and direction of technological change. Drug regulation seems to be one of those. Indeed, I am surprised that it took such a long time for people to agree that regulation, to the extent that it was doing what it was supposed to, was changing the rate at which drugs were introduced, for that seems to be its stated purpose.

There are certain other areas of regulation with similar purposes: regulations affecting pesticides, food additives, and toxic substances. Their whole purpose is to alter the kinds of substances that are introduced into the environment.

It is in these areas of regulation that there are some rather substantial lessons to be learned from the experience in pharmaceuticals. The lessons may be especially valuable because we have had regulation in drugs (and, possibly, food additives) longer than in the other areas; so we have a better history to help us assess both the benefits and the costs of this regulation.

In this area of regulation, I sense a growing realization that the original purpose behind much of it, which was to achieve something approaching zero risk, is unattainable except at zero rate of product introduction. Therefore, we have to strike a balance; we have to run certain kinds of risks to get the benefits of new substances. I think that the drug literature provides some ideas about where we may be going in other areas, provided it is carefully interpreted.

There are other areas of regulation, however, where any alteration in the rate and the direction of innovation is only a side effect. Examples are regulations affecting auto safety and emissions, nontoxic and environmental discharges, and things of that sort. I do not know that we learn very much from drug regulation in these areas, except for what it might tell us about the extent to which regulation alters firm behavior in the broader sense.

In areas such as toxic chemicals regulation, however, where the whole purpose is to change the product introduction and research strategies of firms, I would urge researchers to look most closely at the drug experience and ask some of the questions that Yale Brozen has asked. I am especially interested in learning, with respect to pharmaceuticals, what actual benefits in the form of reduced risks we can document after this period of time. What have we as a nation given up, not just in the way of resources diverted—because I am less concerned about that, perhaps, than some others would be—but in terms of opportunities forgone for new products?

Louis Lasagna, M.D.

One question we have been asked to address is why there has been so much research related to the economics of the pharmaceutical industry and the effects of regulation on innovation.

It is obvious that health, in general, is a sexy political topic. There are hearings going on almost all the time about this; there is a lot of media coverage, mostly about bad news. The public has certain obsessions, such as "cancerophobia." There are only about thirty known human chemical carcinogens. One would think that people might get more upset about the fact that there are actually thousands of pharmaceutical products that can be fatal, in ways other than through cancer, but there is a kind of asymmetry in the concern that people have that is, I think, in large part related to who is beating the drums at any moment.

Many people are preoccupied with the fear that we are a pill-happy society. Malcolm Muggeridge used to paraphrase the King James Version of the Bible: "I will look up unto the pills whence cometh my help."

One big difference, it seems to me, between innovation in the pharmaceutical industry and most other biomedical innovation and discovery is that, at least in my experience, regulation does not seriously affect one's life if one is an ordinary medical scientist but one who is in the drug development game is certainly affected by regulation.

I would have thought that, in fact, we did not have *enough* economic research in this area. At least in the circles in which I travel, I notice the same tired, lukewarm bodies, including my own, reappearing on the circuit and few new voices or new ideas. I would urge those who are interested to get into this field. I am not sure we need much more theoretical research, but it would be important to have some research on the real-life problems that face us all.

As I travel around, I hear many complaints about the costs of good laboratory practice regulations and good manufacturing practice regulations, but it is very hard to get answers to such questions as: How much is it actually costing? How much of it is worthwhile? How much is not?

One hears statements at meetings about the increasing percentage of research and development money spent on noninnovative pursuits, but, again, I am not persuaded that anyone has good data on that point.

The Center for the Study of Drug Development at the University of Rochester was set up to raise the level of national debate by trying to get some of the facts out on the table, including economic data. It was obvious that one of the advantages we had over people in individual companies was that we at least had the chance to get data from different companies and to see which considerations crossed company barriers and which might be more specifically true only for a given company.

Dr. Richard Crout, in Geneva recently, made the point that the drug companies had the disadvantage that they, unlike him, could not see what the filings were from different companies; on the other hand, the companies had an advantage over Dr. Crout and his colleagues in the Food and Drug Administration (FDA) in that they had the chance to see how different regulatory agencies acted in different parts of the world. Our cooperation from industry has been reasonably good, although the slowness with which it provides us information makes us suspect that it had not been paying much attention to this kind of data before we asked for it.

I am convinced that policy-related research in this area has had an impact on the regulators. It was always amusing to hear people like former Commissioner Kennedy say that there had never been any drug lag but that it had been eliminated. That has a surrealistic flavor to it.

The fact that we now have an official FDA policy of putting drugs on a fast track and on a slow track indicates, too, a response by the government to allegations that they are too slow and a desire at least to be less slow than usual about drugs that really look as if they are breakthroughs.

The increasing palatability of data from foreign clinical trials is interesting. Just a short time ago such data were not given much credence, but now we have Dr. Crout boasting that 25 percent of the new drug applications have pivotal data in the form of foreign clinical trials. He admits that they are still demanding U.S. trials as well, which I think has some ethical and legal implications, but the very fact that people are using the data more is, I think, a response to prodding.

The people at the top in the FDA are not so thick-skinned that they enjoy criticism and harpoons from people like those at the Center for the Study of Drug Development, for example. I would say, however, that many of the facts have been ignored by the faceless troops in the trenches of the FDA, who are the real power structure in many ways, because it is not the law that is a problem, it is the regulations or the way the regulations are applied. It is in this area that the individual drug monitor becomes much more powerful than his or her superiors, who have a higher level of turnover in their jobs. The half-life of a commissioner at the FDA is quite short, but the half-life of many of the drug monitors, including some of the most malcontented and obstructive, is very long.

If we look at the Senate bill that was recently passed—Senator Kennedy's bill—and contrast the various provisions there with what is already being done by the FDA, we will find that the bill is largely a legitimization of what is, in fact, already operating procedure.

Now, what about some needs? I think we are in bad shape in terms of quantifying the benefits from drugs. We are not in good shape even with regard to the benefits that are quantifiable with some ease, and when we get to benefits that are not easily quantifiable, we are in very bad shape.

Many of the data are very soft. Physicians do not save lives very often with drugs or anything else that they do. The surgeons and orthopedists do some dramatic things from time to time, but most internists and general practitioners are engaging in holding operations and just trying to make people feel a little bit better.

If we tell someone about a study in which a professional musician, let us say, has been shown to perform better, by his own evaluation or by the evaluation of judges, in a tranquilized state then in an untranquilized state, the reply will be, "I can buy that. That might have some real impact. You might get a job, if they are filling a chair in the symphony, if you are not paralyzed by anxiety." But if we say to such a person, "Well, what about a housewife who finds life a little bit more tolerable in the Valiumized state?" Then the reply is, "Isn't it a pity that she's got such poor moral fiber that she needs that help?"

It is very hard to quantify things like the mayhem and murder that have been prevented at home—around 5:00 P.M.—by either a martini or a Valium tablet. I suspect that many homes have been kept together by alcohol at certain times of the day—but identifying that kind of prophylactic benefit is hard to do, to say nothing of quantifying it.

We could use better data on the reasons for drug delays. I am not at all sure that I can quantify how much of the trouble is due to FDA regulations or their implementation and how much to incompetence on the part of firms, and it would be nice to know because, if we are going to correct those delays and eliminate the unnecessary ones, we need to know where to attack, and I am not sure that we do.

We are never going to find it very easy—and maybe it is impossible—to make precise judgments about the benefits and harms of the drug lag. I, for one, am no longer interested in debating the drug lag because it is obvious that there are differences from country to country in the speed at which drugs are approved.

The real question is whether our society is better or worse off, on balance—looking at *all* the drugs, not just one or two—and it is very hard to come up with data of that sort. We are left arguing about whether the United States is better or worse off, without either side's having good data to back up its views.

Someone has said that it is a good thing that we really cannot have randomized trials of some of the benefits of drug therapy. I am not sure I buy that; I am in favor of doing studies on the "naturalistic" use of therapeutic agents because that is the way the world works, but it certainly would be nice, if we are comparing patients who are on cimetidine and those who are not, to be able to say that groups are roughly comparable at base line in regard to the severity of their disease, their prognosis, and so forth. To the extent that we do not have that, we are constantly trying to parcel out variables other than those of primary interest.

As far as warnings for the future are concerned, it strikes me that we ought to worry more about what is going to happen to devices. The imposition on the device industry of the constraints that we have had on drugs has potentially far more chilling effects than we have seen even with drugs, because in the device industry the inventors often are solo entrepreneurs, working in garages or basements. That may be an oversimplification, but I could write a scenario in which the impact of overregulation would be considerably more deleterious for medical devices.

I am very much concerned about attempts to contain hospital costs by regulatory fiat, be it federal or state or local, in regard to drugs or anything else. Here, again, it would be very good if we could say something about the benefits and the risks of containing costs, rather than just arbitrarily deciding that we cannot afford to spend more than a certain amount on health care and coming to a decision solely on the basis of dollars spent.

I find that most people do not really understand that diagnostic procedures, for example, are more productive of negative data than of positive but that there is a real benefit in diagnostic procedures that reassure the patient that something is not wrong.

Finally, we do not have enough liaison among economists, political scientists, medical researchers, and health care delivery experts. By health care delivery experts, I mean people like Michael Halberstam— good, competent, practicing physicians. We have had too much of an impact on discussions of health care made by the sort of public health types who inhabit schools of hygiene and public health. These folks are often great at planning but not very good at delivery. I am not even sure they like people. They like the Public, with a capital *P*; I am not sure they like people with a small *p*. Often, they are the last people I would hire to devise a health care scheme, let alone to set up the criteria for judging whether it is working or not.

I therefore urge that we try to get more interaction between the types I described above—meeting for purposes of discussion and for planning research among people with very different backgrounds and very different interests and very different talents. They are all needed if we are to attack these problems to better effect than we have in the past.

Highlights of the Discussion

MR. HELMS: Thank you, Lou. First, I shall ask if there is any reaction among the panel members to what the other panelists have said.

MR. COMANOR: I have a question for Dr. Lasagna. This is a question that has bothered me for some time, and since I typically speak to economists, I would like to get some other opinion on it. I think it is fair to say that the evidence suggests a decline in the rate of new product introduction in the last ten to fifteen years. There are two hypotheses given for this decline: one is the effect of increased regulation, and the second is a decline in available basic scientific knowledge.

I should like to hear your comments—admittedly impressionistic comments—on which you think is most important. Are they both important? What can you say about that question, which I think lies at the heart of a lot of economic research on this issue in the last few years?

DR. LASAGNA: I used to pay lip service—and maybe a bit more than that—to the knowledge-depletion hypothesis, and I am sorry I ever did. As I read the medical literature and go to medical meetings, I am struck by the fact that never in the history of the world have we had so many exciting things going on in the biomedical sciences as we have today.

We have certainly not run out of new facts, new ideas. I will admit that we do not always know how to apply them; we do not know how to integrate them into a Gestalt so that the facts will be productive, but we certainly have not run out of leads. I would say, therefore, that the likelihood that *that* is the major force responsible for the slowdown is not tenable.

I should like to mention one other factor, which you did not mention in your dichotomy. One thing that has contributed to a slowing down—although it does not explain everything—is the evolving technology for evaluating medicines. Even if the world had not changed in other ways, it would take longer to work up a drug in 1979 than it took in 1960.

MR. COMANOR: Even with the old law?

DR. LASAGNA:Even with the old law. I found myself, in 1960, testifying at the congressional hearings that there were better ways of evaluating drugs than we were using. I do not believe that we can find many people in the pharmaceutical industry who really would want to go back to the old days and not do proper experiments, which are unfortunately more time consuming and more expensive than the older methods.

There is a great deal of argument about whether there is an excessive demand for data of this kind and whether all the reduplication is necessary; but I think that the evolving state of the art would have contributed to a delay in any case.

PROFESSOR J. FRED WESTON, UCLA: Can you estimate how much?

DR. LASAGNA: No.

MR. COMANOR: These are questions that I think economists have really worried about, and in talking to each other we do not get much of a handle on them.

PROFESSOR BROZEN: There were some trends at work before the 1962 law came along that were the result of the very thing that Dr. Lasagna was talking about, and that is that it was becoming increasingly costly just to do the various tests because of the multiplication of the number, depth, and quality of the tests. Just extrapolating trends would seem to indicate that the costs would have risen at a rate such that Ronald Hansen's estimate might have come out at around $27 million today as against a million or less before 1960 for bringing an average NCE to market.

MR. COMANOR: You and I both know that extrapolating trends is a very dangerous game.

PROFESSOR BROZEN: The point is: What can you beat it with at this point?

MR. COMANOR: I have nothing to offer; I was just saying that it is a dangerous game, and I was glad to hear Dr. Lasagna's comments.

PROFESSOR BROZEN: As Dr. Lasagna said, the indications are that the trend of increasing testing cost was at work, as nearly as we can tell by extrapolating trends. When someone gets a better technique, I wish he would tell me about it.

Bill Comanor draws a dichotomy between static and dynamic efficiency and speaks as if rapid innovation somehow is inconsistent with price competition. I would suggest that innovation is price competition. In effect, when we bring along a cure—let's say a drug cure—that costs a hundred dollars as against a hospital stay that costs a thousand dollars, that is price competition.

MR. COMANOR: We should not argue about definitions. If you define it that way, so be it. It is not the conventional way of defining price competition, but it certainly has to do with prices.

PROFESSOR BROZEN: Let me put it another way. A 10 percent slowing in the rate of innovation, according to one study, has the effect of decreasing the prices of old pharmaceuticals 3 percent more slowly than they would decline otherwise. The innovation, in and of itself, causes declines in the prices of previously existing pharmaceuticals. When we slow down the rate of innovation, we slow down the rate at which the prices of old pharmaceuticals decline.

PROFESSOR WESTON: That was not the issue that Bill Comanor was posing, though. The issue he posed was the divergence between price and marginal cost that appeared to exist on successful products. Do I state that correctly?

MR. COMANOR: I do not want to get into the question of whether the successful drug should cover the costs of unsuccessful ones; there is a sense, of course, in which that has to be considered. One set of literature—whether my studies or some others—has emphasized the differences between prices and costs, and another literature has emphasized the role of innovation. What seems apparent to me is that the two literatures have never really confronted each other as well as they might.

PROFESSOR WESTON: Well, yes. Certainly that applies to one aspect of Yale Brozen's response that the main process by which price competition takes place is the introduction of substitute drugs, which pushes down the price of older drugs. But I wanted to pick up on the assertion that there is a substantial segment of activity where price exceeds marginal cost.

I was going to respond by saying, "That may be true on a certain number of drugs, but it may not be true on others"; that is, on the old and tired drugs, marginal cost, in the long-run sense, may exceed price. This pushes us into an evaluation of overall profitability, and we simply end up there.

When we look at the FTC quarterly data, it appears that the drug industry does a little better than all manufacturing, on average. It seems to me, though, that that comparison is defective, particularly for the drug industry, where there is a high rate of entry and a high rate of exit of companies that are not picked up in the profit data. If we pick up the profitability data on the large number of firms that exit that industry, it is not so clear what overall profitability in the pharmaceutical industry is, compared with all manufacturing.

MR. COMANOR: Since coming to the FTC and having these data originate in the Bureau of Economics, I understand their defects even more than I did before.

MR. HELMS: Okay. The floor is open. Feel free to ask questions or comment on any topic you wish.

DR. JOHN VIRTS, Eli Lilly: I want to continue this last exchange by pointing out that new chemical entities coming from the pharmaceutical companies are not only new therapy but also a means to promote competition. Then I want to say that I agree with almost everything I heard Dr. Lasagna say, but if I had only the choice between some sort of random track for new chemical entities to go through the FDA and this fast-slow-medium track (where the FDA decides on its speed of evaluation on the basis of its assessment of the importance of the new chemical), I would choose the fast-slow-medium procedure. I hope, though, that the FDA, in applying this procedure, does remember that the new chemical entity is an economic entity as well as a physiological-pharmacologic entity and, in some way, gets those economic considerations into the determination of how fast to evaluate a drug.

Actually, I think the FDA has very limited ability to classify new chemical entities by their potential importance.

DR. LASAGNA: If you are lucky enough to get on the fast track with your compound, then that is good for you. If you are unlucky enough to have something that is judged on a slow track, it means, obviously, that you are going to be handled even more slowly than is the case at the moment, and I think the FDA would acknowledge that.

It is interesting that the Canadians have decided that they cannot make these judgments on the importance of new compounds and that it is perhaps not right for them to do so. I think also they may be more aware than others that it may be rather difficult to decide what is an outstanding drug and what is a me-too drug. Certainly, in the past, we could say that it has often been hard to do that. I will admit, however, that our agency is in much better shape than many other agencies would be to do this, because what is really impossible is to make that judgment when the drug first comes in when there are no human data available.

If one works in an agency where most drugs that come along have had a fair bit of human data in other countries, then one's judgment about whether one has an exciting new drug may be much more valid.

DR. VIRTS: Sometimes, though, in a cost-benefit sense, the economic competition aspect of one of these new drugs could even outweigh the pharmacologic benefit of the drug. It is going to be very tough to take this economic effect into consideration when establishing a rational fast-slow-medium track.

DR. LASAGNA: Yes. I do not think we ought to hold our breath before that gets factored into the equation. I think, for the foreseeable future, those judgments are going to be made on the basis of what strikes people as an exciting scientific advance.

MR. EADS: This notion of setting priorities for regulatory processes seems to be in vogue across the government. We are about to undertake an analysis of the EPA air carcinogen policy, not on the basis of which is an exciting substance or which is not an exciting substance but on the basis of which proposes higher versus lower hazards to health. The issue of what priority setting means and what it will actually lead to is something we are going to be looking into fairly heavily in other types of safety regulation.

The concept of setting priorities is a very good one. What it will lead to in practice is a good question, but other regulatory agencies do seem to be reacting to criticisms about their economic effects by saying, "We will find a way of getting at the more important cases first."

MR. EROL CAGLARCAN, Hoffmann–La Roche: My questions—or, rather, my requests for opinions—are directed to both Yale Brozen and Bill Comanor or to anybody else who cares to comment.

In terms of the structure of the industry, Henry Grabowski has presented some tables showing that innovation in the pharmaceutical industry is becoming more and more concentrated; but, in terms of sales, concentration is not yet apparent, and he has explained that there is some lag involved in that process.

I wonder—from your outlook and the outlook of the future of the pharmaceutical industry—what you see happening if there is such a lag and what the situation is going to look like five, ten, twenty years from now, in terms of structure.

MR. HELMS: Professor Brozen, why don't you go first? [Laughter.]

MR. COMANOR: Alphabetical order, of course.

PROFESSOR BROZEN: You have answered part of your own question, I think, in talking about the lag; that is, to the extent that it takes a while for the innovations to change the relative weights of sales, it is going to be a while before they change the relative structure of the industry.

My quick answer is that, insofar as it is true that innovation is becoming increasingly concentrated—I assume I can trust Henry Grabowski's data—that is being offset by the fact that old drugs coming off patent may be picked up by companies other than those that held them on patent in the past. This may contribute to slowing any increase in the concentration of the structure itself in terms of sales.

That is an off-the-cuff answer, though, and I am not sure whether it is correct or not.

MR. COMANOR: I am delighted to say I would support Professor Brozen's statement. It seems to me that that is a reasonable explanation of what is going on, especially since many of the producers of products for which the patent has expired are perhaps the smaller and less research-intensive firms. It seems like a plausible explanation, although we do not have available evidence on that.

PROFESSOR BROZEN: Let me go back for a minute. We certainly have had a decline in the number of pharmaceutical producers, a fairly extensive decline. This decline was moderately slow from 1954 to 1963 and then speeded up after 1963. I use 1963 simply because that is when we have census data.

One implication that could be drawn from that was that the 1962 amendments made life more difficult for the smaller companies relative to larger companies, and that, perhaps, was the reason why the decline accelerated in 1963.

PROFESSOR PETER TEMIN, MIT: If we consider the large firms, the number of firms has not gone down.

PROFESSOR BROZEN: The number of firms *has* gone down, taking the number of firms categorized in the four-digit pharmaceutical preparations industry in the census data.

PROFESSOR TEMIN: I don't think so, and if we look at the trend toward the larger firms—the growth of the share of sales or value added going to larger firms—we see that that started increasing well before the 1962 amendments, and there is no sign of any increase in the rate of growth of their share after 1962.

PROFESSOR BROZEN: There is no sign of any overall trend in that, I grant you that. There have been ups and downs in the share of the four largest firms—or the eight largest.

PROFESSOR TEMIN: Not the share of the four largest, but the share of firms over a certain size; there are more firms in there, it seems to me.

PROFESSOR BROZEN: I have been looking at census data and the way in which the Census Bureau reports this—I must read the numbers differently than you do.

PROFESSOR TEMIN: There are also IRS data by different size classes. The trend, though, is an earlier trend than the 1962 amendment.

UNIDENTIFIED: Is this discussion relevant, though? Individual classes have been fairly concentrated for a long time, and that is the relevant consideration. In some sense, it is like the discussion in economics of increasing aggregate concentration; unless there is some reason for not liking bigness per se, I am not sure it is relevant to the economics of the individual markets.

PROFESSOR BROZEN: Agreed.

PROFESSOR BURTON WEISBROD, University of Wisconsin: I would like to go back to some earlier discussion on the fast track–slow track priority sort of thing, involving FDA policy.

Has there been any very serious thought given—and I just ask this out of lack of knowledge—to the desirability of in fact having different levels of standards or different levels of tests for certainty or confidence levels—however one wants to put it—depending on certain identifiable characteristics of the drugs?

I do not know if my question is too vague. I actually have a small model, which I shall not present here, that suggests that there are good reasons for not using the same kinds of standards for drugs that differ with respect to either or both the expected net benefits per user and the size of the market as measured by the number of users.

I am sure that is not clear, but my point is that I am asking whether there is much thought about using different standards for somehow-defined different chemical entities.

DR. LASAGNA: There is talk about it, and there are in fact de facto differences in the standards applied to different drugs, depending on the feelings of the moment. If we are dealing with an anticancer drug, for example, and especially if it is aimed at a fairly rare kind of malignancy, the absolute amount of data required to get that drug on the market is much less than if we are talking about, let us say, a new antiinflammatory analgesic drug. There are ad hoc philosophies already extant that depend, in part, on the nature of the drug, the difficulty of doing the research, sometimes the ethics of it, sometimes the importance of the drug, sometimes the nature of the bureau or of the section within the Bureau of Drugs.

In addition, there is now more discussion than there has been in the past about certain different kinds of requirements for chemicals that are being studied by, let us say, academic investigators, so-called orphan drugs, where there is a very small market available and where, economically, it is not very attractive.[1]

It has never been clear to me, in the discussions that I have heard in the last year or two, exactly how that process is to be facilitated and what the cuts are going to be that will speed it up. But one certainly hears about tailoring demands to different needs.

PROFESSOR WEISBROD: Is size of the market one of the variables that gets attention?

DR. LASAGNA: In the sense that I just talked about orphan drugs, I would say yes.

PROFESSOR TELSER, University of Chicago: Has anyone actually obtained data from the FDA on NDAs and how long it took to approve them, and so on—a detailed study of that sort of thing?

DR. LASAGNA: There are data available on length of time.

PROFESSOR TELSER: No, I mean something different. Would it be possible to discover what the implicit criteria are from that sort of data on NDAs, to try to do an empirical study based on the evidence of what the effects of the FDA's various rules actually are?

---

[1] Louis Lasagna, "Who Will Adopt the Orphan Drugs?" *Regulation*, vol. 3, no. 6 (November/December 1979), pp. 27–32.

PROFESSOR WESTON: To review their data files, for example?

PROFESSOR TELSER: Yes. For example, if the FDA gets a lot of applications in one category, is it likely to go a little faster than if it is working in a category with few applications? Or is it the other way around? In other words, are there some implicit rules that we could discover that the FDA may not even be aware of itself?

DR. LASAGNA: I think the answer is that those data are not available at the moment. If, for example, you wanted to look at them, you would have a hard time getting them.

I think that, in the past, it was clear from the outside that certain things were going on that had to do with, let us say, the philosophy within a section of the Bureau of Drugs. For several years no cardiovascular drugs were approved, for instance, and that was because there were a number of people at important lower levels within that section who were very hard to please. Given those people in that position, it was hard for a cardiovascular drug to get in. I do not think that was related necessarily to the ease of demonstrating anything or the importance of anything; I think it was due to the individual philosophies of individual monitors.

PROFESSOR TELSER: It seems to me that that sort of thing would be very valuable to study.

DR. LASAGNA: I agree.

RONALD MCHUGH, Bureau of Foods, FDA: I think it is inappropriate to paint a picture of obstreperous bureaucrats going through the morning mail to find out which NDA they can turn down, when in fact they are operating within an incentive structure whose nature guarantees the most conservative regulatory behavior. I am referring to what is almost a type I versus type II error situation, if one can draw an analogy between rejecting a true hypothesis (type I error) and approving an unsafe drug, the operative assumption or hypothesis being that new drugs are unsafe until safety can be demonstrated. An example of a type I error in this case would be the approval of the drug thalidomide. Therefore, regulators, to escape being publicly pilloried, avoid type I or thalidomide-type errors by accepting a high probability of making type II errors, which in this context could be defined as rejecting or delaying approval of effective new drug applications. I wonder, Dr. Lasagna, if you could speak to the question of the incentive structure of the agency and its employees.

DR. LASAGNA: I don't think that it is because people in the FDA are obstreperous, but I agree that it is very easy to get burned for approving a drug that later turns out to have trouble, and I agree that is a very real phenomenon. What we are beginning to see now is a little pressure in the other direction. And when we have an antiepileptic drug obviously being speeded along because somebody goes on the "Today" show with tears in his eyes about his child and other epileptic children, we can see that now there are beginning to be, occasionally, penalties for keeping drugs off the market that strike somebody as interesting and important.

The general phenomenon to which you refer, though, I buy. In addition to that, however, I think that there have been, and probably still are today, individual FDA monitors who do not look on themselves as being obstreperous at all—that is an appellation that might be applied to them by other people—but who look on themselves as public-spirited citizens who are doing their damnedest to keep bad drugs off the market. It is a judgment call, and one can argue about whether their judgments are right. I happen to think that it is bad to have two U.S. presidents treated with Lidocaine for arrhythmia during their heart attacks when we have not yet said that that drug is an antiarrhythmic.

I think it is bad when we have the whole world using Valium to treat status epilepticus and the package insert says, "Contraindicated in patients with epilepsy."

These are obviously important lags that indicate that the system is not working well. It is not always because of the monitors; sometimes it is because a company has not applied for a new indication. We cannot blame the FDA because, until now, it has not considered initiating changes in a new drug application as its charge.

MR. MCHUGH: Right. I agree with you.

PROFESSOR DAVID SCHWARTZMAN, New School for Social Research: Let me return to the issue of research about the pharmaceutical industry. I think that if our major interest is in what factors encourage competition with respect to innovation, not only in this industry but also in other industries, the traditional industrial organization construct of structure-conduct-performance is not very helpful.

I think that it has been misleading in this industry, for example. In the original discussion, the traditional discussion that Bill Comanor referred to and in which he participated himself, this type of competition among drug companies tended to be condemned because these were merely the tactics of differentiated oligopolists: their method of competition was to differentiate their products, and therefore they introduced new drugs.

This diminished the usefulness of the new drugs, and there was some evidence to bear it out because not all drugs are major drugs. It is in the nature of things that not everything is a breakthrough.

So the traditional construct missed a good deal of what was going on in the industry, and I think this has been the trouble with the research of many of the people who have worked in the field, who have approached this industry from traditional industrial organization theory. They have had blinders on; they looked only at certain things.

It is a good thing that economic historians like Peter Temin are coming in and looking at the industry, because this makes for a more open type of inquiry. If we look at the industry itself, there are some obvious things about it that traditional industrial organization types will miss.

One of them is that doctors want new therapy. This is one of their great demands. They are much more interested in new therapy than in anything else. And there is the history of the industry, its period of success in developing new drugs, which propelled it to do more.

So I think it is helpful to try to look at the industry itself, rather than at concentration and therapeutic categories, as we have been doing.

MR. HELMS: Okay. Bill Comanor wants to respond, and then Fred Weston.

MR. COMANOR: I guess I take issue with that, Professor Schwartzman. I guess you are not surprised. [Laughter.] I do not think it is fair to say that those who studied the industry—shall we say, some time ago—including myself, looked on the behavior of firms that introduce new products as a vehicle of oligopolistic action and condemned that behavior. I think we have tried to understand it, tried to observe it, but I think it is unfair to say we condemned it.

As I tried to emphasize, even the traditional structure-conduct-performance paradigm admits that there are other dimensions of performance than static efficiency as in price equals marginal cost. Certainly, the rate of new product introduction as an element of progressiveness is a clear facet of performance, and the difficult questions—for which we do not have any firm answers—are the nature of the possible trade-offs that might exist among the various dimensions of performance.

I agree that it is good to have Peter Temin coming into the field, whatever his background. Maybe we should stop there. [Laughter.]

PROFESSOR WESTON: There was a slight intersection of agreement between Yale Brozen and Bill Comanor on a previous topic that I wanted to link with earlier, when we were talking about the behavior of physicians. If we reflect on the history of the Federal Trade Commission, we see that some years back it was criticized because it was finding a lot of price fixing and so forth, but this was in small industries, small firms, and the criticism was, "Look, it is dealing with trivia. Why doesn't it go after big industries and big firms?" And it started to do that; it started looking at concentrated industries. Now, more recently, it has been looking at some of the guilds, some of the professions.

I am interested in getting Professor Brozen's reaction to the rider attached to the recent appropriations bill that said that the Federal Trade Commission is not to look at a number of professions, specifically the medical and dental professions. This occurred to me because of our talk about the behavior of physicians.

MR. HELMS: We were discussing funeral directors rather than physicians.

PROFESSOR WESTON: Well, I guess that is another part in the continuum of medical care. [Laughter.]

If the FTC is prevented from attacking monopoly where it is, then it is likely to continue looking at concentrated industries, looking for monopoly where it is not. I wondered what Professor Brozen's reaction would be.

MR. COMANOR: I would like to hear Professor Brozen support the FTC. That would be marvelous. I hope I can expect it. [Laughter.]

PROFESSOR BROZEN: I was just going to say "Amen" to Fred Weston, that's all. [Laughter.]

PROFESSOR HENRY GRABOWSKI, Duke University: I thought I would mention a few trends that I think are going to be very important as the industry evolves, that we have touched on and that the panel may want to discuss.

It is very clear that if we look at the public policies affecting the industry right now, some of the major changes are occurring in the distribution and marketing part. The substitution laws and the maximum-allowable-cost (MAC) programs are increasingly, I think, going to create more competition—if one wants to use that word—after a patent expires.

We have more of the cost-reducing innovation (as opposed to cost-increasing innovation), and we have a shorter patent life. We have multiple public policy objectives here. I think we can get established drugs to people more cheaply, and in some sense that may cut down on the incentives to innovation. What we have to ask is, What are the public policy measures that we should seek to give us incentives for innovation, a safe and effective product, and competition?

MR. COMANOR: I think that is the right question, and I think there are trade-offs here that have not been explored.

PROFESSOR GRABOWSKI: I do not know about trade-offs. I was trying to focus on public policies.

PROFESSOR BROZEN: I think, Professor Grabowski, that part of the answer to your question is what has been happening to effective patent life, for instance. On the one hand, we are shortening the effective patent life with the long-drawn-out procedures for getting approval of new drug applications. And, on the other hand, we have the lengthening, so to speak, of the product life, to the extent that a brand-name item continues to be prescribed after the patent has expired, and it continues to manage to hold on to its market, in part because of the information conveyed by the brand name.

I think we ought to face that issue outright. There is a sort of left-handed attempt at it in the proposed drug law, with a notion that a monograph could be filed on a new drug that would protect it for five years.

I think five years is a totally inadequate period. We must think in terms of a somewhat longer period.

On the maximum-allowable-cost (MAC) program, I have very mixed feelings. If we had what might be called a normal market operating, I would simply rely on the market as a cheaper way of spreading the information and as a way of avoiding further intervention on the part of the government, which has its overtones of tyranny. On the other hand, the government is a major buyer, and I think that we want the government, as a buyer, to exercise as much prudence and discretion as it can in doing its purchasing as inexpensively as possible.

So I distinguish between the role of MAC as a device used by a buyer of drugs and the role of MAC that supersedes what would be done in a normal market by the operations of the market.

The trouble is that the health market has stopped being a normal market as a result of the enormous growth in third-party payment, with the government the major third party. It is a very mixed bag.

MR. HELMS: In that regard, why does MAC have to specify that, even if the government reimburses by a generic standard, the patient cannot

329

pay the difference? Why does MAC have to function as a price control mechanism rather than a reimbursement standard?

PROFESSOR BROZEN: That I do not understand.

MR. HELMS: There may be legal rules about that.

PROFESSOR BROZEN: But that is becoming more than the government protecting its own interest as a buyer, and I think that is going beyond the role that is proper for MAC.

PROFESSOR GRABOWSKI: I think one of the explanations is that government is supposed to certify that this is an equivalent product. If people were allowed to pay extra, it might seem as though the government essentially was paying for a poorer product. I think that may be part of the thinking there.

SAM MITCHELL, Pharmaceutical Manufacturers Association: I have a question for Dr. Comanor, based on something he said that I did not understand. If I heard him right, I think he said that he did not want to get into the issue of whether successful drugs should finance R&D. I was confused, because if the successful drugs do not finance R&D, what does? I am sure he did not mean to say that, and I want a clarification of what he meant because he was getting into the issue we just brought up, of what is the optimal way of financing drug R&D.

If we carry MAC and substitution to their ultimate conclusion, we do have a much closer approximation of perfect price competition, but then where do the funds for R&D come from?

MR. COMANOR: I do not think I said that. In fact, I do not think I dealt at all with the question of how R&D should be financed.

MR. MITCHELL: No. My original statement was that you said "I don't want to get into the issue of whether successful drugs should finance R&D or cover R&D." And my question was, "If successful drugs do not do it, what will?"

MR. HELMS: What you said was something about whether they should cover the costs of the unsuccessful.

MR. COMANOR: That is right. That is what I said. That is not the same thing.

Let us take your broader question, which has to do with how R&D

should be financed. In many respects, investment in research and development is like other forms of investment; certainly it is not the typical policy recommendation to promote differences between prices and marginal costs so as to ensure that investment is financed from internal funds.

I do not know whether that is what you were suggesting, but that is not the policy recommendation I think most economists would make. There is always the possibility of external financing of any investment, although one might argue—and probably appropriately—that the riskiness of this investment may be too great to permit external financing. That is a question, however, that I think is still open and needs more research. I do not think there are any firm answers to that precise issue.

MR. MITCHELL: I think it is going to become much more important.

PROFESSOR MEIR STATMAN, University of California, Santa Clara: I think the issue is not whether the funds will come from internal or from external sources. The question is whether investors will be able to earn the normal rate of return or the costs of capital on them. And here we really have a criterion in deciding how far we should go in either price competition, if we want it this way, or the patent period. We should allow as many years as are required for the company to earn the cost of capital on its investment in research and development.

So we have the two elements that were mentioned ten years ago, the trade-offs between high research and high prices, on one side, and low research and low prices, on the other. What will be the optimal solution for that?

Some estimates that I presented in my paper show that if, in fact, price competition takes away the entire market share or the profit margin of companies at the end of ten years, the expected rate of return goes down to about half the cost of capital, which is obviously going to lead to no investment.

MR. COMANOR: I certainly agree with posing the question as you do, and I must confess I have not read your paper to look at the empirical estimates, but I look forward to doing so.

MR. HELMS: I want to get back to the type II error problem that Ron McHugh brought up. This refers to the problem of regulators declaring a product unsafe on the basis of limited information when it is actually safe. As you know, the drug reform bill has passed the Senate and now will perhaps be debated next year in the House.

I would like to ask if any of you—George Eads, Jim Miller, or

Murray Weidenbaum—might want to comment on the general problem of trying to legislate that regulators change their perception about treating risk. I know you three people have thought about this problem in other contexts.

MR. EADS: We legislate that sort of thing all the time, in part because of policy statements, in part because of law. If there is an amendment saying that anything that can be shown by a one-animal test to introduce risk is bad, that is a very heavy type II error.

Since I have not followed the legislation that closely, I was interested in Dr. Lasagna's earlier comment that what is being proposed in the drug reform bill in effect ratifies what is going on in agency practice at the FDA. It has been said that the cancer policy statement that the Regulatory Council got recently in effect just ratifies what is going on in the agencies.

I do not think one should underestimate the importance of sometimes ratifying what is de facto practice and maybe getting it across to other agencies. And, certainly, as the concept that one cannot get rid of all risk without getting rid of the products gains wider currency and people show that it is at least possible to make some of the trade-offs, we may be able to get Congress to go back and take another look at the absolutes it put in the statutes.

PROFESSOR MURRAY WEIDENBAUM, Washington University: Part of the problem may be that it is hard to balance these conflicting public policy considerations without lowering the moral tone of the debate.

Here is what I mean. If an FDA examiner should let a thalidomide through, he or she, and the agency, will be publicly pilloried, and for very good reason. But Bill Wardell, in the current issue of *Regulation,* talks about a beta blocker that has been blocked by the FDA; his estimate is that, if this were in widespread use, more than 10,000 lives would be saved each year.[2] I do not want to pillory the person who is doing that, but I find it personally offensive.

Trading one professional reputation for 10,000 lives is a fascinating trade-off, and maybe high on the research agenda. How does one effectively put pressure on bureaucrats? Maybe the psychologists rather than the economists should answer that. How can we change?

I often say—in the spirit of Bob Helms's question—"Think like a bureaucrat," and I am an ex-bureaucrat; so it comes very naturally. [Laughter.] Maybe I still am a private-sector bureaucrat, but think of

---

[2] William Wardell, "Rx: More Regulation or Better Therapies?" *Regulation,* vol. 3, no. 5 (September/October 1979), pp. 25–33.

the incentives. If one sticks one's neck out, one gets in trouble; if one doesn't stick one's neck out, one will survive.

The FDA process strikes me as the bureaucratic process personified. How do we change those incentives so that the person who is blocking that beta blocker gets strong incentives to change his or her method of procedure?

MR. EADS: The answer is very simple. Make the act of blocking it as much sticking one's neck out as the act of not blocking it. That means that we must, first of all, have a statutory mandate that says that failing to approve drugs that would be good is not considered consistent with the statute, and then we must have a way of getting the information out.

PROFESSOR WEIDENBAUM: This is a serious question based on my limited information about the FDA—to what extent can we amend the basic statute so that we give the FDA a double-barreled mandate? One barrel would be keeping unsafe drugs off the market; the other barrel would be getting new, improved drugs onto the market more rapidly. Is there some effective way of giving the FDA the double-barreled mandate so that it can be judged by both criteria?

MR. HELMS: My question has now been effectively rephrased.

DR. JAMES MILLER, American Enterprise Institute: What Murray Weidenbaum said reminded me of the late Paul Cherington. When he was discussing the proposal for a Dade County airport, another airport in Miami, one of the issues was safety, and he said that, in view of the environmentalists' objection, he recognized there was a trade-off between alligators and people and that was a trade-off that made him very uncomfortable.

Let me say that what strikes me in all of this is that we, as economists, tend to look at individual behavior and think of economic agents responding to incentives. Yet we are not so good at applying our knowledge to bureaucratic behavior, the kind of thing that Murray Weidenbaum was just describing.

The personal experience that I have had—and George Eads has also had—in the president's inflation impact statement or economic impact statement program or regulatory analysis program, is that it is very difficult to get regulatory agencies or regulators or bureaucrats to change their behavior simply by telling them they should do differently.

The incentive structure is simply not strong enough. And that is the reason I have personally advocated that benefit-cost analysis be not only mandated but subject to judicial review—not that judicial review is a perfect instrument; all institutional arrangements are imperfect.

The question, though, is, What is in second place and what is in first place? And it seems to me that—as Murray Weidenbaum said, and I think that George Eads would agree—we have to change the incentive structure so strongly that we change behavior, or we are not going to make very much progress in this regard.

MR. EADS: I agree with changing the incentive structure; I do not agree with judicial review.

PROFESSOR STATMAN: I think that the way to induce innovation in the FDA is really to ask the FDA to take into account evidence that comes from abroad. The entire issue of 10,000 lives saved arises because we have the evidence from—I guess—Great Britain that this is the case.

I guess that there should be some kind of threshold, that if there is so much evidence in Great Britain, then it should be accepted automatically or given fast-track treatment at the FDA. I know that when we export goods to many countries, if there is some quality assurance here or some bureau of standards here, they will accept that standard. I do not see why it should not work the other way around.

PROFESSOR WIGGINS: I would like to repeat a little of what George Eads was saying, and that is that the first step in changing the FDA's procedures has to be changing the legislative mandate.

Looking at various theories of economic regulation, I found that, by and large, regulatory agencies, at least in my experience and often to the consternation of economists, follow the legislative mandate. A perfect example of this is the Civil Aeronautics Board (CAB). Economists screamed for years about the inefficiencies, and in some sense they were right, but the legislative mandate of the CAB was to protect the airline industry, to help it develop and grow. And over time that mandate was changed. The first step in trying to influence the FDA's behavior has to be to try to change the mandate and then worry about incentives. I think, if the mandate is changed, that will have a significant effect on the behavior of the agency.

PROFESSOR BROZEN: Let me add a footnote to this incentive structure. There was an attempt early in the 1970s to remove the onus of making the decision from individual reviewing officers within the FDA and to move it up to a bureau chief or to the committee level, so that the responsibility could get a bit diffused and, that way, putting one's professional reputation on the line would be avoided.

The officers whose responsibility was removed then proceeded to parade before the Kennedy (Senate Health) subcommittee and were made into heroes for avoiding sticking their necks out.

Dr. Lasagna probably knows more about that episode, by far, than I do. I think he tracked it far more closely.

DR. LASAGNA: Yes. What bothers me, as I hear these discussions, is that the FDA is really a paradigm of most of life, as far as I can tell. In the university world, I find that deans and what-have-you behave very much as a high official of the HEW once described he had learned to behave in Washington.

He said he began to feel like a whale. He noticed that whales were harpooned only when they came up to the surface and, if one stayed below the surface, it was hard to be harpooned. [Laughter.] And when he first arrived in Washington, he broke water fairly often and then learned that was not the way to go.

I see this in the university world all the time. If you have a really incompetent medical school or hospital administration, it is easier to stay out of trouble by just letting it go on than to start shaking it up.

When I throw stones at the FDA, it is not that things are so good in my own house. It is just that it is easier for me to throw stones at them than it is to throw stones at my dean. [Laughter.] I do think that the point about the charge is well taken, except that I wonder whether we do not need a more general kind of charge than just a legislative one. I agree that, if the charge to the FDA included approval, with all deliberate speed, of new medicines, that would help.

But I think we also need a mandate from the public, who would say, "Look, we realize that for everything good in this world, there is a price to be paid." There are risks. We are not going to predict all the mischief that drugs do. The very rare serious event will be missed over and over again, for all time.

The long-delayed toxic effect will surface from time to time, and that is part of the price we pay. What I would like to see us doing is encouraging regulators to approve drugs when the evidence is there and can be reasonably assembled.

What bothers me is when more trials are demanded than are needed to approve a drug, when a drug is kept off the market for a couple of years while another 2,000 patients are studied, whereas one could calculate that such a small sample would not pick up the 1 in 100,000 serious adverse effect. It is a waste of time. It bothers me to hear an important FDA official say that, to a man, everyone on the advisory committee knew that such-and-such a drug worked and, to a man, everyone in the agency knew that it worked, but their hands were tied. They could not approve the drug.

When the system is so bad that everybody is knowledgeable and everybody in an important regulatory position knows that the drug should be approved but cannot approve it, then it seems to me we must change the mandate and the climate of opinion in the country.

MR. COMANOR: Perhaps I might add one thing to this debate and talk about a different agency, the Federal Trade Commission.

I think it is fair to say the commission has stuck its neck out in recent years, recent months, and we know where that has got us. [Laughter.]

PROFESSOR TEMIN: It seems to be quite right that in order to loosen up we have to accept the risk—and it is clear the risk is there—of rare events. The question is, What will be the political reaction to these rare events?

One can take two views of this. The current view is that, when we have a rare event, we try to say what caused it. We go back. We typically pass a new law that goes in the opposite direction from what people are talking about here.

It is very hard to take the other tack and to talk to the person who has been hurt very badly or the family of somebody who has died and say, "Yes, well, that's bad luck. You know, it does happen once in 100,000 times. You just have to look at it as bad luck."

And I have not seen the article by Bill Wardell, but the difference between the 10,000 lives that could be saved, as opposed to the one life that is lost, is that we do not know who those 10,000 people are. They are not readily available as a political constituency, whereas the few people who get hurt *are* a political constituency.

Just to go a little further, it would be nice if one could say there is a certain amount of risk in the world—some people smoke, some people drive cars. We have to take a certain amount of risk, and if this is a particularly identifiable one, it is still a risk.

The problem is that if we lived in a world without changing medical technology and without new drugs, we might, over time, be able to convince people there are certain risks that should be seen as acts of God.

The problem, it seems to me, is that we say this year that we have to look at that risk as an act of God, and next year we have a drug that will overcome it. The line between saying, "Well, this is an unavoidable risk, a risk of social progress," and saying, "This is a condition that could have been cured," is a line that shifts over time. The distinction between them is a very subtle one for our political process.

MR. COMANOR: But, Professor Temin, we do this all over, with great frequency. We spend many more dollars in our society to save a specific life, where a person is named, than we do to save ten statistical lives or even more. The ratios are very much out of line, and I think this is in tune not simply with our political processes but with some notion of morality, which is endemic to a society. I think that is the answer.

DR. LASAGNA: We do have constituencies, and they have not been very effective. The Epilepsy Foundation was very effective in recent years in prodding the FDA about this drug or that, and there are other constituencies who could say in strong terms, "Why isn't somebody working on or approving a drug for muscular dystrophy?" or "Why don't we have better anticancer drugs?"

We have tried to mobilize these groups, to constitute what is a very respectable constituency, because it is hard to throw harpoons at people who are sick or at relatives of people who are sick. Doctors are self-serving, and they are money grubbers; the usual pharmacists, the drug industry, they are all suspect, but the sick—if you are suspicious about the sick you are sick yourself. [Laughter.] That is the attitude most people have.

PROFESSOR TEMIN: That may be the way the political contest will come out. It seems to me, in the recent past, the constituency for drugs has been a medical constituency, and people have said, "If you are doing it by proxy, you are suspect." And these other constituencies have not been mobilized.

PROFESSOR WEISBROD: It may be that we are a little too close to the whole issue here. It seems to me we are backing away from it, that this is a conventional problem that is essentially a compensation problem. That is to say—to get back to Murray Weidenbaum's example of the Wardell piece—if we take that at face value, as I think was intended, it is a proposition that asserts that, if properly valued, the benefits from introduction of new drugs exceed the costs. But because we have screwed up incentives, we don't get as many new drugs introduced as we might. I think there are many situations of that sort that pervade the economy.

In principle, it is a clear problem of compensation. In principle, in such a situation it is possible to make everybody better off. In fact, we do not do it. If it is in fact true that 10,000 lives are involved on the one side and some risk is involved on the other side, there exists a compensation mechanism that can make everybody better off. I am only stating an abstract proposition.

PROFESSOR TEMIN: But how does one decide when one is in that category?

PROFESSOR WEISBROD: I thought the problem was not how does one decide but, once one had decided, how does one develop an incentive structure that in fact gets the drug introduced? I think there is that problem, too.

PROFESSOR TEMIN: But it is more complicated because you are not designing a mechanism to deal with this particular drug; you are designing a mechanism to deal with *all* drugs.

PROFESSOR WEISBROD: Let me just be a little bit more concrete. Let us say that thalidomide had been approved. Now, there are others here who know infinitely more than I do about thalidomide. It is my understanding that that was, and is, a fine drug for some purposes. It just ought not to be taken by pregnant women. Is that roughly the case? Aren't there many good things about it?

DR. LASAGNA: It is very hard to kill yourself with it. And, at the time it came along, there was really no drug in that same category.

PROFESSOR WEISBROD: One could easily imagine a system—here I am tying this in with the whole legal-compensation–product-liability issue—for compensating people who suffer losses as unexpected side effects of decisions that are judged to be in the public interest.

I am not saying that I have the solutions, but product liability is one such form. Indeed, the pharmaceutical company or whoever it was that introduced thalidomide in other countries has suffered enormous losses through lawsuits. That is all part of the compensation mechanism. I am not saying that that is the best compensation mechanism. We might, in fact, be able to come up with a better one.

My own feeling—and I have been doing some work in the last year with Joe Cordes, who is at George Washington University, on the economics of compensation[3]—is that there are many compensation mech-

---

[3] Joseph J. Cordes and Burton A. Weisbrod, "Compensating Losers from Economic Change when Lump-Sum Transfers Are Not Possible," Institute for Research on Poverty, University of Wisconsin–Madison, Discussion Paper No. 608–80.

anisms that could be developed—and, indeed, we have them scattered around—that would undercut some of the opposition, because a lot of the opposition is due to the fact that the losses, when they occur, hit certain people very hard and that we have little or no way right now of seeing that these people do not bear the brunt of it; we ought to share it more widely.

PROFESSOR RONALD W. HANSEN, University of Rochester: With respect to the incentive structure that the FDA faces and the importance of either constituencies or public information about a product, I think we have just recently had a couple of beautiful examples of what happens when the public knows a lot about a product and then the FDA tries to ban it.

I point out, in particular, the saccharin case, where the FDA, in applying standards that it would apply to other food or drugs, tried to ban saccharin on the basis of those kinds of tests, and there was immediately a huge constituency that put pressure on to forestall that.

And there is another case—tobacco—which so far has not come up because it has not been classified as a food or a drug. One can imagine the type of constituency pressures we would get if it were ever classified as a food or drug and subject to FDA authority.

MR. HELMS: Just change it to coffee, because some people have suggested that that will be a coming issue.

PROFESSOR HANSEN: I have also heard recently that there is some problem of toxicity due to oxygen. [Laughter.]

PROFESSOR GRABOWSKI: I think, ultimately, in this area, it is a problem of constituencies, and it will be the media and the broader public that will influence things, because I think one hears, over and over, as one congressional staffer said to me, "We are getting polls that people want deregulation in almost every field except drugs, where they want more regulation."

That is part of the popular feedback Congress is getting, and I think, ultimately, Congress will respond to its mail, as it did in the case of saccharin; and as these constituencies are brought forth, I think we can envision a system that could go in the opposite direction. We could have a mandate to get drugs through fast. We could have administrators who push them through. We could have congressional oversight staff calling people on the carpet and saying, "Why isn't this drug out to the public?"

The fact that we do not have that now, I think, reflects the treatment drug regulation has received in the media and other factors. We want to strike a balance, and getting that message to the public is ultimately a big factor in any change.

GERALD ROSENTHAL, National Center for Health Services Research, Department of Health and Human Services: I think there are two issues, which I need to say boldly, because we slip around them.

Essentially, we treat the approval of a drug as a binary issue. We either approve it or we do not approve it, and we do it on the basis of whether it is efficacious or not, whether it is harmful or not.

Since uncertainty is involved, these are stochastic concepts. We test them experimentally in statistically reproducible environments. We place confidence estimates around the likelihood of having something negative happen. And at some point, not predetermined, we decide that we know enough. Sometimes, when we want to buy some time, we say we need to know some more, which is only buying an increment of acceptability.

To get back to the whale analogy, we get the harpooned whales because, ultimately, they have to surface to stay alive. That is the nature of the whale; it cannot stay under water all the time. It has to come up. And at that point, the benefits of coming to the surface far exceed the disutility and the risk exposed in that circumstance. But the surface is always in the same place—there is some control about that.

So we have addressed three issues to which this relates. How do we tell whether a person is doing his or her job? I am a professional bureaucrat, I was in the university—a private bureaucrat, as I put it— and, essentially, there is a law that has a set of goals and objectives, and there are still some bureaucrats who make that a serious commitment when they take their paychecks; that is what they pursue.

But this does not tell them how to do it. It only says that this will occur in an environment that has rewards—positive and negative, if I could put it that way. We live in a world where the unknown never carries as much clout as the individual mistakes one makes. We need to find some strategy—the committee strategy was a process strategy, and I think that is a good example because it was a disaster. It backfired on everybody's presumption that, in fact, we could collectivize it and make it an act of the FDA.

Maybe the answer lies in some staged binary approval cutoff that says that, when a certain set of expectations is reached in a declining expectation of some negative happenstance, we fall into some approval with compensatory eligibility—no fault, just like malpractice insurance in a way. It does not make any difference who did what to whom. As with no-fault automobile insurance, the one whose car is hit pays for the fender regardless of fault.

We have to look for some combination of compensation and analytic method that will allow an individual to say, "At this point I am doing the right thing in terms of my job and my performance."

In the absence of that, we are going to have to rely on some individual's interpretation of a process where the reduction of risk will always be offset by the need for speed. And here we do run into the danger of having small, squeaky wheels divert attention from an agency that has a slow track because it cannot put everything on the fast track, and we may actually be running a higher risk of diverting approvals than we might otherwise want to. That is, it may be that we substitute one really bad criterion for another one.

PROFESSOR WEIDENBAUM: Perhaps we can take a short step toward the kind of possible improvement that we have just been talking about and that Burt Weisbrod brought up.

I get a lot of, not crank mail, but anguish mail from people who do not want more drugs banned but want some drugs available, and I do not mean Laetrile. I mean things like the beta blocker desired by the man with the second or the third heart attack, who says he has a very short life expectancy and he does not give a damn if it is carcinogenic. If he does not use it, he is not going to live long enough to come down with cancer. He wants to take the risk.

There are no second- or third-party effects. It is *his* risk of dying from a heart attack versus *his* risk of dying from cancer; he wants to make that judgment, and the FDA will not let him make it. Are we increasing or reducing welfare by not letting him, with the advice and maybe the consent of his phyisician, make that judgment?

MR. HELMS: That is a very basic question. You are getting back to freedom of consumer choice. Does anyone else want to respond to that?

DR. LASAGNA: I just think that there is one thing that we must not be confused about. For a long time we have been talking about risks to the consumer, but the big hang-up here is the risk to the bureaucrat who approves the drug, and then somebody else gets into trouble. It is not the personal somatic damage that is the restraining process. It is the threat that the bureaucrat is going to get into trouble.

As former FDA Commissioner Alexander Schmidt pointed out, as long as the FDA is asked repeatedly to explain why it let something on the market or why it did not take something off the market, rather than why it has not approved something, it is not surprising that it behaves in the way it does. Anyone would behave in exactly the same way.

MR. HELMS: On that observation, I would like to bring the discussion to a close.

Editor's Postscript

My purpose in scheduling this panel discussion was to bring about an exchange of ideas about what research topics should be pursued in the next few years. I think we are fortunate that this audience included a majority of those engaged in policy-related research on pharmaceuticals. We are also fortunate to have had in the audience some of the country's leading scholars doing research on broader issues of regulatory policy.

I think this discussion has achieved my objective. As is common in these open discussions, we have wandered over a large number of topics and left some interesting ideas dangling. We have reached no definite conclusions about what priority should be given to the various items we have suggested for the research agenda. But I hope the discussion has led some of us to think in broader terms about the process of forming public policy and the type of research on health and safety regulation that is needed to help improve policy.

In summary, this discussion shows that there is still considerable room for more study of the process of drug regulation. As would be expected from a group consisting largely of economists, several economic topics have been identified for future research—topics relating to effects of price controls and market competition on the financing of private research and development. But what is surprising is the emphasis placed on the need for analysis of "politics and behavior" in the regulatory process. That is an area somewhat different from the traditional studies of costs and industry structure that have been done to a large extent by the same economists who are making these suggestions. They are not saying that economic analysis cannot be used to study these broader political and behavioral aspects of regulation—as is illustrated by the discussion of the role of uncertainty in regulatory decision making and the efficiency of compensation principles. But they do seem to be saying, I think, that regardless of who does the research—economists, political scientists, pharmacologists, or perhaps even psychologists—we need to delve more into the behavior of both politicians and government officials. We need to know more about how public attitudes regarding the safety of products are formed and how this induces politicians to pass safety legislation most economists and scientists regard as short-sighted and costly to society. Implicit in the discussion is the suggestion that we should use this new-found knowledge to help design new approaches to safety regulation, approaches through which the good intentions of bureaucrats can be mobilized to use more of the benefits of science.

In short, this group seems to be saying that we should take a more practical approach to regulatory reform in drugs. Since both Congress and the FDA move in these matters like lame Galapagos turtles (who seem to live forever), we need to think of making progress in small steps. We need to write legislation in such a way that we bring a different set of pressures on FDA decision makers. We need to anticipate more fully why the implementation of legislation by the various safety-oriented regulatory agencies has taken such a rigid and costly form. And above all, we need to start from the realization that not all risk can be avoided and that private institutional and legal arrangements can be reestablished that will ensure safety to consumers more efficiently than the present system.

To end the volume on an optimistic note, we know from recent experience with the reform of economic regulatory agencies in transportation and some modest reforms of other agencies engaged in health and safety regulation that some progress can be made in reestablishing market competition and reducing some of the more costly forms of regulation. There is some evidence that the FDA and Congress are beginning to take note of this movement. But, to return to the analogy of the giant turtles, it is difficult to imagine a stampede of a herd of turtles. Still, to keep the slow movement going, it is important that those engaged in policy-related research continue to push in the direction of more efficient drug regulation. As this discussion points out, the stakes in terms of human lives are high. It is important that we take full advantage of what medical science has to offer.

A NOTE ON THE BOOK

*The typeface used for the text of this book is
Times Roman, designed by Stanley Morison.
The type was set by
FotoTypesetters Incorporated, of Baltimore, Maryland.
Thomson-Shore, Inc., of Dexter, Michigan, printed
and bound the book, using Warren's Olde Style paper.
The cover and format were designed by Pat Taylor,
and the figures were drawn by Hördur Karlsson.
The manuscript was edited by Barbara Palmer and
by Gertrude Kaplan, of the AEI Publications staff.*

Selected AEI Publications

AEI Associates Program